How and Why Thoughts Change

How and Why Thoughts Change

Foundations of Cognitive Psychotherapy

IAN M. EVANS

OXFORD
UNIVERSITY PRESS

OXFORD
UNIVERSITY PRESS

Oxford University Press is a department of the University of Oxford.
It furthers the University's objective of excellence in research,
scholarship, and education by publishing worldwide.

Oxford New York
Auckland Cape Town Dar es Salaam Hong Kong Karachi
Kuala Lumpur Madrid Melbourne Mexico City Nairobi
New Delhi Shanghai Taipei Toronto

With offices in
Argentina Austria Brazil Chile Czech Republic France Greece
Guatemala Hungary Italy Japan Poland Portugal Singapore
South Korea Switzerland Thailand Turkey Ukraine Vietnam

Published in the United States of America by
Oxford University Press
198 Madison Avenue, New York, NY 10016

Library of Congress Cataloging-in-Publication Data
Evans, Ian M., 1944–
How and why thoughts change : foundations of cognitive psychotherapy / Ian M. Evans.
pages cm
Includes bibliographical references.
ISBN 978–0–19–938084–8 (hardcover : alk. paper)
1. Cognitive therapy. I. Title.
RC489.B4E958 2015
616.89′1425—dc23
2014031559

1 3 5 7 9 8 6 4 2
Printed in the United States of America
on acid-free paper

For

STAR

Whose two-year-old thoughts confirm the power of words to express feelings, regulate behavior, and promote understanding and joy in those around her.

CONTENTS

PREFACE

Reber and Reber (2001), in their *Dictionary of Psychology*, had this to say about thinking:

> As G. C. Oden put it, "thinking, broadly defined, is nearly all of psychology; narrowly defined, it seems to be none of it." Given the subtle truth of this quip, we might be able to find a middle ground if we treat the term as denoting, most generally, any covert cognitive or mental manipulation of ideas, images, symbols, words, propositions, memories, concepts, percepts, beliefs or intentions; in short, as encompassing all of the mental activities associated with concept-formation, problem-solving, intellectual functioning, creativity, complex learning, memory, symbolic processing, [and] imagery. (p. 748)

Cognitive therapy, a core approach within that collection of psychotherapeutic techniques and tactics known as *cognitive-behavioral therapy*, is fundamentally about helping the client overcome personal difficulties by recognizing and changing maladaptive thinking in order to effect emotional and behavioral change. Among other strategies, it requires encouraging clients to develop skills for rehearsing new, more positive mental habits; to test assumptions underlying misattributions and unquestioned erroneous beliefs and implicit attitudes; to reconsider negative, distorted judgments; to come to recognize that negative feelings cannot and should not be avoided; and to reinterpret ("restructure") memories of past emotional experiences.

Cognitive therapy, therefore, is primarily about changing people's thoughts, both the content and the processes whereby content is most likely to become distorted. Cognitive therapy thus addresses both our conscious thoughts and ideas, of which we are aware and on which we can further reflect, as well as unconscious processes involved in thinking, of which we are and usually will remain unaware. Cognitive therapy might attempt to change a dominant thought (e.g., "I am a failure; I'll never get a job"), as well as changing the process whereby an experience (not being offered a job one has applied for) results in that particular self-deprecating, defeatist assumption, rather than a more adaptive thought (e.g. "I was not really a good fit for that job, so next time I need to apply for jobs requiring my special skills"). Thus the task for the therapist is complex: we need to change the content when the content ("I am a failure") is emotive and likely to be the stimulus that evokes a strong negative feeling (depression, or hopelessness, in this case), as well as further, usually illogical, thoughts ("No one likes a loser"). But we also need to change the process whereby a certain kind of experience (not getting a job one wanted) results in an erroneous conclusion about oneself, the nature of the world, and one's prospects for coping in the future. If this second part of the therapy is not addressed, it is likely that a client making the incorrect inference "I am a failure" will make other incorrect inferences following other possibly negative but certainly ambiguous experiences. It is these thinking styles that cognitive theory assumes to be causal for different types of psychopathology: rapid judgments of threat by people who are anxious, inferences of an unappreciative world by people who are depressed, and assumptions of entitlement by people who are criminal offenders.

Given this latter focus is an essential component of treatment, cognitive therapy does not try to alter every erroneous inference—only those that result in personal, emotional, or social distress for the client. People make erroneous and irrational inferences all the time (Gilovich, 1991). No one is immune from the sorts of cognitive errors that Aaron "Tim" Beck identified so perceptively in depressed and anxious clients; it is just that the ones the rest of us typically make either trigger less strong, more fleeting an emotional reaction, or they trigger feelings that are unrelated to our personal mental health. If someone purchases something in a store and later realize that he or she has been given insufficient change, the plausible but unverifiable inference, "the clerk must have made a simple mistake," should lead to only mild annoyance, compared to the more focused anger evoked by the inference "the clerk was trying to cheat me." In some ways the clinical problem of flawed thinking is no different from the broader societal problems of mistaken judgments, prejudicial inferences, and crooked thinking generally (Thouless, 1932) but with intense personal consequences affecting only the few we see as clients.

Despite the easy acceptance of basic cognitive therapy ideas and techniques within the earlier field known as behavior therapy (Rachman, 1997), the now universally acknowledged hybrid title of *cognitive-behavior therapy* (or cognitive-behavioral therapy, as it is often written) papers over some cracks in the edifice. While it may seem intuitively obvious that how and what we think determines how and in what manner we behave, the relationship between thought and action is by no means a simple one (Wilson, Hayes, & Gifford, 1997). What is the difference between a thought and a belief? How do we find the cause of a thought? Can it really be that thought *causes* overt behavior, or could it be the other way around? Further, is a happy thought truly a thought or an emotion—just a verbal report of a feeling? Do thoughts *cause* emotions, or is that also the other way around? Can one have a sense of self without thought? If clients are taught the rubric that "thoughts are just thoughts, not reality" (Blackledge, 2007), where does that leave a cognitive therapist's thoughts? These are not just pedantic questions. They go to the very heart of what modern scientific psychotherapies are trying to achieve, how they do it, and how they explain it.

Purpose and Aims

The unequivocally cognitive therapies come in various shapes and sizes, with different terminology, theoretical assumptions, and tricky questions, rarely posed. This book raises and attempts to answer some of the pertinent questions in a way that clarifies why thoughts change and how thoughts can be changed—not all thoughts, but those that seem most relevant to relieving psychological distress. Most of psychotherapy has always taken place through words (Staats, 1972); Freud called his new method "the talking cure." So it is inevitable that the how and why of changing thoughts will be central to understanding psychotherapy, even if we end up deciding that thoughts are not necessarily the problem but having thoughts about them might be. I should also declare my perspective right from the start: I do not believe that as they are practiced now it is useful for cognitive therapies to be separated from traditional behavior therapy, or that the novel techniques that have emerged within the cognitive tradition are *sufficient* to meet all or even most of the client's needs for permanent change (Evans, 2013). But if using our words is so often all that we have in therapy, we should at least see how our words might influence others' words and thereby change their thoughts. If changed thoughts bring about happiness or relief from emotional distress or reduced mental illness, changing them must be a worthwhile generic feature of all effective therapy.

Others have come to similar conclusions. Staats' (1983; Staats & Eifert, 1990) call for an emphasis on unifying principles of psychological development and change is now becoming established as the essential requirement for a genuinely scientific approach to psychotherapy (Evans & Fletcher, 2013). More recently, Kazdin (2001) recognized that understanding change processes generically was necessary to progress treatment research. Barlow, Allen, and Choate (2004) started to shift their thinking away from separable treatment protocols toward more unified principles applicable to a variety of syndromes that seem to have much in common in terms of their underlying processes. Hayes, Pistorello, and Levin (2012) convincingly advocate the need for a unified model of change applicable to human beings in general, not just those with depression, anxiety, or personality disorders. As though anticipating this call, Tharp (2012) has presented his "delta theory" as a universal, unified approach to psychosocial influence and change.

The purpose of this book is to reexamine the assumptions underlying cognitive therapy by explaining contemporary developments within general cognitive psychology. One of the things we discover is that by and large errors of judgment are commonplace, and the exact same conditions apply to practicing therapists. One of the great challenges of delivering cognitive therapy clinically, and of training people to do so, is that as clinicians we may have our own flawed ideas, prejudices, and unrecognized biases. This recognition lets us think of therapy not so much as correcting wrong thoughts as replacing the client's dysfunctional thoughts with the therapist's hopefully more functional reasoning—a matter of persuasion rather than revelation (Frank, 1961). These issues are explored in this book on the grounds that by analyzing how thoughts and their function change, the therapist will be in a better position to change them for the client's social and emotional well-being, rather than for encouraging adherence to a particular set of beliefs, including the therapist's. The demonstrated effectiveness of cognitively focused psychotherapy (Butler, Chapman, Forman, & Beck, 2006; Tolin, 2010) suggests that we can, in Banaji's (2007b) words, help people "unravel the contents of their beliefs and even the process whereby they were constructed" (p. 267).

The therapeutic goal is for clients to be able to function better than they do now, not to replace one ideology with another. But that is a real challenge, nonetheless. Does scientific psychology offer any solutions to the challenge? I think so, and I attempt to describe first principles in a way that will be useful to practitioners, as well as those designing and evaluating new cognitive interventions. A widely accepted idea in cognitive-behavioral therapy is that we consider it best practice not to treat all clients with the same diagnosis as equivalents and not to deliver treatments according to a fixed, stereotypic formula. Instead it is recommended that the therapist frames a model or a conceptualization of the client's unique needs and difficulties and goals and uses that model to design a creative plan for facilitating client change (Eels, 2007; Persons, 1989). I attempt to identify the implications for case (client) conceptualization in actual clinical practice.

Outline

The first chapter provides a quick introduction to some of the issues in understanding thoughts as central to our conscious experience and daily lives. I then provide an overview of the key assumptions of the major cognitive therapies, trying to distil their underlying commonalities despite differences in terminology that they have adopted. The third chapter goes back to the psychology of thinking, highlighting contemporary research and theory that is particularly relevant to therapeutic methods. As concepts such as meditation, mindfulness, introspection, and self-reflection are so important for approaching clinical problems, I address these topics in Chapter 4, and in Chapter 5 I consider more extreme disruptions of thought that are key features in many serious psychological problem areas. As the whole raison d'être for cognitive therapies—changing thoughts leads to changes in feelings (mood) and in behavior—the next two chapters critically examine these causal connections. Remember, however, that cognitive therapies do not actually claim that faulty cognitions are a direct cause of psychopathology. We talk instead of "cognitive vulnerability" to emphasize a focus on cognitive processes in the context of stressful life events. Most cognitive theorists assume that cognition, emotion, and action are reciprocally determined and interactive constructs (Bandura, 2006; Beck, 1991). Thus Chapter 8 is an attempt to reflect on the broader principles that have emerged when questioning how and why thoughts change. Finally, in Chapter 9, I reconsider some therapeutic methods for changing thoughts, drawing on the research and theory that has been offered, together with a little speculation. Rather than providing a how-to-do-it chapter, clinically relevant suggestions are made more or less in the sequence that a therapist might find useful to proceed therapeutically, from laying the foundations for change, to dealing with barriers to change, to addressing broad concerns like motivation, to the ways in which thoughts are influenced.

Like my previous book, *How and Why People Change* (Evans, 2013), which was written for a technical audience but designed to be accessible to many, this book assumes some knowledge of modern psychology. I hope, however, that it will be understandable to the nonspecialist, as well as freshly illuminating for professional psychologists and graduate students already quite familiar with the *techniques* of the various cognitive therapies. I try to explain the basics to anyone interested in the way an individual's thoughts are specifically altered within psychological treatment. Sociologists and historians have long been interested in the effects of mass persuasion, in trying to explain how entire societies have come under the grip of ideological influences from totalitarian regimes such as Stalinist Russia, Nazi Germany, or modern-day North Korea. The influence of mass communication—radio, television, and now the Internet—is a matter of great fascination, but while relevant to my topic it is not central to it. This book is not about propaganda, media influences, religious conversion, cults, or similar group phenomena, although they all involve changing thoughts. Rather it is about individuals and how their thinking changes over shorter periods of time as a result of common experiences, as well as unique ones—specifically psychotherapy. It is not about education that gives us knowledge, but it touches on those elements of education that teach us how to think straight and on the barriers to acquiring what logicians judge as rational thought. The focus is on constructive thinking that does us good, solves problems, improves relationships, and leads to better mental health: positive feelings as well as positive behavior change.

How and Why Thoughts Change

1

Introduction

Cogito Ergo Sum

The mind is everything. What you think you become.
—The Buddha (attributed to)

The Cognitive Shift

When people initially approach psychology as a field of study, they think first of the mind, then of feelings, and only finally of actions, unless these actions seem inexplicably strange. As they study psychology formally they are often surprised to hear that psychology is the science of behavior, although the term *behavior* nowadays attempts to encapsulate everything we do, including thinking and emoting. It has not always been so. When psychology emerged as an experimental, natural science in the late 19th century, it was considered the science of *consciousness*. The questions were about how we (meaning other intelligent, verbal adults) sensed and perceived the world around us and how we knew that we perceived it—how we were aware of our own experiences. After all, it is this awareness of ourselves and our own mental life and our ability to reflect on our thoughts that truly sets us apart from all other animal species. Freud qualified these basic questions by noting that not everything that was important to human functioning *was* in fact conscious and that we have feelings, intuitions, and memories that we cannot express in words and of whose presence, especially their influence on our actions, we are largely unaware. And while few of the details of Freud's theories on the origins of personality and psychopathology have stood up to critical scrutiny, the central idea that we are not conscious of much of our own psychological processes is now widely accepted in scientific psychology, and the relevant "dual process" concepts in cognition (aware/unconscious) will form one of our central themes.

At a very primitive level we all know what it is like not to be conscious at all—it happens when we are asleep, when under anesthesia, when knocked out by a blow to the head. An impressive thing about conscious awareness is that it seems to be one of the last true mysteries of the universe, and since it is about us as we are, not some remote galaxy or molecular cell cluster, it is far more personal than any of the great mysteries of astrophysics or microbiology. What is obvious is that consciousness arises in the brain. This has been difficult for science to deal with, in that consciousness is closely related to the essence of our experiences, our humanity, and our minds, whereas the brain is just a mess of pottage. The brain is purely physical, made up of certain kinds of tissue; it is heavy, but not because it is full of thoughts. It has an architecture that has been mapped, and it operates through reasonably well-understood electrical and chemical processes, buzzing and secreting away all the time, which seem psychologically explanatory to many (e.g., Taylor, 2012).

But how can these chemical reactions and the transmission of little messages across billions of specialized neurons generate consciousness, especially having thoughts and being aware of them and thus able to reflect on them? How do we learn a seemingly limitless amount of information, encoded and stored in images, words, and abstract symbols, able to be skillfully manipulated in computational and creative processes (Staats, 2012)? How is it that while brains must all be fairly similar, their contents are so infinitely variable? One day, we assume, our understanding of the physiology of the brain will shed some light on such questions. Until then, however, we may just have to plug away at a less reductionist, more immediately promising level of analysis: the psychological (Shulman, 2013; Staats, 2012; Tavris, 2012). We have to gain a holistic understanding of how thinking comes about, how we mentally translate and revisit emotional experiences, how we can control and manage our thoughts by deliberately accessing them and switching them off, and how we can better use these processes to our own personal advantage and the well-being of our fellow humans.

In my earlier book, *How and Why People Change*, I analyzed the full range of contrived clinical experiences that result in behavior change—for example, learning, motivation, personality formation, social influences, culture, and the physical environment. In trying to understand how people's behavior changes as a result of planned interventions, such as psychotherapy, I wanted to cover the broadest array of relevant psychological processes that shape—in the short term and to our benefit—what we do and who we are. I addressed thought only as the meat in the sandwich, something that often comes between our past and present experiences and our current and future actions (Hurley, 1998). While this analogy is appropriate enough, it is true that for many people it is our thoughts that define us, not our actions (Singer, 1975)—it is the meat that is important, not the bread.

Think (have a thought) for a moment about how often in everyday life we talk about processes such as changing our mind, making up our mind, having an idea at the back of our mind, or letting our mind wander. Our grandparents are certain that thoughts regulate our behavior: "mind your manners," "remember to say 'thank you' to Aunty Mildred," "poor Aunt Mildred; she is out of her mind," "are you thinking of coming for lunch on Sunday?" Even when the actions are highly salient and their consequences devastating, such as the bombings in the streets of Boston at the end of the Boston Marathon on Sunday, April 14, 2013, there is a presumption that thoughts will explain otherwise unfathomable behavior: *The New York Times* asserted that investigators will be trying "to understand the brothers' thinking" (Shane, 2013). What was Mark Chapman thinking when he shot John Lennon? Were his ideas really shaped by his fascination with J. D. Salinger's novel *The Catcher in the Rye*? Was John Lennon judged to be a phony, in his mind?

Thoughts, thanks to consciousness, have an existence that is very real to me; they are my thoughts, I own them, and I am responsible for them. Yet they are often fleeting and mostly inconsequential enough that it is difficult to remember most of their content just a day or two later, sometimes even moments later. I can try to describe them by putting them into spoken words, but those words are rarely my deeper thoughts and certainly not identical to any of them. If I write my thoughts down I inevitably change them while recording them. One of the best recognized concepts in modern psychology is that we cannot explain our mental processes in words very easily (Nisbett & Wilson, 1977). Thoughts produce feelings and also convey these feelings to others. I can be thinking, as I was a moment ago, of the 8-year-old who was killed in that Boston terror attack, and that makes me feel sad, as well as thinking of abstract national policies that have resulted in countless other unknown children being killed in drone strikes, and that makes me angry. Neither the thoughts nor the feelings are likely to drive specific actions as I keep on writing this section at the computer, unless I have personally experienced the tragedy of the loss of a child, and the associations trigger more thoughts and old memories, and I have to stop what I am doing while overcome with grief. Or, more selfishly, my mind can wander elsewhere by association and I can think instead, and almost concurrently, about how good a thick Boston clam chowder would taste and can actively recall where I can find the recipe. That thought exists, although it can be known to others only if I convert it in terms of some sort of mutually understandable signal system. And this does not necessarily result in a change of my behavior, insofar as I will not automatically get up and make soup. I am just thinking about it. But the thought alone could have strong emotional and even visceral consequences that, although trivial, are positive in this case—I can see the succulent chunks of clam and diced potatoes, imagine the rich creamy texture, the hearty connotations of the word "chowder" and its filling associations with the word "chow" make me feel warm and satisfied, my salivary flow is increased, and so on. Recognizing the obvious fact of such potential triggers, many if not all approaches to psychotherapy have a focus on trying to change people's thoughts, with the implicit expectation that it will result in a change in their behavior.

Two Revolutions

Cognitive therapy is a story, like *The Hobbit*, of there and back again. There were good reasons why the abortive 19th century search for the *elements* of consciousness gave way to functionalism and the science of behavior. Behaviorism was the most important and influential advance in psychological understanding, because it provided methods that allowed the subjective to be studied objectively, permitting us to move beyond philosophical speculation. For 40 or 50 years behaviorism reigned supreme, providing enormous insights into our understanding of ourselves and other animals and in the process reducing the tautology of mentalism, in which the mind (how we function) is explained by—well—the mind, or a little homunculus in the brain, or the ghost in the machine.

Behaviorism also gave rise to effective methods of psychological intervention, including therapy, rehabilitation, and education. But then there was a rather sudden shift toward what we can broadly call cognitive psychology, returning again to trying to understand how we receive, process, convert, and use information. George Kelly (1955) was the first cognitive therapist, who saw people as "inveterate inquirers, self-invented and shaped, sometimes wonderfully and sometime disastrously by the direction of their enquiries" (Bannister & Fransella, 1971, p. i). Although the new research methods were not like the old introspective studies of consciousness and relied heavily on methods of objective measurement that were essentially behavioral (reaction times, choices, eye fixations, that sort of thing), the new science of thought, spurred on by analogies with computers, tended to define itself as contrary to behaviorism. As some behaviorists, for instance Arthur Staats (1968), with his behavioral analysis of language, imagery, and cognitive development in children, or B. F. Skinner (1957), with his analysis of verbal behavior, showed, it was not necessary to build cognitive psychology by rejecting behaviorism, but this is what tended to happen. As a result there has been a marked shift in psychological therapies as well, with a much greater focus on cognition than on behavior. The mind, as a processor of information and creator of its own reality, is back.

Modern psychological intervention based on the science of psychology is now known as cognitive behavioral therapy (CBT), although, as mentioned in the preface, the cognitive and the behavioral perspectives within this broad approach are not always compatible. It was this incongruity that I tried to dispel in *How and Why People Change*, by integrating a variety of psychological principles and showing how they are complimentary rather than contradictory. In the process, however, it was not possible to provide a really detailed account of how thoughts might be changed by planned experiences, but given the extent to which we *do* emphasize thoughts and their importance in society, it seems worthwhile to now provide that greater degree of detail. Yet saying cognition is important in psychology is slightly droll—it is like saying sailors have suddenly decided they should take an interest in ships (I stole this analogy from somewhere).

A Clinical Example: Thinking About Crime

We can start this more detailed discussion with a not uncommon but somewhat daunting clinical psychologist's task. Say, working as a correctional psychologist in a prison, you are talking to a 39-year-old man who is a repeat violent offender, convicted of more than one incident of sexual assault, rape. He is coming to the end of his sentence, and your task is to provide a therapeutic intervention that will decrease the likelihood of another sexual offense once he is out of prison. Here is a true test of cognitive therapy, since anything and everything that your therapy consists of will have to be verbal—there are few new learning experiences that can be arranged while he is incarcerated (Wilson, Bouffard, & Mackenzie, 2005). True, there are some social skills he can practice in a group, but the members of the group will most likely be other men committed for similar crimes. There are also some emotional learning opportunities afforded by the relationship you might be able to develop with this client, but you may feel little empathy for someone who is a known rapist, and he in turn may perceive you as part of a hostile judicial system and not inherently in his corner. In addition to distrust and anxiety on both sides, there are typically large power imbalances, as well as educational and social class differences.

You may have been trained to think as a scientist-practitioner, to use only evidence-based methods, and not rely on your intuition. If so, you might as well go home and leave this client to his fate. There *are* no explicit empirically validated methods, although there are some multi-element programs in existence that have reported positive outcomes (e.g., Olver & Wong, 2013). But if you think carefully about known psychological principles, there are many possible extrapolations that could help this client. Notice I have already mentioned "think" twice, just in this paragraph: maybe our dog-Latin should read "cogito, ergo a practicing psychologist sum." So after you have thought, "What the hell am I doing here?" you will need to think, "What am I going to do?" probably accompanied by the most important thought of all if you have a hope of being effective: "No, my training was not useless; I know something about the psychology of human behavior and criminal conduct, and I need to talk to him and find out a great deal more about how, why, and in this case what, he is and was thinking." Some encouragement can come from the fact that that is all you have, anyhow.

Given that you have been trained in interview techniques, I will skip all the obvious information that would be worth obtaining as you get to know this client and focus on whether you can get some sort of understanding of his typical pattern of thoughts and whether prison has changed them for the better (quick hint: not very likely). There are some natural challenges to this task. First, when you ask this client to express his thoughts (talk about his cognitions), you discover he dropped out of school at the age of 14; his vocabulary is limited, and he talks in clichés. Furthermore, he is not used to thinking about his own thinking—he is not at all insightful or introspective (which will be discussed in more detail in Chapter 4). Moreover, you may ask him what he was thinking about at the time he committed his offenses, and that is a memory task, which is hard for any of us. And it is likely that they were impulsive, opportunistic acts rather than controlled or reflective—the dual processes that will be discussed in much greater detail later (Wiers, Gladwin, Hofmann, Salemink, & Ridderinkhof, 2013). Even more important, he may be reluctant to tell you what he was or is thinking, or he will distort his thoughts so as to minimize their content, either because he is ashamed of these thoughts (something he might have learned in prison from the prison chaplain) or because he wants you to like him. It is also possible he wants to impress you so you will admire him or fear him or feel sorry for him, so he will exaggerate, dissimulate, or blame others. Finally, he may not be deliberately distorting his self-reported thoughts but will be doing so unconsciously, utilizing what are generally referred to as defense mechanisms, whose function is to keep highly distressing, unwanted feelings from becoming conscious, painful thoughts. Aggressive clients with histories of assault on their wives are prone to neutralize any self-punishment inclinations by blaming their victims for provoking them (Dutton, 1986). What is often called experiential avoidance in CBT is really a case of the more general avoidance of thoughts and memories that are highly upsetting.

If you turn to a good cognitive therapy text to assist you in formulating interview questions and to help you listen to possibly relevant answers, you will be disappointed. Almost all such texts, except when talking about young children, assume that most clients are reasonably verbal, reasonably well educated, open to psychological interpretation, trusting, and eager to tell you exactly what is on their mind. And probably those who benefit most from conventional cognitive therapy and were clients in the controlled clinical trials are just like that. What cognitive therapy principles can tell you, however, is that if your client has dominant beliefs and attitudes and thoughts that are erroneous, irrational, and hateful, then it is conceivable that changing them would be one constructive part of a more complex rehabilitation program. It is not difficult to imagine what these patterns of thought might be like and why they need to change. Research on the belief systems of rapists suggest some of the following thoughts might predominate in this client.

There are dangerously minimizing thoughts that his victims really wanted sex and their resistance was not genuine. So common was this belief at one time in American culture that women were obliged to develop the unambiguous mantra that "No means no." A related idea, once more common in the cultural thinking of some males, was that a woman agreeing to some actions, like coming inside for a coffee or a drink after a date or wearing attractive and sexually suggestive clothes, were clear signals that she wanted or was willing to engage in sex. If men entertained such beliefs, it facilitated an active thought at the time of the encounter: "she is asking for it."

Then there is a category of thoughts related to rape being justified as a general social good, or something that the male perpetrator feels fully entitled to because of a sense of his own importance and deservingness—sometimes called appetitive aggression. Wealth and social privilege relates to significant power imbalances, which is why servants (including people like hotel maids), slaves, and less dominant prisoners in jails have historically been so vulnerable to rape. Religious beliefs and cultural practices are considered social norms and often are used as cover for brutal ideas—for instance conjugal rape is protected by law in Afghanistan, and in parts of Africa there is evidence of marauding soldiers raping women from another tribe so as deliberately to increase their own group progeny or to destroy a community. Another example of such thinking has occurred in South Africa, when the idea was promulgated that raping a woman (a virgin or a child) who was free of HIV infection would cure AIDS contracted earlier by the rapist (Flanagan, 2001; Meel, 2003).

Third, there are thoughts related to deliberately wanting to hurt, humiliate, terrify, or punish someone (or some society) for supposed evil or wrongdoing. In a more general sense this relates to the concept of rape being a hate crime, not a sex crime. This category can be seen in the cases of "corrective rape," where the victim is a lesbian woman and the supposed purpose is converting them, in attempts to intimidate, such as the frequent rape of female journalists in Egypt after the fall of Mubarak in 2011, as well as in cases of racial hatred where the victim and the perpetrator are of different ethnicities. Misogyny is not limited to extreme visceral hatred, of course, and in Australia, following a speech by the former Prime Minister Julia Gillard the term has been correctly redefined as "entrenched prejudice against women."

You might discover, eventually, that your client does not just have a random collection of unrelated beliefs but instead has an implicit theory about his victims (Ward, 2000). However incorrect the theory might be, it provides explanations of observed realities—how others typically behave, for example, which will be encountered later as the influence of perceived social norms. You should also be aware that what might appear to be rape myths held by the client are really thoughts that have occurred after the offense or while you are conducting the interviews. Minimizing the harm ("I didn't really hurt her"), blaming the victim ("she was asking for it"), or shifting responsibility ("she provoked me," "I was high on P at the time") are all defensive beliefs intertwined with cultural rape myths (Suarez & Gadalla, 2010) serving to reduce guilt or avoid punishment.

It must be emphasized that ingrained thoughts are not by themselves the cause of rape. Rape is far too complex and varied a behavior to be so easily attributed to erroneous beliefs and deceptive thoughts. Many other factors such as lack of empathy and interpersonal social skills, the failure to achieve intimacy and subsequent loneliness, opportunistic behavior, the disinhibiting effects of drugs and alcohol, group pressure from a gang, comorbid psychiatric disorders, and previous occurrences of sexual violence all contribute to this behavior (Lalumière, Harris, Quinsey, & Rice, 2005). But thoughts facilitate the action, and if future prevention (reducing the risk of reoffending) is the goal, then modifying implicit theories and erroneous beliefs and correcting deceptive thoughts comprise a worthwhile therapeutic intervention. An exploratory prison-based treatment program for high-risk rapists described by Wilson, Kilgour, and Polaschek (2013) has yielded promising results. An important part of the program was designed to alter "deeply entrenched belief systems that underpin both personality disorder and offending" (p. 530). Exactly *how* this might be done across a wide range of client problem areas is the central topic of this book.

Distinctions and Definitions

This sex offender example provides numerous illustrations of the phenomena that will need to be clarified before any attempt at describing cognitive change mechanisms is concluded. Beliefs, attitudes, and thoughts about something are all more or less the same thing. Certainly in everyday parlance "I believe it is tea-time," "Four-o-clock! That's the time for tea," and "I think it is tea-time" all mean the same. But beliefs, just like attitudes, have emotional elements that a thought does not need to have. Because of this, in clinical contexts we are often more likely to talk about a client's beliefs, such as an offender's belief that scantily clad women are inviting sexual overtures, or a fearful client's belief that people will make fun of him in a social situation. As is the case with attitudes, and opinions, these beliefs exist as feeling states, independent of their symbolic expression, but when they are expressed verbally they take the form of a thought about something, or the way that something might be in the future. A thought that depicts or defines a future goal is called an intention. A thought that has an element of novelty or creativity or brings together previously unrelated thoughts is often referred to as an idea. When I have the thought that it is lunch time, I will go and make a salad, but when I have an idea about the salad I will then try mixing in pomegranate seeds, edamame, and arugula. Ideas are most often generated in a social context—in reading someone else's ideas, in conversation, in lectures and symposia, in focus groups, and in cyber chat rooms. All right, so Archimedes was alone having a bath when he had his good idea, but he was very keen to communicate it as quickly as possible. It is in individual social contexts, as we shall see, that thinking as new ideas is often changed, but it is in group social contexts that beliefs are often strengthened.

Opinions are personal thoughts, usually evaluative, about a topic or event. Although they can be held firmly, often dogmatically (not easily swayed by contrary opinions and certainly not by evidence), they tend to be devoid of emotion.

"That was a profound movie" is an opinion, whereas "I just loved that movie" is the self-report of a feeling and not truly evaluative (you can love bad movies). Twitter was ideally designed for the expression of opinions, since tweets are purely individual and personal, not the reflection of a group or a movement, and by being limited to 140 characters there is little opportunity for deep thought or conditional clauses. As a result the only tweets of interest to anyone other than the sender are those coming from famous or important people or celebrities, whose random opinions some people may care about. Labeling a thought an opinion gives it legitimacy and discourages further discussion ("I'm sorry, but that is my opinion"). Many people are uncomfortable in expressing a contrary opinion in a social situation, because sharing the same opinion about something is a form of social connection, and having a contrary opinion is distancing. One of the causes of the popularity of Twitter (360 million tweets per day) is by discovering you have the same opinion as, say, Justin Bieber, you are able to feel some sort of personal connection with him. Early in therapy when rapport is being established, it may be unwise for the therapist to express an opinion too firmly, since, as clients are reluctant to disagree, it is preferable to wait to hear their opinions first. At the same time, should you wish to influence a client's opinion, *repeatedly* stating your own will create a sense of familiarity that will lead the client to think your opinion is widely held (Weaver, Garcia, Schwartz, & Miller, 2007).

Opinions, beliefs, intentions, and attitudes are more fixed and consistently held, whereas the essence of free-floating thought is that it can be manipulated, extended, elaborated, and readily associated with other thoughts in creative and novel ways. I might have a belief, based on a long history of being taught the concept in Sunday school and during sermons, that contraception is wrong and against God's will. My attitude toward contraception will therefore be negative, and I will experience guilt when I use a contraceptive device. But my ideas about it all are far less bound, and I can analyze the logic of this Catholic church teaching, learn where the doctrine came from, wonder if the story of Onan in the Bible is relevant to modern society, accept the value of condoms as a means of reducing the spread of HIV infection, and reframe the issue for myself as a personal opinion that the greater sin would be to conceive a child that I cannot financially support. Through such processes of thought, often referred to as reasoning, I can develop for myself new ideas, but when strong emotion is associated with them as beliefs and attitudes, or when the freedom of independent thought has been discouraged, these ideas may be very limited, rigid, or distorted. I can have a well-reasoned perspective on why I personally should use a contraceptive device but feel disloyal for entertaining an immoral thought and if I use the device still feel pangs of guilt as a result of years of conditioning or from the constant stream of homilies from the church as an organization.

The psychology of attitudes, how they are acquired and how they are changed, is a long and complex field of study. It is beyond the scope of this book, but it is worth remembering that there is a large degree of overlap. Many well-known questionnaires confound self-report of characteristic behavior with attitudinal thoughts. For example, if you had assessed the violent client described earlier using a common questionnaire like the Buss-Perry Aggression Questionnaire (1992), it would have included both self-reported behavior items ("I have threatened people I know") and thought items ("Other people always seem to get the breaks"). The content of an attitude, be it positive or negative, is a thought, although typically an unwavering one and tied specifically to the stimulus (in the previous example, "other people"). In the stimulus context of the concept *illegal immigrant*, you may have evaluative opinions or attitudes that are not particularly emotive and might be mildly accepting or rejecting: "they do the nasty jobs that Americans are reluctant to do" or "they should be sent back because they take jobs from people who have a right to be here." In the absence of either strong feelings of hostility (rejection) or sympathy (acceptance), those sorts of thought content can be readily changed by new persuasive information. But if strong affect is the key dimension, it contributes to additional thoughts, especially in ambiguous situations. If you have strong antipathy toward or fear of young black men, it is inevitable that when you encounter one in a slightly unusual context, your automatic thought is going to be "This guy looks like he's up to no good." If you are also vigilant and on edge because you perceive yourself as the local authority, entitled to enforce your ideas of proper behavior and who belongs where, your further automatic thought is very likely to be "[maybe] he's on drugs or something. It's raining and he's just walking around, looking about." Regardless of what you think about the outcome of the trial of George Zimmerman who shot and killed Trayvon Martin, those were the actual thoughts he conveyed by phone to the Sanford, Florida, police. For a psychologist it is only too obvious that such thoughts are related to the emotional responses we call attitudes, in this case a prejudicial one (devoid of any evidence base; Olsson, Ebert, Banaji, & Phelps, 2005). As social psychologist Mahzarin Banaji (2007b) has explained, our precompiled attitudinal processes allow inferences of which we are totally unaware. The simple action of reaching into a pocket could be to produce a wallet, a pen, a cell phone, or a gun.

Although these distinctions are relatively easy to keep clear, I use the terms *belief* and *thought* somewhat interchangeably, because that is what is done in the clinical literature. Beliefs can be more generalized and consistent, much like a trait. The personality concept of "belief in a just world," for example, really relates to the fact that a person will have consistent expectations of fairness, a presumption that people get what they deserve, and thus will entertain specific, situationally relevant thoughts that if something negative has happened to someone, such as being raped, then there must have been some element of deserving it, which results in a feeling—lowered sympathy. When I heard my teenage client's statement that his mother's tenant was trying to poison him, I recorded it in my case notes as a belief and went on to explore a number of suspicious thoughts associated with this belief, such as his thinking it unusual that the tenant was often home on weekends and wondering why she had so many empty plastic bottles in the household recycling bin, which combined to make him feel mistrustful and anxious. The original belief was not deduced from the facts. Instead, the paranoid belief allowed my client to integrate a range of observations (some distorted), thoughts, and feelings, thus making a meaningful, semicoherent (if totally incorrect) composite picture of presumed reality.

The terms defined here—*idea* (knowledge), *thought, belief, attitude*—can be considered content terms. They refer to mental events usually expressed as words. But they also can be nonverbal and nonconscious, and when that is the case we call them *implicit*. A young, preverbal child might have a belief that her favorite toy is in her toy box, and if asked to fetch it that is where she will go to look for it. She doesn't say to herself: "Teddy must be in my toy box, because that is where I last left him." But she acts on that implicit knowledge. There are other cognitive terms—coming up next—that are less about content and more about processing and storage of information and past experience. These are cognitive processes such as judgment and appraisal. They in turn can be distinguished from structural concepts, like schema or memory store. And finally when aspects of cognition are habitual and general, they can be thought of as *traits*, as cognitive styles that define an individual's personality (characteristic way of behaving across a range of situations).

Processes: Attributions and Appraisals

There are two types of thought that are especially relevant to clinical psychology and the science of change (psychotherapy). One of these is thoughts about the causes of events, especially ones that relate to one's own behavior and feelings, or of the behavior of others. These kinds of cognitions are called *attributions*. Attributions can be divided into three broad, general dimensions. One of these is whether a person tends to attribute events to the self (internal) or to external factors. Another is whether the individual tends to attribute events to enduring causes or transitory ones (a stable/unstable dimensions). The third is a global-specific dimension: whether presumed causes are ones that affect many events or just a single event. People who experience clinical problems such as anxiety and depression tend to have attributional processes that are internal, stable, and global (Abramson, Seligman, & Teasdale, 1978). I hardly need spell this out as it is intuitively obvious, but clients who are clinically depressed who have, say, a minor traffic accident, will blame themselves (attribute the event internally to their own carelessness), claim that they are always careless (stable), and assert that they make mistakes in other areas, not just while driving (global). Coming to such conclusions is one common form of irrational thought that depressed clients might exhibit.

The second type of information processing in cognition is especially relevant to clinical problems like anxiety, panic, and stress. This is when we evaluate either a situation or our experience of it as negative or positive, safe or dangerous. This is called an *appraisal*. Widely used though this term is in cognitive therapy, it can be somewhat ambiguous. If we appraise some situation as a threat, then our reaction is likely to be fearful. But some theories of emotion/cognition interaction claim that it is the fear response that helps you appraise the situation as dangerous—in other words your experienced emotion provides informational feedback about the nature of the experience (Baumeister, Vohs, DeWall, & Zhang, 2007). Cognitive appraisals are rarely, if ever, encoded in inner speech as words spoken to oneself, which many conscious, rational thoughts usually are. As such, the concept of cognitive appraisal is a hypothetical one and not always relevant to explanations of anxiety and panic, a point made strongly by Barlow (2004). A child darts across the road in front of you, and you slam on your brakes. It is not very likely that you appraised the situation as dangerous or had any conscious or even emotional regulation of your response to danger. And if a mouse darts across the room and you jump up and scream, it seems unlikely that you appraised it as life threatening. Nevertheless, the concept is a useful one in affirming that cognition is not just about words and thoughts but about the mental processing of information.

Cognitive Structure: Schema and Memory Stores

A collection of thoughts that are all consistent with related attitudes and beliefs and which then have further affect attached to them along with seemingly associated affective memories from the past has become known in cognitive therapy contexts as a *schema* (plural: schemata or schemas). The term was first used by Piaget for the cognitive mechanism whereby we accommodate or assimilate new knowledge. It became part of the lexicon of modern cognitive psychology when defined and described by Bartlett (1932) in his studies of remembering. Bartlett proposed that as we try to remember things, we reconstruct past events in order to fit them into our existing view of the world. Thus a schema is an organized pattern of thought that provides a framework or script for interpreting new events and encounters and combines affective memories of past experiences. In clinical work it is the self-schemas that attract our therapeutic attention. As clinicians we rarely care that a client has a well-organized schema around, say, modern abstract art, with preferences for some artists, reconstructed memories of past exhibitions, delight in viewing a Jackson Pollock, and negative ideas and feelings about realism. But we will be very interested in her schema for the parental role, her emotional conflicts between loving her children and finding them stressful, memories of her own childhood, her feeling that she is not an adequate mother, and her misguided belief that if children are disciplined it will stunt their emotional development. If she has been referred to you for parenting skills training to manage an oppositional child, her parenting schema will be absolutely relevant to any attempt you make, whereas her modern art schema is entirely immaterial.

It was Beck (1967) who popularized the concept of the schema and made it a central principle of his version of cognitive therapy. When using similar ideas with patients described as having a personality disorder, Jeffrey Young (1994) came to the conclusion that current thoughts in such clients were heavily influenced by more complex, emotionally laden schemata developed in the past and often shaped by abusive early experiences. Calling these "early maladaptive schemata," he described them as broad and pervasive memory patterns of feelings and thoughts, particularly relating to oneself and one's relationships with others and that are dysfunctional for the present time, frequently leading to self-defeating behaviors and topsy-turvy interactions with others. As these schemata develop during childhood and adolescence, he opined, the themes connecting thoughts and feelings into schemata were often those of instability relating to abandonment, mistrust relating to abuse and emotional deprivation, and feelings of shame from early messages of inadequacy and defectiveness.

Personality: Cognitive Skills, Styles, and Traits

To finish off this section on definitions and distinctions, I mention a fourth category, that of cognitive personality traits and well-developed cognitive skills (such as emotional understanding), as these terms will occur repeatedly throughout the book. Here I am thinking of the thought-relevant aspects of personality, such as cognitive rigidity, experiential avoidance, introspectiveness, mind-blindness, approach/avoidance motivational style, self-identity, and vulnerability to stress. As these are dimensions on which people show important individual differences but yet cannot easily be identified as personality traits, I introduce them only briefly here; they will be explained later. They are particularly relevant to understanding why it is that different people react cognitively to the same event in totally different ways.

One example might be helpful. Imagine that your client has a personality style of being very systematic in the way she processes information. Such a trait would mean the individual has a tendency to engage in detailed analytical thought. She might not like making snap judgments until all aspects of a problem have been weighed up. She might lack some confidence in her ability to come to correct conclusions and decisions, particularly when she is very involved in the problem or the outcome. This personality trait is the opposite of spontaneity of judgment in new situations. It has been most closely investigated in management studies. If this person were to be confronted with a serious and stressful personal problem that had no obvious solution, her lack of confidence in her judgment about possible risks and her examination of every issue would result in her worry becoming perseverative (Dash, Meeten, & Davey, 2013). Perseverative worry is characteristic of a wide range of clinical syndromes. Prestress cognitive personality style—systematic information processing—thus determines the form (persistence) and content (thoughts about risk) of the client's dysfunctional cognitions. Recently in CBT research, Barlow, Sauer-Zavala, Carl, Bullis, and Ellard (2014) have provided strong empirical evidence that all anxiety-related syndromes reveal a temperamental commonality they call *neuroticism*. This negative emotionality (Gazendam et al., 2014) dimension harks back to the personality theory of my own doctoral mentor, Hans Eysenck (1967), with one unique difference: Barlow et al. are confident that this trait level of cognitive-emotional processing can be directly targeted therapeutically, with "transdiagnostic" benefits.

Thoughts as Independent, Private Events

What else can be said about the concept of thoughts? The great thing about thoughts is that they are yours, unless you are especially vulnerable to having them dictated to by others. This means that we can think what we like, any place, anywhere, but that we have to be continually vigilant to think for ourselves and to expand our thinking by evaluating the thoughts of others. Totalitarian regimes that fear free thinking always try to control access to ideas by burning books and banning writers (Arendt, 1966). The whole purpose of a liberal education is to encourage independence of thought, and the whole purpose of political and religious systems is to discourage it. Scholars of the philosophy of liberal education sometime make a distinction that is useful as the subtext of cognitive psychotherapy: Roth (2014) calls the educational goal of freeing the mind to discover the truth about things "skeptical"; he argues there is a second philosophical, rhetorical tradition he calls "reverential." The latter is exposing the individual to the treasures, achievements, and canonical works of his or her culture so as to foster a connection with a common heritage and inspiration for participation in its future. One might simplify this all as the importance of clients coming to better understand themselves and others—what it means to be human.

While ideas are often shared, thoughts are more usually private, unless disclosed by word or deeds. Fiction and the TV and movie industry love to engage in the fantasy that under certain condition thoughts can be read by others in the absence of their overt, verbal expression. Charles Xavier (Professor X and founder of the X-Men) could read minds, although he promised his foster-sister, Raven, never to read hers. Of the many other media examples I can think of, in the movie *Race to Witch Mountain* (2009), the two alien children, being protected by a cab driver and a space scientist, can easily read minds, including the thoughts of a dog. At one point, becoming exasperated by having their thoughts read, one of the human adults turns to the children and tells them that here on Earth it is considered very rude to reveal or intrude on someone's private thoughts. However, the cabbie comes to value their ability more when the alien girl, Sara, tells him that the brainy female scientist thinks he is very handsome. In the John Wyndham novel *The Midwich Cuckoos*, when the parents of the children conceived by an alien force realize that they will have to be destroyed to save the village, the strategy used to prevent their children from reading their minds and discovering these lethal intentions is to focus fixedly on the mental image of a solid brick wall. In the movie version, *Village of the Damned* (1960), there is a graphic scene in which one of the children starts to break up the protective wall, mentally pulling the bricks apart, in an attempt to discover his parent's thoughts behind it.

Controlling Our Own Thoughts

You do not have to be a psychologist to know that the content of our thoughts can be fairly easily self-regulated or, as we call it in psychology, directed. This is a critical ability for mental health, and distraction techniques should be learned early by children: counting backward, imagery of heroes with brave thoughts, repeating a mantra, and so on. We often say things like, "I don't want to think about that right now," and we then turn our attention to something else. I probably have the same worrisome thoughts as other men in my demographic—how are the adult children going to cope in this economy, am I having greater difficulty remembering names than I used to, will the county give permission to the new landfill being proposed for right down our road? These thoughts lurk in the background, easily activated by a relevant cue—a newspaper report that the Fed is going to stop quantitative easing, telling someone about a movie recently seen and not remembering Matt Damon's name, seeing a garbage truck on the highway. But I don't lie awake at night worrying about them, or stop an activity because the thoughts are distressing; I can readily switch my mind to other, more positive thoughts. Is that the major difference between me and someone with chronic worrying and anxiety—that I have strategies to manage and contain unpleasant thoughts and they do not?

Clients tend to report the content of the dominant thoughts that are salient to them, or that are specifically probed for by the clinician's questioning. But their ongoing mental life, as for all of us, consists of mind wandering as they shift attention from current activities and events to fantasies, rehearsals of things they are going to do or say later, and other musings. If this happens with high frequency, it is obvious that the ability to focus on current tasks and the completion of goals is compromised. For most of us, mind wandering is more likely when the main task on hand requires little executive control (planning, attending, anticipating, reminding oneself of rules and principles), such as driving a car (when an experienced driver; Smallwood & Schooler, 2006).

Early in the history of learning principles being applied to clinical problems, Dollard and Miller (1950) proposed that just as situations eliciting anxiety will be avoided (and such actions then reinforced by anxiety reduction), so thoughts that evoke anxiety will be avoided as well—by *stopping thinking,* in their words. The maladaptive part of such repression of everyday worrying thoughts is first that it reduces exposure to situations that may turn out not to be as threatening as imagined, and second that it interferes with other thinking and reasoning, including talking about these anxious thoughts in therapy. Thus individuals who avoid anxiety-provoking thoughts have diminished opportunities to self-regulate feelings or marshal emotional support from others.

As there is a natural tendency for a cognitive therapist to focus on unwanted thoughts, treatment talk of self-regulation of thoughts is often about these processes of stopping or reducing certain thoughts and certain categories of thought (self-deprecating thoughts, for example). However, therapy often entails adding new thoughts, encouraging clients to have alternative ways of viewing everyday situations, and having new words that they can conjure up whenever they need a little self-encouragement. In such cases the dimension of ease of access to a thought is important. We want to make the client's new thoughts *automatic*—to use a term Beck popularized. Accessibility is influenced by many factors, especially familiarity (a line of a popular song), rehearsal (something you think to yourself everyday), acceptability (if spoken out loud the thought would not be dismissed or criticized by your audience), easily formed because of rhyme or alliteration ("A stitch in time saves nine" is more easily thought than "I should get the job done now before the problem gets worse"), and, for children, a combination of all these features. As Dr. Seuss (1990) wrote: *You have brains in your head, feet in your shoes. You can steer yourself any direction you choose* (p. 3). Clients often benefit from simple aphorisms.

Thoughts Are Worth a Penny

At least that is the way it seems, as we typically offer someone only a penny for their thoughts. But the fact that we offer anything at all reflects the privacy of thinking and that in a social context someone who seems to be lost in his or her own thoughts creates a feeling of discomfort in the others present. One purpose of language is to permit and sustain social interactions (Guerin, 2003), and among the most meaningful interactions are conversations, and conversations require an exchange of thoughts, often with the generation of new ideas in the process. Although we are often encouraged to put our mind in gear before we put our mouth in motion, most of us are not aware, in the course of an interesting conversation, of thinking of an idea (having a thought) and then expressing it. If one really tried to do that, it would be very inhibiting of naturally flowing conversation, even though every now and then one deeply regrets not thinking more carefully about what one is about to say.

It Is *Not* the Thought That Counts

There is another feature to the value of thoughts that suggests that thinking about an action can be judged as valuable, or even more valuable, than the deed itself. Say you give your lover a cheap gift that she probably won't like, and you comfort yourself by saying it is the thought that counts. And she tries to feel less disappointment by repeating the phrase herself. But in a formal study, Zhang and Eply (2012) found that receivers of gifts do not spontaneously consider the giver's thoughts, and they have to be prompted—perhaps by the gift being truly bad. If the gift is very desirable, the thought that went with it confers the giver no extra credit; it is only when struggling to find a reason for getting a terrible gift that the receiver will give credit to the giver for the thought behind it. Only the giver knows if any thought actually did go into the selection of the gift, and only the giver can reasonably expect bonus credit for being thoughtful. It might be useful for good relationships that deeds speak louder than words and certainly louder than thoughts. If you forget to give a gift at all, you will not get much credit for claiming that you thought about it (but ran out of time)—better to admit that you totally forgot. In gift giving, thoughts do not trump quality, nor do they excuse failure to give.

If thoughts do not always count for much, what about thoughts of doing something you know to be wrong? The Bible tells us not to covet our neighbor's wife, but was that because having an immoral thought is sinful or because God, or whoever gave the tablets to Moses, knew that such thoughts can be strong precursors to action? Some of us will remember that just before being elected president, Jimmy Carter, somewhat unwisely, gave an interview to *Playboy* magazine (November 1976), in which he stated, "I've looked on a lot of women with lust. I've committed adultery in my heart many times." The connection, or otherwise, between thought and action will be an important thread of concern throughout this book.

Theory of Mind: Knowing That Others Have Thoughts

If you ask someone what he or she is thinking (about), or assert that a thought is a reasonable substitute for a gift or the equivalent of an action, you are at least acknowledging an awareness that others *have* thoughts, and an understanding that you have them as well. Learning to recognize others' wishes and intentions was undoubtedly one of the first social skills to evolve, as our earliest ancestors first started to cohabit in groups. Recognizing that others have thoughts has become known as "theory of mind," an awkward term that harks back, as so often the case in cognitive science, to the writings of Piaget and even further back to philosophers such as Descartes. It is a "theory" of mind only because we cannot know for sure that others have mental processes akin to our own, these being known to us only through our own introspection. Some psychoanalysts, notably Melanie Klein (1926), suggested that infants cannot distinguish between their own mind and their experiences of their mother. While this symbiotic aspect of the concept may seem unnecessarily tortuous, it is an important part of social intelligence to recognize that other people might have thoughts, beliefs, intentions, and desires entirely different from our own, particularly if they have had immediate past experiences that are different than ours or have had access to less or different information than we have had. Of special interest is the possibility that not having a theory of mind might be what characterizes the thinking of some individuals, especially children with autism. And from there we can speculate that many individuals fail to fully appreciate that others will think differently than they do, and that creates emotional and relationship challenges. In practice there is a considerable overlap with the concept of empathy, which is being able to put yourself in another's emotional shoes, not just their mental shoes, and the ability to adopt another's perspective must be rather similar in both contexts.

There is a simple experimental paradigm whereby theory of mind is tested in children—the false belief task. In this task the child is presented with information that a second child does not have, such as when the other child is out of the room, a marble he or she has seen placed in one location is moved to another. A child passes the test and demonstrates theory of mind if he or she predicts that when the child comes back to the room he or she will look for the marble where he or she last saw it, not where the test child now knows it to be. Children often fail this test until about four years of age, but children with autism almost always fail the test (Baron-Cohen, Leslie, & Frith, 1985). Such findings have caused a flurry of interest in why children with autism have such difficulty in perspective taking and whether that is a cause of autistic cognitive deficits or a result of them.

The mental ability required for pretend play (make-believe) is that two different beliefs about oneself can be held simultaneously. The child playing with a Lego castle knows he is a boy and the castle is not real, but he must also think the opposite: that he is a brave knight and the castle must be defended. Baron-Cohen (1995) went on to develop the idea yet further, calling it somewhat more descriptively "mindblindness." The Hollywood fantasy of reading minds is not so strange after all—we do it all the time, effortlessly interpreting and predicting others' thoughts in all our social communicative interactions. When we do not, either from autism or some other form of intense self-preoccupation, we have mindblindness. As children with autism have difficulty with imaginative play and expressing and understanding emotion, they also very often lack empathy. I vividly remember one of my own clients with autism who got into an altercation with another pupil in a special needs class in his elementary school, and when I asked why he punched the boy my client replied, with no sense of irony, that he didn't like that other kid "because he has a disability." Add to this limited empathy the difficulty with imaginative or pretend play, and the challenge of the false beliefs task seems less and less like an explanation for autism. What is helpful, and useful for all cognitive therapy with any kind of client, is to realize that people have a limited understanding that others think differently than themselves, that will generate secondary social and communication problems. Some of the literature on gender differences in thinking patterns and conversational style (e.g., Tannen, 1990) can be used to help clients with relationship problems practice the art of perspective taking. Politicians determined to bring one nation's ideas of democracy to countries with totally different religious, social, and colonial histories also exhibit a sort of collective mindblindness.

Not only do we need to recognize that other people can, legitimately, think differently than we do, it is also very important to realize that they might feel differently as well—that their needs and desires and goals can be different from ours. Psychoanalytic scholars refer to this as *mentalization* (Fonagy, Gergely, Jurist, & Target, 2002). Developmentalists are more likely to refer to it as *emotional awareness*, a facet of emotional intelligence, requiring verbal skills and the ability to describe one's feelings and those of others. Think how often we ask clients, "And how did that make you feel?" or, if they are describing a social interaction, "How do you think that made ______ feel?" without always remembering that emotional awareness is a cognitive trait with wide individual differences (Lane & Schwartz, 1992). In relating to others, we need to be aware of (and able to describe) what we feel, we need to be able to reflect on those feelings, and we need to feel what others feel (true empathy) and to reflect on those feelings (perspective taking). Clients often are deficient in these competencies—whether that is a cause or a consequence of their emotional distress is much less obvious.

In educational settings there has been some enthusiasm for teaching children better perspective taking, which is usually described as the more complex, cognitive version of empathy. Empathy is emotional understanding, whereas perspective taking involves figuring out what others think as well as feel and predicting their intentions. Perspective taking is the ability to view the world (including the self) from another's viewpoint. In other words the perspective taker's thoughts toward the target become more "self-like," but the target is not necessarily liked more. There seems to be a difference between imagining how another person feels and imagining how you would feel in the same position as the target. The latter type of thinking is more likely to generate positive empathic affect for the target. In perspective taking research, instructions are to listen to what a person is saying and to judge it in a detached, objective way. Empathy instructions ask participants to listen to the same presentation of difficult experiences and to try to feel the impact of the person's experiences and how he or she feels as a result. Perspective taking reduces stereotypic judgments about individuals. This is why the idea has become so popular in schools.

Mind-Mindedness

Another very awkward term that has become popular in developmental studies of parenting is *mind-mindedness,* which refers to parents' (usually mothers') ability to treat their child, especially very young children and infants, as an individual with a mind who has intentions, thoughts, decisions, and so on (Meins, 1997). This quality of parenting is often assessed through the interview in which the mother is invited to talk about her child. In this discourse she might tend to focus on physical features ("he's a really active child") as opposed to mind features ("he is very thoughtful and always considers the feelings of others"). However, mind-mindedness can be inappropriate: mental processes are identified but likely to be erroneous ("he's always thinking up ways to annoy me") or, even if accurate ("he only thinks about himself"), may be fairly typical for a child of a given developmental stage and thus unnecessarily negative.

Interest in mind-mindedness arises because parents that lack this tendency seem to interact with their children in ways that minimize the child's own understanding of different perspectives and points of view. That is to say, the extent to which parents use thought-related explanations for behavior and communicate them seems to predict children's theory of mind understanding. This in turn has interesting implications for children's social understanding and peer relationships. A neat example is provided by experimental studies of children's understanding of making a social faux pas (e.g., Banerjee, Watling, & Caputi, 2011). As we all know, a faux pas is a social slip-up that results in unintended insult. We all make them occasionally, but socially rejected children and adult clients who experience hostility in social relationships tend to make them more often. Avoiding faux pas requires the ability to understand other people's mental states, such as their likely inferences, judgments about ambiguous information, and so on. If parents and teachers are so important developmentally in promoting this ability, we can assume that therapists have a role to play as well. So the recommendation is to interject as many positive, appropriate mind-minded statements as possible in therapy and gently encourage clients to make appropriate mind-minded statements about others with whom they might be in conflict. A comment such as, "I just don't know what he's thinking when he gives me that funny look, but I'm sure it is some hateful thought" may need to be challenged for its appropriateness but reinforced for its mind-mindedness. Mindfulness training encourages clients to avoid judgment of their own thoughts; sometimes they need to avoid negative judgments of the thoughts of others.

Consciousness

Because clinicians are more interested in parental schemas than in Jackson Pollock, we tend to focus on quite a narrow range of current thoughts rather than covering the ecology of a client's mental life. However, in 1977, University of Minnesota professor of psychology Eric Klinger wrote one of the most important accounts of everyday inner experiences. He defined *thought* as the constant stream of images that fill our consciousness as well as the unconscious processes that organize them—the distinction between content and process that has already been identified and that will be a recurring theme of this book. He stated further that

> thoughts are most characteristically streams of inner language, but sometimes thought is made up of mostly visual images and often it includes imagined smells, tastes, touches, and vestiges of movement. The images of thought can tap the whole range of human sensory and motoric experience. (Klinger, 1977, p. 27)

He argued that thoughts are basically sequences of responses and thus those that are conscious operate in an almost unbroken stream, much like bodily acts and equally sensitive to the environmental context. While this inner mental activity may be an unbroken sequence, it is not undifferentiated and like all overt behavior is organized into "chunks" of interrelated activity that can be labeled *segments*. These stretches of homogeneous content can have different levels of generality and include subsegments. For example, if I am planning to go on a family picnic to the beach, which is the most general thought (an intention, in this example), I will have subsegments in which I wonder about the weather, think about what sort of sandwiches I should make, wonder whether I can remember the kinds of soft-drink the grandchildren prefer, and try to remember what I last did with my beach towel. Very often, but not inevitably, these thoughts occur as an internal monologue, as inner speech. This perspective is consistent with one of the oldest theories in cognitive psychology of how cognitively controlled behavior is organized: Miller, Galanter, and Pribram (1960) proposed that people are constantly in the process of following several intertwined plans.

Some of these subsegments Klinger (1977) labeled "operant segments" in the same sense of Skinner's operant behavior: the thought is instrumental or "directed." By picturing how hot the day might be and how much shade there is at my chosen beach, I will know what type of sunscreen to bring along, and by thinking about all the different family members' tastes, I will pack the right kind of food and snacks. This segment is intentional; I will have a subjective sense of trying to achieve something, and all my mental operations should reasonably result in the useful act of a well-planned picnic all ready to put in the trunk of the car before heading off to the beach. One way to measure or monitor these operant thought segments is the think out-loud technique, which has been widely used to try to identify the self-talk that skilled performers, such as chess players, engage in during a task. The verbal reports one elicits in a clinical interview are also think out-loud opportunities, but for life, not for chess.

A slightly different kind of stream of consciousness Klinger (1977) labeled "respondent segments." These include such phenomena as the ones we call day-dreaming, mind- wandering, reverie, and all of the incidental flashes of imagery and undirected thoughts that occupy our consciousness, perhaps for much of the time. As a result it can be argued that respondent segments set the tone of a person's inner life. If daydreaming is predominant when the environment demands more operant thought segments, meaningful constructive activity can be seriously interfered with. My partner asks, "Have you made the sandwiches yet?" and I snap out of my reverie and reply, "Oh, sorry, not yet; I was just thinking about riding the surf on my boogey board at Bellows Beach." I like Singer's (1966) definition of daydreaming: "a shift in attention away from an ongoing physical or mental task or from a perceptual response to external stimulation towards a response to some internal stimulus, *such as the thought of the waves at Bellows Beach*" (p. 3). I added the bit in italics; I'm sure Singer would have done the same had he ever been to Bellows Beach.

Thoughts and Incentives

Eric Klinger (1977) concluded his book with a strong statement:

> Thoughts are about incentives—about selecting them, about the gains and losses to be expected from pursuing them, about the means of attaining them, about hopes and fears regarding them, and about the pleasures of savoring them or the pain of surrendering them. (p. 304)

This summary is only meaningful if we have an understanding of what he meant by *incentives.* We can think of incentives as all events and objects to which a person might react affectively. Affect (an emotional experience or state), as opposed to simple sensory feedback, provides us with a way of interpreting the value of what we are doing. Affect, as most emotion theorists agree, is functional: signaling success or failure, good or bad, threatening or safe, and indicating the value of attaining an incentive and enjoying it once it has been attained.

Of course there are countless possible incentives in our daily existence, and they do not have much influence on our behavior until we are committed to pursuing them, which is then a goal we strive for. The strength of that striving is typically a function of the perceived value of the incentive and the strength of the expectation that it can be obtained—that the goal is achievable. This behavioral principle can be represented in many different ways; Bandura (2006), for example, represented it as an expectancy (belief about the future) that the incentive, when obtained, will be rewarding and the expectancy that one can perform the behavior that will attain it (self-efficacy beliefs). While pursuing an incentive (it has now become a goal), the individual is in a state of what Klinger (1977) calls a "current concern" that persists until the goal has been reached or abandoned. During such a state the individual is especially responsive to anything related to the pursuit—to notice cues, to remember events, and to think about them when not physically present. You will have experienced this state if you have ever been in love. Thus the content of each thought connects or bridges the physical stimulus to the current concern. Note too that "incentive" includes events such as evaluating something new, as well as evaluating the seriousness of a threat—incentives are not only things we know to be positive and strive for; they are also things that we know to be negative or we anticipate being negative that we escape or avoid. When a concern is important, a person's own thoughts trigger other thoughts of the incentive or other things related to it. When this occurs we refer to it as being preoccupied or, more clinically related, being worried or obsessed. Thus at least one principle for changing thoughts that are dysfunctional (do not serve a valued purpose) is likely to be either attaining the goal and confirming one's positive expectations or abandoning it and devaluing the incentive. In such a model, depression is a normal adaptive response following loss or failure, and depression then dissipates as the incentive is devalued and the individual is resigned to the loss. All CBT treatments for clinical depression contain some element of this incentive-disengagement cycle in order to reorganize the client's commitments and strivings toward newly valued, attainable (realistic) incentives. (In Chapter 7 I explain the importance of entertaining both types of thoughts—about the goal we dream of and the barriers we dread.)

Metaphors

For many of us, thoughts are encoded verbally as private speech, but all forms of mental symbolism are possible, as Klinger (1977) stated. Because it is likely to be relevant to clinical treatment, poetic and metaphoric imagery is especially worth noting. When working with children we are quite used, as clinicians, to asking them to draw a picture of their family and using this to probe for thoughts that the child might not easily be able to express in words. (Caution must be exercised not to overinterpret children's drawings or to put words in their mouth, but the same caution is needed when we probe an adult client's thoughts by rephrasing them and trying to get agreement.) Adult clients are sometimes able to represent their thinking metaphorically better than they can with words.

I had one vivid example of this some time ago when I started counseling with a self-referred woman in her late thirties. She had been married a few years, and the couple had no children. She came to the clinic under some duress, pressured by her husband who was frustrated by her lack of interest in sex. Carol freely admitted that she fitted the clinical picture of hypoactive sexual desire disorder (Basson, 2007). She was not concerned about her own feelings but did want to explore treatment as she felt her marriage was significantly threatened. In the interview she expressed no phobic aversion to sex but said she did not have sexual fantasies during sex, which is statistically unusual (Hariton & Singer, 1974), and she simply had no interest. Imagery, however, revealed a rather different picture. I asked her to give me a picture of her identity when she thought about sex, possibly imagining herself to be an animal. This was very easy for Carol because she said she had these images when approached physically by her husband. She saw herself as a delicate fawn, a Bambi, picking her way gracefully through the forest, sensitive and timid but very beautiful with big eyes—a dainty creature who needed to be protected and treated gently.

When I asked her to depict her husband metaphorically she described him as a Pipefish, common in the local seawater aquarium and coral reefs. When he tried to approach her to kiss her, she saw the fish's mouth like a sucker coming at her; Pipefish are described in the Encyclopedia Britannica as "possessing a elongated tubular snout that ends in a small toothless mouth" with a long snake-like body. Her imagery was enough to put anyone off sex for a while, and I can still remember the little shudder her body gave as she described her husband's mouth moving closer to her, and I was glad he was not present at the session—individual therapy was going to be hard enough. Maybe she was not phobic, but she certainly found sex, with this man in particular, highly distasteful. I cannot in honesty say that I cured her (from her husband's point of view) but by very systematically working on the peaceful forest imagery was able to change her dominant imagery, reduce disgust, and improve the marital relationship. She had to work on a new metaphor of herself as a doe, not a little baby fawn, very capable of protection and physical love and reproduction, and of her husband as an innocent buck. I avoided the optional term *stag* because of its machismo connotations—language rules in cognitive therapy.

Implications

We have sauntered boldly through the mysterious vines and foliage in the forest of thought, hoping to see at least some trees if not the woods. But it is a difficult task because the walk is too familiar: thought encompasses so much of our own experiences as human individuals that the psychology of it seems unenlightening. Nowhere on the walk did we bump into someone sitting like Rodin's famous statue of the thinker, with his chin in his hand, generating what we assume to be deep and novel ideas. Clients don't seek therapy so that they can be more creative but because the humdrum thoughts they have are distressing. Only some of what we have discussed thus far would actually help one do effective cognitive therapy, yet it is perhaps informative that there are many terms often used in less than precise ways that can be at least partially clarified. I have also deliberately ignored the one area where we encounter really dramatic thought change and that is in religious conversions, political persuasion and propaganda, and brainwashing of prisoners. This is partly for simplicity but essentially because the goals of therapy are so fundamentally different. Cognitive therapy aims to liberate minds, not to control them—the clinical task is guided discovery, not changing minds.

It will also be seen more starkly as we go on that the psychology of thought is focused on rather mechanical processes relating to the rationality and function of thought. But in clinical contexts the recurrent thoughts of many clients are highly emotional and irrational. Their thoughts relive terrifying, traumatic memories, for example, and cognitive therapists try to identify the nexus of the horrific experience, the "hot spots," they call them. Thoughts are evoked by remembered occasions in which the individual's feelings have been hurt, or form anticipation of future events that fill them with terror, or are composed of recollections that make them ashamed or guilty. Cognitive therapies must address such circumstances, ones that cognitive psychology theories of thought touch on only tangentially.

We have begun to affirm that thoughts are just as real as anything else and do relate closely to subsequent or parallel overt actions. We also can see that the reverse might be true and that actions change environmental situations and these in turn change thoughts. Thoughts have the potential to influence mood, but the reverse is equally true. Thoughts can evoke feelings of fear as vividly as can actual physical threats. Also we can have thoughts about our thoughts—self-reflection or metacognition. All this makes it important for cognitive therapy to recognize the point within that circular chain where intervention might be aimed, especially when specific thought content occurs against an inevitable ecological background of ongoing planning, introspecting, imagining. This chapter should encourage you to explore your clients' everyday conscious experiences, their general mental lives—what they believe, what they think about, what they daydream about. Listen carefully to the metaphors they use and the attributions they ascribe to their own behavior and that of others. How well can they gauge the thoughts of those individuals with whom they may have interpersonal difficulties? This then is a beginning framework for analyzing what happens in cognitive psychotherapy and for setting the stage for viewing what might happen much more effectively in cognitive therapy if we remain focused on the underlying principles of the thought, feeling, and action interface. To start this exploration, we first have to critically examine what theorists say happens in the cognitive therapies and what explanations are provided for their effects. This will be the topic for the next chapter.

2

Changing Thoughts in Practice

The Basic Concepts of Cognitive Therapies

There is nothing either good or bad, but thinking makes it so.
—William Shakespeare, *Hamlet*, Act II, Scene 2

The Cognitive Therapies

While every form of psychotherapy known has significant cognitive elements, the cognitive revolution in behavior therapy resulted in specific theories and methods that can now be branded as *the* "cognitive therapies." The most prominent ones are identified with a particular clinician/scholar who first originated and popularized the methods used: rational emotive behavior therapy (REBT; Ellis, 1962); cognitive therapy (Beck, 1967); schema-focused therapy (Young, 1994); dialectical behavior therapy (DBT; Linehan, 1993); mindfulness-based cognitive therapy (Teasdale, 1993); and acceptance and commitment therapy (ACT; Hayes, 2004). All of them claim that in order to achieve a positive therapeutic outcome (the precise nature of which is not always clearly specified), clients' thoughts, thought patterns, and functions must be changed—directly targeted in the therapeutic exchange (Hofmann, 2011).

One might think that if they are all trying to do the same thing, then their methods would be quite similar. The various originators of these approaches would disagree. And indeed, reading their theories and manuals and methods one will find many differences. Are these differences real, in terms of psychological processes, or are they mere differences in terminology, emphasis, and clinical philosophy? This is the question—rather than the answer—that I hope will be elaborated in this chapter, by presenting the different models and trying to extract their own essential mechanisms. In doing so in an analytic and critical way, I intend no disrespect to the originators of these methods. Considerable intellectual effort has gone into the development of these different therapies, as well as much scientific energy in the form of efficacy studies. The originators have captured the imagination of many who have read their work, listened to presentations, and attended training seminars and workshops. In each case the goal has been to improve the potency of therapeutic interventions and to help clients, and I do not wish to impugn these genuine motives in any way. Since I cannot cover each in the detail that they themselves have offered, my critique might seem superficial and incomplete, but if in the course of looking at what they offer that is unique we can reveal any core mechanisms that are common, the risk seems worth it.

Rational-Emotive Behavior Therapy

As soon as we try to dismantle or analyze critically any of the established cognitive therapies, we begin to see just how impossible that exercise is, because the different name-brand approaches lack procedural specificity, unambiguous definition of terms, and in most cases critical tests of the hypothesized causal mechanisms. These concerns are most easily seen in REBT, developed (long before his death in 2007 at the age of 93) by the ever-confident and charismatic Albert Ellis (1962). The basic premise is that our negative distressing affect is not to circumstances themselves but to our beliefs about them. On the face of it, the basic rationale is simple and convincing. Rational beliefs are those that promote survival and happiness and are likely to be empirically supported. Irrational beliefs are those that are not empirically confirmed or cannot ever be tested (such as the belief that "I'm the worst mother in the world"). Irrational beliefs of therapeutic relevance are not just any and all irrational ideas, such as "birther" billionaire Donald Trump's bizarre claim that President Obama was not born in the United States. Irrational beliefs in REBT are limited to those that are self-referenced and contain many "must," "should," and "ought" statements about personal behavior, about the behavior of others, and about the way the world should be. When personal failures, setbacks, or stressful circumstances occur, these thoughts (really interpretations of degree of responsibility) will lead to unjustified negative emotions, as well as unassertive and self-sacrificing behavior. Note that not all negative emotions in life's vicissitudes *are* inappropriate and undesirable. Sorrow, for instance, is an appropriate, if negative, emotional response to loss. Regret following an action that proved harmful to self or others is a functional emotion that enables us to be more thoughtful in the future.

Therapeutic treatment, it follows, consists largely in teaching clients to dispute their own irrational beliefs. This is done through questioning the evidence for these beliefs, challenging them with logic, and encouraging practical tests of anticipated catastrophic outcomes. The latter strategy bears close similarity to Viktor Frankl's (1959) technique in logotherapy of "paradoxical intention"—intentionally striving for the outcome that one fears or is ashamed of. Ellis suggested that his methods promoted unconditional self-acceptance and eliminated secondary problems such as self-criticism for having problems. Unconditional self-acceptance was defined by Ellis (1977) as "the individual fully and unconditionally accepts himself whether or not he behaves intelligently, correctly, or competently, and whether or not other people approve, respect, or love him" (p. 101).

A major difficulty in evaluating REBT as a distinctive therapy is that there is considerable disagreement as to which bits of it are unique or even which collection of therapeutic procedures can legitimately be called REBT. As Haaga and Davison (1993) concluded, no scientific evaluation of REBT is possible under these conditions. But that is not actually my purpose, as I tend to think that about all brand-name therapies (Evans, 2013). The significant part for the present discussion is whether it can be confirmed that rigorous disputation of a client's beliefs, judged by the therapist to be irrational, does not drive clients away but instead results in a change of those beliefs and that in turn reduces unwelcome emotions. Ellis (1989) certainly made that claim, with specialized disputation techniques being a key feature of the therapy but outright bombast being common. An observer of one of his public demonstrations described it thus: "'Let me tell you why people are always making you so angry', he [Ellis] informed a troubled young woman, one warm evening in 2005. 'Because they're screwed up! They're out of their fucking minds! We're all out of our fucking minds!'" (Burkeman, 2007, p. 1).

In truth we don't know from the research literature the answer to the question: What is it about REBT that changes thoughts and how do they change? Admittedly it does seem plausible that if a client's distress is the result of an erroneous belief or of failing to achieve an unreachable standard of personal behavior that has been inculcated by perceived social norms and cultural expectations, then altering that belief and perception and adjusting those standards should be psychologically beneficial. This is the thrust of many social change approaches, from assertiveness training to decolonization activities for indigenous people. But how do you change people's beliefs, particularly those that cannot be tested one way or another? Something else we do not know in mental health services is just how many clients seeking treatment actually experience distress because of their irrational beliefs. For how much of everyday psychopathology is irrational thought causal? Haaga and Davison (1993) pointed out that people do not tend to come to therapy complaining of their irrational thoughts. These are probed for by REBT therapists, who by virtue of their theoretical adherence are attuned to detect absolutist kinds of statements in a client's discourse. Personally, I think these thoughts of needing to conform to social expectations were much more likely to be seen in British and American clients in the 1950s and 1960s, when Ellis was practicing in New York City, than they are today.

Another interesting question is: What happens to an irrational belief if REBT is successful? Does the thought stop being believed—is it now simply seen as illogical or wrong or even funny and ridiculous? Or does it just disappear from mental experience and no longer influences behavior? Or is it replaced by a more rational, adaptive, or appropriate thought? Ellis seemed to think the latter was what happened. If a client originally claimed that "I should be a perfect mother," the desirable alternative thought is "I would like to be a perfect mother, but that is unreasonable as everyone makes some mistakes in parenting, so I will now try as hard as I can to be a better mother and I will accept that I will not always succeed, and when I do I'll be sure to feel happy and when I don't I will use the incident as feedback so I can do better the next time." A parenting example is apt because this is still one area in modern society where new parents are expected to be perfect. In one of our parenting studies (Couch & Evans, 2011), parents reflected on the changed thinking resulting from therapy. The intervention was didactic instruction (teaching the concept of "balance" between adult and child needs). This was facilitated by mothers watching children play together, reflecting on the developmental principles revealed, and analyzing expectations with other similar mothers facing similar insecurities. To paraphrase a typical subjectively reported outcome of this process:

> I used to think I was a terrible mother if Zoe didn't behave all the time or was ever unhappy. I blamed myself if she was upset, so of course I would get frustrated. Now I can see that there has to be a balance of our needs. I am not insistent on perfection any more—either in her or in me—and being more relaxed about Zoe's behavior and my responsibility for it actually makes everything more relaxed at home, and the transformation in Zoe has been remarkable. (Couch, 2010, p. 85)

Cognitive Therapy

It is easiest to understand the innovative ideas leading up to cognitive therapy if we remember that Beck (1967) developed his approach specifically for clients who were depressed. Depressed people tend to talk a certain way. They are self-critical, run themselves down, easily feel defeated, do not have much hope for the future, and assert that life is meaningless. Hamlet describes Denmark as a "prison" and how "weary, stale, flat and unprofitable seem to me all the uses of this world," while Macbeth, in despair, thought life itself as "a walking shadow, a poor player, that struts and frets his hour upon the stage, and then is heard no more. It is a tale told by an idiot, full of sound and fury, signifying nothing." Clients with clinical depression tend to be uncommunicative and emotionally unresponsive ("flat affect," as it is called in the trade) but can become more animated and anxious when talking about all the things that are wrong with their lives.

Beck (1967) reasoned that biased thoughts like these would darken a person's mood. If the glass could be perceived as half full instead of half empty, mood would become more positive, rewards would be more salient, coping more functional, and motivation to reengage in abandoned activities would increase.

Cognitive distortions are idiosyncratic, unrealistic conceptualizations. The fundamental therapeutic method (at least the cognitive part), therefore, is to target these thoughts and to change them by a combination of Socratic questioning, disputation, practice, and rehearsal of rewritten positive alternatives and real-life experiments to test the validity of the thoughts challenged by the therapist. In addition to a new and effective therapy for depression, the idea led to an outpouring of research on whether people who have a pessimistic view of the world (i.e., the cognitive category of a personality style) and tend to distort their observations are susceptible to clinical depression. In other words, is this cognitive style a causal mechanism for depression when faced with adversity or loss? Beck's clinical work led to similar analyses of the role of cognitive factors in trait anxiety, especially selective attention to threatening situations (Matthews, 2009; Mathews & Mackintosh, 1998; Matthews & Wells, 2000). The research supporting the value of cognitive therapy is impressively comprehensive (e.g., Hofmann, Asmundson, & Beck, 2013).

Each of the well-recognized clinical syndromes has been reanalyzed in terms of the dominant style of irrational thoughts or unfounded beliefs. In anorexia and bulimia nervosa, for example, the irrational belief, put most simply, is the overevaluation of weight and shape (Wilson, Wilfley, & Agras, 2010). Distortions can occur at a perceptual judgment level such as judging oneself to be fatter than one actually is, as well as placing too much positive value on thinness as a desirable and desired body characteristic. In the case of posttraumatic stress disorder, the cognitive "error" is to process the traumatic event and its emotional sequelae in such a way that the individual feels a sense of very serious current threat. This may be due to excessively negative evaluation of the traumatic event and also to disturbances in memory processing (Ehlers, Clark, Hackmann, McManus, & Fennell, 2005).

It has been pointed out by some commentators (e.g., Teasdale, 1999) that Beck (1967) developed these insights without paying much attention to the experimental and theoretical literature in cognitive psychology. As he is a psychiatrist with a psychoanalytic training (Weishaar, 1993), that is hardly surprising. However, two key principles he developed are very much in keeping with important concepts in cognitive science. One of these is the idea of automatic thoughts. In Beck's theory these are fleeting and arise spontaneously in relevant situations. Clients may not have the continuous thought of being hopeless about their future but if asked to plan for the future, for example, might think rapidly and if pressed might reply in words something like "What's the point? Nothing good will ever happen to me." Depressed clients have automatic thoughts not just about their future but about their world and about themselves—known as the depressive triad. These automatic thoughts sustain, maybe cause, negative mood and prevent engaging in activities likely to raise their level of reinforcing experiences. An implicit therapeutic technique in cognitive therapy is to render these thoughts less automatic. This is done by various meta-cognitive strategies (thinking more about one's own thoughts and where they come from) in which the habitual, spontaneous nature of these thoughts can be controlled by raising the probability of less reflexive, more effortful alternatives.

Beck (1991) has written that as a teenager his daughter Judith listened to him expound on his ideas (that is certainly one source of new thoughts!), and she has since become a leading exponent of cognitive therapy in clinical practice. Their standard techniques are very explicit in teaching clients meta-cognitive methods to discriminate between acceptable (in the therapy philosophy) and unacceptable thoughts. Judith Beck (2011) writes, for example:

> From the first session forward, you will encourage your patients to ask themselves, "What's going through my mind right now?" when they notice their mood changing, and remind themselves that their thinking may or may not be true. Initially they may jot down their thoughts (in their Smartphone, on their computer, or simply on paper, in a notebook, or on an index card). Advise patients that monitoring their automatic thoughts can lead them to feel worse, if they accept them uncritically, and that you will do problem solving with them if their thoughts do turn out to be valid.
>
> . . . At virtually every session, you will help patients modify their inaccurate and dysfunctional thoughts and write down their new way of thinking. An essential homework assignment is to have them read these therapy notes on a regular basis. Patients will also learn to evaluate their own thinking and practice doing so between sessions. (p. 296)

A second major construct in Beck's theory is that of the schema, which was partially defined and described in Chapter 1. A schema is not a real thing that can be located in the brain, although the idea that networks composed of emotions, memories, and current attention link known brain areas into a functioning unity is supported by functional magnetic resonance imaging and other evidence from neural recordings. As a structural image, however, it is a hypothetic construct used to account for an associative network of related memories and emotions that is relevant to important aspects of psychological functioning, such as intimate relationships, self-identity, and social interaction. Schemata are structures used for "screening, encoding, and evaluating impinging stimuli" (Beck, 1964, p. 562) and have been likened to mental magnets that pull in and organize experiences in ways that result in patterns of thinking that are hard to change. Beck's concept of a schema is very much in line with memory processes that permit the rapid appraisal of new information. It is patently adaptive to be able to judge (process) potentially threatening social information, based on memory of past encounters, in order to be able to avoid or mitigate potentially harmful interactions with others. As that is so adaptive, it is likely that evolution has enabled us to have these schemata for a variety of negative situations—social situations in the case of anxiety disorders, avoidance of loss and disappointment in the case of depression, and appropriate aggression in the case of anger. So schemata are good to have, even if they are not real. However if autobiographical memories of past harm or threats of harm or unpleasant experiences are too strong, a negatively valenced schema will prevent adaptive thoughts and behavior by allowing the negative automatic thoughts to predominate in ambiguous situations.

The initial interest primarily in depression in cognitive therapy (Whisman, 1993) was soon extended, by Beck and colleagues, to other disorders, especially anxiety, panic, anger, and hostility; eating disorders; and marital conflict, just to name some. It is easy to recognize how in each of these areas syndrome-specific schemata can be identified. In the case of so-called personality disorders, however, what seems to be the dominant feature of a person's schema is the intense emotional connections that are made around themes critical to our early development that can be marred by early negative experiences. For example, in early development it is well established that human infants require secure attachments to consistent caregivers in order to develop a "working model" (Bowlby's term) of their own personal identity differentiated from a reliable caregiver who offers protection and comfort from which one can explore and come to understand one's world. If attachments are insecure, perhaps as a result of abandonment or of abuse, then the schema related to security in intimate relationships will not be a network of positive memories and rewarding interactions with others.

Beck and Freeman (1990) provided a comprehensive analysis of the core beliefs that are likely to be characteristic of different personality disorders. For example a paranoid person's core belief is "Everyone is against me"; a narcissistic person's core belief is "I am special." In each personality disorder there would be related views of the self and of others. Thus the dependent person (whose core belief is "I am helpless") would have a view of him or herself as incompetent, needy, and weak and of others as superior and potentially nurturing. Such a person might need a steady flow of support and encouragement and would thus be likely to cultivate dependent relationships. By 1996, however, Beck was beginning to argue that because cognitive, affective, and behavioral schema seem to be organized into larger, integrated networks, it would be useful to introduce a new construct, that of the *mode*. A mode is more like a personality characteristic, consisting of interrelated elements including core beliefs, compensatory rules, and behavioral strategies. From this original analysis, Young (1994) elaborated on the schema hypothesis and made it more of a direct focus of therapy, schema-focused therapy.

Schema Therapy

Young (1994) proposed the existence of early maladaptive schemas at a deeper level of cognition. He thought these developed during childhood and were elaborated during adult life. If early experiences with parents and families are painful or traumatic, these dysfunctional schemas, which become the core of the individual's sense of self, prevent realistic "processing" (making sense of, remembering) of new information and experiences that are inconsistent with the maladaptive schemata. It has been suggested that one of the differences between the supposed operation of the deep schema Young hypothesizes and the schema Beck hypothesizes is that the former (early maladaptive schema) are unconditional ("I am unlovable") whereas the latter are conditional ("Only if I always please others can I be loved").

Young proposed 18 identifiable schemas that can be classified into five broader domains. To give a flavor of the model, those clients with the predominant domain "disconnection and rejection" do not expect their need for security, nurturance, acceptance, and respect to be met in a constant and predictable way, giving rise to feelings of low expectations of others and hypersensitivity to criticism. The domain of "impaired autonomy" entails schemata around needing constant care, the sense that disasters could strike at any time, and the feeling that one is a failure. The domain of "impaired limits" involves feelings of entitlement and difficulty with self-control—the origin of these schemas might be a family upbringing that was permissive and indulgent. In the domain of "other-directedness," people subjugate their own needs to gain love and approval from others, related to early childhood experiences of conditional acceptance by parents. "Overvigilance and inhibition" is a domain involving an excessive concern with controlling one's own feelings to avoid making mistakes, with rigid standards of performance taking precedence over personal happiness. As one might guess, the supposed family dynamic behind such a schema is one of punitiveness, stringent rule-following, and a harsh devotion to duty and obligation.

Schema therapy concepts are intuitively fairly obvious, with a certain face validity that anyone could construct by thinking of social and interpersonal history and the effects of different parenting styles on development. Every one of these areas has been explored in developmental research in terms of the links between early parental experience and later personality development, for example the well-studied, orthogonal dimensions of acceptance/rejection and control/permissiveness. Not only is schema therapy's terminology very loose, but it also does not clearly relate to established dimensions of personality. Young put together the Young Schema Questionnaire (YSQ; Young & Brown, 1994), based, by his own acknowledgment, on "clinical experience." While the YSQ has been translated into a number of different languages and been widely studied in administrations to both community and clinical samples, most of the findings are ordinary and self-evident, for example the schema of "unrelenting standards" is associated with obsessive-compulsive traits and that of "mistrust" is associated with paranoid personality disorder symptoms (Reeves & Taylor, 2007). The items in the YSQ are in a mixed format; some are self-ratings (e.g., "I don't belong; I'm a loner"); some are judgments of others' perceptions (e.g., "People see me as uptight emotionally"); some are beliefs (e.g., "No one I desire would want to stay close to me if he or she knew the real me"); some are thoughts (e.g., "I must meet all my responsibilities"); and some are feelings (e.g., "I often feel I do not have a separate identity from my parent[s] or partner"). After summarizing the less-than-convincing psychometric properties of the YSQ, Oei and Baranoff (2007) concluded oddly that the instrument "holds a great deal of potential" (p. 86). In a study by Jesinoski (2010), only for Domain 1 (disconnection and rejection) could pathways be shown between specific negative childhood experiences (e.g., neglect, physical abuse), early temperament, early emotional schemas of mistrust, defectiveness or alienation, and current negative affect.

It is not my purpose now to provide a full critique of the theory and its limited supporting evidence. Critical reviews do offer some cautious endorsement (Masley, Gillanders, Simpson, & Taylor, 2012). The main point of mentioning this entire perspective is that it articulates an important notion around thoughts: that is, one's current thoughts, especially those that summarize or make sense of an immediate current experience (notably interpersonal, emotional, and social experiences), are probably shaped by longstanding childhood experiences, which have provided an interpretive, transforming, emotionally charged network in memory. However, as Ward (2000) has pointed out, the way early experiences result in maladaptive schema has never been analyzed or explained in detail. Ward also criticizes Young's 18 schemas as a set of separate entities without any recognition that they might be interrelated and in which distorted beliefs are presented as though existing quite independently of each other.

Dialectical Behavior Therapy

Marsha Linehan's (1993) strategies for working with clients diagnosed with borderline personality disorder (BPD) were the most innovative cognitive behavioral therapy (CBT) methods to emerge in the 1990s. Through DBT Linehan brought into the mainstream of CBT three novel ideas (novel for empirically oriented clinical psychologists, at any rate). These were (a) the self-changing potential of Zen-Buddhist techniques, especially mindfulness training and practice; (b) the emotional benefits of radical acceptance of one's situation as it is, being nonjudgmental about one's own feelings; and (c) the need for distress tolerance—learning to tolerate very painful thoughts and memories. These ideas are now well established across modern CBT approaches.

Some of the other components of DBT are straight down the line behavioral and cognitive-behavioral methods, adapted for the special psychopathology exhibited by clients with BPD. First is the primary importance of the emotional relationship between therapist and client. In a nutshell, the defining characteristic of this as a therapeutically beneficial relationship is that the therapist will never abandon or reject the client, however demanding and difficult he or she may seem to be. The importance of this, Linehan has argued, is because what characterizes the syndrome is a fundamental approach–avoidance conflict between acceptance (which is overly strongly desired) and rejection (which is overly strongly feared). Therapy must be sustained with a client who tests the limits of a therapist's tolerance and patience, or otherwise the client's fears of abandonment will be a prediction fulfilled.

Closely related to this emotional relationship as a therapeutic mechanism is the basic idea of the dialectic. Here Linehan's knowledge of philosophy and her deep intellect has created a complex model of a fundamental dilemma. Here I simplify it. The nub of the idea is this: there is a mismatch or tension ("dialectic" means a tension between two conflicting but interacting ideas) between accepting clients as they are, however imperfect, and at the same time agreeing that they should change, or be changed. "Accept me as I am but help make me different" is a challenging assumptive demand on a professional. Nevertheless, Linehan's use of "dialectic" has a hidden double meaning, since the term also refers to the debate or intellectual discussion that is intended not to refute one or the other positions but to resolve the apparent contradiction by finding the truth in both sides. That is a very different meta-theoretical assumption than those of cognitive therapy (Beck and Ellis), where irrational thoughts are simply wrong and need to be dispelled.

A third, down-the-line behavior therapy feature of DBT is the emphasis on new skills needed to help BPD clients manage their erratic and volatile emotional expression, especially in social situations, and their excessively sensitive and overly analytic judgment of interpersonal relationships. My own understanding of this is that someone with a social anxiety might be hypervigilant for social cues of threat, such as criticism and perhaps rejection or dislike, whereas someone with an intense need for acceptance (BPD) will judge social cues of rejection or dislike as hostile, an experience that will make the person with BPD angry. Anger in social situations will, of course, tend to result in fairly rapid dislike and rejection by others—people with this syndrome are not popular and are often maligned, even in professional contexts, as difficult, insulting, or challenging. Threat of rejection makes a socially anxious person flee; in a person with BPD, it leads to attack.

While this is admittedly an oversimplification of a complex phenomenon, you might be able to see that the theory leads to three types of skill that can be taught in therapy. A potential solution to the discomfort experienced by someone with BPD is intensive meta-cognitive skill training: (a) learning to withhold judgment in cognitively ambiguous interpersonal situations; (b) learning to manage intense and distressing affect; and (c) learning to better recognize social cues and not to come on too strongly and intensely to other people who might not be ready for someone who appears so emotionally needy. In DBT these skills are generally taught in group therapy contexts. Clients learn to distract themselves from unpleasant thoughts, using self-talk, relaxation, prayer, mental imagery, and engaging more fully on the task at hand, all common behavior therapy methods—well, maybe not the prayer part. As these are all ways of changing thoughts, they too will reappear throughout this book. Similarly, emotion can be regulated through better labeling of feelings, increasing positive emotions, and use of mindfulness techniques. And third, the client is taught interpersonal effectiveness skills, such as learning to be explicit in asking for things in social contexts, learning to say "no" nonaggressively (assertiveness skills), and techniques for dampening down interpersonal conflict. All these skills are especially needed in intimate relationships, where the clients' feelings of insecurity and desperation induce overreactions that are unexpected and uncomfortable for the other person. People with BPD seem only too liable to push away people they like and to cling to people who dislike them.

I have emphasized the dynamics of the particular syndrome for which the therapy was developed because it is important to separate a strategy designed for a particular disorder from one that might be considered universal. Beck's theory was very much focused on depression, Linehan's on BPD—a group of clients she started working with because she had become interested in treating suicidal, parasuicidal, and self-harming behaviors (common in people who are diagnosed with BPD). If these therapies are being extended to all comers, then the breadth of the principles may need to be increased. Are Linehan's techniques universal ways of changing thoughts, or are they specific to BPD? This distinction is a conundrum that needs to be remembered—the reader can judge whether it has been resolved by the end of the book.

Mindfulness-Based Cognitive Therapy

It is thanks to Linehan (at least as I remember it) that mindfulness shot into popularity in clinical psychology circles, despite the very staid and rigorous science pretentions of CBT. Suddenly everyone was talking about mindfulness, even those who, like me, had never encountered the work of Kabat-Zinn (1982, 1990, 1994), an American with a PhD in molecular biology who was strongly influenced by a Vietnamese Zen Buddhist monk. He began exploring the use of mindfulness meditation for people with chronic pain and established the Stress

Reduction Clinic and the Center for Mindfulness in Medicine at the University of Massachusetts Medical School. But someone who did know about this work was John Teasdale, who had been wrestling with the rather obvious fact that Beck had developed a remarkable and successful cognitive therapy while being largely ignorant of the field of cognitive psychology. This meant that when standard cognitive therapy for depression either did not work with some clients or failed to prevent reoccurrence of depressive symptoms, there were no obvious additional tactics that could be deduced from the standard Beckian rationale.

Teasdale's attempt to put cognitive therapy on a sounder conceptual footing led to his proposals for MBCT. Its origin is in Teasdale's (1993; Teasdale & Barnard, 1993) complex model of the mind as a multilevel system that has different modes for receiving and processing different kinds of new information, both emotionally and cognitively. Like the other treatment approaches I describe in this chapter, I do the intricacy of the model something of a disservice, although its very density and hypothetical nature make it difficult to begin with.

Teasdale (1993) proposed a model for the mind that involves interacting cognitive subsystems (remember that, like schemas, these are not real things that can be observed directly). The model includes meta-cognitive awareness, which involves the recognition that a thought is something that can pass through consciousness and be identified as a mental event and is not an essential part of the self. I think we can accept that people are aware of their own thoughts and recognize them as products of their mind, of their consciousness. That sounds very close to the theory of mind concept—not just that other people have minds but that one does oneself and as such we should not always presume that all conscious experience represents reality.

The actual therapy techniques that emerged from this perspective (MBCT) are reasonably straightforward, however. They added mindfulness training to cognitive therapy, in particular to try to remedy the tendency of some people with depression to "relapse" (Segal, Williams, & Teasdale, 2002). More accurately, the phenomenon of concern is both one of incomplete removal of depression symptoms and also of depression symptoms returning after having apparently been remitted. In MBCT clients are given more intensive coaching in "decentering" their thoughts. This involves raising metacognitive awareness so that clients are less likely to be influenced by or even have automatic thoughts and are better able to accept negative thoughts and engage in mindfulness. Mindfulness involves a purposeful concentration on sensory and cognitive experience as it is, without judging it to be good or bad. MBCT encourages clients not to get caught up in evaluating the evidence for or against certain thoughts.

Mindfulness has been defined in various ways, but Teasdale's use is very close to that of Kabat-Zinn (1994), who defined it as "paying attention in a particular way—on purpose, in the present moment, and non-judgmentally" (p. 4). Others have captured the essence of mindfulness as not being a thinking process but an awareness process of consciously focusing, broadening, or directing attention.

Bishop et al. (2004), in a determined effort to define this ephemeral thing, proposed that in practice mindfulness has two components. One of these is the self-regulated application of attention to one's immediate experience, which permits the increased recognition of psychological events as part of that experience. The second component is that this concentrated attention is characterized by openness, a sort of curiosity as a nonparticipating observer, and an acceptance of the present moment. The actual training process is quite like meditation, which is described in more detail later but does not require a mantra, as in transcendental meditation. Also, Teasdale argues that instead of focusing on a passive bodily sensation such as breathing, with clients who are depressed the focus can be on a physical activity, such as yoga or walking. In a review of the outcome data on MBCT, Coelho, Canter, and Ernst (2007) were not very enthusiastic about the degree of support for the specifics of MBCT but did propose that it offers added benefit to clients who have had repeated episodes of depression (three or more).

Some concepts are especially revealing about frequently recurring depression. One is that it suggests the previous therapy has not altered the cognitive processing style in which negative judgments in ambiguous situations are the more dominant ones. Another is related to a sort of kindling or sensitizing effect. Each episode of clinical depression will result in strengthened or added memories of the experience of being depressed and thus further evidence of life's adversities. This is a sort of depression about depression not dissimilar to fear of fear, which is discussed again later. It is not just a bias in memory for negative events but also for nonspecificity of event memories, in which the details of a negative incident are not easily recalled but the generalization resulting from them are (Williams, 1996). For example, memories of any specific accident may be hazy, but the generalized idea that one is accident prone is distinct. It is not difficult to see how training in mindfulness allows clients to get beyond all the associations with past episodes and treatments and provides an alternative, focus-free experience that permits them to contemplate a positive future rather than dwell on past adversity.

A major assumption of MBCT is that, while undergoing mindfulness training, clients are instructed to focus conscious attention on their sense of being. It is argued that this focus allows for a cognitive separation of themselves from their thoughts and moods. Personally I find this dualism (the self separated from the self's thoughts and feelings) disquieting philosophically and psychologically. Nevertheless, the message seems to allow the client to escape the power of the mood—to show that one does not have to live according to the mood and the negative thought messages. Even though they continue to exist at the same time, they are in a different dimension. Through the separation of the self and the thoughts/moods, it is easier for the client to modify the thoughts with new, positive ones and to allow new, different behaviors in response to negative moods. These are not my words but are typical of the explanations offered for the effect of MBCT (Teasdale, Williams, & Segal, 2014). It is interesting that very similar and equally amorphous (in my opinion) descriptions of the therapeutic mechanisms of MBCT are offered in ACT, albeit from a slightly different theoretical framework.

Acceptance and Commitment Therapy

This is the last of the contemporary cognitive therapies that I introduce in this chapter. I think it is fair to do so, although its originator, Stephen Hayes, would probably argue that it is not a cognitive therapy at all but is epistemologically a functional contextual form of clinical behavior analysis. It is ostensibly derived from a contextual theory regarding the way alternative symbols for the same object are substitutable ("stimulus equivalence"), with the meaning of symbols determined by their context: known as "relational frame theory." But with its major constructs including acceptance (nonavoidance of experiences, even very negative ones), mindfulness, psychological (essentially cognitive) flexibility, and the self as context, it is certainly a cognitive model, and its assumed mode of influence is through words (from the therapist, as well as from self-talk), although, like all of the other cognitive therapies mentioned, it also involves taking action. That means engaging in new behaviors for their information value and for the resultant changes in positive (reinforced) experiences, which is why the acronym is pronounced "act" and not A.C.T.

Clients with diverse problems are thought to have, as their common or core personality deficit, psychological inflexibility. This inflexibility is thought to arise from two sources. One of these is cognitive fusion, which involves a focus on the content of private thoughts and feelings as though they were true. The other is that such fusion gives rise to distressing internal experiences that the individual struggles to avoid or escape (experiential avoidance), even if the personal and social costs of such avoidance are considerable. To remedy these, ACT proposes a combination of expository (explaining the theory) techniques and the clarification of certain key values. Six interacting concepts relate to psychological flexibility and are thus the foci of intervention: acceptance (as opposed to experiential avoidance), cognitive defusion (described as distancing or detaching from the literal meaning of words and thoughts), contact with the present moment (as opposed to fixed ideas of the past and fears for the future), clarification of values, self as context, and committed action (as opposed to inaction, impulsivity, or avoidance) (Prevedini, Presti, Rabitti, Miselli, & Moderato, 2011).

Given the important concepts that surround the therapy as a clinical method, it is not always easy to distil the essence of the processes assumed to be responsible for change. But there are some essential ideas that pervade the writings of Hayes and his colleagues (Hayes & Lillis, 2012; Hayes, Strosahl, & Wilson, 2012). There is an emphasis on the function of thought rather than the content of thoughts. In terms of emotional experience, there is adherence to a principle that states that negative emotional experiences are as fundamental to human experience as positive ones. Negative emotions provide information, and so clients should struggle less to avoid having them, particularly if such avoidance has been costly in the past. Because thoughts can be combined and interrelated in many different directions, it can be emphasized to clients that a directional reference is not inevitable. The thought "I am a failure" is not so much erroneous (as in Beckian cognitive therapy) or simply uncharacteristic of healthy self-acceptance (as in Ellis's therapy) as not helpful in allowing the client to progress in the direction of their stated values. Taking thoughts too literally is called cognitive fusion, and the intervention to change that is called cognitive defusion. Therapeutically one focuses the client not on the error of the thought but on its function or usefulness—the techniques are designed to detach any importance afforded the thought. (Presumably this is the troubling thought, which calls for complex discrimination on the part of the client, as defusion is itself a cognitive act that requires new thoughts of some kind. And, as will be encountered later, explicit personal values may not represent implicit attitudes regarding the self. Such paradoxes are not examined in the theory.)

In ACT treatments it is stressed that who one is should be tied to the actions and activities one engages in according to one's values and goals for living a "meaningful and purposeful" life. The aversiveness of thoughts cannot simply be avoided in the way one can avoid threatening or painful physical stimuli. Avoiding thoughts is made essentially impossible by the fact that thoughts can be cued by an endless plethora of other thoughts, conversations, memories, even moods. Thus allowing thoughts regardless of their emotional valence (acceptance) is necessary, not avoidance, and will be therapeutic as long as the client takes action to fulfill opportunities for really important experiences that are in accordance with meaningful life goals. Struggling to avoid aversive psychological (mental) experiences intensifies difficulties as these experiences are typically beyond the control of verbal processes, such as self-talk.

The Common Features of the Cognitive Therapies

Despite the link with behavior therapy implied by the accepted term "cognitive-behavioral therapy," cognitive theorists would accept, at the epistemological level, the not-very-behaviorist constructivist view that individuals construct reality not just from external sense data but from within (Mahoney, 2002). Mahoney placed into cognitive therapy Kelly's (1955) idea of the individual as a personal scientist. We do not so much distort objective reality as we create our own—what is often referred to as meaning-making. Constructivists, however, recognize a central core of processes that are protected from external influence and thus limit the flexibility of the first level of making sense of the world. A third element of constructivist models is that our self-identity is stable and allows some degree of steady self-perception and self-evaluation in the face of ever-changing experiences. In clinical work these three notions were forcefully expressed by Mahoney (1993); however, my own reading of the leading cognitive therapists is that they cling to an empirical rather than truly social constructionist view of reality. They are, like William James, pragmatists.

There is another fundamental difficulty in relating theories and principles of changing thoughts to the techniques of cognitive therapy: the cognitive therapies are overlaid with complex clinical procedures and techniques that have nothing to do with their basic assumption regarding how and why thoughts change. Outcome studies of the effectiveness of the therapies do not validate their theoretical rationales (Whisman, 1993; Kazdin & Nock, 2003). Outcome studies comparing one cognitive therapy with another tend to show they are equally effective; a good example of this is a well-designed study by Manicavasagar, Perich, and Parker (2012) in which cognitive therapy and MBCT produced equally good results in treating depressed Australian clients. Another example is Forman, Herbert, Moitra, Yeomans, and Geller's (2007) comparison of cognitive therapy and ACT for treating anxiety and depression. Both therapies produced equivalent gains in syndrome reduction and other benefits, such as quality of life. A similar pattern of results was also found in a large clinical trial comparing CBT and ACT for clients with various anxiety disorders (Arch et al., 2012). Although it seemed like the mediating processes might have been slightly different, these are usually defined (reported on by clients) in the same language that has been used extensively in the therapy. Clients learn our lingo so that differences in how they report their therapeutic experiences (process) are obscured.

It is not even clear how different the therapies actually are in practice, even though their theoretical rationales sound different. There are differences in therapist expertise, and it is rather easy to drift away from adherence to the prescribed methods. Because the cognitive therapies all emerged from a social learning perspective, they tend to have a number of features in common. This is compounded by specific therapies usually having a variety of elements. Emotional processing therapy was developed by Edna Foa and colleagues for the treatment of adult clients with posttraumatic stress disorder, especially women who have been raped (Foa & Kozak, 1986). Foa has argued that the memory structures (schemata) that result from trauma involve very complex patterns of associations, often to stimuli present but only peripherally relevant at the time of the trauma. Such schema also include, in her model, powerful self-beliefs: being unable to handle stress, that the trauma might have been preventable, and that the world is fundamentally dangerous. Their standard protocol illustrates the multicomponent nature of CBT treatments. It contains educational information about common reactions to trauma, training in controlled breathing, prolonged and repeated recounting of traumatic memories during sessions, outside of sessions listening to a recording of those recounted experiences (homework), encouraging exposure (involvement, participation) in those situations that the client typically avoids because of fearfulness, and discussions with the therapist of the thoughts and feelings arising from the exposure experiences (Ehlers & Clark, 2000). That is a lot of elements for a treatment whose essence is based on two dysfunctional cognitions: the thought that the world is dangerous and the thought that one's self is totally unable to handle stress. The "processing" terminology is an attempt to understand the therapeutic mechanism in a way different from the conventional behavioral model of prolonged exposure being an extinction procedure (see Evans, 2013, for a discussion). The first mechanism is the same: fear structures (schema) must be activated. The second is different: information must be presented or experienced that is incompatible with some features of the fear structure and must be integrated in it so that the pathological elements (dysfunctional thoughts) are replaced with more realistic ones. Cognitive strategies involve taking time to understand what one is really feeling and acknowledging emotions as having personal importance and validity. The client must also reduce engaging in the dysfunctional avoidance strategies that emerge from the negative appraisals of the trauma and its sequelae.

The various approaches to cognitive therapy share another feature: they all distinguish between core and peripheral cognitive underpinnings (Safran, Vallis, Segal, & Shaw, 1986). Although for purposes of illustration we all tend to trot out simple examples of irrational thoughts that are very easily mentioned but clinically quite rare (e.g., "I'm a failure"), cognitive therapy more typically deals with slightly deeper mechanisms, often involving interpersonal schemas. Expectations of rejection, feelings of inadequacy, general self-criticism, or being threatened by conflict are all core cognitive elements that may not always be expressed in words or articulated as pessimistic, overgeneralized statements about a harsh, hostile, and threatening world. But their influence is implicit. They will, in the very specific sense of being at the root of, underlie the way interpersonal experiences are judged and interpreted.

When it comes to the delivery of treatments, the cognitive therapies and traditional behavior therapy share some values and methods of actually *doing* therapy, although their focus on what is important to target for change may sometimes be different. Both provide clients with a basic psychological model of internal and external influences. In Beckian cognitive therapy, for example, it is common to start by explaining a "five-part model" to clients of how thoughts, mood, behavior, and biology all interact within an environmental context (Padesky & Mooney, 1990). Like behavior therapy, cognitive therapies also tend to engage clients in practical conversations about their daily lives and experiences as they perceive them. While the therapeutic engagement is warm and genuine, it is help-oriented and much more directive than other therapeutic schools such as psychoanalysis (object-relations theory) and humanistic, client-centered psychotherapy (Keijsers, Schaap, & Hoogduin, 2000). There is a focus on learning new skills, both behaviors and habits of thought, so that the therapist's role is more like a supportive teacher or coach than a healer. There is also an almost exclusive concentration on conscious awareness, and what the client reports is accepted at face value, rather than interpreted for its hidden meaning. Even in ACT, where thought content is less important, the therapist is still dependent on the clients' self-reports of their mental state and verbal descriptions of their emotional experiences.

All of CBT emphasizes current experiences and circumstances, while acknowledging that past history will have shaped a client's expectations and ways of perceiving the world, and these may need to be counteracted in some way. But rather than retracing developmental processes and long-distant relationships, the objective across these therapies is to look ahead to the future and what needs to change in order to resolve current difficulties and meet new goals. All cognitive therapies attend to manifestations of personality style as these are represented in dominants thoughts and beliefs, although these vary by disorder. Thus depressed clients have a pessimistic judgment style, eating-disordered clients are often perfectionistic, and anxious clients perceive themselves as vulnerable to harm. These are not schemas but traits, and their broad effect on clients is often discussed early in the treatment sessions.

All of the cognitive therapies address the meaning that clients ascribe to their symptoms (meaning-making) or the way they interpret their symptoms. The therapeutic goal is to encourage positive reframing—seeing past events in a different light or interpreting current feelings as having some constructive value. Sometimes this is just a matter of providing information, thus instilling new ideas and dispelling myths. Clients with eating disorders are especially likely to have erroneous information about the effects of dieting, natural weight fluctuations, and the futility of harmful diets and strategies that bring about short-term weight loss but exacerbate the problem in the long run (such as purging; Fairburn, 2008). Often this is done using diagrams and simple models of hypothesized factors maintaining the symptoms. This is rather like the clinician's case conceptualization but personalized for the client's own experiences, language, expressed beliefs, and personal goals. At a slightly deeper level symptoms can be reanalyzed by exploring how they have come to dominate the individual's life and self-perception and are interfering with engagement in many other activities once valued and enjoyed.

The empirical evidence for the delivery characteristic of CBT is not extensive, but there are some informative studies. Jones and Pulos (1993) rated verbatim transcripts of therapy sessions from trained CBT therapists and those using brief psychodynamic techniques. So what was the CBT actually like? The 10 most characteristic features of CBT were (a) the therapist actively exerts control over the interaction, (b) the therapist behaves like a teacher, (c) most of the discussion is centered on cognitive themes, (d) the client's current life situation is emphasized, (e) there is discussion of activities and tasks the client should be practicing outside the sessions, (f) the therapist actively asks for more information or elaboration, (g) the client's self-image is often a focus of discussion, (h) the therapist explains the rationale behind the technique, (i) the therapist is supportive, and (j) the therapist restates, paraphrases, and clarifies the client's communications. Goldfried, Castonguay, Hayes, Drozd, and Shapiro (1997) also dissected sessions from CBT and psychodynamic-interpersonal therapy protocols. They noted that CBT tended to be prescriptive, suggesting how clients could cope better with events in the future; in other words teaching active skills, not simply changing thoughts. CBT therapists offered support and encouragement to engage in between-session experiences; if there was a focus on reality, the broad CBT message was "things are not as bad as you think."

The implication for cognitive therapy is that the chief delivery mechanism for cognitive change is that of a verbal dialog, a narrative conversational interaction that involves an exchange of ideas and information rather than the explicit elicitation of feelings. As such, cognitive therapy is a cerebral, intellectual approach, rich in examples, metaphors, parables, self-disclosure, and readings from texts and self-help books. It is possible, although we do not really know much about this, that cognitive therapy tends to be more effective with people who typically analyze situations intellectually and who are aware of their own thinking patterns and can report these in an insightful way. Although their meta-cognitive conclusions are incorrect, they are not mind-blind. Being thoughtful may make it easier for thoughts to be changed. However, one of the implications of this book is that by gaining a still deeper understanding of how thoughts do actually change, it will be easier to achieve change even in people who do not engage in much self-reflection.

From our starting point of changing thoughts, there is another strange feature that cognitive therapies tend to have in common. Compared to outcome studies (did the therapy produce the expected clinical change in clients' mental health?), there are not that many process studies (did those clients who achieved the best clinical outcomes show the greatest degree of change in the cognitive patterns that were targeted in therapy?). The reason for this imbalance in the research is that the field of psychotherapy, stung a long time ago by Eysenck's (1952) provocative claim that there was no evidence it actually helped people, has been more focused on demonstrating results than on revealing the principles of change. But such studies do exist, for example Teasdale and Fennell (1982) found that change in automatic negative thoughts came about when clients were taught to test their assumptions and reformulate their negative beliefs. In other words, thoughts can be changed by thought-change exercises, and with that change comes a reduction in symptoms of depression.

As research designs have evolved to match the realities of clinical practice by observing change within and between therapy sessions, empirical confirmation of process influences continues to grow. They support observations common in clinical practice, such as the occurrence of therapeutic breakthroughs, described in the research literature rather blandly as "sudden gains." Bland or not, a key finding has been that in the session preceding dramatic improvement in clients, expected cognitive changes occurred (Tang & DeRubeis, 1999). Within-session measures of introducing specific cognitive techniques (such as attempting to change client beliefs) or discussing general philosophical principles of CBT, or enhancements in the alliance between therapist and client, in contrast, did not immediately precede sudden therapeutic gains. That does not mean these others are inert features of therapy—they presumably exert their influence earlier in the sessions, although everything is a bit interactive, in that *after* showing sudden improvement, the therapeutic alliance also improves. Naturally, both client and therapist enjoy treatment success. The original findings were replicated by Tang, DeRubeis, Beberman, and Pham in 2005. However when "cognitive change" is referred to in these studies, it covers a pretty broad category of client changes, such as changes in beliefs, schemata, and the acquisition of new "cognitive techniques," which are usually ways of controlling negative thoughts. Even so, the studies are persuasive: it is the specific cognitive effects of CBT, rather than the nonspecifics, that help clients.

Strengths-Based Assumptions

All of the cognitive therapies identified here, especially ACT (Kashdan & Ciarrochi, 2013), are sympathetic toward the positive psychology movement. There is less emphasis on client deficits and disorders and psychiatric illnesses and more on helping clients fulfill their potential—achieving "lives of value," meeting social and interpersonal obligations, and realizing a sense of well-being. These values are not always clearly articulated as part of CBT, since there has long been a tradition of emphasizing the therapeutic techniques that have been validated by outcome studies, rather than creating a meta-theory of what therapy is all about (Evans & Fletcher, 2013). But the values described here can be gleaned from the writings of leading CBT therapists, from video-tapes and demonstrations and from the written transcripts of therapy sessions delivered by foremost practitioners.

Smythe and Dewar (2009), for example, proposed that casting individuals strictly in terms of their *strengths* was a "different way of thinking" (p. 147). How would this come about? First it requires knowledge of what a strength is, in general, and they define it in terms of what a person has to give. They consider strengths to be the familiar things a person already does that fills him or her with energy and drive and thus cannot be defined by job performance measures or be identified by someone other than that individual. Yet there are dangers in these assumptions: Buckingham's (2008) approach is to teach people that their strengths are the activities "that make you feel strong" (p. 43), and this could be perceived as a highly self-centered perspective. One might then need to think about one's own strengths and try to validate them, but actually we usually assume that the approach focuses on the positive abilities and interests that people bring to a task, be it education, psychotherapy, community work, or whatever.

It is also necessary to examine the opposite carefully and to become more sensitive to older mental habits of deficit thinking. It might be necessary to change a common paradigm, for example if working in a mental health clinic and wanting to have a strengths-based approach, the traditional focus on illness, limitations, and pathology, symptoms, and syndromes is counterproductive to language and principles that emphasize people's abilities, not their disabilities, their individual humanity not their label. If deficit terms dominate the discourse and the administrative language of a service, it is very difficult to be consistent on one's strength-based dialogue. So too if the words are the right ones but they do not lead to tangible differences in opportunities for people and the way they are treated and how acceptable they perceive themselves to be.

While ACT makes a special point of stressing values, it is not unique in its focus on empowerment and resisting pathologizing models—consider, for example Ward's "good lives" model (Ward, Mann, & Gannon, 2007) or, in the area of student behavior, the importance of restorative discipline (Meyer & Evans, 2012). A particularly important early influence, although nowadays not considered one of the evidence-based cognitive therapies, was the work of William Glasser (1965), a psychiatrist, with what he called "reality therapy." His focus was on choice, the futility of trying to change others, and enhancing clients' beliefs that they could control their own behavior. He would pose a question that is implicit in a number of the cognitive therapies: "What are you going to do about your life, beginning today?" His message was (he died in September 2013) to be nonjudgmental; to focus on making specific, workable plans for the present; and to emphasize options rather than symptoms. For those of us interested in positive approaches to school discipline, his book *Schools Without Failure* (1969) provided essential lessons in the importance of avoiding coercive methods in favor of fostering a trusting relationship between students and teacher in order to promote personal responsibility in students.

Confusingly, all of the self-consciously "cognitive" therapies described emphasize that in clinical practice they also rely on what they call "behavioral" techniques. Kingdon (2009), writing about clinical work with people with psychosis, states "behavioral experiments, properly designed and carried out, can modify beliefs and assumptions more powerfully than verbal techniques in the office" (p. 4). Young and McGinn (1996) state that "schema-focused therapy incorporates, when appropriate, many well-established behavioral and operant techniques, such as social skills, assertiveness training, systematic exposure, and behavioral programming" (p. 199). Of course they do—there is nothing wrong with introducing a range of tactics for helping people change. It is just that as a result it is scientifically meaningless to evaluate a particular therapy's unique effectiveness when it is essentially no different from any other form of therapy.

What is sometimes presented as a desire to integrate and unify cognitive psychotherapies flounders on the truism that we cannot actually tell them apart.

The Uncommon Features of Cognitive Therapies

There is one conceptually rather confusing way in which clinical cognitive therapies differ, and that is the level at which cognitive events are identified as targets for change. There is a long series of hypothesized processes between initial sensation and perception and the expression of elaborate ideas and beliefs. In cognitive therapy two intermediate levels are often identified—and as a result somewhat confused. These are (a) the level at which information is processed or retrieved from memory (such as selective attention to cues, appraisal of a situation as positive or negative, and misinterpretation of ambiguous situations or memories) and (b) the level of the overly simplistic conscious thoughts that characterize the results of such processing and by which biased or erroneous processing becomes known (to others, especially the therapist). Some cognitive therapy techniques, especially those that are clinically relevant to psychotherapy, emphasize the latter (conscious thoughts and expressed thought content), others emphasize the former (prethought processing), and a few go back and forth between both. Prethought processing distortions have given rise to a newer set of methods called *cognitive-bias modification,* which sounds like a new therapy, but I am not convinced of its novelty except perhaps as a delivery technique (it is often administered through computer software or other learning programs). It is fashionable and thought to be scientifically de rigueur to talk about "training the client's brain" rather than "teaching the client," but either way cognitive-bias modification depends on the well-established phenomenon of transfer of training (Woodworth & Schlosberg, 1954) as a way of altering personality-level tendencies to make cognitive processing errors.

What is rarely discussed but is a very striking feature of the cognitive therapies is that they generally evolved in the context of a specific psychiatric syndrome: depression for Beck's theory (though he went on to address anxiety, anger/hostility, and schizophrenia in much the same way) and for Teasdale; personality disorders and trauma for Young; BPD and self-harm for Linehan; and mixed adult psychoneurotic disorders for Ellis and Hayes. From these syndrome-specific theories, all of them have captured a much wider market of client problems for which their treatment is claimed to be effective, including drug and alcohol abuse, aggression, posttraumatic stress disorder, and psychosis. It is because of these "big-picture" claims that they have become generalized perspectives on adult psychotherapy. At the same time, very important therapy advances have been made with targeted syndromes that have not assumed this kind of brand-name status. The finest example is Barlow's (2002) analysis of anxiety disorders from a behavioral-cognitive-neurobiological perspective, leading to well-developed treatment manuals for panic and generalized anxiety disorder. In his approach there is a very tight connection between psychopathology research and strategies for change. There are other good examples—ones that come to mind are Foa's memory model for trauma, especially sexual assault (Foa & Rothbaum 1998), Salkovskis (1996) and other British writers on obsessive-compulsive disorder and panic, the British group working with CBT and psychosis (e.g., Kingdon & Turkington, 2005), Fairburn and Wilson's (1993) manuals for eating disorders and obesity, Heimberg on social anxiety (e.g., Hope, Heimberg, & Turk, 2010), the late Alan Marlatt on alcohol abuse (e.g., Witkiewitz & Marlatt, 2007), the late Neil Jacobson on marital difficulties (Jacobson, Christensen, Prince, Cordova, & Eldridge, 2000), and Kendall's work with coping strategies for anxious children (Kendall & Hedtke, 2006).

Obviously I am leaving out many exceptional clinical researchers whose work has closely combined what are broadly CBT principles with their cognitively guided analysis of these major clinical problems. And because clients in these different diagnostic categories are all a bit different, so the treatments developed by these notable researchers also use slightly different terms, emphasize slightly different constructs, and describe very different thought patterns that are syndrome specific. Thus they make little attempt to reconcile or merge their theories and often totally ignore major areas of relevant work, such as developmental psychopathology, as Chorpita and Barlow (1998) complained about. As a result we find ideas that are by no means universal across people, cultures, or syndromes suddenly coming into fashion as though they were the best treatments for all comers who have straggled into a clinical service.

Implications

A primary assumption of all of the cognitive therapies is that clients' thoughts are causing their problems, perhaps because they are irrational (i.e., not reflective of reality), or their thoughts are not to be confused with the reality of situations, or their appraisals of situations are erroneous, or their beliefs are unfounded or simply not helpful. Yet there is a large amount of evidence from social and cognitive psychology that the default option—the thinking of people who are not clients—is wildly unfounded and often illogical, easily distorted by past experience, memory failings, and self-preserving (defensive) emotions. We have in everyday society unrealistic optimism, exaggerated notions of the degree of control, and self-perceptions that are unjustifiably positive (Taylor & Brown, 1988). Some have used this kind of evidence, and other experimental studies, to claim that clients with depression are sadder but actually wiser—their views of themselves and the world are actually more accurate than those of the rest of us

(Alloy & Abramson, 1979). But both client pessimism and nonclient optimism could be equally nonreflective of reality. What the boundless optimism illusion does, however, is allow nonclients to distort negative information and make it less threatening (Taylor & Brown, 1988).

In the Jones and Pulos (1993) study, the relationship between what actually transpired in CBT and the outcome for the clients suggested that one CBT benefit lies in helping clients achieve greater control of negative affect through the use of honest, self-reflective intellectual processes. This is always combined with vigorous encouragement, support, and reassurance by the therapist, which enhances self-acceptance. Because traditional behavior therapy techniques also relied on changing covert processes through language and imagery (see Chapter 7), what are generally referred to as the cognitive therapies are not the only methods within general CBT that deal with cognitive events or teach clients internal, meta-cognitive strategies for change. However, the cognitive therapies all have one important feature in common, which is that they emphasize the importance of changing the derivation, the content, and the function of conscious thought. Unconscious cognitive processes are always added, such as automatic thoughts, implicit attitudes, and appraisals and expectancies about people and events. But these unconscious processes are either made known to the therapist through expressed thoughts or inferred from theories of psychopathology, which is a bit circular.

The cognitive therapies, as copartners in the broader business of CBT, all rely on theoretical principles regarding the nature of thoughts, but unless specific process studies are conducted regarding how and why thoughts change, the success or otherwise of these therapies in clinical work does not have much bearing on the adequacy of these theoretical principles. What the cognitive therapies do so conveniently is to provide descriptions of methods that have been used to try to change thoughts. Some of these methods have been described in this chapter but not yet in psychological depth. To complicate matters, methods have been refined for specific categories of psychiatric disorders, so there are syndrome-specific techniques all showing significant degrees of empirical support as defined by typical efficacy trials (Hofman, Asnaani, Vonk, Sawyer, & Fang, 2012).

Anyone who has read clinical transcripts or seen demonstrations of their therapeutic methods by the leading scholar-clinicians, including others not mentioned in this chapter, must have noted that their style for working with clients goes well beyond their basic theory of change. Salkovskis (1996) makes this very point by quoting Christine Padesky's suddenly recognizing from a training video that, when he was actually doing therapy, it was Beck's questioning style that allowed a female patient to develop a clearer understanding of her problems. The insight was that Beck seems to value "client ownership of discovery over dramatic therapeutic interventions that make the therapist look clever" (p. 538). I am sure that is true. Yet it makes it well-nigh impossible to deduce the actual processes of change from explanations of the cognitive principles or to separate them from the generic therapeutic strategy employed. So maybe we have to leave the different varieties of cognitive therapy for a while and just try to address the commonalities of thought change as revealed in the experimental psychology of cognition.

3

Thinking About Thoughts

Angels are pure intelligences; not material, but limited, so that they may have location in space but not extension. An analogy might be drawn from human thought, which is similarly non-material and similarly limited.

—Dorothy Sayers, *The Lost Tools of Learning*.
A talk delivered at Oxford University, 1947

Thought is Nonmaterial

We come now to the really hard part. It is easy enough to paraphrase what a number of cognitive therapists have said about how to change thoughts and why we might need or want to. But defining thoughts and thought processes in a manner consistent with current psychological knowledge and of potential interest to therapeutic practice is another kettle of fish entirely. One can almost sense the relief that J. B. Watson and the other early behaviorists must have felt when they proclaimed that analyzing consciousness had too many questions about the number of angels who could dance on the head of a pin, and from now on psychology was to be about behavior: stimulus and response, with the bit in-between being best consigned, as Skinner argued, to a black box. But if we try to shine our flashlight into the box, what will we see? This chapter lays out some of the general understanding in the psychology of thought that helps connect the principles directly to cognitive therapy procedures.

It is convenient for now to represent a conscious thought (an event we are aware of, can report to others, and reflect on) as inner speech, something that is encoded in words—or some other communicable symbol system. Preverbal children obviously have thoughts, but it is only when children are capable of thinking about something that is not physically present that therapy for them can become *cognitive* therapy. We can, of course, think one thing and say another, but that thought could potentially be uttered in external words, and once done so socially, in the presence of an audience, it has consequences that internal thoughts do not. When you say out loud to someone or some group "Not guilty," "I love you," "That dessert was disgusting," a thought that had no social influence when private has a fundamental impact on what happens next.

As noted in the previous chapter, cognitive therapy treats thought content as words (usually subvocal things said to oneself or reported to a therapist). Sometimes it is presumed that a word alone serves as a cue, and sometimes it is presumed that a string of words serves as a message about reality—what to expect from a situation. If the string of words uses faulty reasoning, the expectation will be based on error, and the expected hurt, or danger, or put-down will not occur but will still cue emotion (depression, fear, or anger) in such a way that the individual essentially experiences hurt, danger, or put-down. But with this slight exception (these misplaced expectancies), cognitive therapy theory has not tried to attribute client distress to nonverbalized thought, such as intuition, gut feeling, or instinct. So, unlike psychodynamic approaches, potentially conscious—usually verbal—inner experience is the focus of therapy and the presumed cause of distress. However, what Beck called "automatic" thoughts, as well as latent beliefs, appraisals, expectancies, and inferences are assumed, in cognitive therapy, to be lurking in the background.

Thoughts as Representations

Is a thought a representation of a mental event, or is it the mental event itself? The question can be posed because the only way we know about a thought is to ask for it to be expressed in words. For example, what thoughts does a child have about his or her mother? Quite possibly none, until asked for one (question: "Tell me about your mom"). Of course the child will have had countless mother-related thoughts ("she'll be cross if she knows I did this," "Mom is busy today," "Mom loves me"), but these are not generalized summary thoughts until called for (answer: "Well, my mom gets cross with me at times, but I know she loves me and she is sometimes too busy to notice things I do wrong"). So, until expressed outwardly as a thought, what is the child's representation of the construct "mother"? The working model concept, a sort of blend of attachment ideas and schema models, suggests that there will be at the nonverbal level a coherent system of expectations, assumptions, and emotional connections that will guide behavior despite the absence of a conscious, verbally complex thought. Thus, in the simple example given, the child's working model would mean that when the child transgresses, he or she will not be very worried about Mother's reactions (implicitly either because Mother might not find out and if she does her love will override her annoyance). In everyday life, therefore, that child will typically not worry about mistakes and errors and feel secure that lapses will be forgiven, even if these thoughts never exist in that precisely articulated form.

These representations in children can be measured by the technique of the prompted narrative, also known as a story stem task, in which the child completes a simple sentence and from the narrative they generate, assumptions can be made about their conceptual framework. With the MacArthur Story Stem Battery (Bretherton, Oppenheim, Emde, & the MacArthur Narrative Working Group, 2003), children are not asked about their own families but instead are asked about what might happen to the family in the story, usually illustrated with dolls and other props. The clinician might start a story like this:

> So, Mommy, Daddy, Mario, and his sister sit down at the table to eat breakfast [clinician holds up Mario doll]. Mario reaches to get the juice, and you know what happens? He tries to get the juice and he spills it by mistake! [knocks over the pitcher] "Oh no!" Show me and tell me what happens.

Another typical stem provides triggers to parental conflict. The story stem might go something like this, while the clinician sets up the dolls:

> Well, here's Mom and Dad and a little girl, let's call her Ruby. Here's Ruby coming into the room and she sees Mom and Dad looking at each other like this [clinician pulls an angry face]. Mom says [using a dramatic tone] "You lost my keys!" Dad says, "No, I didn't." Mom says, "Yes, you did; you always lose them." Dad says, "Well, I did not lose them this time!" Show me and tell me what happens next.

Obviously the child's thoughts need to be carefully coded, but the words used, the themes expressed, and in particular the likely outcomes and the ways of coping revealed all provide the clinician with much information. In some scoring methods the cohesion of the story (planning and sequencing) is considered important, as is the avoidance of distressing elements. Empathy can be scored as well as antisocial thoughts and thoughts about how a parent might sooth and comfort an upset child (Robinson, 2007). When children who have been abused or exposed to family violence provide narrative extensions to the sorts of stems illustrated here, themes of helplessness, threat, and hostility are common. Furthermore, when mothers have been traumatized in violent relationships, their own ability to consistently validate their children's negative emotions (see the discussion in Chapter 6) is compromised. The origins of the schemata hypothesized by Young are only too apparent when the thoughts revealed in these narrative are explored (Oppenheim, 2006).

The Link: Cognitive Distortions

All cognitive therapy, as we learned in Chapter 2, revolves around some sort of method for changing what the therapist judges to be cognitive distortions—irrational thoughts and erroneous beliefs (content), or appraisals, attributions, and inferences unsupported by evidence (process). What is much less certain, however, is where such distorted thoughts and processing styles come from in the first place, other than a rather circular proposal that they come from distorted schemas and that these are created by negative experiences. The attribution is to early childhood experiences and especially (in the case of clinically relevant schemas) of distressing, traumatic, punitive, socially rejecting experiences. While this general position links a great deal of developmental knowledge about the relationship between early experiences and later psychopathology, it does not provide a very satisfactory account of the cognitions that need to be targeted for therapeutic benefit, nor does it explain how and why a therapist can change these cognitions when the client, and his or her social environment, cannot. Nevertheless, as will be seen in this chapter, the schema/working model/implicit theory idea provides one way of thinking about the origins of specific (able to be isolated) individual thoughts when these are triggered by external events.

A pertinent example of this presumption regarding thought origins in clinical practice is the phenomenon that clinicians call *ideation*. This refers to clients having persistent ideas (thoughts) about something, especially suicide. A study of adults who had had traumatic experiences found significant correlations between suicidal ideation and three of the early maladaptive schemas as reported on the Young Schema Questionnaire: Social Isolation/Alienation, Failure, and Defectiveness/Shame (Dutra, Callahan, Forman, Mendelsohn, & Herman, 2008). *Social isolation* refers to feelings of being different and not belonging; *failure* refers to beliefs that one has failed in life and is therefore stupid or inept; and *defectiveness* refers to beliefs of being unlovable, bad, and unwanted.

According to William James (1970), we do not need reasons for our beliefs when there are no challenges to them that must be responded to. We have views and opinions and beliefs that need to be reconsidered only on the basis of new experiences that run counter to them. He suggested we are most likely to accept a new opinion when doing so requires the minimum modification to existing beliefs. Thus a true idea "marries old opinion to new fact so as ever to show a minimum of jolt, a maximum of continuity" (pp. 34–35). Beliefs have a degree of inertia and will tend to be preserved if we have no reason to abandon them. Here we see the epistemic conservatism that underlies the tendency in cognitive therapies to require clients to test their thoughts pragmatically, rather than the therapist only disputing them with clients. A therapist's expressed beliefs, except in special cases, are not fundamentally an incontrovertible challenge to those of the client, who has heard other opinions often before.

Where Do Thoughts Go When We Are Not Thinking Them?

In Chapter 4 I describe in greater detail our mental ecology—the free-floating, rapidly shifting, swirling current of our day-to-day lives. But for now the discussion centers more on specific, contained thoughts that have a semantic coherence (beginning and an end, typically with a self-focus when listening to clients). As proposed in Chapter 1, these thoughts can be conceptualized as being stored in memory. Not only do we store all the sensory and motor information related to particular experiences (episodic memory), but we also store thoughts and ideas and can access them later when we need them (semantic memory). Unfortunately we quite often access them when we do not want to, and the presence of thematically recurring unwelcome thoughts is a characteristic of clients. Traumatic experiences are sometimes laid down in memory in vivid detail, like a flashbulb photograph, and people can experience sudden and unwanted retrieval of them, usually called a flashback. Often, however, only some elements are vivid, so that much of the original experience is fragmented in recall. McNally (2006) argues that memory difficulties underlie many of the symptoms of posttraumatic stress syndrome (PTSD). Clients sometimes have overgeneralized memories of traumatic events, so that some of the painful details are not recalled, thus protecting the individual from even greater emotional discomfort.

Overgeneral memory is assessed by giving a cue or a question. If asked, "What were you doing at the time of the accident?" a client might reply, "We were going to Chicago" instead of "I was driving on the I-94 with my two kids in our Prius, and we were on our way to visit my grandma who lives in Evanston, near Chicago. There was a lot of snow on the road." Maybe difficulty recalling past events in detail makes it difficult to engage in another important aspect of thinking—thinking about the future. This client might want to plan whether to buy another Prius, to get snow tires next winter, or to slow down in bad weather. Without detailed memories of the past, future thoughts are less detailed and less functional and less informative in social conversation. Overgeneralized memory may be a distinctive feature of PTSD and depression (Moore & Zoellner, 2007), but whether clients *typically* overgeneralize or can *only* overgeneralize depends somewhat on how carefully one probes and asks for details and clarification. This in turn, clinically, assumes that one has a therapeutic or forensic rationale for pressing the client to retrieve such details (e.g., Watkins, Baeyens, & Read, 2009). It has also been suggested that one could encourage (train) clients with PTSD and depression to have more detailed thoughts about the future (constructive plans, positive expectations) regardless of their tendency to have overgeneral recall of their past (Kleim, Graham, Fihosy, Stott, & Ehlers, 2014).

More adaptively, when we have a good idea (a new thought) we actively take steps to keep it in memory—tell someone about it, write it down, or mentally rehearse it a few times. Yet it is fascinating to reflect that it is quite hard to remember even our own thoughts if we do not rehearse them. If you are preparing a talk or pondering an upcoming assignment or thinking about what you are going to say to your annoying coworker, and you suddenly have an excellent idea but are somewhere where you cannot write it down or communicate it, you will be frustrated when you discover later that it is hard to recall the details of the idea—only that you had one and that you hope it will come back to you when you have a pencil or smartphone handy. Why is an idea communicated by someone else or in some form of writing or TV documentary so much easier to recall than one's own thoughts? It is because in these informational contexts we have a history of focused attention, rehearsal, and other features of explicit memory that assist in the storage of information.

Memory researchers like to think of memory as adaptive. People differentially attend to and remember threatening information, which would have been necessary for survival over the millennia. With increased importance of social cooperation and the opportunity to focus on gaining pleasure rather than avoiding destruction, social pressure rather than survival success allowed for the same specialization to evolve in memory for pleasure-enhancing information. In Chapter 6 I revisit the topic of adaptive memory as part of the explanation for consistently irrational thought.

All of these features of thought indicate a very close relationship between thought and memory. Memory is a complex topic, but essentially there are three significant components: processing of the information (encoding), storage, and retrieval. As there are processes of decay, various forms of interference (overlaying of other information at different times), and association, retrieval is rarely isomorphic with the original storage. Another important distinction is the difference between implicit and explicit memory. An entire book could easily be devoted to that topic, but for the present analysis the important feature is that, as the words mean, implicit memory takes place without any conscious effort to remember, and it influences our thinking and behavior without any conscious effort at recall. It is the large, submerged bit of the memory iceberg. (When I earlier talked about implicit attitudes and beliefs, the meaning was the same—emotive influences on thought of which we are largely unaware). Explicit memory is the result of conscious rehearsal, as a result of which it is often encoded, once we become verbal, in the form of words but also as images, including very vivid, intense, discrete images like a flash photograph. Autobiographical memories are those directly related to one's experiences throughout life, as opposed to abstract knowledge we have acquire indirectly. As we also store (lay down in memory) the feelings that accompanied an important thought or experience, it seems likely that Beck's model of a schema is really a memory phenomenon—the storage of a thought along with many of its associations, including imaginal (visual images), verbal, affective, and contextual (the environmental situation at the time). If we store information that has been encoded in very salient ways, such as easily remembered words, rhymes, or familiar images, it will be more readily recalled and available for later use. If the information is basically familiar, such as an aphorism, cultural saying, religious dictum, or oft-heard and repeated phrase, it may become overly accessible; but if it is unique and special to the individual it will encounter less interference from later information and experiences and also remain highly retrievable.

Because of the associative networks that seem to characterize memory storage, when we try to retrieve a specific memory we do so, as Jung (1910) popularized, by thinking up associated thoughts as cues. Such cues also trigger other memories as well, sometimes causing people to recall people or events or experiences they have not thought about for years. All forms of therapy, not just Freudian psychoanalysis, rely on this process by encouraging clients to reminisce freely about childhood, family, work, and romantic experiences. Oddly enough, however, we sometimes need to inhibit some intrusive memories in order to access the one we want, and this results in that inhibited memory being less retrievable in the future. The phenomenon is known in cognitive psychology as *retrieval-induced forgetting*. Its relevance to the present discussion is that it demonstrates that the retrieval of memories can be inhibited. And when we have memories of events that are very upsetting, it is sometimes helpful to makes sure that unpleasant thoughts about it do not always come to mind when related environmental cues are present. When clients say they cannot stop thinking about some event, it means that they have memories that are distressing and poor ability to suppress them. We do not know much about the successful strategies people use when they do not wish to be reminded of something, but most of them seem to be the generation of an alternative thought (Levy & Anderson, 2008). We are used to thinking of executive control being the control of overt actions by conscious thought, but it is obvious that conscious thoughts can control cognitive processes as well, and some individuals are better at doing this than others.

That is a common-sense model that grossly underrepresents the vast amount of psychological theorizing and experimentation on the nature of memory, but it is good enough for now. It has some important implications. One is that individual thoughts, both negative and positive ones, are going to be accessed by clients according to the established principles of recall: external cues, internal search strategies, motivation, mood, association. Another, following from this, is that while negative thoughts are often cued by external circumstances, easily retrieved negative memories mean that some thoughts are hard to stop from entering conscious thought or to put out of one's mind, and so clients often engage in destructive activities, for example excessive drinking or compulsive shopping, as a coping mechanism to "help them forget." A further implication is that our autobiographical memories, particularly for a prolonged series of past emotional experiences, may be laid down in a haphazard, incomplete, or overgeneralized way. They may also be more lasting, as past actions and personal experiences will be laid down in distinct "tracks." Therapeutically this calls for something like "reprocessing them," and a number of cognitive therapy approaches suggest how that may be done.

One of the most promising methods, called *narrative exposure therapy* (Schauer, Neuner, & Elbert, 2011) is based on the memory model of PTSD, which asserts that a series traumatic or fearful experiences are associated in memory but disconnected from contextual representations. Recalling only an associated collection of highly aversive physical experiences generates feelings of helplessness, insecurity, and being under acute threat. The growing strength of the associative fear network contributes to the other symptoms of PTSD through emotional dysregulation: lessened emotional control, instability of affect, and impulsive, angry reactions. Narrative exposure therapy "works by anchoring the context-free sensational cues, cognitions, emotions, and physiological reactions that make up the fear network in the temporal and spatial context of the specific traumatic event" (Crombach & Elbert, 2014, p. 3). It achieves this by having the client symbolize every significant experience in life along a time-line rope. Age- and culture-appropriate symbols are used to identify happy versus fearful and traumatic events, without exerting any moral judgment on violent acts or other traumas. Traumatic events are recalled and verbalized in detail from beginning to end, facilitated by therapist questioning, thus ensuring that cues from the fear network are "embedded in context and period and, thus when activated, were understood as reminders of past events and not actual reasons for becoming aroused" (p. 7).

Thoughts Versus Thinking

One quite different way of tackling this difficult topic is to make a distinction between thoughts—the accessible and retrievable content of one's conscious experience—and thinking, which is the manipulation of symbols, especially words, to generate new ideas and novel (for the individual) solutions. Psychologists have spent much more time worrying about thinking than about thoughts, since, as we know from Twitter, the content of most people's thoughts are rather ordinary and certainly very idiosyncratic. What is important is the reasoning process that is used to generate the thought: the logical derivation, the weighing of evidence, judgments about relevance of related thoughts, and the application of previous knowledge.

Cognitive therapy, too, assumes that irrational thoughts come from faulty reasoning, but we all have faulty reasoning (Kida, 2006; Tversky & Kahneman, 1974). As Kahneman (2011) later wrote: "You build the best possible story from the information available to you, and if it is a good story, you believe it" (p. 201). It seems it is somehow a special feature of depression and anxiety, however, that people are excessively prone to make incorrect inferences from limited amounts of information. Perhaps they are also prone to believe it if it is a bad story. Whether that is a cause or a consequence of depression and anxiety will have to await for a later discussion on the relationship between thoughts and feelings. However, clients' tendencies to engage in faulty reasoning are addressed in all cognitive therapy whenever the client's discourse (thoughts expressed in words) reveals the faults. A common one would be overgeneralizing from one incident so that a rule or expectation is created with negative consequences, such as one bad experience with a physician resulting in the faulty cognition that all doctors are quacks and cannot be trusted. This was the conclusion one of my clients who had had a stroke came to; after originally being misdiagnosed, when she later received more accurate medical advice—in this case to quit smoking—she negated *all* medical recommendations. However, with this client, as is obvious, she was also reluctant to accept the advice because it was difficult to carry out. Thus another feature of faulty reasoning is denial, not just overgeneralization. Denial is a defense mechanism in that it serves to protect us from unpleasant feelings. When clients' faulty reasoning is exposed and explained to them, the extent to which this changes their current thoughts is heavily dependent on the function their faulty reasoning serves. If it avoids distasteful, frightening, or difficult tasks and emotions, clients are more likely to cling to their prior thoughts. Therapists know this and will try to ascertain the function of thoughts that seem erroneous to the outside observer but that are preserving some aspect of the client's emotional equilibrium. This is rarely discussed as a deliberate strategy in the cognitive therapies, but because they are all connected, however loosely, to behavioral or social learning ideas, the concept of the function of thoughts is usually understood by cognitive behavioral therapists. We meet the idea of function a number of times before the book ends.

Thinking Needed for Problem-Solving

There is a very different way in which training in more rational thinking processes is a core element of therapeutic intervention. This is the well-developed topic of teaching good problem-solving to clients. Problem-solving requires thinking strategies pursued in a formal rather than an ad hoc way. Popularized clinically by a number of authors but most notably Marvin Goldfried and Art Nezu in the case of adults (Nezu, 2004) and Shure and Spivack (1982) in the case of children, problem-solving training is a technique to enable clients to derive conclusions that are based on reality and practicality rather than prejudicial and wishful thinking. In all methods, the essence of the teaching (the intervention) is to develop the skill of reviewing information and weighing the options before acting impulsively or catastrophizing and not acting at all. The goal of problem-solving therapy is to achieve more rational behavior that serves the client's needs best within a socially acceptable context. However, that behavior change is achieved by means of the generation of a cognitive event—a rationally or empirically derived thought.

The thought might be a decision or a resolution (buy Facebook stock; quit one's job; change one's diet to improve cardiovascular health) that then rapidly guides and directs new actions, but the outcome of the decision-making process is first and foremost a thought about (identifying) the action that one has decided to take. This is one of the many ways that thoughts lead to action that I consider more fully in Chapter 7—not that the thought itself causes the action but that it gives it the green light, so to speak. Because of this, the thought needs to be as specific and well reasoned as possible, just like a resolution to act. It will not permit the required behavior if the thinking process involved in problem-solving yields other equally plausible and sensible-seeming thoughts that are contrary to the rational decision ("hmmm, maybe don't buy Facebook stock as the future profitability of the company is unknown; buy Procter and Gamble instead—everyone needs soap").

One of the things clients are known to do, especially if they have what are called internalizing disorders, is to vacillate between ideas, not make decisions, and worry about how to make up their mind about important life choices. Clients who are depressed cannot decide simple things like what to wear to a party, far less the complex ones like whether to buy a new car. People do not see psychologists in order to make stock market, clothing, or car-buying decisions, but they do raise difficult interpersonal, relationship, and future life-course issues. Some years ago a prominent attorney came to see me seeking marital advice. He had fallen in love ("smitten" was his word) with an attractive young model and minor TV star but still loved his wife and agonized about the possible effects of a divorce on his two young daughters. There is no rational solution to this type of conflict, and while I struggled to help him look at pros and cons, he vacillated between guilt and desire. As soon as he made a decision at the end of one session he came to the next one, having thought up all the problems with that decision in the subsequent week. Part of the active generation of new twists and angles on the basic theme (leave the marriage or stay—at the time the options were clear) was that he was involved in a high-profile trial, which was extremely stressful. In the end, both women made the decision for him—the girlfriend left him for not making a commitment and his wife left him as her affection for him had been steadily eroded. Hamlet might have been able to vacillate for weeks, but partners tend not to afford one the same degree of "space," although in this client's case both women had been supremely patient and tolerant of his conflicted feelings. I was not really able to help him, since the problem was not one of rationally weighing options nor really one of increasing self-knowledge and values clarification, although that was the angle I took—for example, asking what elements of your thoughts are irrational in the Ellis sense (feelings of duty and morality), or based on fear of the unknown (how much the children would suffer versus being able to cope?), or pure self-interest (the financial cost), or concerns around image (what will family and friends think of you?) and unclear goals (how will the decision square with what you truly want out of life?).

The Psychology of Decision-Making

The cognitive psychology of thinking is mostly about material, factual cognitions—things, issues, topics that may be personally influential but that typically do not cause high levels of anxiety, guilt, anger, or joy. The processes of experimental study have included, but not been limited to, problem-solving (usually abstract problems), decision-making (usually hypothetical situations), reasoning (often logic and syllogistic inference), and creativity (the self-generation of new ideas but excluding personal insights, which is the essential goal of insight-oriented counseling and psychotherapy). Every now and then the issues addressed are ecologically valid (based on real life), which helps us understand real clients. A good instance of this is Galotti and Tinkelenberg's (2009) study of parents making decisions about their kindergarten child's school placement. Galotti's previous work on real-life decisions (2007) introduced a five-phase model, with these phases possibly overlapping and not necessarily sequential: (a) setting goals, (b) gathering information, (c) structuring the decision (i.e., enumerating one's options as well as the criteria to be used for deciding between them), (d) making a final choice, and (e) evaluating the decision. It seems that this is a well-understood process, but it is more complex than it sounds—for example, selecting one's prechoice options might indicate that some decision-making has already taken place. My client, the attorney, was weighing only two options—wife or girlfriend—and he had not ever contemplated or included the possibility of another: neither.

Therapies teaching problem-solving, and many laboratory studies of decision-making whether by novices or by experts, have the same expected outcome: the most rational, most adaptive, most beneficial course of action will be adopted. This explains why they have relied on liner models—the assumption that the ideal approach to good decision-making follows a sensible, linear sequence. This is to break the problem or the decision down into different alternatives, generate criteria (pros and cons) for evaluating them, rate all the alternatives on these criteria, and select the one with the most pros and the least cons (Dawes & Corrigan, 1974). If you have ever watched any of those TV property programs in which the show hosts help couples find their dream home, you will know that few people seem to follow a linear model. The show hosts express exasperation—necessary for the dramatic element of the program—when it transpires that one or other of either the alternatives or the criteria was not, in practice, what was stated at the outset, or that it turns out the couple do not agree on the criteria or change them once the range of options imposed on them by budget considerations becomes more apparent.

Some experimentalists have suggested what any of us working with clients would also assume: that actually people adopt different cognitive strategies for decision-making according to context (i.e., the type of decision that must be made; Payne, Bettman, & Johnson, 1993). If asked how they typically make decisions, people generally acknowledge five distinct, nonoverlapping styles: (a) spontaneous, a need to just go for it and get the process over as quickly as possible; (b) avoidant, characterized by trying to avoid making any decisions; (c) dependent, in which there is a search for advice from others to give them direction; (d) intuitive, where the individual relies on gut-feelings and hunches; and (e) rational, which is the supposedly ideal linear process of selecting and evaluating logical alternatives (Loo, 2000; Scott & Bruce, 1995). One does not need much clinical experience to guess that most clients adopt strategies (a) to (d), rather than (e).

So, returning to the parents who were trying to decide to which school to send their kindergarten-age child, Galotti and Tinkelenberg's (2009) study revealed many interesting insights about real life. One is that although the parents had a variety of school placement options (at least six if you include charter schools, home-schooling, language-immersion programs, public versus private versus parochial), they tended to restrict the options very early to just two or three. Second, they came up with a total of about 20 criteria that were relevant to their judgment, all the way from the most frequently mentioned things like convenience, cost, teacher characteristics, and class size down to the least frequently mentioned, such as overall reputation, diversity, physical resources, and keeping their child close to siblings or other friends. Over the six months during which decisions needed to be made, however, the list narrowed considerably, and only *convenience* remained as a primary criterion for the majority of the parents. These authors argued that this sort of decision process had a dynamic quality to it, that the parents used holistic judgment, and that their process did not match their self-reported decision-making style. Remember, however, when trying to generalize such findings to other contexts, all of the available options were potentially good outcomes (none of the schools would be considered bad choices), and also, if things did not work out, it was possible to make changes later on. Many parents will decide that another type of school or teacher would be better for their child, and in countries like the United States, some degree of within-district movement is possible. Contrast this with my attorney client: once he had made a choice (if he had ever done so), it was irrevocable, and that renders decision-making a great deal harder. When that is not so for some types of choices, clients can sometimes be assisted in making a decision simply by helping them recognize it is not binding or permanent.

Two Systems: Fast and Slow Thinking

Much of the previous exploration of aspects of thought, both clinical experiences and research paradigms, can best be understood by a theoretical perspective that includes both reason and passion within the general rubric of thoughts and thinking—what Teasdale (1993) referred to as "two types of meaning." When thoughts and thinking are devoid of emotional conditions, the result seems strange to us, unfamiliar and disturbing. In fiction, one of the most cogent illustrations of this was the role of Mister Spock in the popular TV series

Star Trek. Of mixed human and Vulcan heritage, Spock uses simple logic, uncontaminated with human emotion in his reasoning processes, the result often amusingly revealing the poor reasoning processes of Earthlings. Rational, nonemotive reasoning is, however, something we can all potentially do just fine, and so we can start to discuss thought as reflecting two systems, or possibly polar opposite dimensions, varying from the most rational to the most emotional. At least five somewhat similar distinctions have been made in cognitive psychology: (a) controlled versus automatic processing, (b) explicit versus implicit thinking, (c) bounded rationality, (d) cool versus hot cognitions, and (e) the one I think brings them together, Kahneman's (2011) System 1 and System 2 model. Between them they provide us a framework for thinking and for clinical strategies for changing thoughts.

Automatic/Controlled Processing and Related Distinctions

The *automatic/controlled distinction* is the most general and the oldest of the five models I see as somewhat comparable. It was introduced a long time ago, largely attributable to the work of Schneider and Shiffrin (1977), to show the difference between learning and performing new skills, including cognitive ones, which initially require attention to the task and "thinking" (mentally manipulating symbols) about what one is doing or thinking (controlled processing). Over time, however, and with practice, these skills become more automatic and can be performed less consciously and with the minimum of cognitive effort, which is important for smooth performance, for carrying out multiple tasks (like conversing with a passenger while driving a car, which is hard to do when one is learning to drive and mentally rehearsing all the things one needs to be doing and attending to). Thus automatic processing allows for what is called *parallel processing*, as one can see every day by watching young people negotiating strolling down the sidewalk and dodging traffic while texting at the same time, although there are imperfections (sometimes they bump into you).

When automatic processing involves nonexplicit assumptions about shared information (one might exercise caution walking along a slippery path because other people are doing the same, but one does not necessarily assume that they are having wary thoughts), it can be called *submentalizing* (Heyes, 2014). There are many opportunities for us to be able to make accurate inferences about what others are thinking without consciously doing so, such as sharing an amusing moment with a friend or rapidly clarifying a statement one has made without consciously recognizing it might have been misinterpreted or offensive. People experience social difficulties when they make erroneous inferences about what other people are thinking.

Four features are included in the definition of controlled processing (executive control functions): (a) conscious intention of what the control of mental activity will accomplish, (b) the sense or feeling that one is in control, (c) the expenditure of effort in the control of the mental action, and (d) the monitoring of the control output in a closed-loop feedback arrangement (Wegner & Bargh, 1998). From these defining features we can see that the processes being analyzed in the research literature are mostly complex cognitive skills, such as solving math problems, flying a plane, writing a computer program—tasks that require attention, visual search, retrieval of information from memory, and the like.

I am not convinced that automatic processes in these cognitive realms are exactly comparable to Beck's idea of automatic thoughts, unless he meant "unreasoned"—verbally expressed thoughts that are devoid of thinking and mentally weighing up alternatives. But to the extent there are parallels, however, there are various phenomena that have been revealed in automatic versus controlled processing research that might be of interest to clinicians. For example, complex cognitive tasks that have become automatic are harder to change, to unlearn, than when they were controlled, processed skills. Also, as Schneider and Chein (2003) point out in their comprehensive overview, we are, to belabor the obvious, more in control of controlled processing. Thus, when it comes to the expression of personal thoughts in social situations, control can be a very good thing for peaceful interactions. Automatic processes are harder to control. Controlled processing is more likely to be compromised by stressors, fatigue, and drugs, which means that trying to make clients—stressed by definition—more thoughtful and less reflexive in their thoughts might be intrinsically difficult. Executive control also typically requires inhibitory skills, notably behavioral restraint and blocking distracting input through attentional sets—indeed any suppression of the processing or expression of information that would disrupt the efficient completion of a goal-directed task (Jurado & Rosselli, 2007). This raises a question: Is mindfulness actually an example of controlled cognitive processing? It certainly seems the antithesis of bubbling, babbling thoughts.

Implicit Versus Explicit Thoughts

Although automatic processing may cover the unconscious, nonmonitoring features of what Beck would refer to as automatic thoughts, this classic distinction in the psychology of performing cognitive skills does not quite capture the obvious: that some thinking seems to be emotionally neutral and some is not. Getting slightly closer to that distinction is the idea of *implicit thoughts* (includes instinct and intuition) versus *explicit thinking*. Again, this a quite wide topic. One way it captures something about emotional involvement in thinking is because of the growing understanding in basic psychology of phenomena like implicit attitudes and implicit memory. The concept challenges the basic notion that attitudes have a tripartite foundation: cognitive (thought content), emotional, and behavioral (approach vs. avoidance). While that seems sensible, the trouble is that these three dimensions of an attitude are rarely concordant. People sometimes avoid things they state they like or at least accept. They sometimes say things do not interest them but then show emotional arousal to them.

The concept of implicit attitudes refers to the observation that most attitudes are formed or contained within processes of which we are largely unaware (preconscious). Jung (1967) explained that we often have two attitudes about the same thing, one of which is conscious and very influenced by social forces, knowing what we should be thinking and reasoning, and the other of which is unconscious and reflects (in Jung's notion) neurotic conflict and irrational fears, such as racial prejudice or homophobia. Experimental psychologists have developed an array of clever methods for revealing implicit attitudes other than the old-fashioned way of asking people what they think about various constructs. Thus people with some unconscious doubts about their own sexuality might state verbally on a questionnaire that they approve of gay marriage, or the rights of people to marry whomever they choose, but when assessed implicitly (such as measuring reaction times to recognizing stimuli as reflecting homosexuality or not, or measuring the duration of eye fixations on photographs), it transpires from patterns of avoidance that they have some deep negative feelings toward the topic. They might be genuinely unaware of these underlying feelings, or they might be trying very hard not to be prejudiced and influenced by them in social or public contexts.

As a quick aside, it is rather strange that clinical psychologists, fully conversant with the idea of implicit attitudes, are nevertheless rather at the mercy of the client's verbal, conscious statements of attitudes. Since we have really no clinically validated, practical methods of assessing implicit attitudes, we are obliged to make inferences from related comments the client might make in other contexts. We try to do this by listening very carefully with one's clinical "third ear" for nuances in the words used, for comments that purport to be humorous, or for noting reluctance to engage in behavior that should be in accordance with stated attitudes. For instance, if family members who are going to have to be involved in the care and rehabilitation of a relative are asked for a direct, verbally expressed thought (opinion) as to their support for in-family placement, they will mostly say the generous thing—that they are behind it. However, if their interview tapes are scored according to subtle signs of ambivalence, nonacceptance, or hostility, it can sometimes be shown that these same family members are far from being accepting. One reason this is so interesting is that when family members do show this kind of subtle hostility (negative expressed emotion) toward the discharged patient, that person is more likely to fail in any family-based program.

Bounded Rationality

A third form of the distinction I am pounding away at came from the extraordinarily fertile brain of the pioneer of artificial intelligence research, Herbert

Simon. In his analyses of the limits on the quality of general decision-making and information processing, he coined the term *bounded rationality.* He offered bounded rationality as a "behavioral model [in which] human rationality is very limited, very much bounded by the situation and by human computational powers" (1983, p. 34; see also Simon, 1957).

It is a simple idea, which is true of many of the good ones:

> The fact is if we become involved in a particular activity and devote an important part of our lives to that activity, we will surely assign it a greater importance and value than we would have prior to our involvement with it. It's very hard for us, sometimes, not to draw from such facts a conclusion that human beings are rather dishonest creatures . . . Yet most of the bias that arises from human occupations and preoccupations cannot be described correctly as rooted in dishonesty—which perhaps makes it more insidious than if it were. (Simon, 1983, pp. 95–96)

Simon's model was offered as an alternative to the assumptions of many economists regarding human decision-making. We are bounded by the situation and by emotive influences on our decisions—as Thaler (2000) explained it, we are dumber, nicer, and weaker than classical economics assumes. Putting it yet another way, our recall, willpower, and self-knowledge are all less than perfect.

In developing his model, Simon (1983) made use of the importance of mental representation of symbols in cognitive processes, remembering that symbols are not words alone. He offered planning as a good example of this. Plans can direct the immediate action needed in progress toward a goal, as well as establish a series of subgoals toward a more distant goal. Whether these are followed or not depends on additional sensory feedback from intervening events. When successive actions are made conditional on information about current circumstances, these plans would be called strategies. Simon has argued persuasively that whether actions are based on plans or are executed rapidly according to new situational demands, they all require some kind of symbolic representation of the situation (Vera & Simon, 1993).

Hot Versus Cool Cognitions

When it comes to explaining cognitions that are more relevant to clinical practice, Walter Mischel (Metcalfe & Mischel, 1999) popularized an important distinction that can be made within cognitive systems: hot versus cool. He drew the distinction with respect to one of the topics of most enduring interest to him—the nature of self-control and resistance to temptation:

> The cool system is cognitive, emotionally neutral, contemplative, flexible, integrated, coherent, spatiotemporal, slow, episodic, and strategic. It is the seat of self-regulation and self-control. The hot system is the basis of emotionality, fears as well as passions—impulsive and reflexive—initially controlled by innate releasing stimuli (and, thus, literally under "stimulus control"): it is fundamental for emotional (classical) conditioning and undermines efforts at self-control. (p. 3)

There is a sense in Mischel's writing that he considers hot cognitions to be more problematic for mental health generally, not just self-control. However, another side of the argument is that it is passion and intense feeling that make life worth living. When Emerson said, "Thou art to me a delicious torment," I am pretty sure he was not expressing psychological pain. With love there may come disappointment, rejection, and sadness but more usually great joy. Naturally Mischel knows these things too, and it is important to realize that hot cognitions are not bad unless the affect generating the heat is upsetting and harmful. Also the hot/cool separation is more of a metaphor for categorizing psychological events rather than a model depiction of conditions or temperature of mental life.

System 1 and System 2

The same can be said about the final dual process theory to be considered in this section: Kahneman's (2011) analysis of "fast and slow" thinking, which he considers to be two separate systems. It is a tad presumptuous of me to try to summarize the current perspectives of a Nobel Prize winner in just a few paragraphs. Yet there is a remarkable convergence of ideas across the five models under consideration. In Kahneman's model, System 1 (which is fast) functions automatically, involuntarily with little effort; it evolved to quickly notice and allow rapid reactions to the numerous problems that had to be overcome for survival. System 2 (slow), on the other hand, functions with mental effort and is the conscious, reasoning self. Although these too are metaphorical entities, it is nevertheless rather strange to talk about a mental system as a homunculus that has its own agency and beliefs—or in this case a pair of homunculi, sometimes working together but usually not. System 2 can supposedly, under some circumstances, "*take over*, overruling the freewheeling impulses and associations of System 1" (Kahneman, 2011, p. 21, my italics). The System 1 and 2 terminology was introduced by Stanovich (1999; see also Stanovich & West, 2000), who now prefers "Type 1" and "Type 2" processing labels because the idea of a "system" implies that there is some sort of mapping of these systems directly onto brain processes, which is neither intended nor likely to be correct (Stanovich & Toplak, 2012).

Kahneman's (2011) depiction of System 1 and System 2 makes no attempt to identify any such thing as neural pathways. He says, "there is no one part of the brain that either of the systems would call home" (p. 29). He is also well aware that there is a danger in the homunculus implication. But he does still reify the two systems, often depicting them as two independent features of cognition fighting it out inside one's head. If one system is occupied, the other can gain the upper hand. An example he gives is that when people are cognitively engaged, such as in a digital memory task (System 2 is active), they are more likely to make self-serving choices, use sexist language, and make superficial social judgments (System 1). Other examples he gives of cognitive activities are perceptive. Among System 1 examples he includes "complete the phrase 'bread and . . . ,'" "detect hostility in a voice" (think of expressed emotion), and "drive a car on an empty road." System 2 examples are "monitor the appropriateness of your behavior in a social situation," "compare two washing machines for overall value," and "check the validity of a complex logical argument."

These examples certainly capture the essence of the two systems, and Kahneman (2011) goes on to provide many fascinating observations based on the idea that System 2, which is slow, often fails to check and monitor the rapid responding of System 1. It is the reflexive, automatic, associationistic activity of System 1 that is responsible for a host of biases in judgment, like the confirmation bias, as well as reasoning errors. He also makes valuable observations regarding how people might answer complex questions. As therapists ask clients complex questions all the time, and as System 2 is a lazy system, we might take notice of some of the instances Kahneman provides. Thus if asking a client "How happy are you with your marriage?" it would be easier to convert the question to a more heuristic one: "Have you had any disagreements with your spouse this week?" Clients can generate quick answers to very difficult questions. Self-reflection is one of the functions of System 2, but other functions like planning, choice, and weighing evidence are easily overridden by emotional valence. Cool thinking is overly influenced by hot cognitions. In a sense, affect is another heuristic. Your emotional response to something (your opinion) will impact your reasoned judgment. If you are negative toward genetically modified food, like I am, you will be less likely to think of and express the possible advantages (I read that genetically modified papaya saved the entire crop in Hawaii from being wiped out by the ring spot virus) and more likely to remember stated disadvantages (I've heard the GM papaya potentially cause allergies).

My conclusion is this: No cognitive system operates independently. Driving, which can be quite automatic, is never totally so, since one does monitor speed restrictions, thinks about where one is going to have to turn and prepares to do so, and performs related cognitions like rehearse whether one brought snacks for the journey or if one's sunglasses are in the glove compartment. There is really no such thing as a perfectly cool set of words or thoughts because there will always be affect-laden associations. Anyone's judgment about anything, whether it is of the president's latest policy or his or her spouse's cooking, is entirely dependent on emotional attitudes toward the individual. The task of the cognitive therapist cannot be to make clients rational but only to facilitate their irrational thought being more adaptive for them. If a person likes to eat a papaya for breakfast every day, he or she does not need to worry about ring spot virus; if the person is a farmer growing them, however, he or she should. The goal of therapy is to give the client's System 2 a better chance of functioning to his or her benefit, but only if the fast, hot feeling thoughts are truly negative and need to be restrained. Let clients indulge in joyful feelings even if they lead to less than ideal decisions.

Metacognition: Thoughts About Our Thoughts

There are big differences between various System 2 cognitive phenomena, such as thinking about some content (musing or mulling something over), trying to actively solve a problem, planning ahead, and creative thinking. But all of them can partially involve metacognition—thinking about one's own thinking and deliberately using internal speech/ dialogue to regulate other cognitions.

One feature of metacognition is of special interest in clinical contexts. When asked to think about themselves and their past thoughts, clients are being presented with a very difficult task, as I have already argued. Yet it is one demanded by most clinical questionnaires: for example, in the Trait Meta-Mood Scale (Palmer, Gignac, Bates, & Stough, 2003) are items such as "I try to think good thoughts no matter how badly I feel." Now if a depressed client expresses a negative thought, such as "I'm a bad parent; I just don't give my kids enough time and attention," it is somewhat instinctive, as a cognitive therapist, to try to discount this by seeking contradictory instances. One might reply, "Hmm, that is a bit of a black-and-white generalization, isn't it? Just last week you told me you took the boys to soccer practice and stayed and watched. Can you think of some other instances in which you *have* given the kids lots of your time and attention?" But that is a memory task for positive past instances when the current mood is negative, which we know makes recall difficult. And if the client then has difficulty recalling positive instances, he or she has a meta-cognitive experience that is the exact opposite of what the clinician hoped to achieve: "I can't think of any examples [that would dispel my generalization]." Schwarz (2004) has summarized numerous studies in which "subjective accessibility experiences are informative in their own right and qualify the implications of recalled content" (p. 334).

If we have difficulty recalling a lecture we attended some weeks ago, we could makes sense of that difficulty by stating that it was not very interesting—"in fact I can barely remember it, it was so dull." There are a number of possibilities people can generate to explain their poor memory, like they were not really concentrating that day, or they are just so busy at the moment that they do not want to think about the lecture. In other words, one's accessibility content and accessibility experiences are two very different things. But here is the interesting thing: Being asked to recall just a few instances of something, say, times you were assertive, makes you more likely to judge yourself to be assertive, because if you have to list many occasions and have to struggle to do so (a longer list of exemplars is harder to recall), then you can easily conclude that you must not be very assertive after all. As clinicians we often ask clients to provide examples of the events or actions they are concerned about. What we might forget is that the difficulty this task imposes on clients interacts with their naive theories about how memory works. People tend to think that when thinking of something, or some person, if other thoughts come to mind, they must be relevant; otherwise why would one have these associations? And other thoughts will be perceived as particularly relevant if they come to mind readily. Schwarz (2004) concludes his review of this extensive literature with the truism "that there is more to thinking than thought content" (p. 345).

When people have difficulty recalling things, there are a host of plausible conclusions that can be drawn. In marital disputes in the clinic, a husband accuses his wife of never spontaneously saying something flattering to him. The wife hotly disputes this, saying, "Of course I do; I do it often," to which the husband replies, "Okay, give me a couple of recent examples." Regardless of the actual reality, providing examples from memory is very hard to do, and after some struggling the wife comes up with at best one or two. What can be concluded from this difficulty—what is the meta-cognitive realization? As Schwartz has asserted, it depends on one's naive psychological viewpoint, such as, it is difficult to recall things on demand or when under pressure; it is easier to recall examples of something when there are more of them out there; the wife's idea of a flattering remark or compliment may be different than her husband's; or, indeed, she does not often express out loud things that she really does feel (and thus the challenge is unfair). How this kind of marital dispute will play itself out, therefore, has nothing much to do with the reality of this couple's behavioral interactions.

Metacognition and Personality

I mentioned earlier that Beck's therapy led to much research interest on thinking styles (rather than thoughts per se) as traits. As already explained, different personality dimensions may be associated with characteristic ways of interpreting, analyzing, and summarizing experiences. In other words there are individual differences in meta-cognitive processes. If we look at most trait descriptions within personality theory, we immediately notice that while they sometimes relate to characteristic behavior patterns (the introvert tends to curl up on the sofa with a good book) and characteristic feelings (the extravert enjoys wild parties), a lot of the elements of a trait are cognitive. People who are easily stressed see themselves as vulnerable; those high on the trait of harm avoidance seek out activities judged as safe, even if tedious (Gazendam et al., 2014). People who are open to experience (one of the Big Five personality dimensions) report that they have a vivid imagination and spend time reflecting on things. Those on the opposite end of that same dimension (people who are closed minded) self-report that they are not interested in abstractions, they prefer the obvious over the subtle, and they tend to be conservative and resistant to change. There are times when, if a client's construct system is to be preserved intact, he or she simply cannot afford to be wrong. Quite a few clients in community mental health services fit that description, so maybe they are not likely to receive cognitive therapy. In any event, it has been a long tradition in personality theory that people show significant individual differences in thinking processes.

Social Influences

A slightly different way of looking at individual differences in characteristic emotional expression is to consider the role of parental influences on cognitive appraisals. I use the common emotions of disappointment and resentment to illustrate the point. They may not be as common as the clinical concerns of anxiety and depression, but they can cause distress, often lasting, and interfere with positive interpersonal relationships. Some years ago a student in my lab group at Binghamton University was interested in young people's memories of positive and negative family experiences. We administered an open-ended questionnaire inviting first-year college students to give examples of incidents they still remember with strong feelings, and we were very surprised at the number of times what might be considered relatively minor disappointing events were still remembered and accompanied by strong affect. A classic example was a 19-year-old freshman who described an occasion in which his father had promised to come watch him play in a soccer tournament at the age of 8 but had not shown up. He reported still feeling some resentment toward his father. Here are two common emotions—disappointment and resentment—that are especially tied to cognitive appraisal.

In the case of disappointment there must first be a strong expectation of a positive event, one that is of importance and that one is looking forward to. "Looking forward" to something means thinking explicitly about it, planning for it, and communicating to others about its anticipated happening. When the event fails to occur, disappointment is experienced directly. Whether that disappointment leads to resentment toward others depends on one's appraisal of the extent to which others were directly responsible (causal) for the nonoccurrence. Such appraisals are highly subjective and based on many levels of interpretation (thoughts, reasoning) of events. The young man in our study might have been told by his father than something important came up at work, but the disappointed child could still have reasoned that the father might have found a way to get to the tournament if he had tried hard enough. The disappointment remains the same regardless of the cause of the nonoccurrence of the event, but the next affective reaction depends on a complex judgment: Had the father been cavalier about coming to soccer matches in the past? Had he broken other promises before? Did he seem genuinely remorseful? Did he promise to make amends?

Ordinary lives are full of disappointments, some small, some large. We do not get a job we applied for; our children are not as good academically as we had hoped; it rains torrentially on the day of our outdoor wedding; the "Bachelor" does not give out a rose; we get a B+ for an assignment rather than an A. Managing the negative affect of disappointment requires self-regulatory and coping strategies that require thinking (reasoning) skills that are based on years of experience as a child and the kinds of cognitive strategies suggested to us by parents, teachers, and friends. What are some of these? One is not to have too intense an expectation of the desired event. This might require saying things to oneself that prepare one for the possibility of nonreward: "There will be a lot of good candidates for this position" rather than "I'm a shoo-in for this job." Another set of coping thoughts revolves around a plan to obtain the reward at some later point in time, and maybe it will be bigger and better: "Well, the rain wiped out our spring camping trip, but we can go for a longer time in the fall when the weather is better anyway." A third is to devalue the nonoccurring event, which is cognitive dissonance: "That bachelor was kind of full of himself, and I wouldn't really have wanted to date him anyway." A fourth is simply managing the intensity of the disappointment through perspective taking: listening to comforting words from one's mother: "I know you are disappointed, but a B+ isn't worth getting so upset over—some of your friends actually received Fs; think how they feel."

That fourth strategy is a good one for parents to rely on as it requires a young child learning to discriminate between serious disappointments and trivial ones. There is a big difference between being jilted at the altar and being stood up for a date. Good parents model this in their own behavior by explaining that although unfortunate and regrettable, the situation can be fixed, replaced, or done without. Giving examples of how they have dealt with minor disappointments provides children with thought strategies they can use. Some of these are quite irrational and overly optimistic—"you'll do better next time." Children also sometimes need time to experience the disappointment and come to terms with it on their own—negating it or minimizing it interferes with the opportunity to learn self-management strategies. We call it being a good sport when one takes defeat in a game in one's stride. Children who are poor losers have not been given the kind of cognitive learning experiences that losing is okay, that the winner needs to be congratulated by the loser, that rubbishing one's opponent with hypercritical adjectives (bad-mouthing) is not acceptable, that parental pride and giving rewards comes not from winning but from obviously trying hard, and that defeat is not a time to blame others or have their performance critiqued. It is interesting that standard tips for parents on how to handle disappointment in their children (e.g., http://illinoisearlylearning.org/tipsheets/disappointment.pdf) almost always recommend verbalizing the child's feelings and explaining that the feeling leading to upset is one of disappointment. As explained later (Chapter 6), children's emotion competence is heavily influenced by having verbal labels for feelings—indeed, language competence in general (Beck, Kumschick, Eid, & Klann-Delius, 2012).

We all know that disappointment is easily read on someone's facial expression, so when it is necessary for maintaining social relationships it is often required that one mask one's disappointment. Much of the developmental literature on disappointment revolves around children's growing ability to inhibit overt expression of disappointment. In Western cultures it is expected that one smiles on receiving a gift from someone, regardless of whether one likes it or not. The paradigm usually used in the lab is a simple one—children are offered a reward, a gift, a drink, anything positive really—which turns out to be much less positive than they were led to expect. A promised lemonade drinks turns out to be disgustingly salty; grandma's beautifully wrapped gift is socks and underwear, not the expected Lego set. As children acquire social skills, the importance of not hurting someone's feelings and expressing gratitude even if disappointed becomes more apparent, and so experiments examine factors that make children more or less able to hide disappointment. Gender is a powerful variable: girls are much better at hiding disappointment than boys. There are also cultural differences, with Chinese American children showing less positive expression (masking disappointment) than their European American peers (Garrett-Peters & Fox, 2007).

The transformation of disappointment into resentment, I have argued, is related to the appraisal (judgment) of responsibility for the nonoccurrence of the expected reward/positive event. Such meta-cognitive judgments cannot typically be totally objective, and so there are many opportunities in everyday interactions to develop resentment (and thus anger and from there the desire for revenge). In some of our own studies of children's perceptions of fairness within families, we used parental breaking of a promise (and thus causing disappointment) as the scenario to examine children's perceptions of how this might feel. When children attributed the event to something beyond the parent's control, they were more likely to excuse their mother or father (forgive rather than resent); they would give their own explanations such as "the mom was probably too busy at work to spend time reading to Mary as she had promised to do." However this was slightly less likely when the parent was described as a stepparent: "Her stepmom probably doesn't really like Mary very much and doesn't want to spend time reading to her." The influence of cultural myths regarding stepparents was thus in evidence, although more so for children from intact families than children who actually had experience of a stepparent (Evans & Falchi, 2013).

Implications

Three important ideas about thoughts have been expanded on in this chapter. The first is about how thoughts are represented mentally and stored in memory. Thoughts are not always represented in words, especially not subvocal speech. When clinicians ask clients to describe or report their thoughts there will be a fair amount of editing going on. That is why we always listen for pauses and hesitancy, inconsistencies, attempts by clients to correct specific words as not being quite right, and qualifications of statements made. Thoughts are not encoded as a clear-cut, well-articulated script that is in our minds and available to us at any and all times. We know this from personal experience of engaging in conversation with someone, however impersonal (such as discussing a recent movie) and realizing that our thoughts are being formulated as we talk. Memories are accessed, previous biases and prejudices pop into consciousness, and the friend's thoughts and words trigger both our thoughts and sometimes our emotions—making us think more deeply and feel differently. The German novelist Hermann Hesse commented: "Words do not express thoughts very well. They always become a little different immediately after they are expressed, a little distorted, a little foolish." Often when thoughts are stated out loud to an audience, they are strongly socially controlled—many of the supposedly irrational thoughts uttered by depressed clients ("Nobody loves me"; "I'm a terrible dancer") in social situations serve the function of evoking reassurance, eliciting compliments or caring. Such social support reinforces self-deprecating utterances and does not change them.

When clients talk to therapists, exactly the same processes take place, and in nondirective therapies clients are almost having conversations with themselves, sometimes articulating thoughts in words that they have never dared to admit to themselves, causing surprise or relief, and sometimes coming, through internal reasoning (metacognition), to new ideas and conclusions. It is insight that seems to be therapeutic—when the client clarifies, modifies, or reframes a previous thought introspectively. We tend to think that such a process is more profoundly therapeutic because the new thoughts are owned by the client rather than being imposed on them by the therapist. Cognitive therapy is often more directive, however. Cognitive therapists are implicitly trained to jump in and challenge and correct thoughts that may not be habitual but are being formulated only at the very moment of disclosure.

Whether the therapist immediately reinforces the new insights, interprets them in a different way, affirms their helpfulness for the problems identified, or acknowledges them through silence, talk that reveals buried thoughts or clarifies previously unformulated ones is possibly the essence of all talking cures. Thoughts are negative when the theme is distressing but the thinking contains no antidote. Worries that have no element of resolution, guilty thoughts that are quickly suppressed but still gnaw away at the person, fears of harm that are not contextualized in memory or balanced by cognitive strategies to forestall disasters—all represent the essence of cognitive distress.

The difference between a distinct thought content or idea and a client's discourse (or narrative from memory) can partly be explained by the second major theme discussed in this chapter. It is a widely accepted model that we have two "systems" of automatic, hot, fast cognitions versus reasoned, cool, slower cognitions less influenced by implicit (unconscious) attitudes and beliefs. Reasoning (see Chapter 5) is rarely devoid of emotional influences, as the process requires accessing past experiences that are stored in memory along with the emotions felt at the time. Feelings of resentment or disappointment will influence subsequent thought processes such as appraisal of the actions of others or attributions regarding their cause.

The healing, self-correcting ability to reflect on our thoughts comes about because of our ability to engage in metacognition. This is the third important theme in this chapter. As a coping mechanism, meta-cognitive strategies are most likely learned in childhood and can become engrained as effective thought management strategies through becoming habitual—being part of the individual's cognitive personality style. But whether we are talking about discrete thoughts or thoughts about thoughts, these always occur against a backdrop of every individual's mental life—his or her stream of consciousness. This backdrop will be examined next.

4

The "Stream" of Consciousness

Mind-Wandering, Introspection, Rumination, Meditation, and Mindfulness

> People who learn to control inner experience will be able to determine the quality of their lives, which is as close as any of us can come to being happy.
>
> —Mihaly Csikszentmihalyi, 1997

When Thoughts Flow

The general philosophical position of the late 18th century, from David Hume to James Mill, was that all ideation proceeds in accordance with associations between one thought and the next, although Hume (1739/1962) regarded association as not an inevitability but only "a gentle force, which commonly prevails" (p. 54). Singer (1975), one of the few psychologists who has made a career studying inner experience, stated once that he did not like the metaphor of a stream, arguing instead that "our life task involves an endless effort at organizing experiences and matching them to available schema" (p. 728). That sounds a lot like the rationale for all cognitive therapy.

So, to gain a sense of the themes in this chapter, imagine that you are on an airplane, going on a journey, and observing the everyday human behavior of others. The early behavior of your fellow passengers is quite limited, and their thoughts are focused on the few immediate tasks required, just like yours—finding your seat number, trying to fit your carry-on luggage into the overhead bin, wondering if the person in the next seat is going to keep his arm in your space throughout the entire flight, turning off your cell phone, and so on. Cognitively these are all System 2 functions. With minor variations everyone engages in these tasks in roughly the same way. Once everyone is settled in their seats and the plane takes off, there are even greater constraints on the behaviors possible, and subsequent activity is all essentially cognitive—having a conversation, listening to music, reading a book, watching a movie, sleeping. But some passengers will be engaged in solitary thinking. Some will be planning and generating new ideas, preparing a speech or a pitch. Most, however, will be engaged in those streams of consciousness I first mentioned with reference to Eric Klinger (1971, 1977): mind-wandering, daydreaming, meditating, fantasizing, ruminating, and worrying.

All of this mental activity will be unrestricted by the environment, which is narrowly fixed when you are on a plane, and disconnected to behavior, which is highly regulated in that context. You cannot act on your thoughts in any significant way. Mind-wandering is defined as thoughts that are decoupled from the present environmental stimuli and unrelated to the task at hand (Stawarczyk, Majerus, Maj, Van der Linden, & D'Argembeau, 2011). If a task event occurs on the plane, such as the serving of drinks or a meal, or if a salient stimulus event occurs, such as a disruptive passenger or extreme turbulence, your thoughts are easily directed and focused, sometimes on threatening ideation: themes of terrorism or plane crashes. If you have a fear of flying, or tend to be worried about such events, it is your thoughts that regulate your affect, since most people will not react that way and they are all in the same stimulus situation, so unless you have had a past traumatic conditioning experience, it must be your ease of imagined disasters, inferences, interpretations, and judgments of probabilities that determine the affective response of anxiety, fear, and panic. Even if specific affective triggers do not occur, rumination and worry can be distressing; meditation and mindfulness exercises, conversely, are widely considered mental antidotes to distressing thoughts and have thus come to play a significant role in cognitive therapy.

The Ecology of Thinking

In the previous two chapters I mentioned in passing that the issues of clinical relevance usually pertain to discrete, individual thoughts that can be isolated—meaning that the therapist can solicit information about specific content. Clinical assessment takes the form of questions such as, "What were you thinking about just before you committed the offense?" or "You say that you think your husband can be inconsiderate—what exactly to you mean by this thought?" or "Have you thought about what we discussed in the last session?" or "Tell me more about your thought that you lost your job because you are not as smart as the others in the office." However, one of the most obvious features of conscious mentation is that it is not usually divided up into easily separated discrete elements. The reality of daily mental experience is that it is a constant flitting around the internal dialogue: planning what you are going to say to someone when you next see him or her, thinking about which restaurant you should go to tonight, wondering if the chest pain you are experiencing is indigestion or something more serious, wishing the neighbor's dog would stop barking, wondering if

Congress will approve a strike against Iran, and questioning where you last put down your cell phone. Maybe these were just my conscious ruminations over the past few minutes, but they characterize the "ecology" of everyday thinking. As Klinger (1971) expressed it so well:

> Human beings spend nearly all of their time in some kind of mental activity, and much of the time their activity consists not of ordered thought but of bits and snatches of inner experience: daydreams, reveries, wandering interior monologues, vivid imagery, and dreams. These desultory concoctions, sometimes unobtrusive but often moving, contribute a great deal to the style and flavor of being human. (p. 347)

What has not been very clearly specified in any of the cognitive therapies is how cognitive events targeted for change—particular thoughts and current concerns, specific thinking processes, consistent thematic clusters of ideas and feelings (schemata)—can be isolated from the daily stuff of conscious experience (Evans, 2013). Is there something about these desultory concoctions that contribute to the personality style and uniquely individual flavor of being a client? If we want to change a client's thoughts, surely we need to know quite a good deal about the content and organization of what he or she thinks about, not just the specific thoughts evoked in answer to an interview question.

Mind-Wandering

Mind-wandering is possibly the most neutral of the phenomena to be considered in this chapter, as there is no implication of it being good or bad unless concentration on a task is being interfered with. Mind-wandering thoughts are stimulus-independent and task-unrelated. As these thoughts require some degree of cognitive resource, often the same resources as required by the task at hand, they interfere with many parallel cognitive tasks. However, the evidence for this is uncertain because the methods of measuring mind-wandering during tasks requiring concentration and attention are themselves intrusive. Usually what is done is a probe: the subject is interrupted during a task and asked to report whether he or she was aware of any other conscious experiences at the time of the thought probe (e.g., Teasdale, Proctor, Lloyd, & Baddeley, 1993). One of the difficulties with this kind of approach is that some distracting conscious experiences are task-related and thus not true mind-wandering. "I wonder when this task will end?" is task-related, as are the thoughts of clients who are test-anxious, such as "I'm useless at these kinds of tests; I hope these are the sorts of answers I'm supposed to give." And some consciously reported experiences are not true mind-wandering examples because they are not stimulus-independent: "I was aware that my hand was getting tired," or "I found the chair really uncomfortable."

As a result of the complexity of the differences in type of ongoing conscious experiences, the possibly interfering role of mind-wandering in cognitive performance tasks remains somewhat uncertain (Stawarczyk et al., 2011). There may even be positive effects, since mind-wandering is often related to anticipating and planning the future.

Daydreaming

One of the ways of depicting ongoing thinking, whether it be a stream or not, is to conceptualize it as the activity of daydreaming, We all know what daydreaming is, because we do it, but how should we define it? It is a special type of thought, and it often relates to anticipation of future events. In this way it is quite similar to mind-wandering; indeed it belongs to that category in that it too is both stimulus-independent and task-unrelated. However, daydreaming tends to follow a coherent story or theme of what might be, rather than meandering from thought to thought as in mind-wandering. The themes are frequently fantasy themes, such as imagining oneself in a heroic role, or interacting with a famous movie star, or succeeding at an impossibly difficult task, or imagining how one will spend one's lottery winnings. Because daydreams need have no connection with reality, it is also very possible to daydream about the past and in particular to remember and embellish the positive experiences and reconstruct the negative ones into what might have been. Since daydreams are fanciful, they are usually associated with positive feelings and moods—at least during the daydream period, since having to end it in the face of unpleasant reality brings one down to earth with a jolt, as we say. You may not have read much about daydreaming in formal psychology training, which is odd because it is surely a very common mental activity. Klinger (1977) asserted that for many years psychologists believed that daydreaming was an unhealthy activity and that fantasy was equated with defense mechanisms. The contents, however, are idiosyncratic and personal—we may report them to an intimate partner or a total stranger met at a bar but not to a researcher. Thus it would be well worth asking clients to say what their daydreams consist of. While Freud thought dreams were the royal road to the unconscious, daydreams may be a simpler reflection of current concerns and personal incentives.

We know this from a few studies of daydreaming across the lifespan. Giambra (1979) investigated daydreaming in men from teenage years to old age. Those between the ages of 17 and 23 tended to daydream mostly about the future. From 24 to 64 men tended to daydream about current issues, and after 65 years of age men reported daydreaming more about the past than the present or future. Older men also reported fewer hostile daydreams and fewer daydreams in which they perform heroic deeds, and they report fewer daydreams of any kind overall and are less absorbed in them; despite this, and despite reduced levels of activity, older men report being less bored. These changes and differences are not simply related to age but are confounded with opportunities and competing activities. One assumes it is easier to daydream on an assembly line or laying bricks than it is when one is planning the schedule for the factory or designing the building. Daydreaming keeps the individual somewhat aroused and awake in monotonous situations, and Singer (1966) suggested that we totally underestimate the amount of this type of inner activity that proceeds in parallel to other tasks, including that of being a client—and sometime a therapist! How much of this goes on during any social interaction, meeting, church sermon, or listening to a keynote address at a conference?

Singer and Antrobus (1972) developed a questionnaire to ask people what their daydreams were all about, called the Imaginal Processes Inventory. They found that there were three major factors or types of daydreaming in American college students: tortured self-examination with predominantly negative fantasies of heroic achievement; disorganized, unclear fantasies mostly related to failure and the seeking of external reinforcement; and an elaborate, thoughtful fantasy life, with high levels of acceptance and interest in one's own imagination abilities. It is curious, however, that romantic and explicit sexual fantasies were not included in the reported daydreams. This kind of daydreaming is very focused and has strong stimulus or priming elements. Perhaps there is something different about deliberately imagining something to enhance arousal in contrast to unfocused daydreaming, but if so we need to know more about it. Think how often in psychotherapy, whether behavioral or cognitive, the client is asked to imagine something as a means of increasing motivation, altering the significance of stimuli, or covertly rehearsing some new skill (see also Chapter 7). One of the other potential benefits of fantasy is that imagining oneself in a heroic role makes one more munificent toward others, and this is also found in fantasy video games, such as having (visualizing) a positive heroic avatar (Yoon & Vargas, 2014).

One of the challenges of bringing this topic to the realm of clinical practice is that there now appears to be evidence that people can be quite reluctant to disclose their daydreaming themes honestly. Klinger, Murphy, Ostrem, and Stark-Wroblewsky (2004) reported that 79% of their participants preferred to disclose real experiences rather than their daydreams. Those who were not distressed by revealing their daydreams were people who exhibited lower negative emotionality, higher positive emotionality, and less of a tendency to ruminate. In other words, disclosing daydreams may be more difficult for the very people who are most likely to become clients. However, exploring clients' daydreams is important within cognitive behavioral therapy as the themes offer insight into clients' current concerns as well as goals (Klinger, 2012).

Experience and Thought Sampling

A technique that has been used to identify an individual's predominant thought content is to use some kind of sampling procedure in which a cue is presented and the person is asked to report what he or she had been thinking about at that moment. My partner's question ("Have you made the sandwiches?," see Chapter 1) was a cue, although it did not specifically call for a statement of my thoughts, I offered one anyway as a justification for not getting on with my assigned task. In research studies participants are specifically requested to state or record their thought content when the cue is presented in situ, often by a beeper, a signal from a mobile phone, or a phone call from the experimenter (Hormuth, 2006). This methodology was used by McAdams and Constantian (1983) in a study of 50 university students who carried a pager for a week and were paged seven times a day. In response to the page the participants completed a self-report form of thoughts, affect, wishes, and behavior. Intimacy and affiliative motivation had been assessed beforehand, and those students high in intimacy needs recorded more interpersonal thoughts and positive affect in social situations than students low in intimacy. Affiliation motivation was associated with expressions of desire to be with others when alone. In a revealing reflection of changing mores, 30 years ago those with either high affiliation motivation or intimacy motivation were more likely to be engaged in conversation or letter writing. One might assume that were such a study conducted today, time spent on Facebook would be the activity associated with intimacy and affiliation needs.

Experience sampling methods were used to good effect by Csikszentmihalyi and Figurski (2006). They argued that at any given moment a person's attention is focused on stimuli or thoughts external to the self or is focused on information about the self. A person might be thinking, "I am not looking my best" or "I look better than anyone else in the room" or "I wonder if they are noticing how I look today?" but in each instance it is the person's self that is the focus of attention and the central element of his or her thoughts. This is usually described as self-awareness. Having self-awareness—being both the known and the knower—is undoubtedly one of the complex pinnacles of our evolution, allowing a sense of personal identity. But it has its downside, as can be seen in such phenomena as social phobia where excessive (and negative) focus on self causes feelings of anxiety. In fact excessive self-evaluation interferes with enjoyment and openness to experience. However, it can be argued that a discrepancy between a current condition and an ideal standard only generates negative affect when people feel a lack of opportunity or skill to change their performance.

In the Csikszentmihalyi and Figurski (2006) study participants were beeped at random intervals by a pager, and self-awareness was assessed by their answer to the question, "What were you thinking about when you were beeped?" They were also asked if whether what they were doing at the time was voluntary ("I wanted to do it") or obligatory ("I had to do it"). And finally they rated their mood (friendly, cheerful, and happy vs. hostile, irritable, and sad). When activities were perceived to be voluntary, their affect was more positive, regardless of whether or not they were thinking about themselves. Self-awareness was associated with a more aversive experience (negative mood) but only when the activity was voluntary. It was concluded that the ideal experience is one in which the person is "engaged in an activity voluntarily and is not focusing attention on the self; it is in the voluntary condition—one in which behavior change is presumably easier to attain—that self-awareness is associated with aversive experience" (p. 25).

It should be noted that some habitual, distracted thinking causes little harm or distress, and because we do not typically study the full ecology of what occupies people's minds we do not know how widespread repetitive mental habits are. To illustrate, I had a client once, a retired stockbroker, who happened to mention that he had a strong mental habit that caused him no distress and was unrelated to why he was seeing me. He described that whenever he was sitting somewhere, no matter what else he was doing, if he saw a straight line on any part of the surface of the external environment, like the top of his TV set, or a table in the distance, or a window on the bus, he would try to estimate its midpoint, thus dividing the line in half, and then look for the midpoint of each half, thus dividing it into quarters, and he would continue this until the divisions were too fine grained to hold in imagery or he had to attend to something else. It was as far as I could determine a completely innocuous mental compulsion. I have no way of knowing how ubiquitous such mental habits are in ordinary human thought.

Think of the study by Csikszentmihalyi and Figurski (2006) in which a critical variable was whether the activity accompanying thoughts was voluntary or obligatory. Older men are often retired, and retirees always comment that what they enjoy about their present lifestyle is that they are able to do what they want, not what they have to. Opportunities for flow increase, perhaps, and flow and daydreaming are not compatible, since flow enhances performance, while daydreaming or compulsive mental activity are a distraction for most tasks that require mental engagement.

Flow: The Opposite of Mind-Wandering

Having introduced some of the work of the enigmatic and unpronounceable Csikszentmihalyi (read: six-cent-me-hay-ly), it is time to say something about what he is really famous for, and that is the concept of "flow" and how the state of flow is associated with the greatest levels of happiness or at least self-satisfaction. Flow is a state of effortless concentration that is so deep people lose any sense of themselves and their problems. Sporty people or those who were young in the sixties talk about being "in the zone." Obviously it would be a handy part of cognitive therapy if we could increase clients' experiences of flow.

As already seen, voluntary activities that are intrinsically motivating are most likely to be accompanied by flow. Csikszentmihalyi (1997) found such experiences to be characterized by five crucial elements. There is a state of centering of attention on a limited stimulus field, together with a merging of awareness and action brought about by intense concentration. Two additional elements are that feedback is unambiguous and the person feels competent within the interaction, unconcerned with his or her degree of control over the situation. Finally the focused attention and concentration requires lack of self-awareness (self-consciousness), which is the fifth element. Flow is not limited to highly academic or scholarly pursuits such as writing a book; one can experience flow when skiing, watching a movie, playing a musical instrument, cooking a gourmet meal, or hunting deer. Activating such behaviors is a set of procedures designed to encourage clients across a range of syndromes but especially depression (Addis & Martell, 2004) and anxiety (Chen, Liu, Rapee, & Pillay, 2013), to reduce the avoidance, withdrawal, and inactivity that serve to maintain depressive symptoms and interfere with helpful problem-solving. Doing these planned activities in a state of cognitive flow is ideal. With my strong preference (i.e., bias) for treatments that promote behavioral activation, I have the heretical thought that flow may be as good as mindfulness for mental health.

Mindset and Idée Fixe

Another useful concept is that of the *mindset*, an old term from the earliest 20th-century beginnings of experimental cognitive psychology. What was meant by this term was not so much a fixed attitude or way of thinking (our typical modern everyday meaning) as the mobilization of the cognitive processes necessary for the completion of a task or solving of a problem when intensely focused on so doing. In a sense this is the cognitive mechanism underlying "flow." Gollwitzer and Bayer (1999) proposed two types of mindset. (a) deliberative, which is needed before an action is effected and involves executive cognitions like planning, weighing up options, and seeking additional information; and (b) implemental, the mindset that is involved when deciding on an action ("Should I quit my job?" "Should we update our kitchen?"). The implemental mindset involves different cognitive processes, such as determining how to carry out the action ("I'll look in the job vacancy ads"; "I'll go to Home Depot to pick out the new cabinets.")

The everyday use of the term implies something much more negative than organizing cognitive resources to solve a problem. It is often used to designate a set of firmly held assumptions that are never seriously questioned or readily recognized as incorrect or insufficient. It is a truism that our closest social group members confirm our ideas by reinforcing them with praise or repetition. Therapists (as well as other societal critics like university professors) are sometimes the first individuals to challenge a person's mindset. What renders mindsets so problematic for the group or organization is that, collectively, their minds are closed to data at variance with their assumptions. The classic recent political example of this is the belief in the George W. Bush White House that Iraq and Saddam Hussein were the biggest threat to US national security, despite numerous briefings to the contrary (Clarke, 2004).

A truly focused mindset is comparable to the everyday notion of fixed ideas, or fixations, that are extremely resistant to change through logic, reason, or new evidence. The French term *idée fixe* is somewhat similar to cognitive components of some clinical syndromes, such as anorexia, body dysmorphic disorder, or obsessive compulsive disorder, but the term is usually reserved for its occurrence in people who do not seek help or get referred to mental health services. The concept neatly illustrates the inevitable interconnection (fusion) between an idea that causes emotional distress and leads to actions that reconfirm the original belief in some way and sustains the distress. Thoughts, emotions, and actions become bound up and dominate people's lives in dysfunctional ways, and the train of thought becomes impossible to control.

I knew a professional who illustrated this perfectly. His idée fixe consumed large portions of his life but did not interfere with his practice, and he never sought treatment as he was convinced of the correctness of his belief that he had discovered an unorthodox cause of a common clinical syndrome. When he tried to publish this idea, his initial attempts were rejected by academic journals, as he had no supporting evidence. He became preoccupied with the lack of recognition. As a result, instead of following the usual academic process of research and publication, he wrote to many influential people, enclosing long, unpublished manuscripts, claiming that he was being disrespected by the scientific community. These actions were guaranteed to fail. Not getting replies, and/or being treated as a nuisance, merely confirmed his notion that he was not being recognized as he ought to have been. Believing his theory was important and would help people with the disorder added to the distress of being disrespected and put down. Some colleagues tried to placate him by reading his work and even agreeing that the ideas were interesting, but instead of satisfying him in any way, such feedback simply intensified his hatred for the researchers who lacked such wisdom.

Introspection

Students of psychology will remember that when Wilhelm Wundt opened the first psychological laboratory in Leipzig, in Germany, introspection was one of the most important research methods he used to try to analyze the structure of consciousness. Essentially the procedures involved exposing a research subject to a situation—usually a controlled stimulus of some kind—and asking him or her what was experienced. How intense did a stimulus have to be before it was detected as a sensation? What color was seen after intensely staring at one color and then looking away or at another? How many dots could a subject accurately report apprehending after being shown an array for a period of time too short to allow an actual count? Verbal report, spoken or written, is one of a very few ways that we have for finding out what people are experiencing—or thinking about.

Not only do we all have conscious experiences, including thinking, but we are also aware of having these experiences and can reflect on them. When we report them to someone else, be it an experimental psychologist or a psychotherapist, we are communicating about these experiences. That is the essentially social meaning of introspection and the only method truly available to psychotherapists. Clients are likely to be able to report accurately how many children they have or where they met their spouse but less likely to be able to explain their reasons for having children or what first attracted them to their spouse. Even reporting simple sensations and perceptions in the early laboratory studies was not reliably done by some subjects, and Wundt noted that it was sometimes necessary either to train subjects to be better at self-report or to not use some participants at all. When it comes to the kind of self-reflection and self-analysis that would be important in cognitive therapy, introspection is often extremely limited:

> The ability to be fair in judging others objectively, the ability to act in accord with intention, the ability to treat members of ingroups and outgroups equally, the likelihood of privileging those who come from dominant and subordinate groups—these are heavily compromised mental acts, and invisibly so. (Banaji, 2007a, pp. 264–265)

Thus it could be important to recognize that people differ in their ability to report experiences, either because they lack the necessary vocabulary to report complex experiences or because they do not typically think much about mental experiences or reflect on them or analyze their feelings at the time.

Other individuals, however, seem to spend a considerable amount of time engaged in such analyses, particularly as it relates to their sense of and understanding of themselves: as a cognitive trait characteristic they would be high on something we might call introspectiveness. Everyday parlance has words for these mental activities when focused on our own motives, attitudes, values, and convictions: soul searching; self-analysis; seeking self; self-awareness, and, more crudely "mental masturbation." Self-focused thoughts after a positive event are not likely to cause negative affect, whereas introspection after negative events is likely to do so (Mor & Winquist, 2002).

We thus have two very relevant aspects of this topic as it relates to how and why thoughts change: (a) the differential ability of clients to introspect and report accurately on their inner experiences and (b) the tendency for people to engage in a great deal of noncommunicated personal introspection, possibly in a way that is harmful or at least unhelpful to constructive planning, problem-solving, and finding meaning in their lives through action. After all, it is constructive self-reflection that is important for identity development, especially during adolescence (Adams, Abraham, & Markstrom, 1987; Levy & Farber, 1986).

A recent doctoral student in my lab, Anna Reynolds (2013), was interested in exploring the positive and negative aspects of introspectiveness in teenagers. The first thing she wondered was whether the tendency to be introspective was a unitary trait or could be divided into different styles of introspection. She administered an established questionnaire, Hansell, Mechanic, and Brondolo's (1986) Introspection Scale, to 148 high school students between the ages of 13 and 18. Typical items are questions such as: "How much do you pay attention to your own thoughts?" and "How much do you picture in your mind what your life is like?" Reynolds was well aware that rating scales such as this are open to many sources of error, including scaling and anchoring problems with questions such as "how much" does anybody think about anything? However, her young participants seemed to have no trouble taking a stab at her questionnaires, and she obtained normally distributed scores for all instruments used. She thus had the necessary statistical green light to factor analyze these adolescents' ratings and found there were three factors that accounted for 60% of the variance. She labeled these: Self-Analysis (e.g., "How much do you think about why you do the things you do?"), Psychological Awareness (e.g., "How much do you pay attention to your feelings?"), and Egocentricity (e.g., "How much do you think about yourself when you're alone?").

Reynolds had also measured a number of other aspects of these adolescents' personality, emotional difficulties, and social behavior. Emotional symptoms, peer problems, negative affect, and low self-esteem all correlated only with the Self-Analysis factor and not with either of the other two. Her conclusions were that introspectiveness is not a unitary construct and that it has three broad elements to it. It is the type and duration of teenagers' introspection that relates to their emotional adjustment. This made a lot of sense to us because there has been a long back-and-forth discussion in the literature as to whether being introspective is healthy (Hoyer & Klein, 2000). When adolescents think about what they are like as individuals, this could broadly encourage a strong self-identity and make them more empathic. Thinking about the reasons and motivations underlying one's behavior could assist with problem-solving but appeared, in Reynolds' study, to be much more ruminative and related to higher levels of emotional symptoms and negative affect. Not only are there different facets of introspectiveness, but the kinds of introspective thoughts and the contexts in which they occur determine whether they are adaptive or not.

Reynolds conducted a second study in which theoretically relevant parallel cognitive traits or abilities were also examined as independent variables: mindfulness, cognitive flexibility, and emotional clarity. I have more to say about the first two later, so let me just define emotional clarity for now. The construct comes from the measurement of emotional intelligence and is supposed to reflect individuals' ability to recognize and understand their own emotions. With the dependent variables being the presence of emotional symptoms, Reynolds used structural equation modeling to see how all these variables might interact in predicting psychological difficulties. The model that best fitted the data indicated that introspectiveness had no direct effect on emotional symptoms but did relate to mindfulness (negatively) and cognitive flexibility. The latter two related to emotional clarity, and mindfulness, cognitive flexibility, and emotional clarity all related negatively to emotional symptoms.

It is always a little difficult to get a clear picture of what complex data sets are really revealing, but Reynolds and I think the conclusions are the following. Introspectiveness as commonly measured is made up of different facets. When it comes to adolescents' well-being—having fewer symptoms of emotional distress—those who report being aware of their thoughts and feelings and think about who they are had greater well-being, and those who reported spending more time in self-analysis had greater emotional distress. However, there are other measures of characteristic thought styles that are better predictors of well-being, especially mindfulness, emotional clarity, and cognitive flexibility, in that order. And since self-awareness was related to negative symptoms in the first study, one sees a classic example of interactive effects so characteristic of personality research: if self-aware *and* mindful, adolescents are likely to be low in emotional distress. Thus introspection per se is neither adaptive nor maladaptive—it depends on what facet of introspectiveness one is talking about and what other constructive cognitive attributes the individual possesses.

In educational and training contexts, it is widely recognized that reflective thinking is an important skill. Reflection means stepping back from an experience in order to think more about it and one's performance and thus increase and consolidate learning. The purpose of reflection is to link current experiences with prior experience, thus aiding transfer of simple knowledge to new and more complex cognitive tasks (Bruner, 1960). Just as trainee therapists might be stimulated to reflect on their new clinical experiences (e.g., Rae, 2010), so we can encourage reflection in clients after they have experienced new thoughts in therapy or in guided behavioral practice. This process is implicit in all cognitive behavioral therapy but could be made much more explicit to clients by explaining that "reflection is an important human activity in which people recapture their experience, think about it, mull it over and evaluate it. It is this working with experience that is important to learning" (Boud, Keogh, & Walker, 1985, p. 19). It would be important to make it absolutely clear that reflective thinking demands openness to new ideas and thinking in an upward spiral, bringing in more general and abstract concepts for resolving future life situations (Kolb, 1984). The mulling needs to be positive and constructive; it must not be confused with repetitive rehearsal of mistakes and concerns—what we call rumination.

Rumination and Worrying

One reason teenagers deserve a special analysis when it comes to the stream of consciousness is that adolescence is considered a period of especially intense self-examination, seeking of identity, and forging daydreams of possible futures. Daydreams, however, as Klinger proposes, can intensify into rumination and worrying. An element of thought that has not yet been analyzed in much detail is that an individual's thoughts can trigger new thoughts, about the same thing or about things related to it. This is both a blessing and a curse. It is a curse when the thoughts are worrying or negative in some other way (saddening, for example) or focused on problems not solutions. Because thoughts are not bound by physical reality, events and other thoughts triggering them are not easily controlled. If anxiety is triggered by a situation, which it usually is, especially in the case of phobias, then the anxiety can be potentially reduced by changing the environment and removing the situation—if crowds make you anxious, do not go to the mall on a Saturday. But if an anxious thought is triggered by an earlier anxious thought, and that in turn triggers a related anxious thought, avoidance is not so easy. If a thought that you tend to be careless triggers the thought you might have left a burner on the stove top on, that will trigger the thought that the olive oil was near the stove, which triggers thoughts about fire, which triggers thoughts about whether your homeowners' insurance premiums are up to date, and so on. Unless you can somehow reassure yourself that you did not leave the burner on, by being able to explicitly recall turning it off, you will be obliged to turn the car around and go home and check—even if you do not have a proclivity for such thought sequences that we label obsessive-compulsive disorder. Checking is a nuisance, but it does resolve the anxiety, if only temporarily; other negative thought sequences do not lend themselves so easily to a corrective action.

So worrying is having anxiety-laden thoughts that persist, feed on each other through association, and are not focused on strategies that might reduce the threat. Because anxiety is often triggered by expectations around some future event, like having to give a talk or go for a job interview, worry, being internally primed, is possibly more common than specific phobias. If a person's thoughts contain themes of impending difficulties, future economic problems, and anticipation of failure, then they can, through simple association, run wild, unconstrained by issues of probability or plausibility. Tom Borkovec, a leading clinical anxiety researcher, told me a story a long time ago about soliciting participants for his research on anxiety disorders. He advertised for people who were not mental health clients to be willing to be subjects in his research program on reducing anxiety. As he was at Pennsylvania State University, which is in a small town called State College with a limited nonstudent population, very few people answered his ads for free help with anxiety. But when he changed the wording to ask, "Do you have worries or a problem with worrying?" the response was dramatically different, and hundreds were beating on his door. I may have embellished this story slightly, but the point is clear: ordinary people tend to think of nonspecific anxiety as worry. And worry tends to be encoded in verbal thoughts, not images (Borkovec & Inz, 1990).

There are thoughts other than of threat, such as feeling excessively responsible for some situation. A negative thought sequence, in which for example a woman thinks she might have unwittingly harmed someone, such as being unavailable to her child when she was stressed at school, or a man who thinks he could harm someone, like thinking he might hurt his baby, are also not easily resolved. The thoughts simply trigger each other, with no means of reassurance. This is what we call ruminating: turning something over and over in one's mind. We have evidence that this process maintains anxiety in both people who tend to be chronically anxious and those who do not (Wong & Moulds, 2009). Rather creatively, these authors experimentally facilitated ruminating in their study participants by asking them to think about what it would be like if their anxious feelings persisted (a classic worry about one's symptoms scenario) or to think about how they performed on an anxiety-inducing task (giving a speech). And they facilitated the opposite (which is distraction) by having them think instead about neutral (think about a band playing outside) or calming topics (think about clouds in the sky).

The affect connected with ruminating does not need to be as intense as might be generated by the examples given. We can ruminate about the vacation being somewhat spoiled because the hotel is not nearly as pleasant as the brochure indicated. We can ruminate about the decline in respect for teaching the humanities at universities worldwide. We can ruminate about actions in the past one now regrets. In some ways these kinds of ruminations are simply negative daydreams and not very different from metaphorically chewing the cud, which is where the word comes from. Anxious people ruminate about decisions they have made in the past, especially when they worry about making errors and find it difficult to commit themselves to something in case they are wrong. These are tendencies that personality theorists refer to as *fear of invalidity* (Thompson & Zanna, 1995). Thus in clinical contexts ruminations can be highly distressing and difficult to control. Nevertheless, different cognitive therapy approaches have shown an ability to do so.

We know this from experimental studies. First, there are clinical questionnaires designed to measure self-reported rumination, such as the Response Style Questionnaire (Nolen-Hoeksema, 1991). Attempts to measure rumination in people who are depressed have had a checkered history. Nolen-Hoeksema introduced the idea of response style (a personality variable) in depression, suggesting that a depression-specific response style would maintain or exacerbate depressive symptoms by focusing clients' thoughts on the potential causes, meaning, and consequences of their depressed mood. The Rumination scale of the Response Style Questionnaire consists of 22 items that cover a focus on one's own symptoms ("I think how hard it is to concentrate") and self-focused, self-blaming rumination ("I think 'Why do I react this way?'"), including the devastating consequences of one's melancholic mood ("I think 'I won't be able to do my job if I don't snap out of this'"). The latter two items are perfect examples of meta-cognitive tendencies to worry or to get depressed over one's own "symptoms." Inevitably there has been interest in trying to determine whether a ruminative response style is a trait (a stable way of thinking like introspectiveness) or is simply concordant with depression, such that as depressive symptoms decrease, so will rumination, giving the illusion of a causal connection.

The difference between symptom-focused rumination and self-focused rumination further complicates the picture, since as depression decreases and symptoms become weaker clients would have fewer things to ruminate about. The self-focused thinking style should be more stable if it is a causal risk factor for depression. Both of these expectations have been confirmed in research studies (Bagby, Rector, Bacchiochi, & McBride, 2004). In an exhaustive literature review of her response styles theory, Nolen-Hoeksema, Wisco, and Lyubomirsky (2008) concluded that "rumination does predict depressive symptoms and disorders and does impair thinking, problem-solving, instrumental behavior, and social relationships" (p. 418). These authors also assert—perhaps overinclusively—that, in addition, "new evidence reveals that rumination predicts not only depression, but anxiety, substance abuse, eating disorders, and possibly self-harm" (p. 418).

So much empirical energy has been spent on these questions, it seems to have been forgotten that questionnaires are rather weak ways of obtaining information on typical or chronic thought patterns, compared with the experience sampling methods that were common in the 1970s that have already been described. Since a questionnaire asks respondents to make a judgment about what they are typically thinking when depressed, the fact that they are answering these questions when in a depressed mood would surely influence their judgment. But, be that as it may, it remains somewhat interesting to note that people who are depressed often ruminate about their depression, and that means not only constantly turning things over in one's mind but thinking negative thoughts about one's negative (depressed) thoughts. This is an identical situation to what happens so often in anxiety. Clients have anxious thoughts about their anxiety, allowing them to anticipate anxiety in future situations and to worry about the symptoms of anxiety (not being able to give the speech without shaking or not being able to fall asleep because one is so nervous about getting enough sleep before a major exam; Evans, 1972).

The bottom line is that ruminating about one's symptoms is not productive and can quite possibly prolong them through these sort of fear-of-fear and depressed-about-depression mechanisms. And at this point you should be asking yourself, "Right, sounds good; so how do we stop people from ruminating?" Not surprisingly, Nolen-Hoeksema et al.'s (2008) suggestions are not very different from the various cognitive therapy strategies already developed for depression, by assuming that the mechanism of treatment is through altering or interfering with a ruminative response style. The suggestions include engaging in activities (behavioral activation) that distract people from ruminative thinking about depression; mindfulness training and acceptance (more analysis of that later) that teach people to notice their thoughts without becoming embroiled in them; cognitive therapy strategies that teach people to challenge their negative thoughts rather than passively replaying them; and interpersonal therapy and social problem-solving that reduce sources of rumination (such as about one's intimate relationships). In other words every recognized form of treatment for depression, no matter how different in focus, these authors believe have their benefit through reducing rumination. Some confirmation has been provided by Manicavasagar, Perich, and Parker (2012). Using the Ruminative Response Style questionnaire as one of their treatment outcome measures, these authors compared conventional cognitive therapy, addressing dysfunctional attitudes and negative automatic thoughts, with mindfulness-based cognitive therapy (Segal, Williams, & Teasdale, 2002), designed to foster mindfulness through awareness of current experiences. Despite these methods having very different conceptual rationales, both were equally effective, and both resulted in less rumination. It is hard to escape the suspicion that rumination about depression is not so much a cause of depression as a feature of depression.

One of the most interesting ideas about controlling ruminations, or stopping worry from becoming ruminative, has come directly from the lab and relates to Mischel's distinction between cool and hot thoughts. Kross, Ayduk, and Mischel (2005) conducted ingenious experiments in which the precise context for thinking about negative past experiences was manipulated. Recalled thoughts of negative interpersonal experiences were focused either on "what" questions ("what were the angry feelings like?") or "why" questions ("why did you feel this way?"). But even more important, the questioning encouraged either self-immersion or self-distancing. Self-immersion is the usual way therapists encourage recall of the past. Distancing was achieved by the following instruction: "Take a few steps back and move away from your experience . . . watch the conflict unfold as if it were happening all over again to the distant you." *Why* questioning in a distancing context facilitated a cool, reflective "processing" of negative emotions, allowing the participants to make sense of their experiences and the affect elicited without (re-)activating the original negative feelings.

Brooding

So much attention has been paid to worry and rumination as components of anxiety disorders and depression, we sometimes forget there is third version of this phenomenon that we call "brooding" in everyday parlance. The distinctions are subtle, but brooding is to anger as worry is to anxiety (think Heathcliff in *Wuthering Heights*). We brood morbidly about injustices experienced and the harm others have caused us. Brooding is accompanied by feelings of hostility, as well as thinking about revenge and methods of retaliation or hopes for some misadventure to befall the perpetrator of the insult or injustice. All anger is about a wish for harm to befall the person or object who caused the harm, and brooding facilitates this thought rather than reformulating it more positively within the framework of forgiveness.

That, at any rate, is my view. Other psychologists specifically interested in depression have used *brooding* as an adjective to qualify *rumination* and to separate a form of rumination from a more reflective type. However, I consider brooding about injustice and perceived hurt to be quite a significant issue in the psychology of people with anger management problems, passive aggression, and a history of violence. According to the previous edition of the *Diagnostic and Statistical Manual of Mental Disorders* (American Psychiatric Association, 2000), there are culture-bound syndromes such as *amok*, which is seen in people in Malaysia. Brooding is precipitated by a perceived slight or insult and continues for a period followed by a sudden outburst of aggression or violence (Gaw & Bernstein, 1992). That is obviously not unique to Malaysians. Insulting, hurtful, and unjust experiences are quite common in workplace settings because of power differentials. Brooding on these experiences allows the anger to grow and the fantasized getting even to be covertly rehearsed, sometimes resulting in explosive outbursts that can be very lethal. There is a reasonably distinctive type of mass shooting episode in which the perpetrator has intense feelings of anger and resentment, arising from prolonged thoughts (beliefs) of being grossly mistreated (Knoll, 2010).

Meditation and Mindfulness

Meditation is an attention-based strategy that permits active, unregulated thoughts to be reduced in consciousness while the meditation exercises are being practiced. If it is to be considered a professional part of cognitive therapy, meditation needs to meet some specific criteria: there must be a formal technique and an attitude or mental set with which one approaches the activity; some form of muscle relaxation is involved; there must be little evaluation, in the sense that there should be no intentions to analyze or judge the experience; and there needs to be a self-focused skill component that anchors attention, such as posture (cross-legged), or the mantra in transcendental meditation (Cardoso, De Souza, Camano, & Leite, 2004).

Introducing clients to meditation has been a component of many cognitive-behavioral treatment protocols, where it is interpreted as a stress management intervention if practiced regularly. There is consistent and strong evidence for quiescent psychophysiological changes—reduced activity in the autonomic nervous system, such as lowered heart rate, lowered blood pressure, and heightened skin resistance. Longer term changes in brain processes and metabolism are also commonly reported, but what the psychological (interpersonal, cognitive, and social) and mental health benefits of these might be is not really established, due to inadequate methodology in the clinical trials (Ospina et al., 2008). There is some evidence for benefits for clients with high chronic levels of anxiety. Despite all this the Internet is glutted with articles—many by respectable psychologists—on the benefits of meditation and how it works to "rewire" the brain (e.g., Lucas, 2010). The latter is a slightly odd metaphor as there are no wires in the brain, the functioning of which does not resemble the electrical circuitry found in a house or even in a computer.

Mindfulness is a type of meditation, often using attention to one's breathing as a focal activity. It is different from concentration meditation, as the goal in mindfulness training is to be more open to experience (thoughts and emotions) without identifying oneself with them. When learning and practicing mindfulness, individuals are encouraged to purposefully pay attention to the "present moment" and not be preoccupied with worry or daydreams. This can include concentrating on sensory experience, such as the bouquet of the wine, its deep redness, and its complex flavors. We all too often go about our daily lives thinking ahead, planning, addressing family needs, rushing to catch the bus, without stopping to savor the current experience. Another component is a self-regulatory skill that involves focusing attention on a current experience on a moment-to-moment basis. This supposedly allows greater recognition of the variety of one's own mental processes. A third component of mindfulness training is a very particular orientation toward this self-reflective experience: thoughts and feelings are to be accepted in a nonjudgmental fashion (e.g., Williams, Teasdale, Segal, & Kabat-Zinn, 2007).

All the major cognitive therapies state that they rely to some extent on imagery and on metaphors to change thoughts. Metaphors play a special role in Teasdale's therapy. What he refers to as "implicational mental codes" indicates a level of meaning that is generic and holistic and does not map directly onto the semantics of language. A poem, for example, conveys holistic meanings that are much more elaborate than the specific meaning of the individual words or sentences: "Break, break, break, on thy cold gray stones, O sea" (Alfred, Lord Tennyson) surely conveys thoughts, images, feelings, and memories way beyond the literal splashing of waves on the seashore. Imagery is a major feature of ACT. In ACT treatment for problem anger, for instance, Eifert, McKay, and Forsyth (2006) ask clients to "imagine that one day the headstone in the drawing below will be the headstone on your grave . . . what [epitaph] would you like to see on your headstone?" (p. 128).

Mindfulness meditation for counter-acting stressful thoughts might encourage you to imagine yourself to be mountain, natural and at ease with itself, impervious to the strong winds and dark storms that can sometime swirl around it. As you will discover later, my own preferred imagery for some clients emphasizes not cold, unyielding mountains but flexible and adaptive trees that bend with the wind. The late Alan Marlatt and his colleagues developed a mindfulness exercise specific to the urges experienced by people attempting to control their use and abuse of drugs and alcohol. Suggesting that urges get stronger and stronger but eventually die away, they offered clients the mindfulness image of riding (surfing) a wave, which builds up in strength but if you stay on top of it will eventually dissipate into gentle, harmless spray. As measured by a questionnaire on acceptance versus control of negative private experiences and reduction in cravings, participants in the program showed significant benefits (Bowen et al., 2009), so now "mindfulness-based relapse prevention" is a designated treatment (e.g., Witkiewitz & Bowen, 2010).

As with any other therapeutic technique, much hinges on the rationale provided the client and the circumstances in which clients are encouraged to practice mindfulness exercises. Savoring the present moment, at least while one is in it, makes it more difficult to dwell on negative thoughts. If practiced intensely it is reasonable to suppose that it becomes a more habitual way of experiencing the world, so that the chances of spending conscious hours dissociating and thinking thoughts irrelevant to the task on hand are reduced. Yet exactly why mindfulness training does benefit clients is far from clear, as it evolved as a technique with very little theoretical integration with principles of cognitive behavioral therapy (Wells, 2002). The most frequently cited rationale in cognitive therapy for training clients in mindfulness exercises is that it allows clients' thoughts to be disconnected from automatically associated negative affect, but exactly how that happens remains obscure. The best explicit rationale, based on a relevant theory of just one type of cognition/emotion interface, has been proposed by Wells, and I consider it later (in Chapter 8) once these other features of the interface have been further discussed.

A challenge for researching the specific effects of mindfulness training is that it tends to be confounded with other forms of concentration and distraction, including relaxation training, yoga, tai chi, and guided imagery, where one visualizes peaceful scenes as well as positive actions prior to or during a stressful event. There are websites, such as Inner Health Studio (http://www.innerhealthstudio.com/guided-imagery-scripts.html), that offer guided imagery scripts for up to 43 different purposes, such as headache relief or "finding your authentic self." Mindfulness, with its close ties to Zen philosophy, is also confounded with notions of ancient wisdoms and Buddhist worldviews. The wisdom theme is reflected in Miller Mair's (2012) concept of mindfulness as poetry in our cognition:

> By poetry I do not mean short lines on a page that may or may not rhyme. I am referring to an approach to living that involves imaginative fluency rather than conventional solidity. I am referring to being able to hear with new ears, see with fresh eyes, and becoming able to

> speak with imaginative directness, telling it like it feels and is right now, not in terms of hack phrases or conventional slogans. (p. 185)

Mindfulness training might affect negative thoughts in various situations in which such thoughts dominate consciousness in a less than helpful way: for example, being preoccupied with thoughts about the future or the past or being inattentive to personal feelings of stress or fatigue. Mindfulness is also considered an antidote to attentional failings, such as neglecting valuable social information, like someone's name or description of their family, or recent experiences that one simply fails to process and cannot then recall them later when interacting with that person. But given the absence of information on individual differences in the degree to which people, societal groups, and cultures already function mindfully, as well as no serious data on when clients should use mindfulness practice as opposed to simply trying to become mindful (or for how long), I cannot help but be surprised at the speed with which mindfulness training has come to dominate both cognitive therapy and the popular imagination.

Implications

Because the ecology of everyday thought is not really studied in psychology, we do not know what farmers think about when they are milking cows or putting up a fence, or factory workers on an assembly line, or children walking alone to school. Perhaps their daily musings are so individualized and trivial—hardly worth even a penny—that we rightly focus on discrete thoughts only when they are bound up with distressing feelings of one kind or another. But from this chapter we have seen that it is important to recognize in clinical contexts that the cognitions that most need to be changed in effective psychotherapy are not limited to discrete thoughts. Because cognitive therapy manuals often give examples of particular irrational thoughts that depressed people have, and particular threat inferences that anxious clients make, clinicians well-versed in these approaches probably listen carefully for similar examples in our clients. That's fine. Making client characteristics more salient is probably one of the beneficial results of training in a particular approach, but one has to be careful that that is not all one is listening for in clients' discourse. Thoughts often targeted in cognitive therapies occur within a very definitive mental context—the daily stream of consciousness, which may be more like a hummingbird darting from flower to flower than a flowing rivulet. Sometimes it is the way this incessant mental activity works and works for or against the client's own better interests that needs to be the focus for change. Studies of rumination as a response style, in depression as well as other clinical disorders, highlight the important distinction between adaptive and maladaptive self-reflection and introspection.

There is a conundrum facing therapists who hope to discuss a client's thoughts along a path of reasonableness. Psychotherapy in general puts considerable store on the importance of "working through" clients' negative emotions by encouraging them to express and analyze negative thoughts. But here's the rub. There is a fair amount of experimental evidence that by trying to probe such feelings, and focusing on their causes and outcomes, people become entwined in rumination that increases their negative affect (Nolen-Hoeksema, 2000; Rusting & Nolen-Hoeksema, 1998). Fortunately, however, there are promising ideas regarding mitigating these unintended risks. Mischel and his colleagues have experimental evidence that when individuals ask "why-am-I-feeling-this-way?" questions in a distancing rather than self-absorbed manner, it allows cooler cognitive processes to predominate (Kross, Ayduk, & Mischel, 2005).

Sometimes, then, clients need to be taught cool meta-cognitive strategies that allow them to become much more reflective and to think about their actions and their impact on others. Perhaps they need to recognize better the unconscious feelings and past learning experiences that have given them attitudes and opinions that do not stand up to critical scrutiny. Sometimes the therapeutic goal will be in an opposite direction—to reduce negative, self-absorbed introspection and rumination—and sometimes the goal will be to foster a more positive contemplative, nonreflective style of mentation, at least for some periods of time. There is evidence that when clients, indeed people in general, practice mindfulness and meditative skills, it can have wide-ranging emotional benefits.

The goal for mindfulness is not always apparent, however, which makes it hard to know when and in what circumstances it should be introduced to clients. It is not just a happiness pill that will make one feel good, like oxytocin, legal marijuana, or an afternoon of self-indulgence at the spa. (These are never the control conditions for studies of mindfulness, so how they actually compare we do not know.) Sometimes authors seem to suggest that there are affective benefits simply in savoring experiences—really enjoying the spaghetti carbonara rather than merely wolfing it down. It is hard to get depressed on a cloudy day if you take the opportunity to stroll in the rain, smelling the mysterious scent of wet earth, watching the birds take a bath in the rapidly forming puddles, and letting your dog run happily through the mud without thinking of the mess he will make when you get home. Sometimes the influence seems to be that while meditating or practicing mindfulness one cannot simultaneously be worried about all the things one usually worries about. Creating incompatible behaviors is one of the classic techniques that cuts across all behavior change programs (Evans, 2013). Sometimes the influence of mindfulness is presented as having a deeper purpose—some authors propose that it teaches a generally useful skill of controllability of thoughts, of being able to manipulate thinking so as to uncouple it from its usually related emotions or harmful behaviors.

Except for mindfulness, which involves an extreme focus on current mental state and not on the content of one's thoughts, all of the phenomena considered in this chapter involve thinking about things and events that are real or could potentially happen in the future, even if unlikely. Worrying about fires or burglaries or illness or whether your date finds you attractive may be irrational but not totally implausible. Yet we can also have repetitive, ongoing thoughts about things that could never happen, and these we call fantasies. This is not to be confused with sexual fantasies and other arousing, daydream types of experiences we have described but is more like fantastical or magical thinking. Some people are particularly prone to fantasy, and this is considered a personality trait (rather predictably called "fantasy proneness"). Such a characteristic has considerable implications for thinking and thought content, including daydreaming about things that are not real or did not happen. This fits into another whole type of thinking that will be described in the next chapter.

5

Distorted Thoughts

Last year I experienced psychosis. I was insane. I believed I was a mermaid & turning into a dragon, that I was a witch & a psychic. I thought people could hear my thoughts and that the whole world was secretly laughing at me.

—A blog by "I Have Lost My Mind" on the *I Have Experienced Psychosis* website: http://www.experienceproject.com/groups/Have-Experienced-Psychosis/181537

Thoughts and Reality

Due to the pervasiveness of the Internet, anyone can now read hundreds of personal accounts of the thoughts experienced by people who have been diagnosed with psychosis. Some of these accounts are lucid; some of them continue to show errors of reason and logic and sense. They provide a richer catalogue of unusual thoughts than one will find in the scientific psychiatric literature. But should they be part of our present discussion? It may seem that we are now going backward and revisiting irrational thinking, which has always been the meat and potatoes of cognitive therapies, from Ellis onward. But in this chapter we are going to consider seriously irrational thoughts, so seemingly disconnected from reality or probability that we need a new category, and I've chosen to call them *distorted*.

There are numerous psychological phenomena of thought, not usually linked, that all seem to share the common characteristic of being significantly discordant with reality and yet, unlike some daydreams and fantasies, are held as real and have an undue influence over the reasoning and actions of those who entertain them. I am thinking here of phenomena like hallucinations, the quite different phenomenon of thought disorder (but also typical of clients diagnosed psychotic), unwanted, intrusive thoughts such as obsessive concern with what might happen to you or what you might do, paranoid thoughts, and so on. However, we also need to include the distortions that arise from fallible memory processes and the uneven recall of past events that could serve an adaptive function. And while distorted thinking in clients is often reported as a symptom of psychopathology or a particular diagnostic category, this may prove to be just a matter of degree. I attempt to show that distorted thinking occurs to some extent in everyone's mental life, but overly so in the case of very distressed clients.

Delusional Thought

Delusions and hallucinations are often linked together because they are both characteristic of people who are in an active state of psychosis, although they can occur in people who are not psychotic. Hallucinations, however, are perceptual experiences rather than thought-based phenomena. Hallucinations are visual, auditory, olfactory, and sometimes tactile—for example, a client of mine reported the not uncommon sensation that ants were running up and down inside her legs. Another not uncommon experience is command hallucinations—hearing voices that tell the individual to do something. Thus hallucinations' connection with thought is that people think they have seen or heard something. This is illustrated by some of the ingenious ways that experimental psychologists have devised for studying hallucinatory events in supposedly totally typical people. One of these strategies is called the White Christmas hallucination. Participants in a study using this paradigm are told that they will be performing a task and that, while they are doing so, Bing Crosby's "White Christmas" might be played. They are instructed to press a button every time they hear it or think they have heard a fragment of the song. When they come into the experiment, Bing Crosby's song is actually playing. Then they are fitted with headphones through which white noise is played. They are told to press the button every time they hear the song and that they can press the button for every fragment heard. They listen to the white noise tape for the next 3 minutes, and during this time the "White Christmas" song is never presented. Yet participants will press the button numerous times (Merckelbach & van de Ven, 2001). Given the suggestive power of words on imagery, I am fairly certain that some readers will be hearing "I'm dreaming of a white Christmas" right now.

Delusions, on the other hand, are undoubtedly thought based, as I have been defining thoughts thus far, and are often indistinguishable from an overvalued idea, an idée fixe. Delusions are firmly held beliefs that would be palpably false to the vast majority of people of the same culture. They are often themed around personal threat or persecution, impending disaster, or excessive concern about the malfeasance of well-known public figures. Erotomanic delusions, such as that some famous person is in love with you, is a frequent theme. Grandiosity, such as delusions of power or connection to powerful people, is also common. The philosopher Bertrand Russell (1938) attributed such delusions to all males' craving for power:

> Men who allow their love of power to give them a distorted view of the world are to be found in every asylum: one man will think that he

> is the Governor of the Bank of England, another will think he is the King, and yet another will think he is God. (p. 212)

Delusions are drawn from false inferences based on distorted, neglected, or erroneously judged information. The best documented cognitive bias in people with psychosis is that of jumping to conclusions (Dudley, John, Young, & Over, 1997). If a person has a tendency to draw inferences from minimal amounts of information, it is easy to see how such a bias would support delusions of persecution. We typically distinguish between delusions that are judged bizarre, in the sense that they relate to ideas that are not possible (such as believing the TV is sending you personal messages), and delusions that are potentially plausible (such as your husband is trying to poison you, or the jealous thought that your wife is unfaithful). It is possible that this distinction is only a matter of degree, since "bizarre" is something of a social judgment. For example, I personally think the belief that President Obama was not born in Hawaii is bizarre, with some people even believing that the late Loretta Fuddy, the former director of health for the state of Hawaii, who had originally confirmed the authenticity of his birth certificate, was deliberately murdered when she died in a plane crash off the island of Moloka'i (*Huffington Post*, 2013). However, we could not appropriately describe the many conspiracy theorists who suggested this as psychotic.

Clinicians assume that these errors are different from the ordinary errors of judgment any of us might and do make—such as seeing someone laughing and wondering if they are laughing at us. Instead, delusional thinking must not only involve a breakdown in logical reasoning and relative lack of doubt but reflect very deep-seated fears and insecurities—possibly ancestral, as I suggest later. Because of this, it does not seem plausible that the delusional thinking of someone diagnosed with schizophrenia will be very easily corrected by rational argument by asking the person to test reality through experimentation (as is often recommended in Beck's form of cognitive therapy) or by presenting contrary evidence (Tai & Turkington, 2009). Any such social intervention falls immediately into the trap that allows the person with delusional thoughts to extend those thoughts to the person presenting the alternative arguments—namely the therapist. Delusional thinking is almost certainly functional in some way and serves a range of needs (Birchwood & Trower, 2006). In Donald Trump's case, questioning the tragic death of Loretta Fuddy might really be only a cynical ploy—successful as it so happened—to attract attention from the media.

This analysis leads clearly to the first stage of changing delusional thinking, which is that the therapeutic agent must first establish a level of client trust. This would include *not* overtly or immediately challenging the distorted thinking or implying that the thoughts are truly crazy. When challenging a client's beliefs is initiated as a strategy, it might be possible to start with the more minor, less firmly held ideas to see if he or she can begin to yield on some of these more inconsequential ones. A very gentle, nondirective form of challenge is to make comments such as, "What about . . .? Do you think just possibly . . .?" Similarly, tactics that often work for other clients, such as using humor, irony, sarcasm, or gentle teasing, are proscribed as they are likely to be misinterpreted by clients with this type of thinking. Thus the major foci of cognitive behavioral therapy (CBT) interventions for people with psychosis, especially schizophrenia, is to target the distress that can be caused by the distorted thoughts (e.g., Trower, Birchwood, & Meaden, 2004), to focus on the anxiety and depression that commonly precede or accompany psychotic episodes (e.g., Morrison et al., 2004), and to reduce stress and increase social confidence and self-esteem (e.g., Hall & Tarrier, 2003).

So what then has been attempted regarding the specific targeting of delusional thoughts? Interestingly, this was one of the first demonstrations of the value of cognitive therapy by Beck (1952). As early as 1952 he published a paper on altering delusional beliefs in an outpatient with schizophrenia. Very recently he presented a full account of cognitive therapy for schizophrenia (Beck & Rector, 2005). Not surprisingly, addressing the "core beliefs" of a patient with schizophrenia is commonly presented as part of the overall CBT approach (Morrison, 2009). But the approach is one of curiosity, not interrogation; for those readers with long memories of TV shows, the approach is that of Columbo, not Dirty Harry. To avoid a direct and immediate clash of reason in therapy, one widely used technique is "peripheral questioning." Rather than challenge the client's beliefs immediately or, worse still, dismissing them as symptoms of insanity, therapists ask clients about the specifics of their beliefs in order to better gauge the actual processes of reasoning involved. How were the conclusions we might judge as seriously distorted actually drawn? We can also question what actions individuals have taken with respect to their delusions, such as asking what evidence they have accumulated to support the belief, and at that point slowly introduce alternative possibilities for clients to consider. The idea is to try to reveal chinks in the delusional armor—pieces of the narrative that are strikingly inconsistent and hard for the client to ignore or dismiss.

That all sounds good, but it is very hard to do in practice. Consider one of my clients, a young female Jewish graduate student named Celine who had the delusional belief that her young advisor was deeply in love with her and that the professor and head of her program (in art and design at a leading American university) was a Nazi war criminal. When I questioned her about the possible evidence for this ("Tell me why you think that might be so"), she produced indistinct black-and-white photos taken after World War II of suspected German war criminals. When I suggested the likeness was not great ("That picture is pretty grainy; it is hard for me to see the resemblance you have noticed"), Celine became angry and wondered what was wrong with me that I could not see the obvious. Naturally I backed off and agreed to differ rather than assert I was right and she was wrong. I had better success with pointing out that the professor in question, although indeed born in Germany, was 72 years old, thus making him only a very young child during the Nazi era. As to the junior professor who was her thesis advisor, I was able to ascertain very quickly after talking to him that he was in fact gay and had no romantic interest in her. This chink in the armor was more disruptive to her beliefs than his own direct assertion to her in conversation: his decidedly ineffectual narrative was that although he greatly cared about her succeeding in the program, he did not love her.

A closely related technique was originally developed by Ellis in rational emotive behavior therapy and is called "inference chaining" designed to elicit the personal meaning of the belief to the client (Turkington & Kingdon, 2000). For example: What are the implications for you if your partner were cheating on you? What harm would you cause if you accused him/her and you found out that your suspicions were totally unfounded? What would your advice be to a friend if he/she revealed that his/her partner had been unfaithful? If an acceptance and commitment therapy counselor, you might ask: How has this belief helped you reach your own valued, personal goals? With Celine it was possible to pursue a number of her inferences in a way that potentially revealed some of her more intense emotional concerns. The most revealing inference-chaining questions related to what would happen if she were right about the background of the head of the department ("He'd be fired and would have to leave in disgrace—the department would be a less stressful place.") Why is that? ("He sets the tone . . . Also, he might be turned over to Israel for trial like Adolf Eichmann"). How would that make you feel? ("I'd be recognized as a hero, an angel of justice; Jews would be grateful and honor me. Craig [the assistant professor who was her academic advisor] would be able to finally reveal his love for me"). "Is that the goal you are looking for in life—love and admiration?" ("Isn't that what everyone is looking for?"). So from this questioning, which bypassed her delusions, there were revelations of anger and hostility toward the department, a search for recognition, and a craving for affection—none of them irrational or bizarre desires.

A feature of both peripheral questioning and inference chaining is to assess the strengths of delusional beliefs, under what circumstances they are strongest (most firmly and insistently held), and the degree to which they preoccupy the client's consciousness. The idea of the stream (or hummingbird) of conscious thoughts has already been addressed in detail, and this situation represents a good instance of when the more general ecology of the client's thoughts are worth investigating, rather than maintaining an excessive focus on the delusional beliefs. Are these delusional ideas noticeable, in a less intense way, in the manner in which the client judges other situations? Is there evidence of a general trait of suspicious or paranoid thinking and irrational inferences? If so, what approaches are available to therapists to begin to focus on other, more positive and less distressing aspects of the client's experiences, especially social ones? Some of these will become more apparent as the story of how and why thoughts change unfolds.

For now, however, it might be noted that some cognitive distortions seem to be particularly characteristic of people described as having personality disorders; in fact this proximity to the distorted thinking of people with psychosis is why some clients were described as "borderline" in the first place. Some distortions have widespread influences on how the individual responds to others, particularly in social and intimate interpersonal situations (as Young [1994] and as Linehan [1993] have been particularly effective in explaining). For example, dichotomous thinking involves difficulty in seeing grey areas—believing oneself to be either a success or a failure, with few ideas in between, or appreciation that one's success might be conditional on external circumstances. Overly inclusive and personalized labeling occurs when the individual considers one event represents a characteristic of oneself, such as thinking "I can never do anything right" rather than "Oh dear, I really messed that up." Emotional reasoning is a distortion especially focused on in acceptance and commitment therapy: thinking that the way one feels about a situation reflects reality, such as thinking that because one feels a sense of despair, it means that nothing can be done to rectify matters. Overgeneralization is obviously the phenomenon of thinking in which one event represents how things are and will always be, such as a single occasion of one's partner being inconsiderate means that he or she is uncaring, despite previous examples of the opposite.

Thought Disorder

In addition to distorted themes, we also encounter in the clinic distortions in the generation and expression of thoughts. This "thought disorder" refers to a variety of different problems in maintaining a coherent flow of verbally expressed thoughts (either internal or spoken). Problems like these are characteristic of people diagnosed with psychotic disorders such as schizophrenia, but when I describe some of the common errors seen in thought disorder, it becomes apparent that, at a much less noticeable level, these kinds of interrupted flows are not entirely unusual. An early study from my lab demonstrated that both individuals with schizophrenia and typical controls exhibit greater language disturbance when discussing affectively negative topics, such as family problems or past trauma, than when discussing positive or neutral topics (Docherty, Evans, Sledge, Seibyl, & Krystal, 1994). Many subsequent studies have confirmed that heightened levels of physiological arousal contribute to these difficulties. This effect can be observed when highly experienced and talented actors give their acceptance speeches at award ceremonies such as the Golden Globes or Oscars—many of them are truly incoherent. In the case of any client being interviewed, it is worth remembering that the articulation of clear thought processes is difficult when under stress—both from the unfamiliar context of initial therapy and from the arousal related to the distressing topics of concern being disclosed.

One of the better defined phenomena of thought disorder is called *derailment,* which is a pattern of verbal expression in which ideas slip off track onto ideas only obliquely related or unrelated, resulting in the key idea of the narrative not being reached. It is not dissimilar to another phenomenon of formal thought disorder, *tangentiality,* in which the person replies to questions in what seems like an irrelevant manner, unrelated to the question. In both cases there is a sense that remote and idiosyncratic associations are guiding the thoughts, rather than some process of monitoring the logical development and communication of ideas. (It should be mentioned that in the past, clinicians would treat some of these phenomena as though they were simply a meaningless jumble, often referred to derogatorily as "word salad." But we now know that if the conversational thoughts are listened to carefully, the individual's logic can often be discerned, especially if one knows something about the person's recent experiences, past history, fears, stresses, and traumas.) If you have ever given complex lectures to students about difficult areas of scholarship that you have detailed knowledge of, without using notes, you may well have noticed how easy it is for one idea to trigger another, which in turn leads to a quick aside, that can result in a new reflection you have not had before and the introduction of some ideas and topics that are quite distant from the starting point of the thought. Or maybe it is just me; certainly I know students find it perplexing if they cannot follow my "flight of ideas" (another term from psychiatry that is less than complimentary).

Some other styles of thought sometimes seen in clients showing active positive symptoms of schizophrenia include *neologisms*, words that have meaning only to the individual person, pressure of speech in which there is rapid-fire talk that is difficult to interrupt, and circumstantiality in which it takes the client a long time to get to the actual point of what he or she is trying to communicate. Together these are all phenomena related to the conversion of thoughts to words, but as I have claimed already, we typically do not think first and then speak; rather speaking is simply thought externalized and usually in a social or communicative context. People with psychosis demonstrate this when they talk to themselves, a somewhat disturbing phenomenon when seen in people with obvious mental health disorders on the streets of our cities. Externalizing in spoken words, the flow of consciousness that is so commonly part of our mental life, is disconcerting for others when there is no obvious audience to whom the thoughts should be addressed. It is likely that people will know that they are doing it, but this is true of patients as well: when questioned about it, they often report that they know they are talking out loud to no one. Nevertheless, the phenomenon represents a breakdown in the usual rule of conversational speech requiring that one be silent if having the conversation only with oneself.

The topic of thought disorder, with its various facets, can best be approached through cognitive models of language production, and despite these being seemingly relevant to changing thoughts, the psychology of language production takes us too far afield for me to cover the topic in detail. Typical models include (a) the formation and maintenance of a discourse plan; (b) lexical encoding, which is the grammatical and phonological encoding of the information to be expressed; (c) monitoring both one's own and others' speech; and (d) editing one's speech for errors and finally articulating thoughts (Levelt, 1989). Cognitive language researchers have devised some ingenious ways for measuring each of these elements. One example, a measure of monitoring, requires participants to read some words out loud and read some words to themselves (silently). They are then given the same words, plus another new set, and asked to determine whether each word was previously said, previously thought, or a new word. The advantage of using a language production model is that the processes are not the same as the observed clinical phenomena and thus can be used as explanations of where people with schizophrenia are having difficulties with organizing and expressing their thoughts.

Imagine that a client has very active associative processes or difficulty inhibiting inappropriate associations. A language production model might help account for the emergence of one aspect of thought disorder, remote associations or neologisms. Barch and Berenbaum (1996) explain it like this:

> In a spreading activation model of normal lexical access, the level of activation determines which item is selected for production. A disturbance in the spread or inhibition of activation could result in inappropriate lexical items being more activated than appropriate lexical items. For example, while attempting to retrieve a target lexical item such as treehouse, related lexical items such as bush and cottage may receive inappropriate amounts of activation. If bush and cottage were to be more strongly activated than treehouse, then bush and cottage may be chosen for production, leading to a word approximation such as bush-cottage. (p. 86)

Dissociation

There is such a fine line between the thoughts and thought processes of clients with recognizable syndromes and the rest of us that many psychologists, especially behaviorists like myself, generally think of psychopathology as on a continuum with common, everyday processes and functions we all take for granted when they are part of life and do not interfere too much with goal directed behavior (cf. Dalenberg, 2009). We have already touched on the everyday phenomenon of mind-wandering, where we are supposedly engaged in one task requiring controlled cognitive processes and find our consciousness drifting off onto other thoughts and fantasies. These other thoughts might be those that cause anxiety (worry), those that cause depression (negative mood), or those that cause anger (hostility). (And remember by "cause" I only ever mean "contribute to" in some way.) Mind-wandering is the most common and elemental form of a range of cognitive experiences we call *dissociation* when in clinical contexts. Dissociation can be a coping strategy when its outcome is emotional detachment or numbing of emotional distress. Clients are prone to reduce emotional demands by limiting connections with others, but they can also mentally avoid by actively refusing to think distressing thoughts.

Dissociation, therefore, refers to discontinuities and alterations in consciousness, ranging from its opposite, desirable experiences such as flow, when one is fully absorbed in one activity and totally inattentive to others, to very unusual and clinically extremely rare conditions when one is unable to remember major parts of one's life, or actually functions as two different persona (the much-loved Hollywood phenomena of amnesia and multiple personality). In the old *Diagnostic and Statistical Manual of Mental Disorders* (fourth edition, text revision; American Psychiatric Association, 2000), the essential features of all dissociative disorders was a disruption of "usually integrated functions of consciousness, memory, identity, or perception" (p. 519). Experiences described as dissociative can be positive, in the active rather than evaluative sense of thoughts intruding, such as a flashback or experiences of being possessed, or negative, in the passive sense of thoughts being excluded from consciousness, such as dissociative amnesia (fugue states).

Psychiatrists call the experience of unreality of the outside world, often manifest as intrusive thoughts, *derealization*. *Depersonalization* is a related phenomenon involving the experience of unreality in one's sense of self. Clients describe this experience as watching oneself act and having no control over the situation. Although these are the primary symptoms of the different psychiatric syndromes of dissociative disorder (Spiegel et al., 2011), both can occur in clients' descriptions of other concerns, such as panic. Self-report of dissociative experiences, such as from questionnaires, tend to overlap psychometrically with the perfectly normal and common trait of fantasy proneness (Merckelbach, Muris, & Rasin, 1999). This raises all sorts of intriguing possibilities. One that Merckelbach and Jelicic (2004) put forward is that people who are fantasy prone (and who report dissociative experiences) employ liberal criteria when describing past experiences of trauma and childhood sexual and physical abuse or when endorsing vaguely worded items on a questionnaire.

Other possibilities relate to cognitive therapy. Backtracking for a moment, I think it would be fair to claim that none of the cognitive therapies have addressed dissociative disorders in clients to any great extent, being so focused on the much more common syndromes of depression and anxiety. However, dissociative phenomena and related everyday experiences such as mind-wandering and fantasy proneness are highly relevant to the techniques for the management of thinking patterns that underlie CBT. One might think, for example, that fantasy proneness could relate quite closely to unrealistic expectations about life, friendships, career, family, and so on. One of my doctoral students, Anita Darrah, argued in her dissertation that women expecting their first baby were, in many societies, exposed to powerful romanticized myths about the joys and beauty of motherhood. Fantasy-prone women could be spending considerable amounts of time engaging in daydreaming of how wonderful it will be to have a baby.

While there is undoubtedly magic in childbirth and raising a baby, the reality is that it can also be quite stressful, with experiences of pain, discomfort, sleepless nights, and loss of physical attributes as well as loss of some friendships and socializing patterns befalling women late in pregnancy and in the early months of baby care. Unrealistic expectations and burst fantasy bubbles, Darrah (2012) reasoned, could contribute to postpartum depression, and she designed a brief intervention for expectant mothers to better prepare them for the inevitable losses of autonomy and lifestyle that would accompany having a baby. The preventative short-term intervention was designed simply to explain how commonly held social images and construct around motherhood were shaped by societal imagery and dialogs. Without in any way negating the wonders of childbirth and motherhood, women participants in the training could better anticipate some of the difficulties they would face and that what they could expect were common and more realistic experiences. (In Chapter 7 I describe this important juxtaposition of dreams and reality as mental contrasting.)

It is possible that teaching clients the skill of savoring would assist them in enjoying their baby experiences, whether objectively positive or negative. But would mindfulness training be a good idea for people who are prone to dissociate? We do not know the answer to that question because studies of the benefits of mindfulness have not considered individual personality differences that might relate to its effectiveness.

Obsessional Thinking

Obsessional thoughts are often addressed within clinical psychology because what is called *obsessive-compulsive disorder* is quite prevalent. They are also typical of other forms of somatic delusion, such as the thoughts in body dysmorphic disorder that there is something wrong with some aspect of one's physical appearance. So too there are somatic delusions in psychosomatic anxiety that there is something wrong with the workings of one's body (one's health). Are these kinds of thoughts psychologically any different from delusions? Certainly many obsessional worries such as thoughts one has left the gas range on, or that eating a plate of pasta will make one fat and unattractive, as well somatic concerns about things that might be wrong or go wrong with one's body, are improbable but not quite as implausible as in some psychotic delusions. It is very possible to leave a stove unattended, to accidentally hurt one's child, to have a tumor despite a negative biopsy, or, like one of my clients (Evans & Pechtel, 2010), to have a common surgical procedure leave one permanently damaged in some way. The powerfulness of some clients' beliefs about physical defects suggest that at the personality level, biases predominate both cognitions and more basic perceptual processes when sense data are potentially ambiguous (Clerkin & Teachman, 2008). And as bizarreness is not a defining criterion for delusions, even in clients judged to be psychotic, it would seem that obsessional thoughts are not substantially different from those considered delusional.

First of all, obsessional thoughts are intrusive, and clients may recognize them as unrealistic or implausible. With delusional thinking, the implausibility eventually needs to be challenged because it leads to inappropriate behaviors (repeatedly calling the police because you believe your neighbor is manufacturing terrorist bombs in his backyard). In obsessional thinking we are more likely to focus on the anxiety that results from uncertainty—the possibility that the belief is correct causes distress and motivates compulsive behaviors such as checking. It is the anxiety that the client cannot escape, despite realizing that the probability of the thought being true is quite low—doubt fuels the anxiety more than the threat does. Salkovskis (1989) proposed that when intrusive thoughts are of a threat that the individual is personally responsible for (or for preventing), it results in anxiety and discomfort, which is then temporarily neutralized by the compulsive act.

In children, lack of certainty is not so much doubt about possible eventualities as lack of knowledge and understanding of the complexities of the world. Here parental reassurance about what is safe and warnings about what is dangerous seem to play a large role in modifying—or not—children's erroneous beliefs about harm. For example, McIvor (2014) reported that children with needle-related distress (injection phobias) sometimes had odd cognitions, such as the belief that the needle would make them bleed to death or that it would go right through them. Providing better information as to what will happen is a simple cognitive strategy to reduce anxiety and thus the actual pain (Tak & van Bon, 2005). For children, the information provided by parents is critical. When children worry, providing reassurance ("You will be okay; there is nothing to worry about") is less effective than distraction ("What did you do in school today?"), and vague information ("This might hurt a bit") is less effective than sensory information ("It might feel like a pinch") (Cohen, 2008). Nevertheless, the information and its source have to be credible—children are not unused to being deceived about such things. In a study conducted in my lab we were able to show that hard evidence was more effective than verbal reassurance—being shown that the potentially feared contents of a box were not there. The children were able to see for themselves that the box was empty (Evans & Galyer, 2009). We suggested that doubtful thoughts are better dispelled by positive experiences than by parents'—or therapists'—comforting words.

A good question is whether intrusive thoughts and doubts, commonly experienced by many people, are the same as the negative automatic thoughts proposed by Beck. Obsessive-like, intrusive thoughts in nonclinical samples are also usually of violence, sex, and dirt/contamination and are not similar to the negative automatic thoughts that occur in people with anxiety and depression disorders (Purdon & Clark, 1993). In Purdon and Clark's study, negative automatic thoughts were assessed by the Cognitions Checklist (Beck, Brown, Steer, Eidelson, & Riskind, 1987). Further, there is a difference between intrusive, obsessional thoughts, and worrying (Turner, Beidel, & Stanley, 1992). According to Turner et al., the themes found in chronic worrying or rumination are more usually of common everyday concerns, such as money, family, health, and employment, and occur as a distinct (verbally encoded) thought. Obsessive intrusions, on the other hand, are more often related to religion, sex, aggression, and contamination and are manifest not just in verbal thoughts but in images and urges (the impulse to remove the threat). Worry thoughts are more often triggered by an external event or cue, and because they are of somewhat acceptable common themes, they are seen as potentially more controllable and not as strongly resisted as obsessional thoughts.

Managing Repetitive Thoughts

When I suggested that distorted thoughts such as delusions and obsessions must be considered within the broader context of the client's mental life (stream of consciousness), it helps to focus attention on two different domains of explanation. After all, describing delusions and obsessions and touching on methods for changing them does not really explain where such ideas and beliefs come from in individuals who become clients. There are, however, some concepts we can introduce that might be relevant when it comes to explanation. One area of analysis is that of factors that impose limits on self-regulated, wise, and well-reasoned thought, and the other relates to more fundamental cognitive processes, such as memory, attention, and the evolution of cognitive skills to cope with challenges and pressures faced by our early ancestors. It should be noted that cognitive psychology has tended to focus research on logical reasoning—the syllogistic reasoning rules first clarified by Aristotle. The upshot of all this research is that such reasoning is difficult to do, requires training and mental effort, and is easily thrown off by the nature of the problem presented and the emotion and motivation of the reasoner (J. Evans, 1982; Johnson-Laird, 2012).

Many of the thoughts I have been describing in this chapter are in a sense unwanted thoughts—they cause us discomfort and distress, directly interfere with activities we would otherwise enjoy, and by evoking anxiety result in avoidance of everyday, constructive experiences (see the next two chapters). This is why they are targeted for change in cognitive therapy. But one might expect that in order to reduce these negative elements, we could simply get rid of the unwanted thoughts and not indulge in them anymore. Why don't we do that? The reasons are complex, but we can make a start by considering simply the issue of self-management of thoughts.

First, it is quite possible to put unpleasant thoughts "out of our mind." We do that all the time, often by distraction techniques, such as not sitting around and ruminating but getting on with some other task that requires mental effort, such as e-mailing a friend or reading a book, or sustained attention, such as watching a complex drama on TV. That is an active choice we have to make, and we need to know a little bit about what will work effectively as a distraction. We also engage others by asking our partners or friends not to talk about something or to change the topic of conversation because we find the topic too sad, too upsetting (angry making), too shaming, and so on. We can also stop reading the newspaper article that is making us upset by evoking past memories or switch off the disturbing TV program that will give us nightmares later. We can, in other words, direct most of our thoughts, although exactly how we do this is not always obvious. It mostly requires accessing the external environment, as described, which is why the airplane example (at the beginning of Chapter 4) shows how in many situations one is constrained by the limits on behavioral variability.

It is not easy, however, to suppress a thought just by simply stopping thinking about a topic. There is a famous Bob Newhart YouTube skit in which he plays the role of a psychologist working with a client who has a persistent fear of being buried alive in a box. She says she just starts thinking about it and begins to panic, and it makes her life horrible. Newhart says he is going to say two words to her. And he shouts across the desk "Stop it!" (See the full episode on YouTube, at http://www.youtube.com/watch?v=Ow0lr63y4Mw).

Threats to Wisdom

In CBT there has been a growing interest in an old topic in psychology—wisdom. This has been stimulated by the newfound interest in Zen Buddhism and its concept of "wise mind" as promoted by Linehan (1993) in dialectical behavior therapy. She asserts that wise mind is where the person knows something to be true or valid, where there is no doubt, and when an action or a thought leads to no dread or anxiety. It is the quiet voice of guidance where reason and emotion meet. It is a bit like intuition, in that one experiences it rather than actively generates it. That sounds very nice indeed, so how do we achieve it, for ourselves and our clients? Strategies involve teaching clients to imagine a situation for which they want guidance, then to focus on breathing in a meditational fashion, focus on the moment of pause—of emptiness—at the transition between inhaling and exhaling, then ask themselves the question again while inhaling, and at the moment of transition notice what comes to them in the pause—it could be an image, a thought, or an urge.

While exercises like this have been developed in dialectical behavior therapy, practice, wise mind is not, in fact, something that can be easily taught or learned directly. Rather it occurs as other emotion regulation skills, interpersonal effectiveness, and problem-solving skills are acquired—as one begins to see the whole picture of a situation, rather than just a particular, perhaps upsetting, part. Because wise mind is a state of quiet certainty, acceptance is closely related to its achievement.

The psychology of wisdom, however, covers issues much more general than simply personal feelings of inner calm and self-confident emotional control. Unfortunately for clinical therapists, however, modern analyses of wisdom—as represented most authoritatively by the late Paul Baltes (e.g., Baltes & Staudinger, 2000)—are very much focused on *being* wise: on making wise decisions and on giving wise advice to friends and family. This kind of wisdom, based on experience, knowledge, and good judgment, is what we typically think of when describing people as wise and when we associate "wisdom" with age. But can we foster greater wisdom? In my lab, Judith Campbell (2013) recently completed a small-scale research program examining the assumed wisdom of older people and whether it can be enhanced: When it came to making sound judgments about personal and political issues of relevance to the elderly, would a volunteer group of ordinary senior citizens show wisdom, and, if not, what sort of intervention would allow greater rationality?

In the study we first asked a focus group of elderly persons what sorts of things at a personal and neighborhood level caused them some degree of distress, such as rising crime, reduced government services for pensioners, noisy neighbors, and predicaments experienced by their grandchildren. From this list of issues that preoccupied their thoughts, we generated realistic scenarios regarding situations that they might typically face: (a) personal, such as giving advice to a grandchild having difficulties or talking with a neighbor whose trees were blocking their sunlight; or (b) policy related, such as being asked for an opinion on age-limit changes in the driving laws or what the country's immigration policy should be. Matched sets of both personal and policy scenarios were given to the participants before and after a brief intervention, and these were then coded for degree of irrational thought shown in the elderly participants' proposed solutions.

Understandably, whether a thought is irrational is extremely subjective. So we did not judge the nature (content) of the suggestions, solutions, or advice offered. Instead we scored each answer in terms of a number of features of thought that would accord with the sorts of concerns first identified by the early pioneers of cognitive therapy. A variety of errors of reasoning were easily detected. These included (a) making prejudicial statements based on overgeneralization ("I don't mind British immigrants, but those Asians are a bad lot"); (b) black and white thinking ("If my granddaughter got pregnant I'd tell her she should have been more careful"); (c) catastrophizing ("The crime rate in my neighborhood has never been worse"); (d) minimizing ("I'm too old to have any ideas about that"); (e) meaningless clichés ("The do-gooders want the country to become a nanny state"); (f) habitual thinking ("Young people just don't listen anymore, and my grandkids are the same"). These are just examples; we had 20 criteria for irrational thoughts and ideas, and these were applied to the participants' solutions by two independent judges. It was not that easy to establish reliability—one can see from the actual examples of utterance listed here that they fit a number of categories of irrational thought, so we also asked the judges to give a global rating of the degree of wisdom revealed by these elderly people.

Certainly there are many possible interventions from the clinical literature in cognitive therapy, mostly based on discourse with the person, pointing out where his or her thoughts seemed to reflect irrational judgment. However, as these people were volunteers, not individuals seeking treatment or feeling any need to change, we adopted a different strategy to try to make them wiser. Based on the original focus groups and on our clinical knowledge of elderly people, we proposed that of the many possible causes of irrational thought, two might be particularly amenable to a change intervention. One was based on the idea that when a problem evoked a high level of anxiety or threat, the participants would fall back on simple, but irrational intuitive solutions (Mikels, Cheung, Cone, & Gilovich, 2013). The underlying mechanisms for this might be quite varied, but a plausible one is derived from terror management theory, which asserts, with much evidence to back it up, that when people are reminded of their own mortality (frailty in the elderly), their attitudes shift in ways that increase their sense of security, such as becoming more patriotic. Similarly, when people feel threatened, as Franklin D. Roosevelt reminded America in 1933, they "retreat" and become more conservative, authoritarian, and supportive of right-wing policies and leaders (Jost, Glaser, Kruglanski, & Sulloway, 2003). Thus one of Campbell's (2013) interventions comprised workshops on the self-management of negative emotions around issues and problems that caused stress in participants' lives. By recognizing that they were feeling fear or anxiety, and that this was interfering with rational thought, they could become more likely to problem-solve than to fall back on solutions that falsely offered greater security (such as denying immigration opportunities to foreigners or increasing prison sentences).

Our other idea, based on our observations, was that the supposed wisdom of elderly people is because they have many life experience to draw on, but in practice they do not always do so appropriately. We noticed that when issues were really meaningful to them, they either failed to draw on the most relevant past experiences or they applied rules and strategies that might have been relevant when they were younger but that no longer reflected changed conditions in society. (We hear this failure frequently when interacting with some older people who preface each remark with "Well, in my day . . ." or "When I was young we didn't have . . ."). The principle harks back to Bartlett's (1932) ideas about schemas—mentioned in Chapter 1—as an acquired framework in memory whereby new events and experiences are interpreted. We wanted participants to understand that this is how they were making judgments about new experiences in ways that were not necessarily relevant today. People can use their past experience more effectively if they realize not only that conditions have changed but that in order to apply their knowledge from the past they need to see how it might fit present circumstances in an oblique way. For example, the participant who said that for dealing with crime offenders should be "locked up and the key thrown away," could be asked about strategies they remember working in their day for achieving forgiveness, and they might reply, "Well, when I was young my dad would sometimes pretend he hadn't seen the naughty things we did, and not punish us, but because we felt the guilt we usually changed our ways." When they added the reflection, "So maybe there are ways of getting at young people earlier before they commit a major crime and perhaps help them see the harm they cause," it was possible to point out not that their solution was now wiser or more rational but that by applying their past knowledge thoughtfully they had achieved a new, possibly valuable, insight.

Did these brief interventions work to encourage more thoughtful, more rational, less emotive, and less rigid and prejudicial thinking in elderly people? The basic answer was that they did, or at least receiving *both* the emotional management and the better use of past experience workshops resulted in more rational, wiser suggestions for solving common, everyday problems. Judith Campbell's (2013) research was the first we know of to suggest that while elderly people are not particularly wise and tend to use a good deal of irrational thinking in their approach to life's challenges, they can be offered, if interested, simple learning opportunities that enhance their wisdom. In dialectical behavior therapy, Linehan (1993) encourages clients to understand that "emotional mind" is often in conflict with "reasonable mind," but when promoting wisdom I think there may be additional, metacognitive strategies that encourage people to think about what they are basing their judgments on and whether, if these are from the past, they are still relevant.

Reasoning Influences

From the example of enhancing wisdom in elderly people, we can see the likely role in irrational thought of two variables: (a) topics that are emotionally laden, particularly threatening themes, are hard to think clearly about; and (b) thinking is locked into old habits of thought and reasoning that might have been appropriate once but is less so now, under new and changed conditions. These variables represent possible features of a causal model that would be more informative than simply giving irrational thinking a descriptive label, such as it is "obsessional," "delusional," based on "prejudice," and so on. So too we have seen that language-production models begin to drill down past a restatement of the phenomenon to explain thought disorder, so there are explanatory models of reasoning that can begin to account for many of the errors of logic and coherence that can be seen in ordinary distorted reasoning as well as the obsessional thoughts, intrusive thoughts, worry, and delusions seen in so many clients.

In both the clinical and cognitive literature, when errors of reasoning are noted they are often "explained" by reference to the celebrated analysis by Tversky and Khaneman (1974) of human judgment and decision making. Their paper, "Judgment Under Uncertainty: Heuristics and Biases," is a classic and known to every psychologist, although the work was developed largely around economic decisions. Cognitive biases come about because people rely on what these authors called *heuristics*. They identified three common heuristics that are often useful in judgment tasks but that can lead to biases. One heuristic is representativeness: an event or person that is seen as representative or similar to a general category will be judged as belonging to that category, regardless of other factors that influence probability, such a base rates. Seeing a young woman dressed in a sexy outfit resulted in an elderly client of mine judging her to be a prostitute, because prostitutes try to look sexually appealing; but it would be improbable given the far greater number of young women who dress alluringly on a Friday night downtown compared to the number of street prostitutes working in the same area. As the judgment is not likely to be tested one way or another, the individual having this biased view had an illusion of validity and did not recognize her judgment was fallible.

A second heuristic is availability, which relates to the "ease with which instances or occurrences can be brought to mind" (Tversky & Kahneman, 1974, p. 1127). This heuristic is particularly relevant to clinical disorders, as the retrievability of instances and their salience to clients is exactly why, for instance, a harmless individual might seem dangerous because of the client's bad experience with a similar-looking person in the past. The third heuristic is that of anchoring, in which when there is information on an initial value, or starting point of a phenomenon, it influences the final numerical estimate. If a clinician is told that 10 percent of all veterans have symptoms of posttraumatic stress disorder, his or her prediction that a given client has the disorder will be lower than if told the value is 20%, whereas the judgment should be made strictly on signs and symptoms.

While providing a serious revelation regarding the biased judgments even of experts in a given field, the possible antidotes to biased reasoning were not offered in the original work, other than general suggestions that people need to be better informed about base rates, sampling, the effect of ease of recall of only somewhat similar instances, the crucial importance of getting feedback about the correctness of our judgments and decisions, and so on. And while rarely drawing from this specific literature, some of these same suggestions have been simply incorporated in cognitive therapy techniques and explanations. One good example is the idea that our clients' interpersonal judgments of others (their trustworthiness, safety, romantic commitment) is overly influenced by easily accessed emotional memories (schema) derived from past relationships. One might expect that giving clients insight into these influences on their judgment would reduce their biases, or perhaps most important encouraging them to test the validity of their assumptions and predictions before letting them gain too much credence. However, Tversky and Kahneman (1974) did tend to present their analysis of poor judgment under uncertainty as something of a fact of life—we all use these heuristics because they work most of the time for making rapid judgments. They did not think our limited ability to reason correctly was something that could be easily changed. More popular works, such as Kida (2006), drawing on this experimental literature, offer practical suggestions for challenging unfounded inferences and common urban myths.

Contemporary cognitive theorizing, by examining deeper processes, may, however, offer additional suggestions relevant to therapy. One topic of growing interest is *concepts* as units of thought. Concepts are mental representations of classes of objects we encounter, allowing us to decide, sometimes erroneously, what things are (what properties they have), and they allow classification, inference, and the creation of new conceptual combinations (Fodor, 1975). Concepts are represented by words: *shoe, communist, boyfriend, phobia, fragile*. However, it is likely that people will have these concepts independently of the word used for external communication. Some concepts evolved in human history in order to simplify communication and allow rapid access to important information. Concepts like *predator, poisonous, friend, healer* would link rapidly to motivational forces of avoidance (the first two) and approach (the second two; Delton & Sell, 2014). When clients describe their past experiences, or their concerns, they will apply words that seem to them to identify the concept they are trying to convey. How good they are at that and how closely the word evokes a comparable concept in the mind of the therapist is an important factor in therapeutic communication. Once iconic author J. D. Salinger was described in the media as a "recluse"; that concept forever after defined his identity for the public until his death in 2010. He did not in fact live a reclusive lifestyle—just an unexpected one, as he tried to avoid being hounded by reporters and stalked by fans while preoccupied with religion and writing (Shields & Salerno, 2013).

Concepts have what are called "extensions" and (rather awkwardly) "intensions" (Hampton, 1981). The extension is the group or class of things in the world to which the concept refers. Thus the extension of "scissors" is all those devices with opposing cutting blades. The intension of a concept, on the other hand, is the set of properties that we normally associate with it. The intension of the concept "scissors" might be ideas like used to cut paper or style hair, having rounded points when found in a school, and having handles for fingers. While knowing a concept's extension allows one to make logical judgments (all scissors have two blades), a concept's intension allows for a range of creative and idiosyncratic properties, such as not being allowed on planes, that do not apply to all scissors (small ones, in this case). Without this element to concepts we would have no creativity and no poetry, and we would all be like so many Mr. Spocks.

It is possible that if the intensions of two concepts are combined, a new composite concept emerges. The intension of the concept "hairdresser" has properties such as trimming and styling hair; the intension of the concept "surgeon" includes delicate snipping and healing. Shown a pair of scissors with long handles and short slightly angled blades, one would be more likely to identify them as surgical scissors even if one had never seen such scissors before. "Surgical scissors" is thus a new concept with an extension that excludes hairdressers' thinning scissors, for example. Hampton (2012) uses this model of combined intension to explain one of the most famous reasoning errors identified by Tversky and Kahneman (1983). The following scenario was supposed to show common errors of human logic. Linda is described to participants as a radical student with interests in politics. They are then asked: "When Linda leaves college, how likely is she to be a bank teller and how likely to be a feminist bank teller?" Most people select the latter as more probable, although it is entirely illogical, since "bank teller" must include all types, including feminist ones. However, the emergent features of the two concepts, their combined intensions, give rise to a plausible possibility that Linda will be a feminist (likely) *and* a bank teller (unlikely), whereas our intension of the concept "bank teller" alone seems totally unlikely as it does not fit the image that has been suggested for Linda. Thus, while the logic may be faulty, the judgment makes completely intuitive sense, and we typically use our intuition to understand our complex world. In cognitive therapy clients are encouraged to use their intuition and be less rule-bound. So when they exhibit faulty intuition that seems to be misleading them, therapists can examine the concepts they are using and suggest alternative combinations of intensions (new hybrids). A friend can still be a friend, if sometimes thoughtless and hurtful; a child is still a child even if he is hyperactive.

Adaptive Memory

Schema therapists like Jeffrey Young attribute current self-defeating maladaptive thoughts to the presence of early maladaptive schemas forged in memory by certain kinds of early childhood experiences, especially dysfunctional parenting in which the individual's basic emotional needs were not met (Young, Klosko, & Weishaar, 2003). However, everyone has had varying degrees of childhood experiences that are not always nurturing and ideal. Why might it be that some early experiences are retained in memory to a greater degree than others? It cannot simply be that it is a function of the intensity of the emotion experienced at the time. There is ample evidence that traumatic experiences in childhood are not always recalled in later years (Cordón, Pipe, Sayfan, Melinder, & Goodman, 2004). Other variables must be at work.

One possibility has been put forward by Nairne, Pandeirada, Gregory, and Van Arsdall (2009). Their basic argument is that cognitive structures supporting memory are not simply arbitrary or neutral. They are not just a set of equal capacities waiting for experiences to be recorded in order to influence subsequent thoughts. Rather, cognitive structures evolved to deal with problems encountered by our early ancestors. Cognitive systems that enhanced fitness (reproduction and survival) would give selection advantage to those individuals who were best able to use past experience in the service of the present—our elderly research participants notwithstanding. Memory processes are functional. We already know from a number of anxiety researchers that fear is more readily conditioned to some stimuli that might have evolutionary significance, such as snakes, than to equally dangerous modern threats, such as electrical outlets (Coelho & Purkis, 2009; Öhman & Mineka, 2001). While it is true that snakes and outlets differ in other ways, the fact remains that specific phobias are rarely to hazardous objects like handguns and more often to scuttling creatures and things that go bump in the night. So presumably for our cognitive systems of thought and memory, those processes that facilitated survival would be adaptive—those that helped find food, catch prey, escape from predators, and cured injuries and diseases. Nairne and Pandeirada (2010) describe novel experiments that support this notion, including well-known gender differences in memory, such as for interpersonal information as opposed to navigational information.

Interesting though it may be, what does this have to do with therapy? I think the relevance is for greater recognition that the core beliefs identified in cognitive therapy and the early schemas of schema therapy that ostensibly result in clients' distressing thoughts are not, in the wider picture, intrinsically maladaptive at all. They are "ancestral priorities," so maybe they were once more adaptive than they might be today. But we are still tuned to store and make use of memories that are related in quite a primitive way to survival. Yes, we can learn much information about programming our smartphones or trading in stocks, which has nothing to do with finding our way back to the cave or remembering the cues that a good-tasting root is just under the soil. But the things that clients tend to worry about have been biologically important throughout history: dirt, contamination, domination by others, rejection, untrustworthy relationships, being unattractive, letting the side down. Before the advent of science and the Enlightenment gave us a more rational view of human nature, humankind has for thousands, indeed millions, of years relied on spiritual faiths to manage fears of the unknown, apparently uncontrollable catastrophes, and a terrifying afterlife of pain and torment. It is not chance that causes people in distress to have religious as well as blasphemous automatic thoughts. I do not think any of this is a new revelation, but perhaps clients would benefit from recognizing why they ruminate about being disrespected but not about loss of civil liberties, and why they watch *The Bachelor* more avidly than *Jeopardy*. Maybe it does not matter much what story the client is told, as long as it offers an account of their worries and ruminations and delusions that attributes them to the past, thus helping them to live in the present. They can be told that human cognition has evolved to preferentially attend to and remember threatening information.

Implications

This wide-ranging chapter has essentially been about reality versus fantasy, reason versus the irrational: thoughts based on some degree of empirical evidence versus imagination, bias, and false beliefs about self and others. It is not conventional to put unusual "psychotic" thoughts on a continuum with irrational ideas, superstitious beliefs, and emotionally based errors of judgment and limits to wisdom. It is certainly possible that delusions in psychosis or magical thinking in obsessive-compulsive disorder are qualitatively different symptoms of thought distortions that require unique analysis for different syndromes and different patients. In terms of their functional relationships and the psychological change strategies that influence them, however, such a continuum makes sense. We seem to be prone, as humans, to a great many distortions of rational thought and a profound lack of wisdom, which in most cases is not disastrous. It is a manifestation of a common set of conditions, centered around how prior early experiences have laid down expectations and how emotional experiences have created the biases, prejudices, fears, and dreads that implicitly shape the clarity and goal-directness of our thinking.

One of the practical implications arising from this focus on highly statistically unusual thoughts is that very often clients are aware of the extent to which their thoughts are quite strange. Clients in this category quite often ask what it means if they are having these thoughts. When this happens it represents an additional layer of meta-cognitive awareness, in that having unusual thoughts often evokes another automatic thought. People with schizophrenia are often anxious about "being mad" or being possessed, or have the thought that they will never get better and that they will end up on the streets. While these thoughts also represent incorrect inferences, such as magnification, catastrophizing, and black-and-white thinking, they are not without some potential validity, thus this level of meta-concern can be addressed by reassurance and a focus on practical coping skills (e.g., Tarrier et al., 2004).

There are two additional, very important lessons we can learn from this chapter. One is that narrative interchange and verbal discussion with clients, even those with the most severely dysfunctional and distorted thoughts, does have the effect of helping those clients manage their thoughts and thus reduce their distress. However, the nature of this verbal interaction is very complex and is a long way removed from simple disputation or argument. Padesky (1993), in her discussion of Socratic questioning as a way of guiding self-discovery, points out the danger of cognitive therapists waiting for irrational statements and then pouncing on them to prove how wrong they are—a sort of "gotcha!" mentality. Yes, arguments are made in cognitive therapy, but they are not confrontational, and they should be designed on the basis of an understanding of the function of these thoughts. Function refers both to their controlling variables and their likely origins in terms of common and long-standing stressors that have been part of the human condition since the dawn of time.

The second lesson is that current and past stress seems to underlie much of the more distorted thoughts we have been considering. The personal reports of people with psychosis that I mentioned at the beginning of the chapter are replete with accounts of the economic, social, and personal stress they experienced prior to having a psychotic episode. The formal research supports the idea that prior trauma (such as sexual abuse) and other stressors contribute significantly to the manifestation of thought disorder. Much of the evidence that delusions and other thought distortions are understandable reactions to life events and circumstances has been marshaled by John Read and his colleagues (e.g., Read, Mosher, & Bentall, 2004). In virtually every case it is partially the intrusion of strong emotion that distorts thinking, at least when we judge the thoughts of others as unreasonable, illogical, bizarre, or however we wish to depict them. Yet the premise of cognitive therapy is the reverse—it is the distorted thought that causes the negative affect. The next chapter further examines this puzzle.

6

How Thoughts Influence Mood and Feelings—or Is It the Other Way Around?

What's in a name? That which we call a rose
By any other name would smell as sweet;
So Romeo would, were he not Romeo call'd,
—William Shakespeare, *Romeo and Juliet*

Thoughts and Feelings

The basis for cognitive therapy lies in the assumption that thoughts alone can evoke emotions that are distressing to us or to others, such as anger, sadness, fear, or jealousy. This assumption holds even when the therapeutic rationale focuses on the information processing biases that generate thought content. It also holds when the negative emotion relates to an objectively distressing or psychologically harmful event, in that all experiences must ultimately be interpreted (constructed) regardless of how automatic and unconscious the very first reaction to the event might have been. That is to say, cognitive behavioral therapy (CBT) is grounded on the premise that thoughts *cause* feelings, just like words can make one happy or sad or angry or aroused, and if these feelings are undesirable or unwanted or a source of additional distress, then they can be alleviated by changing the thoughts that produced them. Beck and his adherents are always adamant that, although the influence can be bidirectional (emotions influence thoughts), the essence of the cognitive therapy model "is the fact that emotions are strongly, and causally, influenced by the perception of events or situations" (Hofmann, Asmundson, & Beck, 2013, p. 200). Evidence has steadily accumulated that when the balance of negative and positive cognitions shifts in a positive direction, it results in decreases in depressed mood (Whisman, 1993), not simply decreased symptoms.

Redefining Emotion

Thus far throughout this book I have been a bit cavalier in the use of terms like *affect, emotion, feeling,* and *mood*. In fact I have used them somewhat interchangeably, with the exception of *mood*. Moods tend to last for days or even weeks and are "free-floating" in that they may have antecedent events but are diffuse, with no focused object (like a fear *of* something that threatens self-preservation, or sadness *about* a loss, separation, or failure). So now is a good time to be more explicit about the meaning of these terms. *Emotion* is really the most general term for subjectively experienced excitatory states that have objects. *Feeling* refers more directly to the subjective experience part and thus seems often cognitive in the sense that it requires words for recognition. For example, one of the characteristics of borderline personality disorder is "chronic feelings of *emptiness*." Is that a thought, a feeling, or an inseparable amalgamation of the two? *Affect* is virtually synonymous with emotion but early in the history of experimental psychology tended to be used with reference to the difference between positive (approach-related) and negative (avoidance-related) feelings (Russell, 2003). Today affect is still used to identify personal values: "the goodness or badness of things" (Clore & Huntsinger, 2007, p. 399). As a result, the positive or negative valence of affect can be thought of as providing us with information.

Positivity and *negativity* of affect/emotion/feelings is another dimension I have bandied about as though the distinction is always apparent. We tend to assume that emotions such as love and hope and joy are positive and ones like hate, jealousy, and anger are negative. But there are some emotion theorists who have contended that the distinction can be misleading. Solomon (2006) has emphasized that there are many more complex polarities than positive and negative. Love may feel positive but cause one to behave in harmful or immoral ways. Anger, which results from obstruction to one's goals, tends to have behavioral consequences such as conflict with and aggression toward others, but righteous anger is sometimes necessary to achieve positive outcomes. Gratitude would seem to be a positive emotion but may leave one feeling indebted to a higher being (including a deity) that falsely makes one feel special and superior to others who are no less deserving of the higher being's bounty. Clients quite often report such confusion: "I know I should feel grateful to my boss for the large raise I received last month, but I'd rather feel I earned it instead of being singled-out for special favors." Yet we judge negatively people on whom we have bestowed some largesse if they do not express gratitude.

The Swiss Center for Affective Science (Fontaine, Scherer, & Soriano, 2013) has proposed that there are five components of emotion, which cover the various ways emotions are measured. Paraphrasing slightly, they are (a) appraisals, the process whereby the value of a situation is perceived or judged; (b) bodily reactions, the changes in excitation that are physiological, usually regulated by the autonomic nervous system; (c) expressions, which are both facial expressions and manifestations of the emotion that can be judged by others, including verbal statements; (d) action tendencies, those reactions for which the emotion is preparing, such as approaching, avoiding, or escaping; and (e) feelings, the subjective experiences that can be consciously identified and usually labeled. Cognition is tied up closely with at least three of these components: appraisal is cognitive, expression is often in spoken words, and feelings are often self-identified in words.

Cognitive Appraisal Shapes the Form of the Emotion

Given these interconnections, we have not yet completely resolved—but hope to in this chapter—the extent to which a thought (e.g., "I feel sad") *is* the negative emotion or merely the recognition of an inner psychophysiological sensation (e.g., tearfulness). If we express the statement to someone else, it is usually considered merely the report of a feeling, so if we just think it, is it also merely the self-recognition of a feeling, perhaps with a little self-clarification ("I'm sad, but not angry, that she left me")? Furthermore, we all accept that environmental (external) events and situations trigger emotion, and there is no reason to exclude words, thoughts, and ideas (internal) in that category of potential antecedents. But even when the trigger is external, there is usually a cognitive mediator—a conditional rule—that determines how one feels. Someone you know well gets an award (event) and instead of being pleased you feel jealous (emotion/negative affect). Presumably some cognitive processing of the event is necessary for that feeling to occur; in this example you must both covet the award *and* believe that you deserve it more in order to have jealousy be the emotion rather than delight in your friend's success. These two cognitions (I wanted the award and I deserved it) may not be consciously, well-articulated thoughts. The only thought might be "I'm jealous," which will not be the cognition that made you jealous but might be the cognition that ensures you now feel negative. Jealousy does not feel good.

Resentment, as I have already discussed, requires the prior cognition that one has been wronged, especially humiliated, by someone's actions, and judging that one has been taken advantage of or one's achievements have not been recognized. The negativity of the affect may not be that different from jealousy or hostility, but the cognitions that encapsulate, define, and maintain resentful feelings are very different. In managing school discipline problems, Meyer and I (Meyer & Evans, 2012) consider resentment in young people to be a significant harmful trigger for reactions against authority and requires the perceived insult (being disrespected) to be addressed, whether intended or not, by the perpetrator. The function of resentment, Solomon (2006) argued, is to preserve one's self-respect, but the negativity of the feelings harms subsequent relationships, with teachers, partners, or work supervisors. Yet there is little empirical literature evaluating how resentful thoughts might be changed in cognitive therapy.

The available suggestions follow common sense as much as anything: ask probing questions that help the client articulate precisely what the hurtful slight was, since the client cannot always identify it or is ashamed to admit it, as it often appears petty. Then perhaps the client can, as in many approaches to psychotherapy, be asked to think of what the future would be like if the feelings of resentment were "let go" (resentment involves metaphorically clinging on to something, so that imagery of letting go and throwing it away may be particularly useful). A common follow-up suggestion is for the therapist to suggest the client write a letter to the source of resentment explaining his or her feelings and the circumstances but then to throw the letter away (not send it). The goal is forgiveness, but that is complicated by the high probability that the insult was not fully intended and that the offense is as much in the interpretation by the client as grounded in reality. That is a delicate communication to clients—asserting that they are not fully justified in feeling a certain way represents the dialectic identified by Linehan (1993). Telling clients too bluntly that they should not feel a certain way clashes with the importance of empathizing with their feelings.

Personality/Environment Interactions

If it is the case that there are direct links between therapeutically changed thoughts (less automatic thoughts, fewer dysfunctional attitudes, more positive memories more easily accessed, and especially new attributions) and improved affect, it creates a theoretical conundrum for approaches such as acceptance and commitment therapy, which purports to provide a unified model of behavior change (Hayes, Pistorello, & Levin, 2012). Hayes et al.'s therapeutic approach adopts the strongly contextual behavioral position that thoughts are not causal of other behaviors—including feelings—and that if people find their thoughts distressing, recognizing that thoughts are thoughts and not necessarily representations of reality should render distressing thoughts less meaningful and less threatening. Outcomes of treatment studies cannot confirm or disconfirm the theory. The fact that acceptance and commitment therapy might sometimes produce good outcomes for clients does not take away the reality that cognitive therapy also has good outcomes for clients, using a different rationale and a dissimilar set of therapeutic processes. So it may be that *either* changing thoughts from negative to positive *or* encouraging people to minimize the impact of their most distressing thoughts *both* result in more positive affect (and, over time, improved mood). The issue is not that one strategy is correct and the other wrong but that there are different ways of ensuring that a client's negative thoughts are less able to evoke and foster negative feelings.

Perhaps one common denominator in different cognitive therapies is how a cognitive event mediates the sequence between external circumstances and how one responds to them affectively. My example of jealousy is a good illustration. After all, semantically negative thoughts ("I am" and "a jerk" occurring in the same internal sentence) leading to depression problems do not occur in a free-floating fashion, although they might in introspection and rumination. Rather, negative thoughts more usually occur in response to an environmental event as a stressor of some kind: for depression it is failing at something, losing, not getting an expected reward, and so on. It is not so much the event itself but the way it signals loss—loss of something valued like a cherished belief about the kind of person one is. Anxiety problems are a little different. While one might have a propensity to undifferentiated, semantically worrying thoughts ("I am" and "not secure" in the same internal sentence), the perception of threat occurs in situations that are easily construed as dangerous or potentially unsafe—meeting new people, having to perform in public, flying in a plane, dealing with a fierce-looking dog, or having to go to the dentist.

This theoretical perspective is one of personality/environment interaction that in CBT theories of psychopathology is called the cognitive vulnerability model. When stressful events occur, people prone to depression interpret them in ways that, as Beck (1964) argued originally, have implications for their self-worth and for their future well-being. A cognitive style such as this is considered a trait characteristic of those people who experience depressed mood in the face of even mild adversity. It would be nice to know exactly where such a trait comes from, both for prevention efforts and for tailoring therapy more precisely than just arguing with clients that their interpretation of events is wrong (misguided, misattributed).

One origin is surely the verbalizations of significant others (parents and teachers) during early development. In one of my end-of-year high school reports a teacher wrote "Evans' poor performance at math is because he is bone idle and he will never be successful." Fortunately I had parents who said, "Don't worry, Ian, it is just one teacher's opinion, and look, you did quite well in English and history—you may be a bit lazy but you are not stupid"—or words to that effect. Countless verbal interactions of this kind build up characteristic individual differences in self-labeling, attribution style, locus of control, and all the other cognitive traits that interact with later challenges. We also have some evidence that cognitive vulnerability is not set in concrete. Listening to how friends talk and interpret events can alter cognitive style, especially during periods of transition such as going to college when the older influences of teachers and families give way to new relationships with roommates and professors (Haeffel & Hames, 2014). There must be times when this "contagious" effect of conversational interactions is particularly strong—when making new and intimate friends, when seeking new truths (like going to college or to a workshop or to a guru on a mountain top), and when engaged with a therapist.

Words Can Always Hurt—But Can Comfort As Well

The origins and shaping of characteristic cognitive styles needs further elaboration, but for now let us continue to think of mechanisms connecting verbalizations to affect. One of the best illustrations of the power of words over feelings is a phenomenon we are all familiar with—that of having our feelings hurt. Forget the sticks-and-stones nonsense about what really hurts. A very prevalent example is that people judged to be overweight by others are often called names and subjected to verbal insults (Puhl, Andreyeva, & Brownell, 2008). Hurt feelings seem to be a blend of fear and sadness, and the connection to physical pain is not simply symbolic. Yet the emotion of hurt feelings cannot be easily reduced to other emotions and is usually related to the experience of rejection. When people give accounts of hurtful episodes, the dominant episodes (the external stressors) involve betrayal, criticism, and explicit rejection, especially verbal messages from those who are close to you. The associated vulnerable thought is the appraisal that the perpetrator does not view his or her relationship with you to be as valuable as you do (Leary & Springer, 2001). Feeney (2005) has elaborated on this notion somewhat by proposing that hurt feelings arise from threats to a belief that one is worthy of love and challenges the conviction that relational partners can always be relied on. Having both of these beliefs negated disrupts one's certainty that support can be counted on when needed, which is a feeling of insecurity whose importance clearly evolved as our earliest ancestors formed social groups for mutual survival.

The most widely accepted theory of emotion generation today is a cognitive, *appraisal theory* of emotion (Lazarus, 1966; Scherer, Schorr, & Johnstone, 2001), which has a vast research literature supporting it. The assumption is that emotions occur if an event or situation is appraised in a motive-relevant manner as relating to the actual or potential fulfillment or frustration of desires and wishes. The emotional arousal and its varied forms (the actual feeling category—joy, hate, jealousy, sadness, etc.) are therefore a function both of the event itself and the way the individual appraises it. The tricky issue is that this appraisal, though we can think of it as a cognitive event, often happens well below the threshold of a conscious thought. Fear is an immediate response to looking outside the airplane window and seeing the engine on fire; the thought "we're going to crash, and we're all going to die" may escalate the emotion to panic, but that conscious-reasoning process did not precede the first physiological alarm response (Selye, 1956). There was also some kind of preliminary appraisal that allowed the person to discriminate between a trick of the light reflecting off the wing and incontrovertible evidence of flames. If one believes the words when the pilot announces "we are shutting down the port engine, but there is no cause for alarm as this plane flies fine on one engine," one will remain anxious but not terrified. A range of coping and emotion-management skills come into play (Lazarus, 1966). These cognitive stages have been well described in the literature, and the distinction between conscious appraisals (thoughts) and unconscious appraisals triggered by basic perceptual processes can be found in all of the different theoretical models of emotional disorders (e.g., Barlow, 2002; Lang, 1985; Ortony, Clore, & Collins, 1988; Teasdale, 1999).

Furthermore, the repeated conscious, unmodified appraisal of the same event could, like repeated motor skills, eventually become rather automatic, meaning that the emotional arousal is repeated and sustained over time. Thoughts allow us to relive the stressful event and, because that is unpleasant, reexperience the emotional discomfort—what Eysenck (1968) described a long time ago as *incubation*. Neuroscientist Robert Sapolsky (1998) explains "why zebras don't get ulcers." Simplifying greatly, he says they have no cognitions to carry affect/stress over from one dangerous encounter to another. All this may help explain why emotions to situations most of us would judge as neutral or benign are easily triggered in clients and may explain the phenomenon of moods, which, as I have stated, are emotive experiences that persist across time and situations. Although moods often seem to lack concrete external objects or events as triggers, clients, when pressed, can usually report some pervasive general life situation that they see as causal in lowering enjoyment—difficulties in a marriage; not liking a job; long periods of cold, wet weather; and the like.

The chronic accessibility of cognitive structure relevant to all this appraisal going on can be conceptually tied to "structures" such as memory schemas (Higgins, Bond, Klein, & Strauman, 1986). So, for example, if one has previously been in a terrifying airplane accident or near-accident, one's schema (network of memory associations) of airplane dangers will allow much more rapid activation of threat appraisal than for other people. Another important individual difference (personality influence) is related to holding very general beliefs that will influence appraisals. A good example of such a category is optimism, which is a generalized expectancy for positive outcomes. One's trait of optimism will support an appraisal of the airplane danger as "maybe we will have a crash landing but be saved," rather than "we're all going to die." When the emotional situation is one under people's control, a generalized self-efficacy belief (Bandura, 1977) will allow them to appraise a challenging situation as one they have the ability to master and will even help them achieve their goal. Emotional situations for individuals who have hostile beliefs as opposed to general interpersonal trust will be appraised in a manner likely to evoke anger. It may be that these generalized beliefs studied in personality theory are similar to the cognitive therapist's concept of a (maladaptive) schema or Ward's (2000) idea of an implicit theory. However, personality theory suggests these characteristic beliefs are quite widely held within society or a given culture and have not clearly evolved from specific and unique experiences, such as trauma, sexual abuse, or early parental mistreatment and neglect.

Emotion Categories

At this juncture you might have noticed a rather close parallel between the different categories or elements of emotion and the different categories of thought I proposed earlier. In Chapter 1 I suggested that these thought (cognitive) elements were content (theme of the thought), process (meta-cognitive analyses of the content), structure (how thoughts are retained or held in memory), and personality elements such as general cognitive style. Now we have encountered very similar categories for emotions. There is the content of the emotion (what it is one is feeling), the processing of information that shapes and regulates the feeling (meta-emotion processes like appraisal or judging and making sense of a feeling), the structure that holds past emotional experiences (schemata and sensitivity of specific channels of emotional expression), and personality dimensions that relate to ease of emotional arousal (stability/lability [neuroticism], ego-centricity, callousness, and so on). If emotions have elements that parallel cognition and thoughts have elements that parallel emotion, we are likely to see these two psychological phenomena intricately entwined.

Throughout the previous discussion, and this book overall, is the inevitability that we talk of thoughts with reference to their emotional valence. We talk of "negative thoughts," or thoughts that are distressing, or positive (happy thoughts or thoughts that make one feel happy—is there a difference?). This could indicate that thoughts evoke feelings through semantics, or it could mean that thoughts *are* feelings, in the sense that the semantic, verbal representation of a thought is stored in memory along with its associated affect. There are at least two ways of understanding the inseparability of words and feelings that have been considered in psychology. One of these is the emotive property of words themselves, and the other is a similar notion but more explicitly tied to the simultaneous activation of two memory stores: the semantic meaning and the valence of the words.

Thoughts Have an Emotional Valence: The Connotative Meaning of Words

Thus far, the assumption has been that the thought processes (judgment, appraisal) that mediate between an external event and one's emotional response to that event is itself affectively essentially neutral. The feeling hinges on the meaning of the thought. It is the syntax and meaning of the thought "she doesn't love me anymore" that evokes hurt. In the analysis made by Beck (1964) of the role of thinking in depression, for example, if someone stated, after being fired, his or her thought was "I am a loser," the depressogenic affect arises because the full thought has to be considered in terms of its elaborated meaning. The client thinks: "I myself am something unpleasant/undesirable, a loser, and that recognition makes me no longer willing to try to succeed, makes me sad because it is a negative judgment about me and puts me in a category of individuals I have always judged negatively in the past." The client's attributional style permits causal assumptions for failure that are internal and stable. Thus if the same person had the very different thought, "I'm going to be unemployed because the management of my company decided to downsize its workforce" (external attribution), then even a thought containing negatively valenced words ("unemployed," "downsize") will not necessarily elicit strong negative feelings about him or herself. The problem with the thought "I am a loser" is that not only is it an incorrect inference, but it contains words negative in valence, semantically transferring that valence to oneself. The correct inference (implicitly: "my job loss was due to downsizing and is no reflection on me") should have no negative impact on the person's coping—willingness to seek another job—even though in both cases the actual experience (being temporarily unemployed) is undoubtedly negative and highly stressful. However, the conclusion must still be that words, either by themselves or in semantic structures, have the capacity to serve as direct stimuli for moods and feelings, both positive and negative.

In the formal study of the connotative meaning of words and concepts, the semantic differential has proved to be a useful technique. Originally developed by Osgood, Suci, and Tannenbaum (1957), it involves rating concepts according to any potentially relevant polar opposite adjective (e.g., hot–cold, safe–dangerous, calm–excited). Factor analysis of semantic ratings reveals that the affective qualities of all words and concepts all fall into three dimensions: evaluative (good/bad), activity (active/passive), and potency (weak/strong). Of course within these dimensions any set of polar opposite qualities can be rated on the classic semantic differential 7-point scale. Thus, for example, if all your clients were to rate the concept "my therapist," their average scores might reveal (a) high ratings of trustworthy versus corrupt, warm versus cold, demanding versus easy going; (b) neutral ratings on cheap versus expensive and on easy versus difficult; and (c) low ratings on distant versus close and on cruel versus kind.

The closer the link between verbal appraisal and something intrinsically threatening and thus fear-arousing, the more the words themselves become affectively laden. "Looks like there is a problem with the engine," "We're going to have a crash landing," "We're all going to die," represent not just stages of reasoning and appraisal but increasingly affectively loaded thoughts. Words like "loser" or "downsize," "unemployed" or "crash" have negative connotations in addition to their denotative meaning. We also have a potent self-reinforcing effect in evidence when we apply positive words to ourselves and our own behavior, yet people differ considerably in their tendency to do so, especially when depressed or prone to depression (Heiby & Staats, 1990). On the other side of the coin, anxious and depressed clients are particularly good at self-punishment, using negative and hypercritical words in conjunction with their self-identity.

There is much substantiation in psychology that simply a word or phrase itself, such as "sweet," "crash," or "doesn't love me," has emotional power, regardless of its use in more complex, self-referenced statements and internal dialogue. The justification for the thought–feeling causal direction in cognitive therapy is, ironically, heavily embedded in standard behavioral theories that assert that words, whether spoken to us, spoken by us, or read, serve as simple stimuli in much the same way as the object represented by the word serves as a stimulus. Thus for many people the sight, smell, and taste of bacon are stimuli for a pleasant gustatory sensation. The word *bacon* has similar, if less intense, eliciting properties. We know this from experiments in which the word *bacon* elicits responses such as salivation and the desire to approach, whereas the word *square* is essentially neutral in terms of any such triggering effects.

That the word *bacon* often has positive emotive properties (except, obviously, for those people with religious prohibitions, cultural beliefs about how pigs are farmed, and personal distaste) can be further demonstrated by a simple "classical conditioning" type of arrangement, in which a previously neutral word (let's say *square*) is regularly paired with the supposedly emotive word *bacon*, such that after a number of trials, the word *square* now evokes some vestiges of positive affect—eliciting salivation, being more readily approached than before, or being judged as a more pleasant word than before the conditioning experience. *Square* is also an adjective, and the association *square bacon* does not sound very appealing. We would obtain a stronger conditioning effect if the conditioned stimulus was *crisp*, but *crisp* is not a previously neutral word (*crisp hundred-dollar bill, crisp cracker, crisp fall morning,* and so on; Evans & Weiss, 1978).

This reasonably summarizes a great deal of similar research that was conducted by Staats and his students over many years (e.g., Lohr & Hamberger, 1990; Staats & Lohr, 1979). In some ways these observations and demonstrations seem rather simple and obvious, but in other ways they provide a behavioral basis for the acceptance that words have connotative properties as well as denotative (meaning) properties and if the connotations are positive (or threatening, or disgusting), then words elicit emotions, and words said to oneself can and will do the same.

One of the commonly cited examples of this effect is one demonstrated by Velten (1968). He showed that when people were asked simply to read negative statements, it affected their feeling-state (short-term mood). This occurred even when the statements were completely unrelated to themselves, such as "Poverty in Africa means children go to school hungry and malnourished." Negatively worded statements made people feel negative. You may have experienced the consequence yourself simply from reading that one isolated sentence about hungry children. It is quite a powerful effect—so much so that Velten statements are now used in research studies as a way of mildly manipulating people's brief moods in order to study the effects of mood on other psychological tasks, such as memory for unpleasant events or expectations of reward.

The behavioral notion of words, or semantics (the meaning of sentences), having the power to evoke feelings, leaves uncertain where this power comes from. Conditioning theories imply that the effects are all through association (Eifert, 1987). The word *cancer,* for example, has negative affective properties because it is associated with disease, pain, disfigurement, and premature death. *Obituary* is also about death but contains connotations of the celebration of a life well lived and a person missed. And one does not need to have had any actual experience of cancer and death or cancer and pain but simply to have been exposed to hundreds of learning trials in which these written and spoken associations have been made. There is nothing intrinsically threatening, fear-evoking, or negative about the word *cancer.* For non-English speakers the word would have no meaning (not represent a life-threatening disease) and thus have no affective properties.

In English, the word *rose* has a strong positive valence. Where does that come from? The answer is learning experiences: from smelling a rose when little and being told how delightful it is, from poetry, from being given a rose in a romantic context, from seeing it embroidered on the jersey of a winning English rugby team, from knowing a charming young woman called Rose (we do not know any nice people called Cancer), and so on. The opportunities and options are innumerable. Despite their thorns, our culture values roses—we like their appearance and say so, we like their smell and try to replicate it, and we know that Juliet was slightly wrong that any other name would do—if roses were called *bogwort* they simply would not be as positive, even if they smelled as sweet. There would have to be a lot of poems extolling the virtue of bogwort and a lot of Hallmark cards depicting bogwort as the symbol of love before *bogwort* acquired the same positive properties as *rose.* Say the words out loud slowly and you will know that I am right.

If the connotative meaning of words comes from direct and modeled learning experiences combined with onomatopoeic properties, then individual experiences are very important in creating affect. Also, since we do not experience every possible learning opportunity ourselves, our culture provides opportunities not only for shared meaning (the meaning of our language) but for shared affect associated with words. And if affect is passed on through association, it shows how easy it is to create negative (or positive) associations with other objects simply by labeling them. Thus prejudices and biases arise from the words used in association with objects for which we have no direct experience whatsoever.

Word Connotations Are Sometimes Ambiguous

An endemic problem when listening to clients is that they will report saying things that they claim later they did not really mean. This is a common occurrence in any emotionally charged situation, so that, for example, during a domestic conflict people may say words that they wish they had not. They retract these words, but often the emotional consequences cannot be quite so easily withdrawn.

The full cultural complexity of emotion words has been documented in intriguing work by Fontaine, Scherer, and Soriano (2013). They point out that in British and American English, people can say they love you, they love ice cream, and they love football, whereas in Spanish the same verb is not used to designate what is enjoyed and what is loved romantically. An emotion like pride means different things in the north and south of Italy, somewhat as one might expect in the United States: in the north it is used for feelings about what one has done oneself, but in the south it can also refer to things done by others to whom one is loyal, like kinfolk. Angry, hostile clients use pejorative terms openly in psychotherapy sessions, and it behooves the cognitive therapist to attend to these words and judge their significance.

Changing Words

Language style matching refers to the phenomenon in which two people in a conversation subtly match each other's speaking or writing style (Gonzales, Hancock, & Pennebaker, 2010). It is an unconscious process and leads to romantic interest and the likelihood of long-term relationships. Perhaps the correlation is the other way—if one wants to be liked by the person one is talking to, there will be some coordination of behavioral styles, and we certainly hope that this is true for the psychotherapy situation. However, Ireland et al. (2011) reported that verbal matching of function words predicted romantic interest and relationship stability, regardless of participants' stated perceptions of similarity and satisfaction with the relationship.

If each individual word (in addition to its place in semantics, the meaning of an utterance) has potentially emotive properties the way theorists such as Staats (1972) have described, it suggests that encouraging the use of new words, not just new ideas, may be a good starting point in therapy. Constructs, as explained in Chapter 3, carry strong associations, condense complex thought, and can be represented by a single word. As a result, single words are relied on in propaganda designed to associate neutral or positive concepts with potentially negative ones. The radio talk show host Glenn Beck frequently calls President Obama a "racist," "dictator," and a "sociopath"—he does not have to provide evidence, examples, or any form of reasoning—the association is sufficient. In society we are very used to the opposite influence: adopting less emotive words in order to make ourselves feel better. Americans, for example, call what the British might call a lavatory a "bathroom." A surprised Australian might say "crikey" rather than "Christ," and instead of "shit," "hell," and "Jesus," a Minnesotan might say "shoot," "heck," and "jeez"—sometimes called the Shirley Temples of swearing. Today, "OMG" must be one of the most common acronyms in modern tweets and e-mails. Calling graffiti "urban art" or a vagrant a "homeless person" or an investment banker a "job creator" alters the emotional valence of the construct. The Japanese government likes to call killing whales for sashimi "scientific whaling." Euphemisms are everywhere in social discourse, and we may be thankful for most of them, since there are many words that in past usage have had extreme emotional connotations. I am sure the reader can think of racial terms once common and now no longer used. In disability studies we have moved from *moron* and *cretin* as legitimate technical terms to *mentally retarded* to *intellectual disabled*. While some conservative members of the public love to chide others of us for being "PC" (politically correct), the reality is that if one is sensitive to people's feelings, one works hard to find words and labels that will not cause offense to others or knowingly hurt their feelings.

The self-same process can be applied in psychotherapy. Negative words that elicit negative emotion almost always have synonyms that are less distressing or opposites that are more uplifting. The client who tells the therapist he had a terrible *problem* that week might be encouraged to say he faced a significant *challenge* (synonym) or was presented with a valuable *learning opportunity* (positive opposite). There are different ways in therapy whereby this change in language can take place. It starts with the therapist noticing the negativity of words used and gently correcting the client by interrupting and suggesting an alternative word (or set of words). That degree of directiveness might be preceded by very careful use of positive words by the therapist—a simple modeling effect that gains some of its traction from the rapport or relationship with the client, so that the therapist's words are being carefully attended to. After correcting the client, the therapist might explain why he or she did so—by commenting again on the way the words used affect feelings, however small the trigger, and that if the client were to use different words, feelings would change. The client has to accept the legitimacy of this notion (and therefore must begin to buy into the overall theory of cognitive therapy) and then make an effort to use the alternative words more regularly. In order to change verbal habits the client needs to practice: initially the therapist offers feedback, catching the client and making note of the word so that the client corrects it, and then helping the client self-correct; eventually a new verbal habit is instituted through this simple practice effect.

The initial feedback given to clients when the therapist notices them using undesirable words can be quite subtle. I once had a client, a college dropout, with what might be called a narcissistic personality disorder. Some of his earliest, most grandiose comments related to how he very soon was going to be a success in business and own a Lear jet. I labeled this his "Lear jet talk," and later, when he started to drift into grandiose thinking patterns, all I needed to say was "that sounds like Lear jet talk," regardless of the actual topic, and he would roll his eyes and smile and make an effort to drop the extreme self-important discourse and focus on more practical, meaningful, and accomplishable objectives, for which he would be praised. This was not in and of itself treatment, since the origins of this self-important personal style needed to be addressed, but it was one component of a plan to change his dominant verbal thought process, especially those boastful words used in social discourse, which had the immediate effect of turning his audience (his potential friends) off.

For many clients it is useful to offer a meaningful theoretical rationale for changing their terminology. I personally have found the philosophies articulated in the positive psychology movement to be perfect for this. Not only is this perspective very respectful to clients and affirming of their basic acceptability, but it also reduces mention of problems and emphasizes the positive aspects of people's lives. Seligman, Rashid, and Parks (2006) have proposed a variety of simple techniques under the rubric "positive psychotherapy." One suggestion is for the client to keep a Three Good Things journal, in which he or she records nightly some of the day's positive events. For clients who have been wronged, a forgiveness intervention might be considered, with the purpose of letting go negative feelings toward the transgressor (not necessarily reconciliation). The suggested process is first to recall the details of the transgression. Then to focus on empathy for that person, followed by a commitment to forgive and efforts to hold on to that forgiveness. The importance of developing a sense of personal meaning by forming a coherent narrative of one's life can be translated into exercises such as writing an analytic essay on the most important elements of one's past life. All of these strategies (there are others) are designed to provide new words and ideas to the client's everyday consciousness—his or her ecology of dominant thoughts and thinking.

Thoughts Have an Emotional Valence: Shared Affective Memory Stores

Anyone who is a psychotherapist will have had experience of another function of words that is often encountered with emotion words. The client might, with reasonable composure, have told you of a distressing incident or failed relationship, and you might have asked, in a reflective way "Did that make you feel sad?" At the mention of the word "sad," the client then and only then starts to cry. Thus there is a second major way in which thoughts and emotions are not easily separated. Like the connotative meaning of words, it is most likely based on associations between concepts and affective experiences so that both are laid down in shared long-term memory stores. It is worth mentioning before delving too far into these stores that the descriptive language of this is entirely hypothetical, and the actual way in which affect and verbal symbols are stored in memory and retrieved in a relevant circumstance (into working memory) is unknown. However, models of the process can be constructed for theoretical convenience and, with contemporary neuropsychological analyses, tested for their general fit with measurable neural and psychophysiological processes.

Beliefs and Expectations

Of the many ways in which culture shapes the significance of language, an important influence is that of beliefs. In the Māori culture in New Zealand, there is potent mythology surrounding the appearance of a little bird called a Fantail (or pīwakawaka in Māori). These little birds flit around the bush using their fan-like tails to help them catch insects. As someone walking through the forest disturbs insects, these delightful birds often appear and fly quite close to humans. But if they appear in or near a window of one's house, it is considered a warning of a future death. I had a Māori client who claimed not to be superstitious or a believer in legends who came to a session seriously disturbed at having had a fantail fly onto his kitchen windowsill. He kept saying, "I know it is just an old superstition, but I'm scared and I think I should have the house blessed." His knowledge of the mythical story, heard over countless occasions, changed the meaning of an event and raised doubts, however irrational his thinking self knew them to be.

Much of our discussion thus far has been focused on the way current thoughts regulate emotion. We have not yet spent much time considering the process elements whereby current beliefs and expectations (which are themselves emotive) influence emotional responses to actual experiences likely to occur in the future. From a therapeutic point of view, this is an important directional relationship: many clients, feeling depressed and seeking help with family relationships such as marriage or the arrival of a new baby, express as a major theme their disappointment with current experiences. Negative feelings about the present may not necessarily be due to misconstruing current reality but are more closely connected to the difference between what was expected and what is experienced. The target for therapy, therefore, is not quite the same as changing the client's perceptions of the present, or even of asserting that past expectations were unrealistic. The therapeutic emphasis may need to be on reconciling past expectations with current realities, so that the client can feel hopeful instead of disappointed.

When I earlier considered the assumptions of rational-emotive behavioral therapy, it seemed reasonable to argue that people's thoughts that they "ought" to feel something or that they "should" do something were simply irrational, based on some sort of excessively moralistic reasoning or overly idealistic ideas about the world. The cognitive intervention in rational-emotive behavioral therapy is to try to persuade clients that these thought-based standards are irrational. However, the analysis of prior expectations allows us to reformulate this simplistic idea. Expectations about one's own behavior and feelings, as well as about the appropriate behavior of others, are not intrinsically irrational. They may be somewhat unrealistic, but that does not mean they are not desirable. Motherhood should be a glorious time. Love should be forever. People should keep their promises. The intensity of these expectations is undoubtedly created mythically—that is to say repeated early messages from many different media sources promote the expectation in a way that is possibly too strong, because it is unqualified. The Hallmark Valentine's Day card does not say "I will love you forever, but of course the intensity of those feelings may decline in time and with familiarity but that doesn't mean that I won't stop thinking you are the best thing that ever happened to me." So myths create expectations that are not intrinsically irrational or wrong but are simply overstated and unqualified. They are optimistic. But excessively pessimistic levels of reality are wrong too—the person who says, "Wait till your baby is born and then you will know what it is really like, sleepless nights, messy diapers, no time for yourself any more" is creating an equally erroneous set of expectations—only some of those things will happen only some of the time (Darrah, 2012).

Disappointment, then, emerges from a contrast between experiences expected and experiences experienced (see discussion in Chapter 3). This contrast may not be conscious, in that the person does not actually think, "I thought this, but I found that." Instead, the emotional effect of an event—a crying baby, for example—is not qualified by the expectation that all babies cry and is contrasted with the myth that babies are perfect at all times. Thus the task for therapeutic change is to make these juxtapositions more salient, so that the comparison thought to which reality is contrasted needs to be one that is qualified, not declared irrational or wrong. Here we can think of a process like cognitive dissonance, which is actually a theory of how prior expectations that are unmet result in reappraisal of what is actually experienced. People should have positive expectations, and when they are not realized they should be able to engage in those reappraisal exercises and find the remaining positive features of the experience that failed to be as good as expected. It is when people cannot do this cognitive coping exercise that negative affect like depression can emerge, and one then dwells on the negatives of an experience rather than, through cognitive dissonance, finding the positives or lowering the value of what was expected. Since we do not want mothers to lower the value of their babies or lovers to lower the value of their partners, the strategy of emphasizing the positive features and deemphasizing the negative ones seems the best therapeutic approach.

The Other Way Round

There are many everyday emotional experiences that get us thinking new and repetitive thoughts. Grief is a good example. While the circumstances surrounding the death of a friend or loved one serve to focus all of one's thoughts on recall, recollections, and sometimes regrets, it is the emotional intensity that makes it hard to make decisions, form rational judgments, or express thoughts in meaningful spoken or written words. We are all very familiar with the effects of negative and positive moods. When people are in a generally bad mood, perhaps arising from stress at work or some negative experience, such as being criticized or failing to be appreciated, they are likely to have thoughts that are more hostile or blaming in a completely different situation. This phenomenon was reported frequently by the participants in one of our studies of stepfamilies (Falchi, 2008). The overall study is complicated, but the gist of this evidence was that when we asked parents to give an example of when they had misjudged a situation at home or responded in a harsh manner to their children, it was often because they were in a "bad mood" at the time. The house might be untidy, but it was the children who get yelled at. The intermediate thoughts parents reported were self-pity ("I shouldn't have to come home to a huge mess after such a rough day"), disappointment ("They know I've had a bad day; surely they could have tried to tidy up"), and hostility ("These kids are so goddamned lazy"), and they could hear these themes coming out strongly in the reprimands they gave the children, none of which were entirely accurate, fair, or justified.

Some parents recognize that their verbal outbursts are excessive for the situation and try to change them. They use those terribly helpful meta-cognitive strategies I first mentioned in Chapter 2. Recognizing they are in a bad mood, they think ahead to how they will not react negatively when they get home, and just go with the flow. But this is hard to do unless the core belief or personality schema is recognized. Self-pity is based on the core belief that one is often a victim, disappointment is based on unrealistic expectations (in this example, of what children are likely to be doing when adults are not at home), and hostility is based on the prejudicial perceptions that the children's behavior is deliberately annoying (and, in our family study, that because they are stepchildren they are especially likely to be inconsiderate).

Challenging such schemata and prejudices can be assisted by targeted thoughts, not just random counter-thoughts or a determination not to have these thoughts at all. The targeted antidote to self-pity, for instance, is gratitude for what one *does* have, enjoys, and experiences positively. The targeted antidote to disappointment is lowering the bar on that which is expected. And the targeted antidote to hostility is expression of affection (approach) for the positive aspects of the person engaged in a perceived attacking mode (in our study, thinking of all the positive feelings associated with the stepchild). This latter strategy can be suggested to teachers as well, when they are judging the misbehavior of a student overly harshly. Sometimes it is hard to get teachers to generate effective positive discipline strategies when their only schema for that child contains negative memories of past annoyances. But simple tactics like positive affective priming—requiring the teacher to remember good qualities of the student or generating images of the student as perhaps a younger, innocent child—can begin to shift the schema *naughty student who gives me a headache* into one more complex and multifaceted and involving positive elements as well (Evans, 2010).

State-Dependent Retention

In 1981 Gordon Bower summarized all of his and others' experimental work on mood and memory in a paper that had a considerable influence on CBT and our understanding of common forms of psychopathology. He presented all of the evidence for two important cognitive phenomena. *Mood-state-dependent retention* refers to the tendency to recall an event better if during recall one reinstates the mood or emotional state one was in during the original learning. A second, closely related phenomenon is the *mood congruity effect*: that people are more likely to attend to and learn more about events that match their emotional state at the time. There is a large body of evidence supporting the validity of these two phenomena. In one example, Bower's (1981) participants read a vivid, realistic story about two people, one of whom was happy because everything in his life was going well, and one of whom was sad because nothing was going well. When asked who they thought was the central character in the story and with whom they identified, happy readers thought the story was about the happy character and sad readers thought it was about the sad character and claimed there was more information about that character, although in fact the information was carefully balanced. The next day, when in a neutral mood, participants who had been sad when reading the story could remember many more facts about the sad character—and vice versa. This is a mood congruity effect. Information that matches one's affect is more salient. Anxious clients notice threatening stimuli much more readily than nonanxious people and are more able to formulate possible negative outcomes to seemingly neutral activities—the origin of paranoid ideas. Maybe apprehensive novice therapists notice more about their clients' anxieties than they do about their strengths.

The mood-state-dependency effect is shown in classic studies in which participants are exposed to verbal information when in either a happy or a sad mood and later asked to recall as much as they could remember when in the same mood or in a different mood. It is a memory influence, rather than an original learning influence, as the measure used is simply the difference between what they first learned and what they could recall later (almost always less, of course). Participants who recall in a different mood than the learning mood recall the least, regardless of whether their mood is happy or sad—it is the different mood that interferes with recall and demonstrates the phenomenon. How does one change mood in volunteer participants in the lab? The answer is by making them recite self-referent Velten statements such as, "Things have been going badly for me lately" and "I'm feeling very lonely, isolated, and depressed." These are the very things that clients say to themselves all the time for real, and, equally interestingly, what we as clinicians *ask* them to say. The expected role of a client is to come in and pour out his or her troubles. Not surprisingly, in light of these phenomena, depressed clients asked to recall happy or sad personal events find it much harder to retrieve pleasant memories (Lloyd & Lishman, 1975). Bower's (1981) explanatory model for these effects was a simple associationist one, in which what he called "emotion nodes" are the central element of a network of expressive behaviors, verbal labels, stored events, and memories of actions. While an emotion node might be a specific emotion, such as joy or anger, emotions share certain broader features or constructs: such as joy and acceptance could both be categorized under a construct such as love and therefore connected, like friends of friends on Facebook. Thus emotion nodes are connected to each other through association networks. Such a network is very much like the cognitive therapy structural concept of a schema. Semantic-network theory also proposes that mood will influence snap judgments—exactly as proposed in two-systems theories such as Kahneman's (2011). We can see that our elderly participants in the wisdom study had to be understood in more complex ways than whether they simply had or lacked wisdom. They, like all of us, have different thoughts (judgments, beliefs, ideas) about things depending on how they are feeling at the time. And for explaining the persistence of affective states in clients, the mood dependency phenomena provide some clues. Bower (1981) expresses it well in everyday terminology:

> Thus, a person in a depressed mood will tend to recall only unpleasant events and to project a bleak interpretation onto the common events of life, and these depressing memories and interpretations feed back to intensify and prolong the depressed mood. Thus, the vicious circle of depression spirals. A similar circle can occur with anxiety and worry. We see this in the worrywart, the hypochondriac, the chronically overprotective parent, and those of us who awaken in the middle of the night worrying over some item, which leads to worry over another and another. The mild negative tone of one worry primes and makes more available the negative aspects of some other personal concern, and so one free-associates through the recent worries of one's life. (p. 145)

Thoughts and Emotion as Information

There is a substantial research literature indicating that when people receive information that indicates a problem exists (either in them or in their situation), they are likely to engage in a processing style in which they will attend to, store, and easily recall all the negative information that is available and perhaps seek more of its ilk. Conversely, when people receive information that is neutral or good, they are likely to engage in a processing style that relies more on past habits and simple heuristics. Adaptively, this all makes sense, as when there is a problem to be addressed we need to think more carefully about the information and rely less on snap judgments and stereotypes (Schwartz, 2004). That in turn is in keeping with Kahneman's (2011) ideas about two "systems" and how quick judgments and implicit attitudes come from below consciousness. But if reasoned versus hasty judgments happen more often in problem situations, the snag is that more negative information is then sought. So here is yet another model of ruminating, brooding, and worrying, so characteristic of clients. Could it be that one reason mindfulness training and meditation seems effective for some clients is because it serves as a distraction to getting moody about their depression or worrying about their anxiety?

There are two lines of research that offer further detail on how emotion influences thought. The first of these is the affect-as-information theory of Clore and his colleagues (e.g., Clore & Huntsinger, 2007). The idea is quite simple. Our attitudes and judgments about things come not only from the properties displayed by those things; our evaluations can also reflect the information that is provided by our own affective reactions, even when the source of those reactions comes from somewhere else. The defining experiment involves showing people a movie evoking strong positive emotion and finding that they are attracted to, say, another person, over and above their cognitive information about that person. The affective cues of emotion and mood provide information as to how a participant feels about the object being judged. People's reports of life satisfaction vary—in the expected direction—depending on whether it is cold and rainy or warm and sunny outside when they are asked about their life. The effect disappears if we first draw their attention to the good weather, because now they have an alternative source for feeling good—the good feeling no longer provides the only source of information about their life satisfaction. Affect provides us with information about the value of things even if these things also directly evoke liking, disgust, fear, or any other specific emotion.

The second line of research comes from positive psychology. It is the not entirely new idea that positive affect broadens cognition and also builds resources. Frederickson (2003), who has promoted the "broaden and build" idea, has conducted a host of experiments. Together they support the principle that positive emotion broadens individuals' cognitions, allowing them to make more creative connections and a have wider range of ideas and thought–action repertoires. Working with clients, we more often see the opposite effect. Negative thoughts feed on themselves in clients the way they do not in zebras. Think how often depressed and anxious clients can think of little other than themselves and their own circumstances. This narrow, negative preoccupation is so pervasive that I have even suggested that a sign of clinical progress is when clients start to do things for others, think about other people's feelings, and enquire empathetically about how the therapist is feeling (Evans & Fletcher, 2013). But Frederickson, Garland, and their colleagues (Garland, Frederickson, Kring, Johnson, Meyer, & Penn, 2010), by focusing on the positive side, have shown that having (even inducing) positive emotions allows better attention to the current situation, more creative problem-solving, and greater trust of others.

Positive reappraisal is the essence of effective coping—being able to evaluate situations as positive and positively assess one's ability to deal with them.

There is a slight danger of stating the obvious here. Do you want your clients to feel better? Tell them to have positive thoughts! But in the very broadest sense, isn't this what cognitive therapists have been asserting from Albert Ellis onward? And what rescues the Garland and Frederickson approach from sophistry is that there are some interesting new ideas contained in their perspective. One of these is the idea that emotion works in self-perpetuating spirals—downward in the case of negative feelings and upward in the case of positive. Much of the cognitive research described thus far has suggested different versions of the same idea: that positive emotion ferments in the interaction of emotion, cognition, and behavior like a yogurt culture. Thus even a little positive affect has direct benefits because cognition is broadened, more positive behaviors occur, and more positive affect results.

Cognitive therapists take advantage of the positive feelings they can instill with a good relationship, lots of reassurance, and positive social reinforcement, which in turn help clients to behave ("act") a little different the next week and so come in to the next session ripe for more praise and encouragement and self-reports of better outcomes, and so the spiral spirals upward. Garland et al. (2010) attribute this upward spiral to the underlying neural circuitry, and they may well be right. But for the clinician the more interesting question is this: What sorts of manageable experiences can be offered a client that will maximize the upward spiral? When I first tried systematic desensitization with clients in the early 1970s, we always added to the progressive muscle relaxation instructions suggestive calming thoughts and images such as, "Now I want you to think of a peaceful pleasant scene. Imagine yourself swinging gently in a hammock between two coconut palm trees [I was living in Hawai'i at the time]. You can hear the sound of the ocean in the distance and feel the soft breezes of the trade winds on your skin. You feel calm and relaxed, calm and relaxed." What could be more positive than that? Could it be that that was all that was needed for fearful clients to start an upward spiral of progress?

Are Feelings Encoded in Words?

We have seen some complicated research that clarifies that feelings influence thoughts (this is the "other way round" from conventional cognitive therapy ideas that to change emotion one must change thoughts). But what if we go one step further and suggest that feelings *are* thoughts—that there is no nuanced feeling that does not contain the relevant verbalizations, either internal or external speech. This is a very hard topic to discuss and explain. First I attempt to explicate why it is a meaningful question, and then I present two rather different areas of research that suggest that the experience of emotion is more about knowledge—words—than we often realize. When in therapy we ask clients how they are feeling, we are using the same sort of simplistic psychology as we use in everyday human interactions. When people talk about their feelings, our naïve model is that we have a feeling, an emotion, which is experienced as a sensation, the proprioceptive feedback from physiological changes in the autonomic nervous system. Thus fear is sweaty palms and pounding heartbeat; sadness is tears; anger is muscular tension in clenched fist and gritted teeth; anxiety is butterflies in the stomach. This is a simplified version of the James-Lange theory of emotion; William James and Carl Lange independently proposed that it was afferent proprioceptive signals from visceral bodily changes that we report as our feelings (and behave in accordance with them) (Cannon, 1927). When we report these sensations we do so not in physiological terms (although we occasionally might—"my heart beats so joyfully you'd think that he could hear," sings Tammy in love), but as a verbal report of what we are feeling—sad, angry, scared, and so on. Our cognitive statements are likened to some sort of talking barometer, simply reporting atmospheric pressure, the true feeling.

The difficulty that psychologists have had with this naïve view is that it has proved difficult to isolate discrete emotions, even supposedly very different positive emotions like love, from negative emotions like hate. Yes, there are facial expression differences, no doubt, but even then people are not always able to judge the emotion someone is feeling from photos of facial affect. One of the most classic experiments in psychology sustains this difficulty. Schachter and Singer (1962) gave participants injections of either a placebo or epinephrine, which causes generalized physiological arousal of the autonomic nervous system. What people stated they actually felt, however, was entirely dependent on the context, which in the experiment was being in the presence of a person, a stooge, who was acting in either a euphoric or an angry manner. Differentiated feelings are isomorphic with how we appraise the situation.

Children's Emotion Competence

Quickly switch gears and consider an area of research that provides additional understanding to the origins of language expression capturing emotion experience: developmental psychology's interest in how children become emotionally competent in the first place. No syndromes, even dramatically caused ones like posttraumatic stress disorder, just appear out of the blue. All individuals have histories of emotional experiences, resulting in different emotional responsivities, control and regulatory mechanism, and subsequent opportunities for social support—this is one of the most basic understandings we have of psychopathology. There are large individual differences in children's abilities to understand emotion in themselves and in others, and this difference impacts all sorts of features of their subsequent psychological development, including socialization, self-concept, self-control (especially regarding emotional outbursts), and pro-social behavior. Emotion knowledge includes being able to verbally label their own and others' feelings, recognize facial expressions, predict the emotional consequences of different experiences, and recognize likely causes of emotion. Emotion knowledge predicts children's social competence, including their peer relationships, successful adjustment to school, and academic achievement. By contrast, limited emotion knowledge is associated with internalizing and externalizing problems throughout childhood (Denham et al., 2002; Ensor, Spencer, & Hughes, 2011).

Children's emotion knowledge is associated with their language skill and develops within the context of parent–child conversations. The reasons for the well-established relation between language ability and emotion knowledge are likely to be multiple, including the linguistic component of the assessment tasks and the essential role of symbolic and representational skill in reporting and differentiating internal experience. When observing families, Brown and Dunn (1996) found that children whose parents engaged in high frequencies of feeling state and causal talk manifested superior emotion knowledge and that experiencing causal talk predicted children's understanding of ambivalent feelings at the age of six. My colleague Karen Salmon and her team have shown how subtle both the nature of causal emotion talk and its consequences can be. In a teaching context Salmon, Evans, Moskowitz, Grouden, Parkes, and Miller (2013) showed young children picture stories accompanied by the following sort of discourse: "Tommy starts to run down the hill with his net in his hand. He is looking at the frog and he has a big smile on his face. How is Tommy feeling here? (Yes, that could be it or . . .). He feels happy, doesn't he? How come Tommy's feeling happy? (Yes, that could be it or . . .) Tommy feels happy because he's going to catch a frog." Training in understanding causes without identifying feelings ("Tommy is running downhill because he is going to catch the frog") did not have the same positive impact on knowledge of emotion identification.

The general evidence from many sources is that it is through a variety of affect-laden verbal experiences that children learn the skills to identify emotion, label them correctly, and make inferences as to plausible causes. Thus they learn to understand other children's feelings and to empathize. Cognitive therapy has the liability that it is a short, sharp experience compared with hundreds of prior learning opportunities and occurrences, with family, peers, at school, and throughout life in general.

In CBT we often talk about the thoughts that precede fear or anxiety as irrational or dysfunctional but that judgment should be modified—especially with children—when recognition is given to the evolutionary history of threats to individuals in our species (Boyer & Bergstrom, 2011). And to some extent the developmental stages that fears tend to go through in children do seem to recapitulate phylogenetic development. In infancy (period of helplessness), the absence of caregivers creates strong anxiety. Toddlers are anxious of strangers, and slightly older children (who are beginning to explore the world on their own) of monsters and wild animals that are ready to pounce and lurk in the dark. Parents are often surprised when children fear relatively harmless creatures like sheep. As they develop a greater cognitive understanding, true dangers, germs, pathogens and contagion, illness and yucky things become salient. (One 10-year-old boy visiting Hawai'i was engrossed by Hansen's Disease [leprosy] and the story of Father Damien on the island of Moloka'i and said to me, "I'm not afraid of anything—except disease!") With adolescence, fears of loss of friendship, rejection, and low peer status become more likely as precursors to social anxiety disorders. These developmental sequences of fear targets are surprisingly similar and consistent across cultures. We might conclude that a client trying to explain the nature of their fear or obsession in words will mislead a clinician into thinking that seemingly irrational interpretations of a construct that is no longer a realistic threat is a causal mechanism rather than an attempt to explain an evolutionary-determined response that is dysfunctional more in terms of intensity than content.

That some things are more threatening than others may, however, be less a matter of innate disposition and more a result of social learning, as it is well established that children's fears can be inculcated through verbal information (Muris & Field, 2010). Children are exposed to a vast amount of parental, educational, and media information indicating that certain objects and situations are dangerous. The effects of dire warnings are quite persistent over time. So ubiquitous is this pathway to clinical phobias that one would assume verbal counter-information would significantly reduce fear—a perfect example of a truly cognitive intervention. And indeed it does. Factual, realistic, comprehensive information about threat is a cornerstone of almost all CBT programs for children with emotional disorders (Ollendick & King, 1998). Yet considering the complexity of estimating the risk of anything—from having a car accident to an earthquake to being bitten by a snake to contracting bird flu—it is clear that probability estimates do little to convey threat level up or down, especially to children. And it is telling that in experimental studies, factually accurate information is potentially more effective in altering verbally expressed beliefs than it is in reducing avoidance (e.g., Kelly, Barker, Field, Wilson, & Reynolds, 2010). This has echoes of Unger et al.'s (2003) observation that experimental participants could verbally report that they knew the occurrence of a threat stimulus was not possible but they still made avoidance responses to a warning stimulus. Once you have the idea that there might be an intruder hiding under your bed, how much self- or other assurance do you need before you get up and roll a baseball under your bed to see if it comes out the other side?

Implications

There are certain quantitative dimensions to emotion that have been identified in both theory and research. One of these dimensions is the level of arousal or activation associated with any emotion. Clients who present for psychotherapy tend to be experiencing intense arousal or low thresholds for becoming aroused. We refer to this as agitated, excitable, or irritable. Another qualitative dimension is pleasure versus displeasure. If these are considered core affect, the finer-grained identification of an emotional feeling is what results from appraisals of context and processes of social construction. Fitting into this broad perspective is the idea that there are some emotions that are basic—fear, anger, sadness, happiness—requiring uncomplicated appraisals of value and preparedness for action (approach or avoidance). There are other emotions that are complex and require elaborate cognitive (not necessarily conscious) appraisal—jealousy, gratitude, and embarrassment, for example. It is possible that in psychotherapy allowing clients to examine and make more explicit the cognitions that underlie these complex emotions is necessary before their alternatives can be practiced. To turn resentment into forgiveness, maybe it is first necessary to make the cognitive appraisals that result in resentment very explicit. You might, for example, want the client to be able to articulate the thoughts that "I can see my resentment of my husband's taking a job in Wichita is because it seemed that he felt his career was more important than mine. I felt demeaned. It seemed so unfair, particularly as he gave me few options, and in the discussion he made me feel selfish for wanting to stay in Seattle. But holding onto this feeling is unhealthy and is not helping my adjustment to Kansas. By accepting it really was a great opportunity for him, I no longer feel that that forgiveness makes me a weak person who is acting like a doormat."

The connotative (emotive, attitudinal) meaning of words is one way in which our own thoughts, either expressed or internalized in words, influence our feelings and moods. Advertisers and marketing experts know this full well. Words like "handcrafted," "organic," and "artisan" have a comforting feel, Starbucks call their smallest coffee "tall" (originally that was the name for their large size), and pizza parlors make customers feel less greedy by calling a large pizza "family size." The point is that we need to listen carefully to the precise words used in clients' thoughts and suggest alternatives that are less negatively emotive ("challenging" for "impossible," "tolerate" for "dislike," "forgiveness" for "getting even"). The reverse of this is that we also have to listen for euphemisms that indicate self-deception: admitting to telling a "fib" rather than a "lie"; "having a few too many" rather than "getting drunk; "gave her a love pat" for sexual harassment; "adult entertainment" for pornography; or "eight going on eighteen" for inappropriately precocious. Some clients minimize thoughts and feelings by using litotes such as "not exactly thin," or "I was more than a little annoyed."

To elaborate and understand our complex feelings requires that they be put into words, thus making them both conscious and able to be further reflected upon. And using words we can create new complex feelings. Cognition and the feeling side of emotions (how we interpret them) are entirely intertwined—they are not so much caused by each other as they *are* each other. In this way feelings can be modified by examining the implicit cognitive rules that determine them. For example, we might think happiness is an uncomplicated emotion, but that is not entirely so—there are conditional rules as to when one can feel happy. These cognitive rules are culturally derived, which is why understanding clients' reasoning behind their feelings is so important. Across cultures happiness results from succeeding in one's goals. But in American culture, happiness is related to feeling in control and experiencing a moderately high level of arousal; in Japanese culture happiness is more related to the fulfillment of other people's expectations and is accompanied by a degree of quiescence (Fontaine, Scherer, & Soriano, 2013).

We have seen other closely related processes that underlie this interconnection. We have seen that for children to acquire emotional understanding of their own feelings as well as those of others, it is helpful to have the words that identify different emotions. It is helpful for their feelings to be validated by the grown-ups around them. Also, at a simple lexical level, words themselves have emotive properties—maybe we have to call these attitudinal properties. Words regularly used in thoughts, both internal and externally expressed, can have a direct influence on the individual's feelings. Thus cognitive therapists pay close attention to what a client is saying and may through feedback or direct instruction encourage the use of different words with different connotations. Most complex of all is the evidence that emotions, especially moods, influence judgments, decisions, the way experiences are stored in memory, and how they are recalled. Motivational forces powerfully influence cognition (Neuberg, Judice, & West, 1997), as well as behavior (approach or avoidance), thus requiring us to ask whether there is a direct connection between a thought and a response. This seemingly simple question will be considered next.

7

How Thoughts Lead to Action—and Why They Sometimes Do Not

Beliefs guide our desires and shape our actions; when we form a belief, we acquire a disposition to act in some distinctive way.
—Charles Sanders Pierce, 1878 (cited in Hookway, 2010)

Thinking and Doing

The fundamental assumption of the cognitive-behavioral model follows the principles of pragmatism as proposed by Charles Peirce (1878) and later William James (1907/1975): that thoughts (ideas, attitudes, attributions, and beliefs) not only define who we are and how we feel but also play a key role in determining our actions, which is how we judge their reality. Thought content can only arise from experience (sensations and perceptions) of the outside world, but as symbols representing external reality they can become mental substitutions for the external world and be mentally manipulated to form new percepts not yet experienced. We have already seen that thoughts can be controlled by other thoughts, but thoughts can also control goal-directed actions. This is often described in the literature as *executive control* since the ability also requires coping with changing environmental demands. Thus this chapter addresses the issue of thoughts as internally generated stimuli that trigger (instigate), inhibit, and guide overt behavior. It also offers the view that this is not a unidirectional relationship: actions alter cognitions, some of them designed to make cognitions more efficient.

I had expected this to be a nice, tidy, short chapter essentially elaborating that notion. But the experimental cognitive psychologists somehow got themselves involved and stirred it all up in a very messy way. By now you may have realized that the reason cognitive therapists have not paid much attention to cognitive psychology is because cognitive science can be quite abstruse and often does not have much to say of immediate relevance to clinicians. Similarly, we practitioners do not really have time to worry about particulars and prefer a sort of naive folk psychology that ordinary people can understand. Ordinary people presume that you first have a mental process related to a goal, and then you go and carry out the action that will achieve that goal. If I get up and go to the phone and order a pizza, it was my goal intention to eat pizza for dinner and that "caused" my behavior of ordering one.

Not so fast. First, for a thought, in this case an intention, to have *caused* a behavior it must mean that a mental event was responsible for an action that would not otherwise have occurred, which raises the problem of dualism (me and my mind separate from me and my actions). Then there is the physical movement in the action of dialing the number (intention in action), although these days it is pressing buttons. That is surely a voluntary act we know to be essential for obtaining a pizza delivery; it was enabled by us saying the number to ourselves (self-talk), but the physical motor response is not one that we can consciously direct. Others can easily judge our intention from observing the action (although in this example they might need to know that the number I was entering was Uno's Pizzeria). This might be the closest we can ever get to actually mind reading, or understanding others' mentation from observing their behaviors (Grammont, Legrand, & Livet, 2010).

One thing is clear to all of us. There is a large difference between what we do and what we intend to do, and a large difference between what we say and what we do, despite clinical psychologists' heavy reliance on self-report and questionnaires to make behavioral predictions. Something else is clear as well. Ill-conceived (for want of a better word) thoughts sometimes have horrible behavioral consequences, ones that take us rather abruptly from the mundane ordering of a pizza. We can all think of countless examples, both contemporary and historic, but as a sad recent example contemplate the brutal death of smiling four-year-old Zachary. His mother, Jessica Analani Dutro, beat him to death because she thought he was gay; her Facebook message to her boyfriend read "He walks and talks like it. Ugh" (http://www.oregonlive.com/tigard/index.ssf/2014/03/jessica_dutro_murder_trial_mot.html). We can also identify widespread cultural beliefs that are irrational and scientifically unfounded that have devastating behavioral consequences. An apt example is the belief in the different healing properties of tiger body parts in traditional Chinese medicine. Combined with the growing financial resources of Chinese consumers, these beliefs translate into demands for products that in turn result in trade in tiger parts leading to rampant poaching and the steady elimination of wild tiger populations. No doubt you can think of other superstitious ideas in your own culture that promote socially or ecologically damaging behaviors (Gilovich, 1991).

Self-Talk

One of the most psychologically direct ways that thoughts serve to regulate if not cause behavior is through the mechanism of self-talk, in which internalized words serve as self-instructions for action—about what to do and how to do it. Pavlov (1935/1961) called this the "second signal system." Its influence can be demonstrated by a lab preparation such as the following: a person is taught to press a button when a stimulus like a buzzer or tone is presented. If he or she does so, a reward follows, but it will not follow a press in the absence of the tone. After a while, button presses reliably occur when, and only when, the tone is sounded. This is a nice, simple example of an external stimulus controlling a behavior—once the tone functions this way, we call it a *discriminative stimulus*. Now substitute the spoken word "press" for the tone. No surprises here: the person presses the button only when he or she hears the word. Not unexpectedly, the number of trials needed for that verbal stimulus to control pressing is substantially fewer than when the stimulus is just a tone. Now set up the procedure where the discriminative stimulus for pressing the button is the spoken words "don't press." Thinking of words just as neutral stimuli like buzzers, there is no reason to suppose it would take any longer for those words to control pressing. But obviously they take much longer. The verbal stimulus "don't press" has a long-established, acquired inhibitory meaning for the person—a meaning that is contrary to pressing. The modern version of this task is also conducted with affect versus verbal control. What this looks like in an experimental set-up is when the participant is asked to judge whether faces are happy or fearful while at the same time ignoring an irrelevant superimposed word—HAPPY or FEAR. None of this requires much elaboration. It is obvious that during infant development one of the earliest language skills acquired is for action words to direct behavior: "sit," "look," "hold," "put." The power of these words as stimuli to elicit responses is nicely illustrated in the children's game Simon Says—if you follow a directive that is not preceded by "Simon says," you lose. Affect words direct affect, often to counter negative emotion: "be brave," "cheer up," "stiff upper lip."

Spoken words can facilitate or inhibit overt behavior and can do so perfectly well when they are generated by the same individual performing the act. Just as words' connotative meanings evoke emotion, so their denotative meanings, when they are action words, evoke overt behavior. And, if we are pragmatists like Peirce and James, it is not just action words, since for our thought of anything, if it is to be clear, "we need only consider what conceivable effects of a practical kind the object may involve—what sensations we are to expect from it, and what reactions we must prepare" (James, 1907/1975, p. 29). I can only guess that when he wrote that, James was thinking of the object "pizza." That the denotations of words regulate actions is the essence of a whole raft of therapeutic approaches, especially with children: teach children to talk out loud, using words that will guide and facilitate behavior, and then train them to use these words covertly. Cognitive behavioral therapy (CBT) as a movement may hardly recognize this as a cognitive technique, but it could not be more so. Don Meichenbaum (1977; Meichenbaum & Goodman, 1971) popularized that rather modest strategy for impulsive children, notably those with attention deficit hyperactivity disorder. The way to inculcate this thinking process and to show that tasks always have the potential for controlled processing was to coach the child clients to first say the words out loud: "Okay, I need to take my time. Let's see now, what's going on here? What do I have to do?," then actively say the same words to themselves subvocally. The goal was that with sufficient practice these appropriate, self-guiding thoughts would become habitual and planning strategies ingrained.

For children there is a well-known link between having poor self-regulatory strategies—in terms of hyperactivity, impulsivity, and inattention—and exhibiting conduct problems. Yet self-talk is not as simple a mechanism for behavioral control as might be assumed. The precise language that is used by individuals—or is taught them in clinical treatment to use in complex situations—has an impact on the effectiveness of covert self-instruction. One reason for this is that, as emphasized earlier, words always have two sides, both denotative and connotative meanings, and one side cannot easily be switched off. A nice demonstration of this problem was reported by Fox and Houston (1981) using cognitive therapy to improve anxious children's overt speech performance (recitation in class). The children—who were being videotaped to mildly increase their stress for the study—were taught self-statements designed to decrease anxiety by making the situational demands less aversive. An example was a self-statement such as, "Even if I don't do this correctly, nothing terrible will happen." The children in the treatment group, relative to controls, actually became more anxious and worse in the recitation tasks, rushing through them. The authors suggested, and I would agree, that this outcome was because of the negative focus of the self-statements (*not* doing something correctly). One might call this a negative self-priming effect. What is so interesting about this finding is that that sort of self-statement is exactly like what many a parent, teacher, or therapist will say to a child with performance anxiety.

Note that it is not just action words like "stop," "go," or "I've got to draw this letter *S* to look like a curly worm" that facilitate behavior. Self-instruction that simply provides information about a behavioral standard is equally important. Here I give the simplest example I can think of. When I make my coffee in the morning, I have to put a certain number of tablespoonfuls of ground coffee in the filter basket. For the amount of water I poured in, I know from experience that I need five spoonfuls. I could probably train myself to perform the task unconsciously as five simple repetitions (making a five-spoonful sequence an automatic rather than a controlled action), but of course I do not. What I do is count them out to myself. When I label (purely internal dialogue) the scooping of the fifth spoonful as "five," that becomes the cue to stop and seal up the packet of coffee and turn the machine on to brew. My internal verbalizations—my thoughts in this context—regulated the action. Why do these simple thoughts change? Because if I had thought "four," the coffee would be too weak and if I had thought "six," the coffee would be too strong. There is no such simple consequence (feedback loop) for the person with a drinking problem who says to himself he is going to have five drinks at the bar and then stop and go home. And so for this person's behavior to be better regulated by thought, he needs to express this intention in a different way—as an implementation intention, not simply a self-limit ("I'm only going to have five drinks") or a goal intention ("I'm going to walk out of this pub stone-cold sober."). So let us consider intentions in a little more detail.

Intentions

Intentions are action-focused thoughts and are not the same as hopes. You cannot say you *intend* to win Lotto. You can say you *hope* to win Lotto. You can say that you intend to buy a Lotto ticket (without which, as you know, you have no chance of winning). If you think about winning Lotto but have not bought a ticket, we call that wishful thinking—wishful thinking is used only when it is pretty certain that your hoped-for outcome cannot possibly be achieved or you are taking no actions that could bring you even slightly closer to your goal. If you have a client who engages in a great deal of wishful thinking about success, love, happiness, career, you should as a clinician try to redirect those thoughts toward intentions that will lead to goal-achieving actions while not totally shattering the impossible dream, without which the client has no quest. This is loosely what acceptance and commitment theory recommends as "committed action"—taking the intentional steps toward realizing one's most highly valued life goals. It is also similar to the clinical insights that can be derived from Prochaska and DiClemente's (1983) famous stages of change model. Unless people show some signs of making an actual change in behavior, there is reason to think they are only contemplating change rather than making an intentional commitment.

Thoughts, like all other behaviors, have a function. We want them to work for us, to promote healthy, intrinsically enjoyable, or goal-directed activities and to help us avoid potential barriers by thinking ahead and planning. There are parallel ways in which thoughts can inhibit our actions, and that is not whether they are wrong or illogical but whether they function to negate or neutralize a positive intention. Wachtel (1977) provided some perceptive illustrations of how a particular thought functioned for a male client complaining of loneliness and difficulty falling in love. After describing a particularly positive experience with a young women on a date, he stated he probably would not see her again. When challenged that this seemed inconsistent with the meaningful time he had had, he replied, "Yes, it was a profound experience, but I can have it with other people too." (Wachtel, 1977, p. 195). As Wachtel explained to his client, the accuracy or inaccuracy of this thought was irrelevant—what was problematic was how such a thought served to diminish what might have been rewarding, intimate, further social experiences. As Wachtel described it, clinical work in such cases "must rely largely on pointing things out, gaining the patient's attention, trying to interject different thoughts and perspectives in the sequence of his acts of attention" (p. 198).

Intentions are most likely to lead to goal-achieving behavior when they are implementation intentions. These can be described as cognitive structures that link an appropriate goal-directed response to a suitable situation in which to perform that response. This becomes a second level of specificity of the thought by including *if-then* plans that specify when, where, and how the individual will initiate actions that make it more probable the goal will be reached. My thought might be in the form of "If it is a sunny day tomorrow, I'm going to pack a picnic lunch in the morning and then I'll take the grandchildren to the beach." Important research by Gollwitzer and colleagues (e.g., Gollwitzer & Bayer, 1999; Gollwitzer & Sheeran, 2006) demonstrates that implementation intentions greatly facilitate the translation of general intentions into actual behavior and achievement of outcomes in a manner that the intensity of the intention alone cannot predict.

Not Able or Unwilling to Be Specific

Valuable as this work on implementation intentions is, there are some issues when trying to apply the concept in the clinic. We can help clients rephrase a vague plan into an effective one by encouraging them to specify the implementation requirements. But one of the major difficulties of doing so clinically is that people do not always state accurately to others (including self-disclosure to therapists) what they are thinking about. For instance, clients are often reluctant to state clearly that they have had thoughts about killing themselves. Or it may be that they genuinely are unaware of the seriousness of a suicidal thought and when they report these to a therapist might easily be able to minimize the thoughts by adding "of course, I know I will never do such a thing." This is likely to give inexperienced clinicians a false sense of security, and so it is common practice to probe the client's thinking and ascertain the specificity of any possible implementation plans. The question usually takes the form something like, "Well, if you were ever to think more seriously about hurting yourself, what might you actually do?" There is a slight tendency for novices to avoid asking this question for fear it will help the client actually construct a plan, but more experienced clinicians will point out that clients will have had many such thoughts already, and the therapists' finding out about them will not be very novel. I do not know the accuracy of this clinical lore, but it is fair to say that it is worrisome if the client who denies the likelihood of taking his or her own life actually has a detailed, workable plan of how to do so. That is why we commonly distinguish between passive suicidal thoughts that may be fleeting ("I wish I were dead") and active ones that include plans, methods, and ideas about possible disposal of personal possessions.

Similarly, when asking aggressive or potentially violent offenders whether they have thoughts (intentions) of harming others, such clients might be well able to deny the presence of violent thinking. A better question might be, "You have said that you are very angry at your ex-partner. Most of us, when we feel such anger, also have ideas of getting even, how to get back at the person in some way, or doing something that will really hurt them. What's the most serious thought of harm that you have had, even if you know you would never carry it out?" A particularly tragic case in point was the interviewing by FBI agents of the young man who later went on to explode two powerful bombs at the end of the Boston marathon in 2013—the incident I mentioned at the beginning of Chapter 1. Tamerian Tsarnaev had previously been interviewed by FBI agents after they had received a tip-off from the Russian counterterrorist agency but were satisfied that he posed no threat. We are not likely to find out what they asked him, but clearly he was able to assert that he had no thoughts of terrorism—and perhaps at that time he did not have a well-developed implementation plan. But he certainly had destructive thoughts and would be well aware of emotive attitudes, such as resentment towards US foreign policy, which could potentially facilitate later actions. (In the previous chapter the implications of brooding for revenge fantasies was discussed as an emotive disposition but most often includes possible implementation plans.) And Tsarnaev would also be well aware of the danger of revealing them. So it is for these reasons that predictions about behavior might be aided by subtler means of questioning intentions. In the case of suicide, for example, it has been possible to show that a measured implicit association between death and self was indicative of a greater risk of suicide attempts over the next six-month period (Nock et al., 2010).

Choice

We know that thoughts are related to making choices (responding one way rather than another) because we understand the phrase "make up your mind." It refers to two states of affairs. One is where you are presented with a simple option, such as at a restaurant where you are vacillating between ordering the salmon or the steak, and you know that fairly quickly you have to make up your mind and select one. A choice such as that has no particular consequences, but in areas such as health promotion, choosing a fruit salad rather than the chocolate cake is the sort of consequential choice that health psychologists might like their clients to make. As Shiv and Fedorikhin (1999) put it, the heart and the mind are in conflict. In order for the mind to make more rational choices, they propose, the person has to allocate cognitive processing resources to the task, which supports Kahneman's (2011) observations that under distraction conditions when cognitive processes are needed for some other task, responses are most likely to be automatic, fast, System 1 reactions. This will be considered further in the next section.

The other form of making up your mind as a precursor to action is more closely related to making an incentive into a longer term goal and identifying an activity that will achieve that goal: "I've made up my mind that I want to be a hairdresser, and I am going to enroll in the hairdressing college on Monday." This sense of the phrase implies that there has been a period of thought in which you were wondering what you would do next, and also, now that you have decided, you are not going to renege or turn back—it is a statement of determination. Having an intentional plan of that kind is often very helpful for achieving one's life goals, and so clients can be encouraged to vacillate less—something usually related to anxiety about unknown outcomes. On the other hand, there can be misdirected dogmatic decisions in which once the client's mind is made up there is less opportunity to dissuade him or her from a course of action that might be risky or harmful, because for him or her there is certainty in a decision and that reduces anxiety, as already discussed.

One of the great benefits of conscious thought, especially metacognition, is that we can imagine different outcomes to our actions and work through a planning process mentally. This allows us the unique ability to weigh up one thought against another and eventually opt for one choice. Choice behavior does not *require* such prior mental rehearsal of the options and the issues. Animal research, and work with preverbal infants and people with very severe intellectual disabilities, shows that when presented with alternative stimuli, an organism will approach (choose, select) or avoid (reject) the one that is most or least desirable, respectively, based on prior learning experience in most cases but also species-specific stimulus salience. When verbal human individuals impulsively select one stimulus over another, we deplore the lack of thinking that preceded the action, and so encouraging more reflection and prior mental rehearsal of outcomes is a major therapeutic tactic across a whole range of attempts to reduce risky ("thoughtless") behavior.

The goal for parents, teachers, and psychotherapists is to try to instill positive planning and rehearsal thinking as a mental habit. Middle-class parents and teachers in the United States use the concept of choice as a positive discipline strategy. Instead of a simple reprimand or telling off, they will say to a child who has done something wrong, "You made a bad choice; make a better one next time." This has the potential message value that they are in control of their own behavior and that there is always the potential to think about something before doing it. Covert rehearsal to increase the likelihood of performing a desirable action in the real-life context was an early technique in behavior therapy. We cannot clinically simply negate or devalue in our clients the very concept of thought, as some cognitive therapists propose—it is a critical part of the essence of our humanity and our species' carefully evolved escape from simple stimulus–response automatisms.

Self-Control: Inhibiting Impulses

The thought–action sequence we have been considering addresses the relationship between thinking about something, thinking about doing something, and then doing it, triggered or guided by the thought (values, beliefs, and ideals all included) rather than the external situation. There is potentially an opposite process: thinking about not doing something despite a strong external stimulus trigger, or thinking about something else as a distraction or substitute for the real thing or for a course of action. *Resisting temptation* is a more common way of identifying the phenomenon. We have many self-control strategies available to us, and these are discussed in *How and Why People Change* (Evans, 2013). Among these are thinking strategies, which are often necessary when the more obvious strategy of avoiding exposure to a tempting stimulus is not possible, such as when your friends are ordering another round of drinks, or someone is holding out the box and offering you one of your favorite chocolates. We would like to encourage clients to regulate their behavior more by rational thought than by emotion in a wide range of areas. The clinical implications are once again obvious: to decrease the influence of automatic thoughts in interpersonal and emotional situations where self-control is important, the client needs to ensure that cognitive processing (thoughts) are focused on relevant features of the situation, not distracted by completely different cognitive tasks. Cognitive resources allocated to Task B makes it more likely that Task A will be performed automatically and thus under the influence of nonconscious, implicit emotions.

The children's television program *Sesame Street* used to have a nice illustration of thinking ahead about likely consequences, depicting a child who was about to do something reckless (as I remember it, it was rolling a large ball downstairs). The child on the program was shown thinking about what would happen, first the ball would bounce down and gather speed, then it would crash into the parrot's cage, knocking it over; the parrot would fly off in terror, and the child's mother would trip over the fallen stand and hurt herself. (These may not be the precise details, but you get the idea.) So the key message for the young *Sesame Street* audience was the value of thinking through actions, anticipating outcomes, and taking one's time to do so before acting.

Teaching these thoughts has been a part of CBT for a long while. Since, as we have seen, thoughts do not have to be represented in inner speech (words), the intervening thoughts in choice situations could also involve visual imagery. You look at the cupcake and imagine your belt tightening; you look at the apple and feel a healthy glow. Or you recall the words (thoughts) of others; my doctor said, "Eat more leafy vegetables like kale and spinach," and I remember these words while checking out the cheeseburgers on the menu and opt for a green salad instead. Better still you access memories of the words of famous people: you remember watching on TV when Michelle Obama offered comedian and talk-show host Jimmy Fallon a kale chip instead of a potato chip. In the *Sesame Street* lesson the self-talk was accompanied by graphic images of the squawking parrot and the mother tripping over it. Thus it was in early behavior therapy that cognitively represented negative outcomes became a popular method for change, relying on the association value of one strong emotive image deliberately juxtaposed by the client with another one. The rationale for this technique—covert punishment—is a little different from that of self-talk, as it is designed to change the affective value of an incentive (reduce its goal-directedness) rather than rehearse an action mentally before performing it, but the result should be roughly the same: the client weighs up options before acting overtly.

The early work of Mischel (1974) initiated this line of research. He conducted interesting studies on children resisting temptation when presented with a wonderful treat and asked not to eat it. When his young research participants were told not eat the delicious-looking ice cream sundae that was placed in front of them, those who were encouraged to think about eating it and how good it would taste were far less successful in resisting the temptation and quickly broke the rule of desistance. A much more successful strategy was to think about something else entirely. Practicing such responses in an imaginal (thinking) task has been used quite considerably in clinical treatments designed to increase self-control. (I should add that these types of experiments are not about compliance or following commands. They are typically delay-of-gratification tasks—"you can eat this little sundae now, or if you wait a while and don't eat it, you will get a much bigger one.")

Recently this classic experiment has been updated by looking at the thoughts generated in a temptation situation. Hofmann, Deutsch, Lancaster, and Banaji (2010) used a particularly delicious type of white chocolate as the tempting stimulus. Participants were asked to focus their thoughts either on how wonderful the taste of the chocolate would be or on how the chocolate might be used in other ways that had nothing to do with consumption. The latter group later showed less automatic positivity toward the chocolates. In a second study these authors also looked at an imagined scenario in which the participants thought about being in a tempting situation but resisting and covertly rehearsing a refusal response. Participants were asked to think about the following:

> Imagine that you have the goal of not eating chocolate. Therefore you are motivated to resist chocolate in situations in which it is being offered to you or otherwise available. We would like you to visualize such "tempting" situations and to form a clear intention on how to avoid eating the chocolate in these particular situations. For instance, you may envision yourself in a cinema sitting next to a friend who is eating chocolate and offers you some of it during the film. In this case you may say to yourself: "If my friend offers me chocolate during the film, I will say 'no thanks' and concentrate on the film." (p. 21)

As Gollwitzer and Bayer (1999) would predict, such implementation intentions were even more effective than a nonconsummatory transformation of the stimulus chocolate when it came to reducing the automatic positivity of the chocolate. The implication is that self-control can be enhanced by changing conscious attitudes—this we have seen already—but also, as behavior theories predicted long ago, by changing the hedonic appeal of stimuli at an unconscious, automatic, hot level of stimulus evaluation. But we can also fall prey to automatic thoughts when in a situation of complex cognitive processing. We all recognize from experience how easy it is to do fast, automatic thinking and impulsive actions when fully preoccupied with a completely different and complex cognitive activity—yes, sadly, I did reach for the chocolate-covered macadamia nuts I had sworn to myself not to touch while in the middle of writing this chapter. This general principle is not at odds with Mischel's (1974) ideas about self-control, where it seemed that distraction was a better strategy for children's ability to delay gratification than focusing on the temptation itself. This is because in his and countless other examples, the cognitive focus was on hot cognitions such as how good the yummy temptation would taste, which is not a helpful strategy. And the distraction, to the extent that it involves cognitive load, should be a *relevant* one, such as thinking about the rules of the situation that have been imposed ("If I wait and don't eat this, I'll get a bigger/better one later") rather than a distracting but irrelevant cognitive demand such as solving math problems in one's head. The latter is, as one can now predict, less effective as a self-control tactic.

Implementation intentions (if-then action plans) may not only be harnessed to strengthen the initiation (e.g., Gollwitzer & Sheeran, 2006) or shielding (e.g., Achtziger et al., 2008) of one's goal strivings, but also to weaken the power of the temptation at hand in the first place. This interpretation accords well with recent research from the stereotyping domain (Stewart & Payne, 2008). The tragic case of Trayvon Martin being misjudged as dangerous is a sad example of the problems of negative racial stereotypes. Stewart and Payne argued that stereotyping reflects automatic thinking and that an implementation intention might counter this. For example, a male who has an implicit gender bias (and we know there are plenty of those out there) might show a reduction in his negative attitude by thinking that when judging a person he will explicitly ignore her gender.

In a typical implicit attitude task, Stewart and Payne (2008) showed that when primed with a black person's face rather than a white person's face, participants were quicker to judge an image of an ambiguous object as a gun rather than a harmless tool. Clearly the stereotype among the white majority is that minority ethnicities are more threatening or dangerous. But when instructed to explicitly think the word "safe" whenever perceiving a black face in the study (they were told, "By thinking the word 'safe,' you are reminding yourself on each trial that you are just as safe interacting with a black individual as with a white individual"), participants showed a reduction in the negative stereotypic bias as measured by their reaction time task. Findings like these show implementation intention effects on the automatic hedonic processing of stimuli, suggesting that implementation intentions may not only reduce overlearned stereotypic responses (Stewart & Payne, 2008) but even "tame" consummatory processes relating to fundamental biological needs such as eating behavior for which highly specialized reward systems have been identified (e.g., Berridge & Kringelbach, 2011). As Stewart and Payne expressed it, we do not have to think that because some psychological processes are automatic they are also uncontrollable. Stereotypes are automatic thoughts. If their influence can be reduced by five minutes of imagining the opposite (say, thinking of strong, powerful women; Blair, Ma, & Lenton, 2001), can this be applied in clinical situations? If a client's automatic thought is "I am weak," will that self-stereotype be reduced by five minutes of intense imagining of themselves as being strong? It seems very possible.

Thoughts as Motivators

If we want to take seriously the relationship between thoughts and subsequent actions, then simply assessing people's ideas about future or demanded behaviors should surely be revealing for the planning of any intervention program. The idea of listening to the client's "voice" has a slightly hokey ring to it in the tough-minded world of CBT; nevertheless, from a motivational point of view how people think about what they need to do therapeutically or in life must be significant. This seems especially true with child clients because it is a little harder for any therapist to have mentalization insights for children's thoughts. A nice example of this was provided by Macdonald, Rodger, Abbott, Ziviani, and Jones (2005), who asked Australian children what they thought about the connection between physical activity, health, and their bodies—a topic that most adults have some loose, scientifically derived notions about. These seven- and eight-year-old children were motivated by activities that they thought were fun and that they could do with others, and they did not care that much about winning or competing. As a cognitive rationale for physical activities, they repeated information that teachers had given them about the health-related purpose of regular exercise: "it helps you get skinny;" "you get a lot stronger;" "you get big muscles." Girls were more likely to mention benefits for bone growth and development, and boys mentioned muscle strength and speed—this despite the fact that none had negative body images. When asked if there was a magic wand that could change their physical appearance or bodies in any way, one little boy said, "I could do with a pair of wings!" (p. 205).

One important way that thoughts change behavior is not through direct influence on current actions but on the clarification of long-term goals (future intentions rather than immediate, directed actions). We know from hundreds of personal experiences that dreams and thoughts of the future motivate people to take particular career pathways or work for long periods of time on tasks that prepare them for the future. In news interviews with people who have won Oscars or an Olympic gold medal, the interviewees commonly explain how the thought of that moment of glory guided and motivated specific skill-development behavior over many years. The actual winning of the race, which they will have had numerous experiences of, is less useful as an incentive thought than the moment on the raised podium.

Cognitive theories of motivation explain these phenomena in a number of ways. We have already considered attribution theories (Weiner, 1972): if an individual's appraisal of the causes of an event or outcome attribute it to external forces over which he or she has no control, motivation to change personal actions will be limited. There is some similarity between that idea and Bandura's (1977) self-efficacy theory: an individual's belief in his or her capacity to perform a task mediates the likelihood of engaging in the task.

Possible Selves

At a less lofty and yet much more everyday level, thoughts of what one might become, as well as concerns about negative life outcomes that one would hope to avoid, have a powerful effect on behavior when made less implicit and more explicit. This phenomenon has been studied in social psychology under the catchphrase "possible selves." It is yet another example of the value of converting vague, undifferentiated assumptions about oneself and one's future into conscious, explicit thoughts. The theory of possible selves proposes that the collection of thoughts about both the positive and negative identities one could possibly become (a mother, a teacher, a doctor, a criminal, an addict) serve as schemata whereby young people interpret the relevance and value of current experiences. This concept is slightly different and more complex than simply having a vision or a dream, which is sometimes neither plausible nor possible. If a student's possible selves schema includes being an airline pilot or making money on the stock market and excludes marrying a wealthy partner or going to prison, such a schema would enable him or her to appraise (not necessarily consciously) a calculus class as valuable and studying hard for it as relevant.

The possible selves theory was introduced by Markus and Nurius (1986) and has been studied extensively by Oyserman, Bybee, Terry, and Hart-Johnson (2004). A representative and clinically interesting study based on the theory was reported by McElwee and Haugh (2010), who examined college students' future thinking, planning, and affect. The salience and hoped-for possible selves, as well as the vividness and clarity with which these young people thought of themselves in the future, correlated with positive affect and constructive thought content. In contrast, those who simply thought a great deal about their futures had greater anxiety, negative self-conscious thoughts, and a greater number of feared possible selves. Planning and guiding goal-oriented behavior is facilitated by the clarity and quality of possible selves representations.

Lucia Muñoz Larroa (2013), a doctoral student in my lab, looked at the treatment implications of introducing different possible-selves thinking for increasing the behavior of school engagement. Her participants were high-school students considered at risk for academic failure by their teachers. In an after-school workshop format, she taught the students to identify possible selves more explicitly. The cognitive intervention also provided instruction in how to link their vision of their future possibilities with the outcomes offered by school classes. The latter is something adolescents do not always recognize, and yet in an earlier part of her study Muñoz Larroa had shown this to be a cognitive understanding (series of thoughts) that influenced school engagement.

Although the study did not conclusively demonstrate the value of the brief workshops for improving school *grades* (always a hard call), the influence on individual students was interesting. The possible-selves model is extremely flexible; in this study, for example, three future dimensions of possible self were explored—as a person, as a student, and as an area of personal interest. These were represented in the workshops as the main branches of a tree, and the conditions that fostered growth in the tree or threatened the life of the tree or any of its branches were identified by each client. One of the Māori students, Ngaire, wanted as a person to be a better sibling, as a student to have better time-management skills, and as a personal interest to be a model. As this latter possibility had been originally expressed as being a famous artist, the greater specificity of the opportunities and threats contained within her personal "tree" self-concept allowed the formulation of much clearer implementation intentions. In Ngaire's case this was to enroll in modeling and drama courses available to her academically. So again we see that for thoughts to really produce personally meaningful positive behaviors, they need to be clear and plausible, likely barriers identified, and the content focused on implementation strategies. That is quite a useful summary for cognitive therapists to remember.

Future-Oriented Thinking

The interesting concept of possible selves is probably a special case of a more general cognitive style (trait characteristic), which has been called "future-oriented thinking" in the developmental and evolutionary literature (Aspinwall, 2005). Because we spend so much time thinking about our futures and planning what we have to do next—either in the short term or long term—we rather take for granted that this is likely a unique human cognitive ability that has evolved as a way of being prepared and making good choices. Humans can think of possible consequences for the self and can think about likely future emotions. Both sets of thoughts underlie important clinical phenomena such as worrisome anticipation of future depression or fear, or dreading the outcome of erroneous decisions and thus not making any. So future-oriented thinking is a broad aspect of our cognitive prowess. Some evolutionary psychologists (see, e.g., Suddendorf &

Corballis, 2007) have come up with a catchy name for this ability: mental time travel!

Although everyone thinks about the future at times, there appear to be individual differences in the degree to which people actively engage in it. If that is a trait characteristic, I would tend to judge it not as an ability, since anyone is *able* to think about the future but may not always do so in a constructive fashion. Given that one can engage in thoughts—whether focused or mind-wandering—themed for the past, the present, or the future, another version of the same general idea is "time perspective," for which self-report inventories are available (e.g., Zimbardo & Boyd, 1999). The issue is whether clients could benefit from a future perspective in circumstances when it would improve decision-making and taking action that has long-term advantages, such as delaying gratification in order to reap a later, more desirable reward. Also, we cannot really claim future-oriented thinking is always a good thing, if the thinking focuses on unlikely possibilities of negative outcomes, impending problems, and imminent threats. It is the excessive and unreasonable focus on an overly negative future (pessimism) that many CBT approaches try to neutralize by encouraging clients to live more in the moment (mindfulness training).

Despite these minor qualifications, the general research literature on future-oriented thinking has something useful to offer clinical practitioners. You might approach it, like other topics we have introduced, as a background idea, perhaps explaining to clients some of the desirable personal attributes that have been associated with greater tendencies toward future-oriented thinking. These include less risk-taking in driving, greater focus on life goals, greater disaster preparedness, and making beneficial decisions about one's own health care. However, these relationships are not all simple. In a particularly interesting series of studies, Eskritt, Doucette, and Robitaille (2014) found that future-oriented thinking in teenagers enhanced reflective decision-making (System 2) but not more intuitive decision-making (System 1).

There are other complexities to making future-oriented thinking beneficial for clients. Achievement of future outcomes is less likely when one merely imagines them than when one holds expectations of attaining them (Oettingen & Mayer, 2002). That accords with what we now know about the importance of implementation intentions. And then there is the question of how good we are at judging what we might need or feel in the future. Can newly employed young people trying to save for retirement really estimate their financial requirements 40 years hence or anticipate a life without a regular income? Or can you really say how you will feel at age 67 about the exotic Celtic love knot you had tattooed across your back when you were 18? Do we have any idea about what we might be promising to have and to hold "in sickness and in health"? Making a decision about medical treatment might relate to one's ability to imagine a future with a certain level of disability, as well as having accurate information about how likely a physical handicap might be as a result of the selected treatment.

How well could any of us anticipate the future demands—as well as the joys—of bringing up a child with Down syndrome when faced with the decision of aborting a fetus with a known genetic anomaly?

Many clients who seek therapy, regardless of their formal diagnosis, are stuck in a rut. Threatening thoughts are usually associated with passive avoidance responses, not successful coping strategies (Le Doux & Gorman, 2001). Angst and ennui, unhappy interpersonal relationships, dissatisfaction with their physical appearance or working conditions, and self-injurious habits of drinking or gambling are all examples of conditions that keep clients immobilized and unable to move forward. Not surprisingly, getting on with the life one wishes for and values is a major exhortation of all the cognitive therapies—they are just a bit less explicit on how to do it. Future-oriented thinking is one way almost all clients can be helped, but fantasizing only about a better future does not seem to help much.

Think back to our hypothetic client in Chapter 1, about to be paroled after serving his sentence for sexual assault. He might well be fantasizing a future that involves family and community acceptance. He imagines getting his old job back, and having a decent salary that allows him to buy a nice new car. He's "done the time" and now he can reestablish his sense of worth by helping out at his local church. He fantasizes a loving girlfriend who is attractive and sexy and the envy of his friends. Maybe they will get married and have kids. If all those things were to happen, we could reasonably expect his risk of reoffending to be low (Scoones, Willis, & Grace, 2012). But the reality is likely to be very different, and he knows that too. He will struggle to find work and will be living in a halfway house on release. He has few dating skills and no opportunities to meet women except at disreputable bars and strip clubs. His family are ashamed and embarrassed by him, and his local pastor, although sympathetic, is wary of having a known rapist involved in church activities. A group of concerned citizens who think his sentence was too short will be agitating for the local police chief or sheriff to keep close tabs on his whereabouts, making him feel powerless and resentful of being picked on. His chances of leading a normal, fulfilling "life of value" are remote.

What a therapist might do is to encourage him to have fantasies about both positive and negative futures. These thoughts may need to be stimulated based on all his expressed hopes and his expressed fears, while taking seriously his areas of expertise and respecting his human needs (Thakker, Ward, & Chu, 2013). There is no point sugar-coating his future by saying that he has tried hard in prison to change and once he is out things will be fine. They will not be. But they may not be disastrous. If he has changed his ideas about women, he might well find a supportive girlfriend, even if she doesn't look like Beyoncé. There are programs that provide job training and help the chronically unemployed with interview skills—as long as his salary expectations are not unreasonable. If he saves he might eventually be able to afford a used pick-up truck to get around in.

One would not try to verbally convince him of these compromises but rather encourage the positive fantasies of the things desired *and* the negative fantasies of the outcomes he fears—or should fear. This is not dissimilar to the possible-selves therapeutic strategy in which young people used the tree metaphor to see how they might grow as well as recognize the threats to that growth. There is a tradition in cognitive therapy that proactive coping (taking charge, seeking challenges) is usually preferable than preventive coping (preparing for adverse events, saving resources for future needs), because the latter seems motivated by anxiety. Mental contrasting, however, promotes the concurrent use of both types of coping strategy. The experimental literature is quite consistent: having *contrasting* fantasies in which a positive future is contrasted with impending negative reality, and at the same time having fantasies about a negative future contrasted with impending positive reality, is what leads to commitment to self-improvement goals (Oettingen, Mayer, Thorpe, Janetzke, & Lorenz, 2005). Applying contrasting fantasies is a simple metacognitive procedure using mental imagery and his own words, just as one would construct an imaginal hierarchy in traditional systematic desensitization. The result is like the advertising phrase used by the real estate company RE/MAX: "Dreaming with your eyes open." The offender client might like that phrase as a reminder of his contrasting fantasies.

I have encountered clients whose goal intentions require seeking help beyond my therapeutic efforts (which I would strongly encourage) but who resist on the grounds that getting help seems to reflect weakness or places too much demand on others. At the same time and in a seemingly contradictory mindset, these clients often feel a need to be more proactive in helping others, especially friends and family, but are uncertain that they have the necessary skills and resources. Thus they make little commitment to achieving either of these outcomes (low goal pursuit) or start with enthusiasm that quickly fades (what we might call a relapse). Experimental studies by Oettingen, Stephens, Mayer, and Brinkmann (2010), specifically targeted help-seeking and help-giving relationships. They demonstrated that fantasies of successfully seeking or offering help, mentally contrasted with realities that might stand in the way of seeking or offering help, resulted in stronger commitments to helping relationships. Using the participants' own words generated from interviews of both positive and negative anticipation of a helping experience and excuses for nonengagement (e.g., positive "feeling relieved," "life satisfaction" versus negative "being rejected," "not having the time"), the fantasy instructions were

> Think about this aspect and depict the respective events or experiences in your thoughts as intensively as possible! Let the mental images pass by in your thoughts and do not hesitate to give your

> thoughts and images free rein. Take as much time and space as you need. (p. 496)

Mental contrasting seems to offer a promising mechanism for making and maintaining commitments, a crucial feature of motivating behavior and relapse prevention.

Remember too that not all client goals, however positive, *should* be pursued. So the process of disengagement is just as much a part of the relationship between future-oriented thinking and motivation. Anyone who has had to counsel a graduate student out of a clinical training program will know how difficult this can be unless the student is able to come to understand on his or her own that the time has come to abandon a long-held goal. People in a negative or defensive mood are less likely to seek out information about their own limitations. This self-knowledge has to be accurate—after all, it is excessive reflection on one's own limitations that is considered causative of depression in cognitive therapy. Few people have only limitations and few have none; this is why either set of thoughts is considered irrational in clinical contexts (depression or narcissism). Few goal outcomes are uniformly idyllic, and so creating a positive mood allows people "to juggle work and play successfully, with no loss in the quality of their performance on dull-but-required tasks and with greater enjoyment of interesting tasks" (Aspinwall, 2005, p. 210). The lesson for clients is clear: worrying about the future reduces well-being compared with thinking of future goals and planning how to achieve them in the light of anticipated barriers.

Social Norms Theory

It has been suggested that when people believe that a certain behavior is normative in society, they will then be more likely to engage in it. The classic illustration of this is the notion that young people greatly overemphasize the extent to which their peers are using and abusing drugs and alcohol (Borsari & Carey, 2001, 2003). As a result of this false belief, young people will then increase their own usage in order to "catch up" with peers. The implications of this phenomenon have emerged as a major approach to prevention, particularly in the area of drug and alcohol deterrence, called social norms theory (Perkins & Berkowitz, 1986). Berkowitz (2004) describes the general idea thus:

> When drug prevention emphasizes problem behavior without acknowledging the actual healthy norm, it may foster the erroneous belief that drinking problems are worse than is actually the case and inadvertently contribute to the problem it is trying to solve. In contrast, interventions based on social norms theory focus on the healthy attitudes and behavior of the majority and try to increase it, while also

> using information about healthy norms to guide interventions with abusers. (p. 6)

There is considerable evidence for the value of cognitive intervention based on the theory, although Pape (2012) has questioned the extent to which this supposed overestimation actually occurs.

Beliefs about others does represent one of the most important areas of false judgment. I discussed this when considering erroneous inferences in many judgment situations. Remember the sexually assaultive offender used as an illustration in Chapter 1. Believing that other men are also likely to be accepting of the rape myths I described would be a factor increasing his proclivity for sexual aggression (Bohner, Siebler, & Schmelcher, 2006; Dutton, 1986). Pluralistic ignorance is a common alternative misperception. Individuals often assume falsely that they think differently from most of their peers, whereas in fact their attitudes and beliefs are similar. This judgment error allows clients to behave differently from the way they think and feel, without realizing that similar discrepancies will be true of others. When corrective information is provided, the changed thinking makes it easier for young people to act on the basis of their values and remove anxiety or embarrassment about appearing different. A false sense of uniqueness is somewhat similar and occurs when individuals think the difference between themselves and others is greater than it is. In the drinking prevention context, correcting this misperception is helpful as it makes it easier for individuals who are abstainers to participate in social events involving alcohol. Another common bias is the self-serving belief that others are very like oneself when in reality they are not. This allows clients to continue to deny that their attitudes or behaviors are problematic and in social contexts allows individuals to express beliefs dogmatically as though they speak for others (in their peer group). One can see the relevance of these beliefs to people making erroneous judgments about the attractiveness of thinness to others, of misogynous or racial attitudes, and homophobia.

Cognitive Enactment and Reenactment

When in an earlier section I denied ever lying in bed worrying about problems, it was not entirely true. When there is a crisis, or a significant problem, or you are made aware of problems being experienced by someone close to you, it is very natural to turn these matters over and over in your mind, and of course I do that the same way as everyone else. If this sort of thinking is well directed, a couple of processes can occur. One is that you revisit a past event, perhaps thinking about how you might have handled it better, or perhaps imagining the things you could have said differently. For many types of emotionally upsetting past experiences and memories, it is possible that reenacting what you might have done has the benefit not only of preparing you better for dealing with a similar event next time but actually starts to reframe the whole experience somewhat. Constructive measures, even if not performed at the time, are formulated, mentally rehearsed, and added to the total memory structure of the event, thus beginning the process of reprocessing the overall memory. I described this as reflective thinking in Chapter 4.

Another process is thinking about what you are going to do in the future to deal with the problem—and this process has been very carefully studied under the rubric of problem-solving (or problem-solving therapy). The possible solutions for any problem are varied. By thinking through a problem it is possible that you can come to the conclusion that there really is no problem, or maybe there is no problem you can do anything about. Alternatively, you might make strong plans for what to do next and the specific steps you are going to take to mitigate the problem. Often accompanied by visual imagery, actually thinking through exactly what you are going to do is known as covert rehearsal—the very clear imagining of the actions you will be taking.

Covert rehearsal is somewhat like mentally rehearsing a particular move in some skilled performance, such as a sporting skill. When rugby players are about to do a place-kick, they stare up at the goal posts before they start their run up to the ball. Once they have started the run up to the kick, they have to be looking at the ball, not at the posts. The prior intense looking at the posts involves the kicker imagining the ball flying neatly between the uprights. There is a substantial literature on this kind of covert rehearsal of skilled performance, and it is well established that when people engage in this imaginal thinking, their performance is greatly enhanced.

While focusing on the desired goal (excuse the pun) of the action to be performed is critical, focusing one's thoughts on the mechanics of the action itself appears to be quite detrimental. In sports parlance, this interference is called "the yips"—a golfing term for a phenomenon that is less likely when there is no time to think about a physical action, such as batting in baseball. While there are various possible explanations, they basically all revolve around the idea that once skilled performance becomes truly automatic and no longer requires explicit thoughts as a form of cognitive control, reintroducing such thoughts results in interference. The phenomenon is somewhat different from "choking," which is crumbling under pressure. In sporting competitions it is fatal to start thinking about winning or losing or what one is going to have for dinner that night (Beilock, 2010). Extraneous thoughts that distract people from the needed thoughts for monitoring, problem-solving, retrieving information from memory, and so on, are going to interfere with many complex tasks in life.

A long time ago, when I was a consultant to a university counseling center, I had numerous performance-anxious clients graphically describe to me the experience of what they called their mind "going blank" when starting a test or an exam. When probed, what this really meant was that they would stare at the test material but instead of responding to the words in the questions, their dominant thoughts would be of something else entirely. Usually these interfering thoughts were self-directed, as happens to people with social anxieties, thinking about their own inadequacies or in these cases their lack of knowledge. The experience of not being able to focus on the intellectual content of the test then evoked a sense of rising panic, which made it even harder to get into flow with the cognitive material in front of them. Many people will have experienced something like this when performing stressful cognitive tasks. It is possibly a more specific case of the general observation that anxiety impairs attentional control so that the anxious individual allocates attention to worrisome thoughts or to external distractors, in this case the various environmental stimuli associated with being in a test-taking situation (Eysenck, Derakshan, Santos, & Calvo, 2007).

Thought Chains

Before leaving the whole topic of thoughts as motivation, both enhancing and disrupting current and future behaviors, we have to reaffirm that thoughts contribute to feelings and feelings to actions. When these actions are ones that have occurred in the past, or are new mistakes that can be brooded over, there is typically a sequence or chain of relevant thoughts and feelings. This can be seen especially clearly when the thought is not the explicit plan of action but more of a disturbance, whereby thoughts increase negative emotion, which disturbs rational thought, and the action then does follow—seemingly logically—from the thought. To make this argument a little more explicit, consider the case of the US Army psychiatrist, Major Nidal Malik Hasan, who opened fire in a medical processing building in Fort Hood in 2009, killing 13 soldiers and wounding many more. These, of course, are the kinds of incidents that police and security forces would dearly love to be able to predict from prior thoughts, attitudes, or overt expression of ideas.

As a plan, this killing spree was almost certainly premeditated, in that Hasan had purchased the semiautomatic pistol, had returned to buy extra ammunition, and had practiced at a firing range. What do we know about the prior thoughts? Obviously not much; however, there are some interesting clues, in that he sent e-mails 13 days before the attack to his supervisors asking for suggestions about how to handle three cases that had greatly upset him. The distressing information was in the form of revelations by some of his patients of atrocities against Iraqis by US troops. As investigators searched for evidence of earlier relevant thoughts, three things were noted. While a resident at Walter Reed Army Medical Center two years previously, he had given a grand rounds presentation stating there was a risk that Muslim Americans in the military might attack their fellow troops. He had labeled the United States as the "aggressor" in Iraq and said that "we shouldn't be in the war in the first place." He had also asked to be classified as a conscientious objector and once told classmates that his religion took precedence over the Constitution. *The New York Times* misrepresented these not unreasonable thoughts as "radical beliefs" (Fernandez, 2013).

Here we see the relationship between upsetting experiences resulting in thoughts about the way fellow Muslims were being treated. The circumstances are not dissimilar to the ingenious plot of the TV series *Homeland*, where the tragic killing of an innocent child led to grief, then anger, then hatred for the perpetrators most responsible, followed by a desire for targeted revenge as legitimate form of justice. What we do not know is how Major Hasan's experiences resulted in thoughts that in turn led to the "plan" of killing US service personnel—who seemed not personally guilty of war crimes. In the absence of facts regarding his thought sequences, respectable journalists wrote very psychologically naïve analyses. For example Nancy Gibbs (2009) in *Time* magazine described Hasan as matching "the classic model of the lone, strange, crazy killer: the quiet and gentle man who formed few close human attachments" and Phillip Sherwell and Alex Spilius (2009) stated in *The Telegraph* that Hasan's characteristics of being "withdrawn, unassuming, brooding, socially awkward and never known to have had a girlfriend—have also applied to other mass murders."

Absurdly inaccurate as these comments are, "brooding" is probably a correct description. We know most about these sequences or chains of thoughts and feelings from the research carried out on "offense chains" by forensic psychologists. Ward, Louden, Hudson, and Marshall (1995) analyzed, using a thinking-out-loud method, the offense chains of men in prison for sexually molesting children. A reasonably consistent pattern emerged for each man, with rather more planning than in the case of Hasan because the goal-directed behavior was much clearer. The first stage of the typical sex offender's chain was upsetting thoughts about himself and his circumstances, past conflicts, and current mood. The second stage was distal planning, not necessarily always conscious but increasing likely contact with a victim about whom he had thoughts of possibilities ("I might have sexual contact with her"). In this stage the offender's distorted cognitions were particularly relevant, involving thoughts that suggested the potential victim was willing or likely to initiate a sexual act. The third stage involved behavior patterns that increased contact (opportunity) but not sexual approach. The fourth stage followed logically from the increased contact. By now getting to know the child better, further distorted thoughts could occur, such as deciding the victim needed special attention as he or she was being ignored by friends and, if acknowledging arousal, using thoughts that assuaged guilt ("The child is willing" or "I have no control over my arousal"). The fifth stage was proximal planning, accompanied by very strong feelings of arousal (perhaps hatred in the case of Major Hasan). The seventh, eighth, and ninth stages are all post-offense and are important in terms of understanding what might be addressed in treatment to prevent future offending. Stage 7 involved considerable cognitive restructuring, changing the situation so as to minimize what he had done. Stages 8 and 9 were somewhat similar depending on whether the man had negative feelings such as self-disgust (resolving never to do it again) or positive feelings if he judged the victim to have enjoyed the experience. Both outcomes lead to the risk of reoffending—obvious in the positive case and, in the negative case, the feelings of guilt and remorse led to feelings of worthlessness and depression, thus reinstating the original Stage 1 conditions to some extent.

I once worked with a client with a chronic gambling problem. He showed the same kind of "offense" chain when I probed for his thought sequences. He had originally claimed that he responded to a strong urge he described as like an "uncontrollable addiction." But that proved not to be entirely true. He started by thinking of how meager his financial resources were, triggered when he and his wife could not afford some small thing they wanted. He then thought of past wins that had yielded quite substantial payouts. He actively blocked memories of losses and argued to himself that he had had net gains over time. He thought about the casino he might visit and strongly visualized the gaming tables and the general atmosphere. He went to the bank and took out a sum of money, just in case he was near a casino. Weeks later he made arrangements to have a day off work and hid this fact from his partner. He told himself he was a fool, that he was sure to lose money, but he was beginning to feel the excitement of memories of winning and these thoughts negated his self-criticism. He drove to the casino and played the tables. He lost the cash he had withdrawn and also some funds from his credit card that he had originally decided to leave at home but had not done so. He went home, deeply self-critical, calling himself names and expressing to himself a determination never to gamble again. Changing this typical thought–action sequence required interrupting the chain at a number of key links.

Although a simple descriptive model, the offense chain concept is profoundly important, revealing that there is not some simple thought–action or thought–feeling association in real-life complex actions but an elaborate and prolonged interaction between thoughts, feelings, indirect enabling behaviors, and revised thoughts, new feelings, and more direct actions. Had Major Hasan been properly interviewed by cognitively sophisticated clinical psychologists who understood such thought sequences, the way his life experiences unfolded the three or four weeks before the killings might have been easier to comprehend. The incident could thus have been avoided and therapy initiated to redirect his concerns about the treatment of fellow Muslims in a more constructive, less personalized direction that could contribute to solutions.

Thought–Action Fusion

It is not possible to talk about the relationship between thoughts and behavior without mentioning another intriguing phenomenon referred to as *thought–action fusion* (Shafran & Rachman, 2004). This is the tendency to equate thinking about something with actually doing it. I have already mentioned Jimmy Carter's assumption that thinking lustful thoughts was the same as committing adultery. Rachman (1998) identified that type of thinking as "moral thought action fusion." Thought–action fusion seems to be something of a cognitive style, like a personality trait, possibly related to highly moralistic and other religious beliefs rather than some sort of universal truth about human cognition. Its relevance is enhanced by the phenomenon of metacognition. Because we can think about our own thoughts, there is the possibility that for some individuals—those with obsessive-compulsive disorder (OCD) being the prime exemplars—the fact that they can think about an obsessive thought makes it possible to reason that having the thought makes the threat more likely to occur ("likelihood thought action fusion"). For example, by merely thinking that you might harm your baby, you will be more likely to do so, or worrying about a loved-one being in a plane crash makes such an event more likely to occur—a type of magical thinking. We have a number of similar constructs for the vast possibility of illogical thought sequences. As one person with OCD blogged

> I believe that thought-action fusion is at the centre of my own OCD. My OCD worries focus on doubts about whether a thought of performing an impulsive harmful act towards someone in my vicinity means that I may have actually performed that act even though I have not wanted to. To me these are very frightening and unsettling doubts as they make me think that I may have committed crimes that are abhorrent to me. (Anonymous, written by a "sufferer," 2012)

Of course it is not inconceivable that worried, obsessional thinking about ordinary everyday actions does in fact increase risk of harm, since so many of our everyday behaviors will be impacted by focused attention and anxiety. For example if a person is worried about having a car accident, he or she will drive more consciously (paying attention to actions that should be automatic and not monitored—the yips effect) and more hesitantly, thus increasing the risk of a crash. Anxious driving, which is a bad thing, is not the same as defensive driving, which is a good thing. Worry about harming one's baby becomes a sort of fear of fear experience, making someone possibly overly cautious, stiffer, and more hesitant when picking the baby up; and by thinking of things like "are the knives well out of the way?" it increases one's focus and attention on dangerous objects without actually avoiding them. Furthermore, as result of another well-researched phenomenon, we also know that attempts to suppress these thoughts about potential harm only results in them becoming more salient. Also, people might be more prone to try to suppress such thoughts if they are intolerant of the negative feelings that are common for all of us when having intrusive thoughts (experiential avoidance).

Once again, then, we encounter the complex effects of metacognition on thinking (we appraise our own negative thoughts). It is with respect to OCD that the appraisal of our negative thoughts has been most comprehensively studied. One of the defining features of OCD is that the obsessional thought is resisted—the person attempts to put the thought out of his or her mind. Such clients report that their usual ability to control a given thought is compromised. If a person believes strongly that thoughts can cause harm and also feels obligated to prevent such harm, the pressure on him or her to control negative thoughts can be intense. There is also the well-known phenomenon in which when people are told *not* to think about something they not only find that hard but actually think about that thing more than they would have otherwise. In the early studies by Wegner and colleagues (1987) the "thing" that participants were asked not to think about was a white bear, and the phenomenon of the paradoxical effects of attempts at thought suppression have been called the "white bear phenomenon" ever since. However, the phenomenon seen in OCD clients goes beyond this simple effect, partly because for people with very negative thoughts the appraisal that they cannot be controlled adds to their anxiety. So too does the self-questioning, "Why do I have thoughts like this?" (Purdon, 2004). There is also the possibility that we have not previously considered, which is that clients with OCD are especially attentive to their own stream of consciousness. Many people with anxiety disorders are hypervigilant to external threat cues, so it is reasonable to suppose that some disorders are accompanied by hypervigilance to distressing themes in their own thoughts.

The Other Way Around

I ended the last chapter with a section that considered not how thoughts influence emotions but the other way around: how emotions influence thoughts. What if we took the same stance when thinking about behavioral actions? Could it be equally plausible to suggest that our actions change our thoughts? Of course they do. If you have a woman client who is concerned about family problems and you have come to the conclusion that she lacks important child management skills, you might suggest that she read some of the material published by Matt Sanders described as the Positive Parenting Program (Triple P). This is a good suggestion, as there is a great deal of empirical support for the principles explained in the program. But what you are doing, clinically, is asking the client to engage in an action (read a manual) that you fully expect will give her new ideas and change her beliefs and assumptions about effective parenting. As a result of these changed thoughts, of course, you fully expect the client to change her parenting behavior, which is not always quite so easy. But certainly the action of reading the manual will impart new ideas, change thoughts, and alter beliefs.

In fact, most of cognitive therapy proceeds on the pragmatic assumption that the purpose of behavior is to affect the physical world, to achieve some external goal. This assumption is in accord with basic behavioral theory; for example the definition of an operant is an action that operates on the external environment. Even in behavior theory, however, there are plenty of responses whose only function is to enable some other response—a principle made popular by Staats' (1968) insistence that a behavior can be, and often is, the independent variable for another behavior. So, if that is the case, what about behaviors whose function is to enable cognitions? In terms of other cognitive processes such as attention, this phenomenon is patently obvious: we engage in all sorts of actions to aid concentration and focus attention, including possibly useless ones like scratching one's head or wrinkling one's brow to aid recall. We also know the benefit of recreating the stimulus under which something was learned or thought—not only is it mood that serves as a stimulus but going back to where one first thought of something is a standard technique to jog one's memory by stimulus control. The action of going back to another room, or trying to picture the face of a movie star whose name has been forgotten, are all actions that influence thought. They are called *epistemic actions* (Kirsh & Maglio, 1994).

Kirsh and Maglio (1994) developed the concept by studying people playing Tetris, a complex electronic game, and thus the immediate relevance to cognitive therapy is marginal. But what is interesting is recognition that some actions are designed to affect the external world and some are designed to affect the internal word. Take the widely used strategy in cognitive therapy of guided discovery in which clients are asked to perform little, personal experiments to test the validity of their (erroneous) assumptions and beliefs about themselves and the world. We have traditionally described these like hypothesis testing, or reality testing, and the expectation is that based on a favorable outcome the client's assumptions about the world will have to change. But the function of the activity suggested is only marginally to obtain a positive outcome for the client; it is mostly to challenge the veracity of the client's thoughts.

Does recognition that this standard feature of cognitive therapy requires epistemic rather than pragmatic actions make any difference to anything? The answer is only in one way, and that is precisely how performing the suggested experimental tests is put to the client. The rationale for personal experimentation is important, so as not to falsely confirm a negative belief inadvertently. Imagine suggesting to clients with social anxiety that they test reality of inferences about rejection by asking someone they have encountered, maybe at work or at college, to join them for a casual interaction, like getting a coffee together. We say to the client that the point of the exercise is not to actually get a cup of coffee but to observe more closely how this other person reacts as a test case. The clients are advised to make the invitation as low-key and as unrefusable as possible but *if* rejected or brushed-off in some way, that gives new information as to how to approach other possible friends more successfully the next time. So we try to make it clear that the precise outcome of the action is not important; it is how it will affect their thinking that matters. If actions help people play Tetris, maybe mental rehearsal of other problem-solving methods will assist clients to change their thoughts. I am not sure that it would be useful therapeutically to tell clients these suggestions are "epistemic behaviors," but maybe for clinicians it reinforces the simple principle that when clients do things, cognitions change, and not only the other way around. The metacommunication this might make for the client is the recognition that it is possible not just to change the physical world but to change cognitions so that the world can be adapted to more easily.

Implications

We now have solid recognition that thinking, acting, and emoting (valuing) are not easily separable psychological processes. I have tried to keep them separate by having one chapter on thoughts influencing feelings and another on thoughts influencing behavior, but we keep bumping up against the reality that thoughts influence behavior by influencing feelings and behavior influences thoughts. For a very long time in psychology the distinction between behavior, emotion, and cognition has served us quite well, but it is increasingly obvious that these are not three different categories of psychological reality. The distinction between thoughts and deeds was highlighted even more strongly with the cognitive revolution in psychotherapy. Cognitions mediated between the external world and our functioning—even simple associationist phenomena like classical conditioning were interpreted cognitively: the organism, it is claimed, comes to *expect* that the unconditioned stimulus will follow the conditioned stimulus.

At the same time, however, the core idea that words (internally expressed as thoughts) have a very direct stimulus function is still viable and clinically useful. We can encourage clients to talk to themselves as a strategy for exercising restraint and inhibiting impulses, as a strategy for raising motivation by articulating clear goals and identifying barriers, and as a way of using that motivation by forming implementation intentions. We can encourage clients to use their thoughts to think ahead and plan and make wiser choices. They can try out a course of action in imagination without having to risk the consequences of making real-life errors of judgment. Sometimes these action thoughts are so real to individuals that it can be confusing: Did I think about doing that or did I actually do it?

On the other side of the coin are those behaviors whose function or purpose is not to change the environment but to enable cognitive processes. This is not often discussed in CBT, but it is implicit in a whole variety of strategies that cognitive therapy has essentially inherited from behavior therapy: asking clients to do things that will enable more effective, better coping cognitions, from homework strategies designed to rehearse alternative versions of the client's personal narrative to mini-experiments to test their assumptions about life. So the fusion between thought and action turns out to be a surprisingly complex blend, and emotion is inextricably mixed up in it. In the next chapter I review the theoretical implication of this psychological cocktail for thought change.

8

General Principles of How and Why Thoughts Change

Break, break, break
On thy cold gray stones, O sea!
And I would that my tongue could utter
The thoughts that arise in me.
—Alfred, Lord Tennyson, 1842

Therapeutic Change

We can now draw together some principles of how and why thoughts change. I should probably have added "clinically relevant thoughts" since this book is about cognitive *psychotherapy* and not about every conceivable way that thoughts are modified throughout our lives. But possibly all thoughts are changed through roughly the same mechanisms: new experiences, especially social interactions, with exposure to ideas that have to be accommodated and the acquisition of new words and concepts for the tongue to utter. Thoughts change—when they do—as a result of Socratic argument and persuasion, because of new compelling information, because of exposure to media influences, because of the impact of popular culture, because we learn that they are not functioning well for us, and because of developmental and cultural shifts as one grows older, or makes new friends, or changes occupations, or has a family, or earns more money. This chapter is about these universal influences, and in the next one I try to relate the fundamental principles to specific therapeutic practices, both those currently endorsed in cognitive therapy and some new variations that might be tried.

External and Internal Influences

Earlier, when I was attempting to clarify various meanings of a thought, I proposed that the concept of an *idea* might be better left to identify those very abstract and intellectual cognitions that concern complex matters rather than more personal thoughts about oneself. As a result I have not been discussing ideas very much. But the distinction has some limitations. For instance, we saw that fixed ideas (idée fixe) are well recognized in psychiatry and called "ideas" even though they may exclusively concern the person holding them. Similarly delusional thinking often consists in ideas about the world, such as "9/11 doubters" (they think the US government orchestrated the 9/11 attacks) and Holocaust deniers. Where we might usefully position ideas in cognition is that they are very much social phenomena. I have rather ignored the obvious fact that many of our ideas, both intellectual and delusional, arise from exposure to the ideas of others, usually those whose opinions we value for many reasons. Psychiatry has long been interested in *folie à deux* phenomena, in which two people (often close friends, partners, or family members) share a delusion, but I would suggest that with the Internet allowing rapid and dramatic sharing of ideas the phenomenon is quite widespread in our society thanks to the power of social media to influence thoughts. Just one look at websites devoted to 9/11 doubters or Holocaust deniers will show the way in which one-sided information and irrational arguments shared within a small group overwhelm any meaningful analysis.

In the past, the process known as "brainwashing" (Lifton, 1961) appeared to require confinement in a cult or capture by enemies intent on extracting confessions, using social isolation followed by intense social pressure. However, modern digital media has the capability to replicate some of these cognitive influences. For example, the principles of conversion that Lifton summarized included manipulations that now occur regularly on social media sites and Internet blogs: (a) coincidences and chance events are represented as omens or prophecies to support the delusional argument; (b) a group's dogma is presented as the absolute truth; (c) the language of the group is reduced to clichés that prevent further thought; and (d) there is a demand for purity and conformity to black-and-white ideological thinking. Lifton rather presciently foretold the modern media sound-bite thus: "The most far-reaching and complex of human problems are compressed into brief, highly reductive, definitive-sounding phrases, easily memorized and easily expressed. These become the start and finish of any ideological analysis" (p. 12).

We also have to consider dogma and the circumstances in which thoughts do not change or are especially hard to change. We usually see the more dramatic examples with respect to ideological beliefs. So if we turn to the social psychology literature on the motivation underlying fixed and unchanging beliefs, we gain some insight from the emotional function of political and religious ideologies. Jost and Amodoi (2012) argue that these beliefs offer certainty, security, and solidarity. Security is perhaps existential, with ideological beliefs permitting a way of coping with anxiety about one's mortality, and solidarity occurs because ideologies bring together individuals with shared beliefs and shared perceptions of reality. Therapists can no doubt think of individual clients whose thoughts seemed especially difficult to change, and it is likely that such resistance is based on similar dynamics and social barriers.

In order to better understand how to change thoughts, we concentrate on the two primary sources of influence. One is external and related to social and environmental influence processes—new information, convincing arguments, exposure to media, enhanced experiences, and so on. These influences, if they are to be specific, such as psychotherapy, need to understand the function of clients' thoughts and the emotional dynamics that make it hard for them to change. Many aspects of these impediments to external change have been described in the previous chapters. It would be a mistake to think that because these influences are external they are not under the potential control of the individual. External influences can still be self-regulated. Everyone is familiar with the kinds of behaviors one can engage in that are specifically designed to change thoughts—reading a self-help book, listening to an inspirational sermon, and taking a course that challenges one's biases or presuppositions are all examples of efforts that can be carried out by an individual in order to externally modify old habits of thought.

The other crucial source of influence is internal—the fascinating aspect of human consciousness that because we have a "theory of mind" we have the capability of manipulating and controlling our own thoughts—usually by other thoughts (true metacognition—thinking about our thinking) but also by conscious strategies such as redirecting attention (distraction), by diminishing their credibility or importance through reason, and by reframing memories through adding new elements while reminiscing in writing (narratives) or in daydreaming and mind-wandering. Conventional cognitive therapy's most basic recipe for change, which is having the client inhibit a negative thought and rehearse an alternative, is sort of halfway between external and internal influence: it is externally imposed by the skilled therapist but requires faithful internal application efforts by the client. Therapists cannot literally change someone's thoughts the way they can manipulate external environments; they can only create the conditions under which thoughts are likely to change (Kazantzis, Fairburn, Padesky, Reinecke, & Teesson, 2014).

Cognitive psychotherapy has to condense the same kinds of learning experiences that any of us might have into a much shorter time frame. But fortunately it is not responsible for changing all thoughts clients express—only those that seem to cause, contribute to, or exacerbate clients' distress or the distress they create in those close to them. If the cognitive therapist can also inculcate positive thoughts that add to clients' sense of purpose in life and general well-being, that is an added bonus.

The Essence of Durable Cognitive Change

The primary goal of verbal psychotherapy is clear: to change the individual client's internal narrative. That does not mean that all therapies are the same—far from it. Cognitive-behavioral therapy has evolved a large range of techniques and methods, each of which has obtained some degree of empirical, scientific support, especially when tailored to syndrome-specific thought distortions. Nevertheless, the broad focus of all cognitive therapy is on the individual's recurrent thoughts, in two very specific domains: (a) to change content—the running internal dialogue that is largely disconnected from the current situation or task demands but that can be suddenly brought into painful focus when primed by stressful situations and tasks, and (b) to change process—the way the individual implicitly responds to, or explicitly interprets (meaning-making), the current situation and task demands, drawing on memories of past experiences. I have also proposed that both habitual thoughts and feelings can be identified in terms of structures that support them and personality traits that sustain them. However, structures and traits are most likely harder to change in short-term psychotherapy.

The running dialogue commonly occurs in private, in social isolation—not that no one else is around, but no one else is engaging one in a demanding verbal interaction that requires focused attention. We have seen that it is perfectly possible to maintain dissociatively an internal dialogue completely unrelated to the task or the social interaction, but if the latter is verbal (conversational), the level, originality, and responsiveness of one's discourse will be limited. We are all familiar with this: we have all had verbal exchanges with people in which from their utterances and clichéd or predictable statements we get a strong sense that they are not really listening to what we are saying and they are not really engaged or present in the conversation—for which they will sometimes apologize and state that their mind was elsewhere. Having one's own private running dialogue is not in itself pathological or harmful—it could not be, since it is universal. What is harmful is when themes within the dialogue are distressing (contribute to negative emotion) or require so much preoccupation of consciousness that they interfere with other tasks that require attention, active problem-solving cognitions, or goal-directed actions. This interference through misdirected executive control refers both to work-related tasks such as flying a plane, grading assignments, learning medical facts, and so on and to social tasks such as communicating with, instructing, and generally relating to another person or group of persons.

In these contexts it is the content and the pervasiveness of the internal dialogue that is potentially problematic. In the second way that thoughts need to be modified (process change), it is not so much the thoughts as the thinking that must change: the manner in which errors of thought production result in distortions of reactions (e.g., taking offense when none was intended), of judgment and choice (e.g., coming to the conclusion that one is not lovable), and of memory (e.g., easily recalling a family disagreement when there were many more instances of happy family togetherness).

Cognitive psychotherapy attempts to alter both of these aspects of cognition—content and process—but they are connected. Daydreaming, for instance, contains both content issues (imagining some unattainable outcome, which interferes with more reasonable and adaptive goal attainment) and process issues (permitting mind-wandering that disrupts needed cognitive tasks such as studying, managing an office, or relating socially in a meaningful and empathic way). The therapist's task, therefore, is to understand as best as possible the cognitive habits, the origins of the errors, and the functions of the inappropriate cognitive styles so as to be able to alter them through both the actual therapeutic interaction and the suggested alterations and modifications that the client might need to make in practice.

This latter distinction is what has often caused some confusion in the psychotherapy literature, especially around evaluating and valuing the importance of both process and outcome (Evans, 2013; Evans & Fletcher, 2013). It seems well established now that in psychotherapy there are *two* major avenues of change: (a) the consequences of the special, focused, meaningful, trusting interaction between therapist and client—sometimes confused with concepts such as rapport or therapeutic alliance but really referring to the way the conversation or narrative molds the client's thoughts and how the positive emotional relationship implicitly shapes new verbal habits, and (b) the changes that the therapist recommends in the client's day-to-day activities, including the actual therapy interactions, that should enable change in thinking processes via new experiences and contexts, new testing of hypotheses (beliefs), and new or improved social interactions that require surrendering past prejudices and negative attitudes. Both avenues seem to require techniques that work in that not all therapies are equal or, if known to be good ones, are not equally well delivered. What is likely to work can be partially deduced from treatment outcome studies, but only partially, because all such studies contain peripheral components that are hopelessly confounded with the truly critical ingredients. So another source of understanding what is likely to work are the known principles of cognitive change and influence—the principles and explanations that dominate this book, such as trying to better understand the source of reasoning errors, the effect of behavior on thoughts and vice versa, whether emotion determines thoughts or the other way round, and the social force of persuasive communications.

Limits to Verbal Assurances

Cognitive restructuring is still a fundamental technique in cognitive-behavioral therapy (CBT). It does not involve telling clients their thoughts are wrong; it encourages, through verbal but not manipulative argument, paying attention to one's own thoughts, recognizing when they seem irrational, learning to challenge them, and practicing replacement ones. Typical self-questioning that is encouraged usually covers five internal inquiries: (a) What is the worst possible outcome of the issue I am concerned about? (b) Could such an outcome be unbearable or truly harm me and those I love? (c) What evidence do I have for my concerns, and is it possible I'm looking at the situation the wrong way? (d) What personal resources do I have to handle the situation even though I am still full of self-doubts? (e) What can I start to do to change the situation? It must be emphasized that the answers come from guided reflection. As therapists we do not proffer answers to these questions, however much we might be itching to do so, but we do reinforce the answers we agree with.

For a client to be able to address such questions, emotional barriers to rational analysis still need to be reduced. It is often assumed in the cognitive tradition that information alone is responsible for the acquisition and extinction of the emotions and habits of thought that are dysfunctional for clients and cause further distress. The resurgence of cognitive theories in psychology described in Chapter 1 ushered in explanations for learning and conditioning based on concepts like "expectancy." However, there have been repeated demonstrations that human conditioning can occur without awareness (Evans, 1976). Furthermore, the major theme of the two-systems model is that emotion influences attitudes, implicit values, and judgments at a level well below consciousness. Associations based on past experiences influence our thoughts, not the other way around. There is also a small but consistent body of literature that reveals that while verbal information about a future contingency aids the acquisition of learning and conditioning, providing information that an aversive consequence will no longer occur does not automatically result in reduction of a learned emotional response. Unger, Evans, Rourke, and Levis (2002) provided convincing evidence that a fear-motivated avoidance response was not eliminated simply by information that the feared event would no longer occur. And this was not simply a matter of mistrust of the experimenter: even the removal of the shock electrodes was insufficient to extinguish the conditioned fear.

Similar findings had been reported earlier by Hugdahl and Öhman (1977) using the galvanic skin response as the conditioned response. As long as the conditioned stimulus (CS) was fear-irrelevant (like a flower), verbal confirmation that there would be no more aversive events (a mild shock) completely eliminated the conditioned response. However, it had no effect on the conditioned fear when the CS was relevant to threatening themes (like a snake). Note that it is not just stimuli to which we have been prepared to be fearful through evolutionary history. Similar effects are seen when the "relevant" CS is a culturally determined threat, such as a pointed gun or the face of a person from an ethnic group other than one's own (Olsson, Ebert, Banaji, & Phelps, 2005). In more recent experiments Öhman and Soares (1998) showed that conditioned fear was possible when the CS was masked and the participants were unable to recognize it—illustrating nonconscious conditioning. I have already described our studies with children given a verbal suggestion that a box might contain a creature (a monster or a kitten), but the box was actually empty. The general conclusion is that verbal reassurance of safety is not typically an effective way to reduce strong emotion. In *Watership Down* (Adams, 1972), the unusual novel about rabbits, one of the toughest rabbits, General Woundwort, sees his soldier rabbits fleeing at the sight of a dog and he shouts at them, "Come back! Come back you fools! Come back and fight! Dogs aren't dangerous!" As psychotherapists we all know that telling clients things they fear are not dangerous would be equally ineffectual. But rational self-questioning without experiential evidence is also difficult for clients.

New Experiences

New experiences that are especially salient and memorable challenge old assumptions, add novel elements to long-held beliefs, and elaborate earlier ideas. They might have this effect immediately, such as when new and incontrovertible facts are encountered that if not dismissed through some process requires ideas to change. But they can also have a long-lasting effect by virtue of their storage in memory and their subsequent recall when needed in resolving problems or any other form of thinking. The fact that visual and auditory experiences are laid down in memory means that the recall of verbal and visual images rather than thoughts encoded in words provides an individual with new sources of inspiration and positive or arousing feelings. A classic report of such an influence is Wordsworth's well-known poem "Daffodils" in which he describes an encounter with a golden display of wild daffodils growing by a lake, "fluttering and dancing in the breeze." The relevant theme for us comes in the final verse where he describes how the memory of this scene can bring joy:

> For oft, when on my couch I lie
> In vacant or in pensive mood,
> They flash upon that inward eye
> Which is the bliss of solitude;
> And then my heart with pleasure fills,
> And dances with the daffodils.

Unfortunately clinical phenomena such as posttraumatic stress disorder reveal the opposite phenomenon—vivid recall of terrifying and terrible experiences evoke thoughts and feelings of great distress, and much of cognitive therapy is designed to counter the effect of traumatic memories on current mood. We have seen that trying very hard not to think about (recall) negative past experiences is not easy and may be paradoxically iatrogenic. So what can we do? The usual suggestion is that these stored memories need to be "reprocessed" in some way so that they fade in intensity or are modified in terms of their content, such as trying to remove catastrophic labels from the experiences and make moderating, neutralizing thoughts and images part of the overall schema. Having new experiences in similar contexts or around similar themes is one important way of merging old traumatic memories with newer, more positive ones. One of the unique benefits of the cognitive therapies is that such experiences can take place, or be lived out, in fantasies, substituting verbal and sensory imagery for real-life experiences.

Epiphanies

Throughout this book, influences on thoughts and thoughts' influences on other psychological phenomena have been pursued, but in an odd kind of way these extensive topics and their supportive research literatures do not address radical thought change in a direct way. In traditional behaviorism *change* is a very tangible phenomenon, since alterations in behavior (including emotive expression) and its properties (e.g., rate, intensity) represent the dependent variable directly. Clients start to act differently in their daily lives. But in CBT research, cognitive change is typically more of an assumed mediating variable. Of course practicing therapists will be only too aware of how their own clients' thoughts *have* changed because their discourse is different and they express new thoughts within sessions. But in the research literature crucial cognitive changes are still often inferred from treatment effects on symptoms (behavior and emotional expression). Even when nonlinear clinical change is the research topic, the early or sudden shifts commonly seen in clients are measured by means of symptom-rating scales like the Hamilton Rating Scale for Depression (Hayes, Laurenceau, Feldman, Strauss, & Cardaciotto, 2007). Thus *thought* change has not always been front and center in treatment research.

A phenomenon that better typifies thought change is that of the epiphany: a striking realization that results in a discontinuous change in thought and allows situations to be seen in a new and deeper way. Since that is pretty much exactly what cognitive therapy hopes will happen to clients, it is somewhat surprising that there is not a more extensive psychological literature on the topic. Jarvis (1996), in a qualitative study, noted that self-reported epiphanies often followed a period of internal conflict and feelings of alienation, which may be why the feelings of liberation might be so salient when an individual's deeply held beliefs about self and the world are transformed. She suggested, reasonably, that the impact of epiphanic experiences was manifest across the individual's entire system of assumptions and previously unquestioned beliefs. The effects are transformational and life-changing.

While this may be true of the profound, rarified epiphanies recorded in religious and literary history, there may be somewhat less dramatic but nevertheless permanently thought-changing experiences that are more common. Certainly in everyday accounts of experiences that have changed a person's thinking, change is attributed to some emotionally significant feature of the first encounter with something very different than what one is used to. An example I happened on while thinking about all this was reported in the Honolulu newspaper in March 2013, when providing a brief biography of a distinguished Korean American labor lawyer, Peter Sung Ohr, whose first job was working with Native Hawaiians to settle land claims. There he learned to appreciate how they viewed their island lands and how they treated one another:

> He recalled how people who had been mistreated for generations still remained respectful. [Ohr explained,] "That kind of shapes how you see the rest of your experience. . . . They were so incredibly generous with their thoughts and how patient they were, just a calmness." (Shikina, 2013, p. 3)

As another very different example, Martin Seligman tells a personal story of how he came to see that raising children was not about always correcting them but about nurturing their strengths of understanding and awareness that allow them to self-correct. His moment of epiphany, he relates, was when weeding his garden with his five-year-old daughter Nikki, who was being a bit of a bother, fooling around with the weeds so that Seligman yelled at her, at which point she walked away and then returned and said

> "Daddy, I want to talk to you."
> "Yes, Nikki?"
> "Daddy, do you remember before my fifth birthday? From the time I was three to the time I was five, I was a whiner. I whined every day. When I turned five, I decided not to whine anymore. That is the hardest thing I have ever done. And, if I can stop whining, you can stop being a grouch." (Peterson, 2006, p. 28)

The underlying impact of an experience that is relevant to an individual's current conflicts and disquiet fits my general notion of what causes change. However, it is possible that epiphanic realizations can come about through intentional self-examination. This is the argument presented by McDonald (2008). Based on a review of the scanty literature, McDonald summarized the six core characteristics of an epiphany: (a) an antecedent state of anxiety, depression, and inner turmoil (although I would suggest this can be a much less intense state of apprehension or growing unease in the case of everyday epiphanies, such as Seligman's); (b) the new insights occur suddenly and abruptly; (c) the thoughts relate to self-identity; (d) the epiphanic thoughts are new and illuminating, not anything previously considered by the individual; (e) the new thoughts have direct relevance to the person's life; and (f) while the thought change is sudden, momentary recognition, the personal perspectives (self-referenced thoughts) are permanent or at least long lasting (paraphrased from McDonald, 2008, p. 93).

The notion of a sudden new way of thinking about an issue, or about oneself, or a growing realization that a belief may be false, or the acceptance of a new idea seems very like the phenomenon of gaining insight. I have mentioned this construct freely as we all more or less know what it means. But I have not tried to formalize it because in traditional psychotherapy it refers to a specific process that is the goal of much of therapy. Its origins lie in psychoanalysis. In psychodynamic models that still undergird much psychotherapy, clients gain insight when they become conscious of underlying motives, buried feelings, and historical incidents to which their current behaviors and distress can be ascribed. In all schools of therapy, including CBT and classic behavior therapy, such new understanding about oneself and the origins of one's distressed feelings is considered therapeutic. But in behavior therapy and in cognitive therapies insight is not considered sufficient to eliminate problems and is thus not the primary goal of therapy.

At the same time, as a goal of cognitive therapy is to change thoughts and gaining insight is one route toward change, it is worth examining the process the same way as I have suggested epiphanies are worth examining. In therapy, insight is identified when clients accept the therapist-guided explanation for their current thinking or feeling. At some point in cognitive therapy this concordance of the therapist's and client's thoughts is expected to occur. The client in acceptance and commitment therapy (ACT), for instance, eventually says something like, "Aha, I understand what you are saying—my struggle to avoid distressing thoughts is actually making me more distressed. If I accept these feelings and accept that my thoughts do not reflect reality, I can focus my energies on the sorts of things I want to do and that match my values for a meaningful life." Any ACT therapist would surely affirm the statement and express strong approval. The client has gained insight into two hypothesized mechanism of ACT treatments. Of course that dual acceptance may have to actually happen for treatment to proceed successfully.

Some obvious means for facilitating such insights include trust in the therapist and confidence in the evidence supporting the treatment model. The client being open-minded, engaged in the process of therapy, and ready to listen to the therapist's discourse are also important. Having the ideas expressed in a language that is easily understood and that matches the client's level of intelligence, education, and cultural assumptions are vital. To aid that understanding, the use of analogies and metaphors and easily remembered slogans is important. It is particularly important that the client has an implicit model of psychological influence, however naïve it may appear, that is *not* primarily religiosity ("I feel this way because God is punishing me"), magical ("I'm a Taurus, and this is the way we think"), or fatalistic ("It's just human nature to have these thoughts"). I have heard these or similar statements from many clients, which is why trying to instill insight cannot be a matter of persuasion to one's own therapeutic model and has to be a process of reflective self-discovery. However, for those clients whose lives are going badly downhill, acceptance that their thoughts and beliefs have not been serving them well seems to help initiate a radically new cognitive direction. Being frank with clients that what they have been attempting cognitively has been a failure for them can be a harsh but necessary message to get across. Defensive thoughts need to be loosened and sometimes tricked into permitting variants and alternatives. Finding those chinks in the client's armor was introduced when talking about the very distorted thinking that might be uncovered in someone diagnosed psychotic, yet it applies equally compellingly to almost every client.

Embodied Thoughts

Far from the cognitive, mentalist assumption that thoughts are purely internal, and the radical behavioral assumption that thoughts are subordinate to context, is the claim I made in Chapter 7 that thoughts are closely related to actions and tools. Writing an essay on a computer is not a matter of having independent thoughts and then letting one's fingers type out the necessary sequence of letters on the keyboard. The typing, the keyboard, and the computer are all part of the process of creating and thinking (Clark, 2008).

Ward and Casey (2010) have proposed a view of distorted thinking that incorporates many of these same ideas, albeit their theory is specific to sex offenders. I find these ideas highly cogent. Consider, as one example, that peoples' (in this case sex offenders') distorted thoughts about the world (their implicit theories) are not simply internal mental events but include their physical environment as extensions, such as the availability of pornography or strip clubs. Their social environments may include subcultures that relate to their thoughts about others and themselves, such as contact and social interaction with certain types of women. Similarly, their beliefs about themselves and who they are will be influenced by other people who are either accepting or denigrating, so that the manner in which they have to explain their past behavior can either contribute to unchanging self-justifying thoughts or facilitate new and changed thinking.

We have also considered the role of epistemic actions (Kirsh & Maglio, 1994), which are directed at finding or extracting information in the world that is likely to improve decision-making and the achievement of goals. These are not actions that pragmatically allow goal achievement but allow better inference about another person's feelings or mental state, or allow more awareness of one's own sexual arousal. In ordinary life, these are actions like sorting one's nuts and bolts before beginning an assembly task, or scouting around a campground before deciding where to pitch one's tent. (That action alters one's informational state but gets one no closer to the actual goal, the pragmatic action of actually pitching the tent; these are both Kirsh and Maglio's examples). Thoughts themselves are often articulated in a social context. A client's social and communicative skills enable this context (talking to a friend or a therapist) to shape belief systems and implicit theories, thus allowing new thoughts that are less distorted and more likely to facilitate appropriate behavior.

Another complexity arises from the fact that feelings always have to be communicated by overt expression. Among the forms of expression such as facial appearance, psychophysiological changes like blushing or sweating, and body language, verbal statements of feelings are the most common and most usually relied on by others. Faith in the accuracy of verbal statements is not always justified, as we all know from discrepancies with overt behavior, facial and physiological change, and knowledge of the antecedents. Nevertheless, therapists are very dependent on verbal report as the expression of feelings, and so the words the client knows and the thoughts he or she is capable of using in a complex way determines our understanding of client feelings, whether thoughts are feelings or merely reflections of them.

Background Structures for Conscious Thought: Unnecessary Reductionism?

Three hypothetical concepts about cognitive structures have been introduced that seem to me to be almost identical in terms of functions: internal working model (Bowlby, 1969), schema (Beck, 1996; Young, 1994), and implicit theory (Ward, 2000). These are cognitive representations surrounding a particular theme (relationship with a parent or caregiver in the case of an internal working model), built up by experiences retained in memory, incorporating emotional memories as well. They serve the function of facilitating the appraisal of new experiences, providing rules for interacting with and expectations regarding the behavior of others (especially people of emotional importance), and organizing beliefs and attitudes around the central theme of the structure. Such themes for clients are often ones such as the nature of friendship, how authority figures might treat someone, or what a failure experience means for future opportunities and outcomes.

Is there any real explanatory value in hypothesizing such structures? Do they allow for predictions of thoughts (attitudes and beliefs) and feelings that are any different from simply knowing the individual's specific attitude/belief about any individual topic? Does this lower level of cognitive structure suggest processes any different from the activation of a specific individual thought? Does the structure mediate between the original experience encoded in memory and the way current experiences are judged, reacted to instantly (automatic thoughts), and appraised so that possibly erroneous conclusions and incorrect emotional reactions result from contexts that others would appraise very differently? Does the structure idea offer any insights different from saying people are shaped by their experiences and their behavior is a function of past learning? I think the answer to all of these questions is a slightly hesitant yes. But the fact that the structures are often vague, their rules of engagement uncertain, and their occurrence unpredictable suggests that regarding theoretical precision we have a long way to go. The value of the structure notion (working model, schema, or implicit theory) is that it proposes beliefs are not merely a random collection of attitudes and information but are predictable and are linked by common underlying themes, which are, in fact, not unlike cognitive personality traits, such as pessimism, empathy, neuroticism, or suspiciousness. Such traits would similarly promote and support a variety of more specific beliefs around the larger themes of life—relationships, threats to security, achievements, self-identity, and so forth.

In terms of practical implications, there is a need to know what clients are doing, what experiences they are having, with whom are they conversing, what they are reading, and what TV programs they are watching. The range of these epistemic actions and the sources of thought embodiment must be considerable and highly individual, and much of it not uniquely relevant to the client's psychological distress. Yet I do think that there is a danger in cognitive therapy of attributing dysfunctional thoughts purely to intrapsychic forces—distorted memories, traumatic experiences, and traits like irrationality, psychological inflexibility, or neuroticism—instead of thinking of the client in his or her social and ecological niche. When the treatment is of a family or a couple, we are much more likely to take notice of the sources of social verbal influence than when seeing clients individually and having to rely on their own self-report to figure out what sort of influences on their thoughts they are customarily exposed to. It is helpful to frame routine questions in therapy in approximately the following manner: "Who have you talked to about these beliefs of yours?" "Who in your family or among your closest friends agrees with your perspective? Who disagrees, and what do they say to you?" Have you had any arguments with family members about these ideas and beliefs?" "When you read an editorial in the newspaper, does it ever make you stop and think?" "Have you recently posted something on your Facebook page that any of your friends rated that they did 'not like'?" "Has your minister at your church given a sermon that really made you reflect on your life?" "When was the last time you sat down with your kids and asked their opinion on whether therapy seemed to be helping you cope?" These questions are not to be posed verbatim; they are examples of probes that help a therapist discover more about the dominant sources of current influence (or not) on clients' thoughts from their social and natural environment and from their own preferred epistemic behaviors. Some clients simply do not have or take opportunities to be overawed by a host of golden daffodils.

What We Think About Thoughts Matters

The "we" in this heading refers both to clients and therapists. Our mutual understanding of what thoughts are and how they function shapes both the focus (design) of therapy and how it is received by the client to effect change. It is not surprising that we do not have better descriptions (ecologies) of naturally occurring and typical thoughts the way we do of behavior, because thought content across all of humanity must rival snowflakes in individual uniqueness. Since the evolution of cognitive therapy, however, what we do have are some revelations about common thought content and patterns related to specific clinical syndromes. The most obvious examples, thanks to the descriptions from Ellis and Beck, relate to unassertiveness and depression, where thoughts are dominated by themes of obligation and self-criticism, respectively. Ward (2000) and other forensic researchers have, as already described, identified common thought sequences prior to and during criminal activity. Misconceptions about food, weight, appearance, and guilt that are impervious to common sense have been mapped for people with eating disorders. There are also interesting analyses of common thought patterns in traumatized combat veterans, such as survivor guilt.

People who have been sexually abused as children are reported to have distinctive "sexual cognitions," a term used by Renaud and Byers (2006) to essentially mean erotic fantasies. These are unfortunately measured by questionnaires, which ask people to report the frequency with which they have had certain thoughts (from *never* to *frequently during the day*); as one might assume, males report more frequent sexual cognitions than females. While a range of thoughts are offered in their questionnaire (Renaud & Byers, 1999), just for now let us focus on those involving *submission*, such as "Being overwhelmed by a stranger's sexual advances," "Being seduced as an 'innocent,'" "Being tied up," or "Engaging in a sexual act with someone who has authority over me." Renaud and Byers note that simply knowing someone has such thoughts does not automatically indicate whether they find them positive or negative. Thus in their research program they have been asking participants to report these affective properties. Interestingly, both men and women tend to rate the four examples given here as positive. Both men and women did rate other items like "Being forced to do something sexually" as negative, even though they both reported having such cognitions. Renaud and Byers concluded that some women may have been socialized to experience fantasies of passive and submissive sex as erotic. But for many women these cognitions are negative, whereas for men they tend not to be. In addition, both men and women who had experienced sexual abuse in childhood tended to report more frequent positive thoughts of sexual submission.

The research findings are complicated. Submission thoughts represent only one possible thematic category: others are intimacy, exploratory, dominance, and impersonal. The results described here were reported for Canadian college students. Endorsing questionnaire items is very different from providing details of sexual fantasies, and sexual fantasies occur both before becoming aroused and during arousal—either masturbation or intercourse. Quite often they are not so abstract as the wording described here and are likely to involve particular people or memories of especially satisfying past experiences. Sexual thoughts are interesting in terms of their controllability, since they can be deliberately activated to elicit or sustain sexual arousal. (That is one of the most compelling examples of the power of metacogntion.) Repeated conjunction of a fantasy, including words and images, with sexual pleasure and orgasm has a conditioning effect (Leitenberg & Henning, 1995), and the same may happen with repeated exposure to pornography, with its seemingly endless varieties easily available on the Internet. In terms of the effects of sexual abuse on fantasy life, the sexual fantasies of victims are not necessarily atypical and are experienced with pleasure, despite what one might assume to the contrary (Strassberg & Lockerd, 1998).

Whether people find their sexual thoughts positive or negative further illustrates the point of this section: people have feelings about their thoughts and thoughts about their thoughts: the ubiquitous phenomenon of metacognition. People—not just Jimmy Carter—can feel guilty about sexual thoughts very easily, as there are rather carefully proscribed social rules as to the content and themes others consider acceptable. Fleeting thoughts of committing suicide can be very frightening, and the anxiety then makes the thoughts harder to dismiss. Thus in clinical contexts beliefs about worrying thoughts sustain and intensify the worrying thoughts—a model that Wells (2000), a particularly inventive cognitive theorists and therapist, has developed into a viable treatment protocol for generalized anxiety disorder. Like all other cognitive therapies, his metacognitive therapy is most apropos for one particular type of perseverative thinking style in clients. Wells calls this style "cognitive attentional syndrome." This refers to what has been discussed a fair amount in this book: the phenomenon in which the client engages in excessive amounts of rumination and worry.

Dynamic Traps

One of the most profound principles in traditional behavior therapy is that dysfunctional behaviors are maintained by negative reinforcement—the reduction in highly aversive, negative feeling states. Dysfunctional cognitions often seem to be sustained through a similar mechanism. We have considered quite a few examples of what one might call dynamic or circular traps that maintain negative cognitions through preventing emotion from being managed by reasoning or being neutralized by evidence of safety rather than fear, or hope rather than depression. A good example of a circular or emotion-sustaining process that shapes thought content is that anxious people judge ambiguous social events as being negative and threatening (Kanai, Sasagawa, Chen, Shimada, & Sakano,

2010). Since people who are socially anxious are easily threatened by the possibility of negative reactions from others, it is simple to see how this process becomes self-sustaining. It may not explain either the original fear of social disapproval or rejection, or the origins of the interpretative bias in judgment, but it shows how a person becomes trapped in this dynamic.

Worrying, a common cognitive trap, has a comparable dynamic. Worrying a little bit is functional—it motivates people to do things better and to more constructively achieve goals and avoid failure. But what if people worry that they will not achieve their goals and will not avoid failure or other problems? Then worry is especially unpleasant and leads to conflicting metacognitive beliefs—"I must worry in order to achieve goals and avoid threats, but the fact that I worry means I am going crazy." It is because of this model of a cognitive trap that Wells (2002) proposes that any treatment that simply tries to inhibit worry (such as a relaxation procedure) fails to address the key need. The key need is for clients to realize that whether they worry a lot or a little, terribly bad, catastrophic damaging things will not happen—at which point, paradoxically, the worry declines. The essential metacognitive understanding to be achieved in therapy, according to Wells, is that the nonoccurrence of catastrophe had nothing to do with controlling one's worry. In fact almost all cognitive therapies, but especially ACT, have come to recognize that dynamic cognitive traps need to be defused. There are various ways of doing this, one of which is communicating to clients that it is their ongoing struggle to control negative emotions that is the problem, not, paradoxically, the negative emotions themselves.

In Wells's (2000) model for generalized anxiety, clients with this disorder worry, like the rest of us, when confronted with an imminent threat. As already argued, worry can to some extent be functional in a positive way, since it is one way of coping with the threat by leading to problem solutions (remember our discussion of helpful versus unhelpful introspection). But for clients with generalized anxiety disorder, worry also becomes its own problem, when they appraise the worry as uncontrollable and seriously detrimental to social and emotional functioning. This is worry about worrying. The presence of both positive and negative beliefs about worrying results in typical efforts by clients, such as trying to suppress worrying thoughts and constantly seeking reassurance from others. Wells would argue that, to the extent such strategies work for the client, they prevent the discovery that worrying does not lead to catastrophes like going mad or having a nervous breakdown—that negative affect is tolerable (can be accepted, in ACT theory), or, if one is a rabbit and always running from them, that dogs are not dangerous! The treatment is still a persuasive one but is focused on the metacognitions of the client, not the irrationality of the thoughts. This requires persuading the client that worry is controllable, worrying is not dangerous, and there are other better techniques for coping than worrying. The approach is similar to ACT, in that the therapist, instead of asking the rational-emotive therapy question, "What evidence do you have that you are a failure?" might pose the question, "What is the use in analyzing your failings; can you reduce that cognitive activity?" (Wells, 2009). A benefit of not having to focus on the *content* of the client's worrying is that anxious clients rather easily generate new topics of concern that they bring to therapy (Wells & King, 2006). We have all seen that in clients—as fast as a therapist neutralizes one worry content with logical reason, another pops up the next session.

Wells's (2000) model of the typical metacognitive features found in generalized anxiety disorder allows him to make much more precise statements about the possible mechanisms of mindfulness training as an intervention. I grumbled about the lack of plausible mechanisms for this increasingly popular therapeutic cure-all when it was first described in Chapter 4. But the metacognitive model might influence clients in a number of tangible ways. It might be a general experience that demonstrates to anxious clients that they have the ability to control worry. That is slightly different from its use as a way of reducing stress, although many studies of its use by nonclients indicate that that is its major outcome (Chiesa & Serretti, 2009). Conversely, following the reasoning of metacognitive models, mindfulness should not be used as an anxiety management technique, because then it will fail to serve as a way of convincing clients that anxiety does not lead to catastrophes (Wells, 2002).

It has become a bit of a slogan in contemporary cognitive therapy that "thoughts don't matter but your response to them does" (Wells's blog, 2011, http://psychology-forum.com/counselling-and-psychotherapy-forum/theory-and-nature-of-metacognitive-therapy-by-adrian-wells/). Wells goes on to quote a patient who is describing what she learned in cognitive therapy: "The problem isn't really that I have negative thoughts about myself, it's how I've been reacting to them. I've discovered that I've been pouring coal [*sic*] on the fire." The logical problem here is that the word "negative" is being used two different ways. The therapist uses "negative" to mean noncorrecting erroneous, dysfunctional, or irrational thoughts, whereas the client uses "negative" to mean evoking distressing feelings and self-punitive thoughts. The reality is that distressing feelings—negative affect—are important, just like pain is a signal that something is wrong, perhaps one's actions violate one's own moral code and need to be changed. So distress evoked by a thought is not inherently bad. Similarly, a negative thought that gives someone information not to repeat a behavior, never date that person again, or abandon that stressful career path can be pretty useful in guiding future actions. We need to be careful about concluding that "thoughts don't matter."

Clients interpret therapists' attempts to reduce the emotional impact of their own thoughts in a variety of ways. As one person exposed to this ACT style of therapeutic reasoning wrote in his evaluation of the experience: "I have now learned that I don't have to believe what I am thinking!" I think that summarizes rather well the type of relief that some clients have when they come to accept that thoughts do not automatically equate with external realities. Yet such prior assumptions are a rarity. Clinically we want clients' thoughts to function well for them. We want thoughts to entertain, to lead to better choices, to weigh pros and cons, to enrich communication, to enhance understanding, and to steer goal-directed actions. The statement "I have now learned that I don't have to believe what I am thinking" is logically absurd, because if it is a new thought it should not have to be believed. Surely the goal of therapy is to assist clients to better recognize that their thoughts can and should be questioned, examined, and directed.

Converting Principles to Practice: The Example of Tolerating Negative Feelings

In the past, critics, including myself, have pointed out that while behavior therapy clearly emerged from the science of basic conditioning and learning, cognitive therapy was not derived from experimental cognitive psychology. The theories behind cognitive therapy are more like common sense or folk psychology (Ravenscroft, 2010), with a basic sense of *ringing true* simply because they use everyday language and easily accepted interpretations of thinking that sound right. Cognitive psychology does not tell therapists exactly which thoughts need to be changed, how thoughts can best be changed, and whether, if clients' thoughts are changed, their problems will be decreased. Much of formal cognitive psychology tends to be about hypothetical information processing and highly abstract models of reasoning and thinking. Cognitive psychology has been less interested in the role of emotion or in the content of thoughts. The social psychological literature on attitudes and beliefs and prejudices and how these may be altered is more relevant for sure but even then does not identify precise new techniques or directions for therapy.

On the other hand, as summarized in this and previous chapters, many scientific principles related to thoughts and their change that are potentially relevant to the therapist's task exist in the research and theoretical literature. Cognitive therapy tells clients a comprehensive story about how their thoughts are contributing to their problems—not so much their experiences as the way they interpret their experiences. One of the best-documented phenomena is how people who have experienced psychotic episodes dread having relapses, having been traumatized by their experiences of both symptoms and hospitalization (Berry et al., 2013).The narrative in cognitive therapy takes a few different forms, from the attempt in ACT to diminish the presumptive value of thoughts and tell clients they are not important, to attempts in Beckian-style therapy to get clients to work on changing their inner talk, to attempts to show how their childhood experiences have implicitly shaped their thinking (Young, 1994), to the array of Zen-inspired ways of intruding into the ecology of thinking by helping clients better manage their stream of consciousness and their ruminations and worry (e.g., Linehan, 1993; Teasdale, 1999). All of these approaches have merit, but not always for the precise reasons offered by their protagonists.

There is a mismatch between cognitive therapy protocols, as described in the many excellent handbooks, and the broad principles of cognition and thought change. As this is no comprehensive super-manual, I think that for day-to-day procedures and treatment formulations you would be best advised to stick to the empirically supported techniques you have learned or read about. An excellent source is O'Donohue and Fisher's (2008) edited collection of over 70 CBT techniques. Most of them are closely tailored to specific syndromes, which is a helpful start when a client's symptoms fit a particular diagnosis precisely. But we can add a little polish to those techniques by making them generalizable—capturing those principles that can be applied "transdiagnostically" to a whole range of clients, of diverse ages, cultures, past experiences, and psychological concerns.

Let me offer an example of how the broader principles might apply at this level of analysis. I can pick on ACT. This is largely because it has a very bold meta-theory driven by the creativity and enthusiasm of its major proponents. Take the simple assertion that it is not the content of thoughts that need to be changed. The important thing is for clients to realize that it is their thoughts that are getting in their way of living the kinds of lives they hope for and aspire to. "Get out of your mind and into your life" is one of the favorite mantras. It is clever enough, but what does it mean? And if clients accept this mantra, haven't they been given a new thought, or at least a new way of thinking about their old thoughts? If this discourse diminishes the extent to which clients' thoughts are locked into worry, rumination, and repeated reexamination of traumatic experiences, then that is by all accounts a good therapeutic strategy, and living a life of value is a great outcome. But that is pretty much what all the cognitive therapies are trying to do. Once we actually accept the realities of mental life and how it works to sustain affect and guides or interferes with behavior, then mental events (thoughts) become legitimate targets for change. However, as in Wells's (2000) metacognitive approach, it is not just the *content* of a negative thought that must be changed but the client's interpretation of it: the belief that a negative thought indicates (signals) true threat because these worrying thoughts are uncontrollable and dangerous.

Let us look at another ACT concept and see if it is a change principle. Acting—behaving in new ways that are desired by the client's hopes, dreams, and values—is the crucial goal of therapy: *committed action* it is called. But that is a philosophy, not a treatment plan. The ACT treatment plan contains standard behavior therapy elements such as what are the barriers to changing behavior, what changes are possible given the client's life circumstances, how motivated is he or she to change, and to what extent is change difficult because his or her current behavior is functional in certain strange ways? Behavior that causes distress in the long run, or lacks the vitality of action that makes life fun and meaningful, is nevertheless present in clients because it is functional for them.

The major function, I would suggest, is one we have considered since the days of Dollard and Miller (1950) and two-factor learning theory. These behaviors (or nonbehaviors, inaction) serve the function of reducing or avoiding emotional distress, even if they lead to other problems.

A simple strategy to change these functional but harmful behaviors is to reduce the valence—the negativity—of the emotions that are being avoided. And, I could argue, as ACT does, that these emotions are inherently neither good nor bad. They are judged bad by those clients who have strong "experiential avoidance" tendencies. These are assumed to be at the level of cognitive personality traits. Questionnaires designed to measure this cognitive style (e.g., for adolescents; Greco, Lambert, & Baer, 2008) include items such as "Feeling scared or sad is bad," "I try hard to stop feeling nervous," and "I try hard to erase hurtful memories from my mind" (p. 96). If the client can be encouraged to stop trying hard to do those things, negative feelings might dissipate, and there are many different ways of achieving this.

One way is simply to get the client to embrace alternative, incompatible ideas. That is a persuasive communication, supported by metaphors, analogies, and lots of other ingenious communication strategies therapists might use. One of them is like paradoxical intention: stop fighting the distress, as that only makes it worse; reevaluate it and it will decrease. But an equally viable way to reduce intolerable feelings is through desensitization, one of the oldest techniques in behavior therapy. Another might be to ask clients to test the extent to which experiencing these feelings is as bad as they anticipate. This is pretty much the way cognitive therapy as proposed by Beck (1975) in the old days conceptualized personal experiments by clients, although he saw it more as testing the reality of irrational beliefs about consequences. But fear of fear, depression about depression, and worry about psychotic experiences are realistic beliefs—they are just not overwhelmingly bad unless one lets them be so. It is the dynamics of thought–emotion–behavior interaction that allows for dysfunctional patterns that clients cannot get out of. Those self-defeating dynamic spirals need to be interrupted.

In the end, the problem is that clients' thoughts are unhelpful. They are illogical, they rely on poor evidence and show lack of wisdom, and they are emotive and influenced by implicit underlying cognitions. We can call these schemas or automatic thoughts or implicit attitudes, but what it means is that emotive processes of which we are not consciously aware are influencing our judgments, choices, appraisals, and expressed beliefs that we assume to have high validity and correctness. How do we de-fang cognitive processes of which we are unaware?

Implications

Can all this help you when you are sitting in front of a client and deciding what to do next? You could perhaps be following a nicely itemized CBT protocol, but even then decisions have to be made on a moment-to-moment basis. I am not sure if clients are aware of how much of psychotherapy happens on the fly—I know we like to call it artistry—or if they would be appalled to know that your latest therapeutic suggestion has only just occurred to you. It is because I personally think much of effective psychotherapy has this rather ad hoc, seat-of-your-pants sort of quality that I think having some generally sound background ideas about the current psychology of thought change is useful as a conceptual framework.

Much as I am pleased that the field of CBT has recently reverted back to thinking broadly about general processes that are common to many psychological disorders, I am still struck by the fact that most contemporary cognitive therapy is based on theories of how clients with particular disorders typically go about processing information. Ward's (2000) analysis of thought chains in people who are sex offenders really is different from Rachman's (1998) descriptions of thought–action fusion in people with OCD, and these are different from the incorrect appraisals of threat Salkovskis (1996) reported in people with panic disorder, and they are in turn different from Beck's (1964) pioneering recognition that depressed people express irrationally negative thoughts, or Witkiewitz and Marlatt's (2007) observations that mindfully "surfing" urges helps reduce substance abuse relapses. Is it possible to delve beneath these extremely helpful but syndrome-specific or trait-specific process changes and come up with more general ones having application across the many unique concerns that clients present in therapy?

The following is an example of how I think we might be able to do this in a practical way. I have given quite a degree of prominence to the simple idea that there is a difference between controlled and automatic cognitive processes: the latter allow us to do a number of cognitive tasks simultaneously and reduces the cognitive load. But we also know that, when needed, an individual can usually engage controlled processes quite rapidly. How is this shift achieved without postulating yet another homunculus-like causal mechanism? The prevailing explanation is called "conflict monitoring" (Yeung, 2013). The suggestion is that there are evolved neural processes (in the anterior cingulated cortex) whose function is to detect "competition" (i.e., conflict) in information processing—making an error, for example—and to signal the need for cognitive control. This means that errors can be useful things, signaling it is time to get away from automatic thinking (System 1) and do some reflective self-analysis (System 2). Can that idea be usefully explained to clients? They can be reassured that when they come in and report some minor catastrophe from the previous week, this can be used as a marker for a more "mindful," contemplative, controlled analysis for what might have been done better. This and other practical strategies based on general principles are offered in the next and final chapter.

9

Can Cognitive Treatments Be Enhanced?

> The happiness of your life depends upon the quality of your thoughts.
>
> —Marcus Aurelius, *Meditations*, 167 AD

Thoughts and Distress

Everything included under the umbrella of "cognitive therapy" is about changing thoughts—how we manipulate them, modify them, make them less ambiguous, test them with behavioral experiments, store them, recall them, and put them to work. But for various reasons, as suggested at the end of the last chapter, the developers of these as therapeutic methods have tended to emphasize only those thought-change principles of direct relevance to the distinctive treatment strategies they have designed and promulgated. In order not to be restricted to simply implementing just one of these treatments, it is my contention that clinicians, both experienced and in training, can benefit from connecting with the more general principles of cognitive change in order to have a flexible *foundation* for the more specific, well-developed treatment protocols. There is good evidence that even when following formal protocols clinicians are nothing if not innovative. Broad principles can offer the a priori knowledge to guide and support this creativity.

When seeking the common rationale of all cognitive therapies we find it is that clients have erroneous thoughts—about themselves, about others, about the nature of their world and their emotional experiences in it—that are not working for them and need to be adjusted or neutralized. But all of us share many of the same limitations to wise thought; we too are often irrational and illogical as we try to make meaning out of ambiguous situations and confusing experiences. The problem for clients is either the more persistent and repetitive nature of potentially distressing thoughts or the probability of less-than-helpful thoughts as the reaction to potentially distressing situations. Thus the primary goal of cognitive therapy is not to eradicate all "bad," flawed thoughts but to ensure that clients' thinking serves their pursuit of positive goals rather than derailing them with increased negative emotion and undesired, maladaptive direction in life. Self-relevant thoughts, our private, inner consciousness about ourselves, need to better serve our higher order needs and desires and values—to mediate in a positive constructive way, irrespective of their logical correctness or peculiarity. Clinical psychologists practicing cognitive therapy are not trying to restrict thoughts in any specific form. The melodies are infinite; clients are enabled to turn more pages of the song book.

What we think about and when causes or exacerbates the kinds of emotional distress for which clients seek therapy. It may not be the fundamental reason, as causation always follows a means–ends chain, but it is a direct contributor. If you are feeling very worried about, say, finances, the cause of this might be that you are threatened with being made redundant, which in turn might have been caused by the US federal government's budget sequestration of 2013. These are actual negative life events, not psychological constructions. But how you label the event ("It is a total disaster"), how you process the meaning of job loss for your sense of self-worth ("I'm a failure"), how you reinterpret your self-identity ("I'll be unemployed"), how you generalize from the experience ("I'll never work again"), how you berate yourself ("I should have tried harder at work"), how you cope ("I'm going to have to economize"), how you plan and problem-solve ("No use sitting around feeling sorry for myself; I need to start shaping up my CV"), how you manage your constant angry ruminations ("I'm going to do some meditation and then go and talk to my friends"), how you revise your memories ("The last time I was panicked about money I remember managing my depression and anxiety by talking to a financial advisor"), and how you minimize your worry ("My unemployment insurance will give me a cushion") all represent the thoughts and thinking processes that will determine whether or not you continue to feel overwhelmed by stress, anxiety, and melancholia. Some of the most emotion-laden ("hot") cognitions may not be formulated in words initially, so it is definitely not simply a matter of what words you consciously say to yourself. But they are still mental interpretations that are in response to an event and that determine your appraisal of the event, how it affects you emotionally, and what you are going to do about it—possibly in that sequence.

The Set-Up

The ubiquitous presence of errors of judgment and reasoning that I have described is not a pessimistic commentary on human thought. Half-Vulcan Mr. Spock may have been very logical, but he did not write love sonnets, or stimulate children's imagination with what was on the other side of the looking glass, or compose inspirational music like *Imagine*. But limitations to wisdom highlight the probability that unbounded thoughts are not going to be easily changed. Clinically, therefore, we need to do what we can to reduce the barriers—to prepare the soil properly before we drop in the seeds and give them a little water.

We know that dysfunctional thoughts are intensified by general interpersonal and even environmental stressors (e.g., Ellet, Freeman, & Garety, 2008). Thus one suggestion emerging from the cognitive literature is that we need to foster as much positive affect as possible prior to or very early on in cognitive therapy. That may sound back-to-front, since the whole purpose of doing the cognitive therapy interventions is to foster positive affect. However, it is a matter of facilitating change. The literature strongly confirms that when people experience positive affect they have increased cognitive flexibility (Fredrickson, 2001). Cognitive flexibility is a prize commodity in therapy because it facilitates thought change by making clients more open to new information. This in turn promotes what traditional behavior therapists valued (Evans, 2013): enabling clients to engage more constructively with their environment, thereby building new personal and social resources. This is particularly important for clients who are most self-preoccupied and socially disengaged, such as those with seriously distorted psychotic thoughts. Thus the overall implication is that even when doing cognitive therapy, you need to do what you can to make the client's environment more stable and comfortable (Liu & Wang, 2014). The recommendation would be to facilitate some social support and problem-solving before directly addressing maladaptive cognitions.

The relationship between positive affect and cognition also depends, however, on the person's major style of motivation. Motivation for goal-directed activities can be driven by approach motivation, striving for success, and if so then cognitive perseveration and focus would be more advantageous than flexibility. Alternatively, goals may be pursued through avoidance motivation: striving to avoid failure and preferring safe activities. When we describe clients as having experiential avoidance what we mean is that negative experiences are not well tolerated. Avoidance-motivated clients are more alert and vigilant and pay attention to and remember upsetting details. That sums up the motivational/cognitive style of many clients, in my experience. Trying to change a client's motivational style might be difficult, but Roskes, Elliot, and De Dreu (2014) have suggested the following strategies for reducing the negative consequences of avoidance motivation: (a) removing distracting stressors, like time pressures to complete tasks; (b) providing structure and focus, such as giving clients quite directive and specific recommendations to follow; and (c) allowing individuals to "clear their minds and replenish their energy on a regular basis" (p. 136), which I would interpret for clients as teaching meditation or mindfulness strategies.

The Therapeutic Relationship as Verbal Influence

These concepts are examples of strategies that might precede direct cognitive change treatments. So too are building up our verbal influence over clients. We left Chapter 2 with the simple summary that a common feature of all cognitive therapies is to shape new patterns of thought by discursive communication. Other experiences cause thoughts to change, but they are not always within the reach of psychotherapy as a social intervention. Change transpires within a distinctive relationship between client and therapist. If clients have long-standing schemas that are historically relevant to emotionally charged interpersonal situations, as Young (1994) has asserted so persuasively, it must follow that they have schemas regarding therapy, its nature, its effectiveness, their past experience of it (if they have been in therapy before), and their response to the gender, age, status, ethnicity, and dominance of the therapist. And if that is true, then surely therapists will have a few schemas of their own, about the type of person the client is, the type of diagnosis he or she has, and their experiences with other clients, perhaps similar, in the past. This notion was one of the original cornerstones of Linehan's (1993) dialectical behavior therapy (DBT) with clients diagnosed with borderline personality disorder. She recognized immediately that many psychologists and counselors would have encountered challenging clients previously, as a result of which they might tend to be wary, rejecting, harsh, and controlling, and engage in other sorts of power tactics designed to protect their own sense of self-worth and safety. But these emotive thoughts, beliefs, and attitudes result in an interactional style that is the exact opposite of what will benefit someone with this disorder. These clients need stable relationships, acceptance rather than rejection, and reassurance that the therapist will not easily abandon them (Linehan, 1993; Linehan, Cochran, Mar, Levensky, & Comtois, 2000).

Computer Delivery: A Challenge to the Interpersonal Influence Model?

All of the major cognitive therapies implicitly place great value on the therapist–client relationship, but only DBT specifies the exacting requirements for how the relationship is to be managed. If it transpires that the common mechanism of all other cognitive therapies is some sort of verbal exchange of ideas, could it be that an actual therapist is not needed at all? Verbal influences on thought change come in many different forms. People can read a book or a newspaper article, see a movie, go to a lecture, and their ideas can be transformed. They can go to a sermon, experience a loss or disappointment, pray unsuccessfully, and their beliefs can be transformed. They can do an experiment, read a research paper, witness injustice, or be helped by a stranger, and their attitudes can be transformed. So it should be no surprise that delivering cognitive behavior therapy by computer, usually over the Internet, has rapidly become a popular idea (Mewton, Smith, Rossouw, & Andrews, 2014).

Donker et al. (2013) described their online cognitive-behavioral therapy (CBT) modules for a worldwide nonclinical sample as "identifying negative thoughts, tackling negative thoughts, and undertaking behavioral activation," which is a bit vague. Also, the various programs that have been trialed differ in the amount of homework included, the degree of access to a skilled therapist who makes phone calls or posts comments on a private forum, assessment tools, and interactive feedback provided. Where computer-delivered methods are most explicit is when the software is designed to offer a specific training or learning experience—essentially computer-assisted instruction. The idea is that if the cognitive biases underlying anxiety disorders are like a cognitive trait (having poor or erroneous information-processing skills), then exercises designed to reduce such bias will have a generalized effect. As there are different forms of bias hypothesized for different disorders, the retraining of cognitive information processing is supposed to match the type of bias the client exhibits. If, for example, the presumed bias is attending more to negative than positive information, the training procedure reinforces selective attention to positive and avoidance of negative stimuli (words or images in the computerized tasks). If the bias is an interpretive bias (finding negative meaning in ambiguous situations), the training involves allowing participants to complete only positive responses to an ambiguous context (e.g., the word *growth* might relate to a child having cancer or getting two inches taller; MacLeod & Mathews, 2012). Cognitive biases, however, are difficult to pinpoint precisely, as illustrated in the phenomenon of selective attention to threatening cues. The bias might not actually be in greater vigilance but in the time taken to disengage: redirecting clients' thoughts away from any threatening stimuli to which they have already attended (Wenzel & Rubin, 2005). Cognitive therapy can be considered a verbal influence process, not just a social one: new information, from whatever medium, can change thoughts, at least some of them some of the time. But we still have to know what the prior thoughts are. One of the things we need to try to discover in assessing clients' dominant thoughts is what they are actually verbalizing internally.

Disclosure and Trust

In the clinical literature authors provide brief examples of the things that clients with different diagnoses supposedly say to themselves or hold to as personal beliefs. In the case of social anxiety disorders, Clark and Wells (1995) proposed that there are three types of beliefs held by clients: (a) high standards for social performance, (b) conditional beliefs regarding social evaluation, and (c) unconditional negative beliefs about the self. Examples of the first type might be, "I must be able to convey a favorable impression to everyone," of the second type, "*If* people see that I am anxious, then they will think that I'm weak," and of the third type, "People think poorly of me." Anxious people endorse these sorts of items on a questionnaire; Wong and Moulds (2011) have constructed just such a questionnaire (the Self-Beliefs Related to Social Anxiety Scale) and confirmed that the items tend to fall into the three clusters of beliefs suggested by Clark and Wells. But while they may endorse items on a questionnaire, clients, when interviewed, do not actually come out and say these things—at least not in my experience.

As a clinician, if you assume that the presence of these beliefs are somehow causal in the elicitation and maintenance of anxiety, and if you expect to be able to change them, then it would be important to know precisely what the beliefs are and how firmly they are held and whether they come into consciousness in response to a situation deemed to be threatening. If there is a trusting relationship, clients should be able to disclose these beliefs, or they might be assessed in an open-ended way using a thought-sampling procedure. If clients seem unable to articulate any beliefs related to the three cognitive styles proposed by Clark and Wells (1995), you could have them complete the questionnaire and see which items they endorse and use that as the beginning of a conversation. There is always a small risk that you are putting words into their mouths, but, despite that, further questioning is called for. This is because having a belief in the importance of high standards of performance does not intrinsically lead to anxiety unless one is also motivated by failure avoidance, and it is certainly not an irrational thought in people striving for excellence (approach motivation). So too, how the person may be judged if anxiety is displayed is not automatically negative—exhibiting anxiety can evoke sympathy and offers of support and expressions of understanding. Careful questioning regarding the exact implications of a belief is necessary. The clinician's question, "Okay, so if showing anxiety when giving a talk will be interpreted by your audience as a weakness, what will that mean for you personally?" might reveal a concern that he or she will be made fun of (worry about rejection), will not be picked for a demanding task (worry about job security), will not be able to continue the presentation (worry about being unable to perform the task—fear of failure), will be worried that anxiety will be expressed in the form of shaking hands or dry mouth (fear of fear), or will be reevaluated as an individual (worry about self-image).

Why is trust of some kind so essential for this kind of probing? The answer is because there is a paradox in clinical work. I continue to use social performance anxiety as an example. If a client fears rejection, fears being unable to do the task required (failure avoidance), or is protective of his or her self-image, the same worries can pertain to the therapy situation. Feeling safe in therapy can mitigate a client's reluctance to show his or her vulnerability. Trust is not the only relationship quality that might be important. For depressed clients, confidence in the therapist's abilities, therapy-focused optimism, and long-term commitment is needed to mitigate their apprehension that therapy is a waste of time. Fearful clients express thoughts that therapy itself is scary; depressed clients express thoughts that therapy is pointless; people with guilt recognize the risk of opening Pandora's box; socially anxious clients worry about the impression they give the therapist.

Assessing the Function of Thoughts

As in all psychotherapy, cognitive therapy requires some sort of assessment of the thoughts that the clinician hopes to address or change. Having the client keep a thought diary or thought record is a standard feature of cognitive therapy à la Beck (Greenberger & Padesky, 1995). Examining the client's thought record allows the therapist to find underlying themes that are core beliefs and can be used as a tool to encourage clients to rate the belief ("How much do you believe it?"), which supposedly decouples the belief from the self and their problem. Asking the client to give evidence that the belief is true permits consideration of evidence that the belief is not true. However, I have suggested in various places that obtaining knowledge of a client's mentation requires a number of strategies that are more insightful than checking off items in a questionnaire, keeping a record, or probing for thought sequences.

Remembering ancestrally relevant threats allows us to tap into the deeply ingrained implicit beliefs that form the client's schemata around emotionally intense constructs, such as identity, the nature of friendships, the importance of success, the security of parental and family relationships, or having a moral and ethical code. If past experiences are encoded affectively in memory, those memories and associated feelings need to be explored. It is especially valuable, while listening to their content, to judge clinically whether new processing of these memories is taking place or whether the client is merely rehearsing the same recalled content over and over again. New processing occurs—and can be encouraged—when the client questions his or her own prior assumptions, sees that a new way of thinking about a past event is possible, or links one negative schemata to a more positive one so that negative affect is neutralized. The following is the kind of client musings I have encountered in therapy that illustrate the reframing of old memories:

CLIENT: I've noticed that each time I've told you about how my ex-husband James treated me, and how angry it makes me to think about it, you didn't disagree or challenge my appraisal; you just asked a question like, "What were you expecting?" And that has made me think about one episode in particular when he really hurt my feelings. I know I was expecting him to support me better because I was under pressure at work. So I've begun to ask myself why he did not. And I've been wondering if it was because I never explained to him how I was feeling.

THERAPIST: Was it your responsibility to be that transparent? You were stressed yourself at the time. Perhaps he should have recognized that himself?

CLIENT: You're right up to a point; I'm not beating myself up about it. But as I rethink everything that happened I realize there was some fault on both sides. I've learned from that. I can think back on that incident and I can now feel some empathy for him. It was a bad time and he was doing his best. I want him to be happy. He's still the kids' dad and that is important. But I can tell you that when I start to judge Mark (my new boyfriend) negatively, I force myself to remember some of these terrible arguments I had with Jim, and that helps me focus on being really clear with Mark as to what I am really feeling. I remember my mom always saying "men are hopeless, they just can't read minds."

THERAPIST: Phooey! What an overgeneralization!

CLIENT: Don't get defensive! [Both laugh]. But the truth is one has to communicate feelings. I think I am much more open—I've got some new ideas about intimate relationships: there are always going to be some storms, but if you think about what the other person might be feeling, the sun will always come out afterwards—I know that sounds a bit corny.

THERAPIST: Corny or not, I'd tell you to write that down and stick it on your fridge, but I know you are not going to forget it. Just be sure you say those words to yourself when you are really upset about something—that is when we all tend to react in the hot, automatic, reflexive way I've been talking about!

Islands in the Stream

One of the issues we have run up against repeatedly is that the ecology of everyday thinking is not well researched or understood in psychology. This may be partly because the contents of an individual's moment-to-moment inner dialog is not terribly interesting. It becomes more relevant clinically, however, when daily thinking is made up of mostly egocentric introspection, negative ruminations, worry, hateful and angry thoughts, destructive fantasies of revenge or self-harm, or magical thinking that is divorced from reality. These are, to use laptop-computer jargon, the wallpaper behind more specific thoughts that might be expressed in therapy. The clinician cannot really judge how dominant specific negative thoughts might be unless he or she has a much better understanding of the background. Specific thoughts are islands in the stream of inner experience, consciousness. Are they part of the stream? Are they everywhere, or do they emerge when the client is stressed? Are they only uncovered by the clinician's probing questions? Cognitive therapists' questions are often leading, because such clinicians are attuned to the types of content that theorists and researchers tell us dominate the thinking of people with different syndromes.

Where the stream and its islands come from is also a matter to be assessed, since we also think—in cognitive theory—that the problem for clients is not restricted to thought content but relates strongly to thinking styles (processes and structures). We assume that clients arrive at misguided or distressing content because they appraise information in erroneous ways. We also assume that they have selectively processed and stored past experiences, and these, with their emotional nodes (emotional experiences are so easily remembered), provide the dynamics that influence the function of their thoughts. These emotional memories are the underlying schemata that have the potential to distort current experiences. They are System 1, hot, fast processing that enables snap judgment, automatic thoughts, and unreflective opinions, such as the prejudices and biases that we might be able to discount if we were thinking more coolly.

It is often pointed out that the information-processing biases associated with different clinical syndromes result in thoughts whose content is characteristic of the essential concerns manifest in each syndrome. This has been called "pathology congruent information-processing bias" (Savulich, Shergill, & Yiend, 2012). It is very relevant to clinicians to better understand the different cognitive biases that have been studied to the extent that these biases explain distorted thoughts. But as a causal explanation for the syndrome itself, there is a certain circularity in the observation, as I have already implied for explanatory theories of depression and anxiety. Nevertheless, the greater the precision regarding different biases that emerge from psychopathology research, the more likely it is that cognitive therapists can first assess and then find ways of counteracting the bias rather than simply disputing the expressed thought. For example, if people with schizophrenia have a reasoning bias of jumping to conclusions, treatment would involve providing them with lots of different information from different sources. And rather than offering this information directly, the therapist could encourage clients themselves to seek more information before making a judgment—about anything.

Another difference between surface thoughts and more global underlying beliefs that clinicians might consider during assessment is the relationship between a syndrome-specific negative thought and a general negative thought. A syndrome-specific thought in a client with an eating disorder might be "If I am not very thin, I won't be attractive." We might judge that as an irrational cognition leading to or representing a fear of weight gain. But a more general thought might be "People tend to judge me in a negative way that might make them reject me," revealing a fear of negative evaluation. Logically a fear of negative evaluation is a more general category that encompasses within it fearful thoughts of being unattractive and within that the explicit syndrome of negative thoughts about gaining weight. Thus it is not surprising that fear of negative evaluation is evident in different clinical syndromes, such as both eating disorders and social phobia (McClintock & Evans, 2001). This is a further example of a personality trait level of influence on expressed thoughts.

Cognitive Traps and Executive Control

Over and over again in the preceding chapters we encountered the fact that many clients are locked into vicious cycles of thought that are very like other dynamic relationships in behavior. Wells (2000) describes this kind of processing as the object mode of cognition: thoughts equate with reality, threats are real, and thoughts must be acted on to reduce threat, which becomes the primary goal in life. To achieve this goal, threats are monitored and evaluated but not tested, and the associated worry leads to threat-reducing actions, with the result that maladaptive "knowledge" (erroneous ideas) is strengthened.

But not all thoughts have these kinds of functional relationships with negative emotions. Everyone has negative thoughts at one time or another. But most of us can control them through metacognitive processes, such as deliberately not thinking about something and making an effort to forget a thought or idea that seems distasteful because it is not in keeping with our values. When effective, these self-control processes are like executive control processes in the steering of complex skills, because they require executive functions such as attending to something else, distracting oneself, and providing one's own counterarguments as to why a thought should not and will not be acted on. People seek clinical help when these cognitive executive control processes are not working for them or they have never acquired the ability to use them. Individuals expressing a declarative belief that they are a failure could be argued with in therapy, but it is still not obvious why one person uses the thought to plan and problem-solve and another ruminates about it and becomes a client.

It is additionally distressing not to be able to get destructive thoughts of what one might do in the future (like "I might hurt my baby" or "I might kill myself") out of one' consciousness. However, nonclients are able to construct plans that would decrease the likelihood of such things happening without these preventative actions becoming obsessively reinforced by reduction in the distress. If you think of the danger of having sharp knives around while the baby is playing in the kitchen, you might find a drawer where they can be kept securely, rather than on the counter in a knife block. But if you refuse to have any sharp object in the house because that makes you feel less threatened, that behavior has become overinfluenced by uncontrolled anxiety thoughts and the need to reduce them somehow. Thoughts about things you have done in the past that you know you should not have done generate feelings of regret or guilt. Adaptively, such feelings should motivate you toward acts of restitution or making amends, whereupon the negative feelings should decline and be replaced with self-compassion. Thoughts of how you have been wronged or disrespected evoke feelings of anger and hatred. It requires executive control skills to engage in very different thoughts of forgiveness. In all cases adaptive functioning requires executive control processes that are metacognitive: the ability to think about your thinking and not to be overreactive.

When Not to Probe; Just Listen or Reflect

All verbal psychotherapy depends on clients revealing their thoughts without self-censorship. Cognitive science warns us that relying on what people say to give us insight to their mental world is perilous We have seen that cognitions and feelings are always intermingled (a new term: "thought–emotion fusion"?), although there are strategies available to make conscious thoughts less subject to emotional distortion. The fact that inner thoughts do not necessarily precede spoken thoughts helps us understand why everyone can have vaguely defined feelings of discomfort, self-doubt, and anxieties about others. This uncomfortable combination of diffuse negative affect and unarticulated thoughts can be remedied by speaking them out loud to someone else. As the unspoken thoughts are not well formed and may be filled with contradictions and emotional ambiguity, it often takes a little while for a greater sense of clarity to emerge as the person struggles to represent them in words, reflects on how they sound in words, and changes the words if need be. Sometimes these thoughts are modified by writing narrative accounts of them, sometimes the struggle is aided by a well-placed reflection from an audience, and sometimes it is neutralized by simply letting the person express uncomfortable thoughts in a safe manner. By "safe" is meant that the thought, once articulated, will not shock or otherwise deter the listener and so can still be reflected upon. If the thought has no immediate consequence for the listener, the speaker is able essentially to try out different versions of the thought, think further about each of them, and use the affect experienced as information. Allowing the person to do this, and interjecting comments that only lead to clarification and not to censure, is what we mean by being a good listener. Thus, through spoken words to an important other person, one's own thoughts are clarified, using ourselves (especially our emotions, as Clore and Huntsinger, 2007, demonstrated) or the other individual as a feedback system—especially if this is one's therapist (Kohlenberg & Tsai, 1991).

Barriers caused by such individual differences can be minimized in therapy in a number of ways, all of them designed to help the client be more open-minded and self-reflective. Explaining what you are hoping to achieve can be useful, along the following lines:

> You have said a number of times that you feel confused; you don't know what to think, or what your future direction should be. That is a not uncommon experience. I think it might happen because your thoughts are often bundled up with different feelings. Some thoughts you may not even want to express to yourself as they will evoke unpleasant memories or cause unpleasant emotions. All of us avoid thoughts that cause us distress. But one of the outcomes of therapy should be that you become clearer about your own thoughts, be clearer about what you want out of life, and in the future be able to reflect more clearly about your own thoughts and perhaps better recognize the thoughts of others and how they might be different than your own. So in our initial conversations I will be trying to make that clarity more possible. To begin

> with, the thoughts you express may be vague, even contradictory, or even unacceptable to you. So I am just going to listen, without criticism, and you should try not to censor any of your thoughts—as you trust me, let's get everything out in the open at first and then we can together decide what to make of it all.

Mentalization-Based Treatment

Let us assume that some clients, especially those with a diagnosis of borderline personality disorder, are poor at reflecting on their own thoughts or reflecting on the thoughts of others or even that others have thoughts. This is what we have been calling difficulties with mentalizing. Mentalizing is the opposite of mind-blindness. The ability to make accurate appraisals of the thoughts of others is connected to but a little different from empathy skills, which require the ability to accurately recognize others' feelings. This ability to make sense of other people's mental processes is an essential attribute for therapists. We should not try to demonstrate our sensitivity by saying to clients, "I know what you are thinking right now," because we are not space aliens and never really do. What we want to achieve is their greater reflection on their thoughts and feelings, not simply putting new thoughts in their heads and affirming that we can entertain contradictory thoughts at the same time. Because mentalization-based therapy has recently emerged as part of modern psychoanalytic approaches (Bateman & Fonagy, 2006), it has not figured prominently in cognitive therapies, but it is implicit in much of the social skills development components, especially in dialectical behavior therapy. Our explorations of how and why thoughts change have certainly led to the recognition that metathinking (adaptive introspection, for example) is useful for clients to acquire, and by the same token helping them with ways of discovering what others are thinking should be of value, particularly in intimate relationships.

In mentalization-based treatment it is assumed that the relationship between therapist and client is the agent of change, as the therapist is able to model for the client the nature of mentalizing:

> The therapist's ability to use his [*sic*] mind and to demonstrate a change of mind when presented with alternative views is internalized by the patient. Gradually the patient becomes more curious about his own and others' minds, and is consequently better able to reappraise himself and his understandings of others. The continual reworking of perspectives on self and others in the context of an intense attachment relationship is the key to the process of change. (Bateman & Fonagy, 2013, p. 601)

The Two Systems: Easy (Fast) Versus Difficult (Slow) Thoughts

However we describe them—fast/slow, hot/cool, conscious/unconscious—the differentiation between two types or systems of cognition is fundamental to contemporary understanding of thoughts and thinking and to changing them. We have seen this repeatedly in previous chapters. In traditional cognitive therapy clinicians have tended to identify clients' automatic thoughts and to give them corrective feedback, either that they are wrong or dysfunctional. But the strong convergence of experimental evidence on fast versus slow, hot versus cool, and all the other models of dual processing can give therapists a stronger rationale for reducing automatic thoughts than simply asserting that they are irrational or irrelevant. This is an especially honest approach, as we have seen that everyone has automatic (fast, hot) thoughts and we need to have them, oftentimes, in order not to spend our mental lives lost in reflection and introspection. There is no exact formula for how to deliver this rationale, and clinicians must find their own words, but the message might go something like this (assuming a client with chronic social worries and low self-esteem):

> In psychology, a lot of research has shown that some of our thoughts are really fast, a bit impulsive if you like, and usually quite emotive. Think of the times you have made a snap judgment, or blurted out a remark that you later regretted, fired off a furious e-mail, bought something on impulse, or yelled at your child. I know I've done it; we all do it. Some of our other thoughts, however, are cool, and slow, and deliberate; sometimes we even think about our thoughts in reflective, constructive ways, not worrying about them! I am sure you can recall times that you have been contemplative, weighed up the evidence, checked the reviews on Yelp before picking a restaurant, asked some questions before you assumed someone was being dishonest, done your homework on the best investments. We really do need both kinds of thinking. Fast thoughts are absolutely necessary so we can get on and do other cognitive tasks; slow thoughts are needed so we make fewer errors of judgment in life. The problem is, however, that fast thoughts, because they tend to be based on emotion rather than reason, can get you into trouble at times. This is what I think happens to you a lot of the time: you are very quick to make self-critical comments to yourself, or quick to judge others, or quick to judge a situation as threatening, especially a dating situation. Because fast thinking is driven by hidden emotions, often based on your past experiences, you will not always be aware of why you have these thoughts. You say that you think being "fat" (your word, not mine) is disgusting—that's your automatic thought when you look

> in the mirror. Where does such a hot, fast thought come from? I don't know precisely, but probably from all times you have been teased, or from times you've gazed with envy on pictures of glamorous thin models or movie stars and thought you could be like them, or maybe you were embarrassed in a store trying on jeans that clearly didn't fit you. All these negative emotions are stored in your memory, not precisely but as general negatives and part of what we call a schema around ideas of weight, appearance, self-esteem, and so on. So I can't just say to you, "Stop having these negative thoughts!" They are automatic. But what we can do is look at ways of making some of these thoughts slower, cooler, more reflective, more rational, and, in your case, more accurate. And before we start I'm going to tell you another little fact from psychological research: when you are in a bad mood, or thinking negative thoughts, or feeling really depressed, guess what? The negative schema about your appearance becomes a little stronger and your automatic self-critical thought becomes even more likely. This is the curse of human consciousness: bad thoughts make other bad thoughts more likely. Zebras don't get ulcers, someone said! Why? Because between real-life episodes of danger—like being chased by a lion—they are not reflecting negatively on their experience, regretting going over to that patch of grass, blaming their mothers for not training them to run faster—hey, you get the idea. But the good news about human consciousness is that the same "priming" of new negative thoughts by current negative thoughts works just the same way in reverse: positive thoughts make it easier to remember other positive thoughts. I'm going to tell you how.

Rationales, even long-winded ones like these, I think are useful in therapy because they explain why a technique is being introduced and they engage the client in the model of treatment being used. They are respectful, because they assume that clients want to know as much as possible about the purpose of the therapeutic suggestions. Although rationales are still not precisely treatment, they sometimes have a beneficial effect as they give clients hope, give them an alternative narrative for their problem, and, as in the previous example, tell them why something might change without telling them they are foolish, or wrong, or sick to have the thoughts they disclose.

Explicitly Counteracting Closed-Mindedness (Cognitive Inflexibility)

I have mentioned a number of times the well-established CBT technique of suggesting to clients that they perform "experiments" to test their assumptions about the world, especially the anticipated reactions of other people. A particularly practical version of this approach is to somehow encourage engaging in daily activities that have been avoided due to the intense fear engendered. At the same time, we have seen that their erroneous thoughts are rarely derived from a lack of information. Rather, they are based on long-established habits of thought with attached emotional properties that sustain beliefs *despite* evidence to the contrary. So it would be naive to expect people's beliefs just to suddenly change, either because a therapist tells them they are incorrect or a practical trial is set up to disconfirm them. So simply setting up experiments for clients is no guarantee that they will alter firmly held thoughts. How can we get to the underlying factors that might promote thought change?

The status of the source of the new or contradictory information is important. Instead of asserting that as a therapist you know what you are talking about, or pointing to your degree certificates hanging on the wall, you first ask your client if he or she accepts your credibility as a source of information. The same idea of a preparatory "set" can be applied to the personal experiment technique. You ask clients to design their own test of their assumptions. If you simply give clients a way of testing their suppositions, they can (and do) easily come back later and argue it was not a valid experimental test. Clients offer rationalizations like, "Well, she reacted the way you predicted, but that is just one instance and she probably felt sorry for me rather than genuinely likes me." Best to establish ahead of time that the way evidence is going to be sought has validity and credibility.

Motivated Closed-Mindedness

Remember when talking to clients that while a warm, genuine relationship with a skilled professional of good reputation (that's you) may make the client more amenable to new thinking in therapy, clients by definition have many of the features that support closed-mindedness. Although common, you cannot really assume that this cognitive trait will be present, so there is an assessment task that needs to be inserted about here. There are instruments to measure closed mindedness, but you can assess from interview information the prevalence of causes of closed-mindedness. These include stress, depressed mood, high levels of rumination, and lack of outside social contacts who provide feedback and reassurance. A major causal influence on cognitive inflexibility is also the fact that certain negative ideas and thoughts can protect the client from even more distressing insights and memories. Jost (2006) called this "motivated" closed-mindedness. Not all clients have all of these features, of course. But most will have enough barriers to more rational thinking that direct persuasion is often difficult. As Dale Carnegie said, "A man convinced against his will is of the same opinion still." Anyone engaged in CBT will surely have had the experience of a client nodding earnestly in agreement while we deliver excellent advice, reassurance, or rationally alternative ways of looking at a situation, only to have the client return to the next session with the same (irrational) thoughts as before. Even if you are skilled in motivational interviewing, clients may state enthusiastically that they do see how they need to change yet not be able to alter long-practiced dysfunctional cognitive habits.

If closed-mindedness can be considered "motivated"—that is to say its function is to defend the ego from threats to security—telling dogmatic clients that they are closed-minded will not get you very far therapeutically. What is likely to be more successful is what Linehan (1993) in dialectical behavior therapy refers to as "wise mind" training (see Chapter 5). Wise mind is surely the opposite of closed-mindedness and puts the issue on the obverse side of the coin, as recommended by the positive psychology movement. Linehan's techniques to encourage wise mind in clients mostly revolve around entertaining new, positive, contradictory ideas simultaneously. By claiming closed-mindedness results from insecurity, social psychologists go further and propose that people have a need for self-integrity—to see oneself as basically good and virtuous. If you challenge a client's sense of identity, which does often happen in therapeutic contexts, particularly with clients whose behavior has been reprehensible, you threaten self-integrity. So it might be helpful to allow them to affirm their self-integrity in some other context. This is somewhat like a priming task. You can ask them to read a list of positive personal characteristics and life accomplishments and to rank them in terms of their personal importance, or you can ask them to write a brief report on their most positive feelings of self-integrity. The experimental evidence supports such procedures as a way of reducing inflexibility and closed-mindedness (Cohen et al., 2007). Depending entirely on the constellation of client concerns, it might also be necessary to first increase self-esteem, offer general reassurance, and talk the language of positive psychology—how you are going to focus on establishing the individual's strengths.

Opening Closed Minds

What else can be done to mitigate the barriers of closed-mindedness? First, it is worth assessing whether the client has a rigid personal rule like "never give in" or "don't accept excuses." To some extent these may simply be examples of cognitive inflexibility, but given our understanding of metacognition such implicit rules may contribute to fixed ideas about unwillingness to entertain alternate perspectives. Second, general stress and any sense of threat or foreboding needs to be reduced. There are so many stress-reduction strategies I do not try to list them, but the recommendation is simple enough. Before you attempt any serious work on cognitive change and restructuring, find strategies that reduce the client's stress, through supportive relationship building, practical environmental change, relaxation and meditation, and so on. Feelings of uncertainty are particularly likely to result in closed-mindedness (Kruglanski, 2004). Change and certainty are contradictory states.

Many people have a strong need to avoid uncertainty—in other words it is not simply experiential avoidance that is seen in clients, but uncertain experiences are particularly aversive. Kruglanski (2004) popularized in personality theory the need for closure, the preference for any answer on any given topic over confusion and ambiguity. Openness to experience is only one of three elements of uncertainty avoidance; the other two are need for order and intolerance of ambiguity. When combined with high and salient levels of threat perception, such as anxiety about death and perceiving the world as a dangerous place, the individual's political attitudes are likely to be conservative rather than liberal (Jost et al., 2007). Jost et al.'s theory is that conservatism as a political ideology is made up of two core components, resistance to change and opposition to equality, as these two attributes reduce uncertainty and threat, respectively.

Third, a therapist needs to try to discover the function of irrational thoughts and beliefs. It seems slightly paradoxical to be seeking the function of dysfunctional thoughts, but the term "dysfunctional" relates only to short-term negative effects for the client, whereas their function, in the traditional behavioral sense, refers to what deeper emotional protection these erroneous thoughts provide. A simple example might be the teenage girl with an eating disorder, whose irrational belief that she is too fat is "dys"functional in the sense that the belief contributes to very harmful behaviors, such as unhealthy dieting, excessive weight loss, and harmful vomiting. But the function of this belief could be that it counteracts the thought that she is unattractive and unacceptable to the opposite sex and diminishes the threat of being socially isolated. The traditional functional analysis is a way of probing, by careful questioning, what historical schema is fuelling these automatic thoughts and beliefs. And, as suggested in Chapter 3, when thoughts are expressed in words to an audience, there is a strong probability that the thought has a social function. Expressed thoughts like "I can't live without you" or "I never do anything right" are not simply irrational. They serve to elicit sympathy or reassurance, or they manipulate other people's feelings.

Treatment manuals are not always explicit about what sort of cognitive groundwork is needed prior to persuasive cognitive change. Take the case of juvenile offenders. One of the best validated programs, Aggression Replacement Training was designed originally by Arnold Goldstein and updated by Glick and Gibbs (2010). It advocates a three-pronged approach: increasing social skills, anger management, and, of special relevance to this discussion, "moral education"—teaching moral reasoning and increasing empathy for others using stories of classic moral dilemmas. There are four common cognitive distortions one might typically find in young people with histories of delinquent behavior: being self-centered, minimizing and mislabeling negative consequences, blaming others, and assuming the worst. These can be assessed by a scale constructed by Gibbs, Barriga, and Potter (2001) called the "How I Think" questionnaire. However, some underlying System 1 cognitions are quite complex: in appetitive (instrumental) aggression, thoughts of the victim's pain and distress are associated with feelings of power, excitement, self-efficacy, and pleasure (Elbert, Weierstall, & Schauer, 2010). Delinquent youngsters have a code of conduct that needs to be reframed. One of my clinical research students, Diana Paki (2012), argued and then demonstrated that New Zealand youth's transgressions when with peers, and their ease of manipulation by antisocial friends, were related to either one of two possible functions. These were fear of rejection (thought: "My friends will despise me or think I'm a coward") or a sense of loyalty to others (thought: "It's right to stick with your mates; all for one, one for all," or, since they had never heard of d'Artagnan or read Alexandre Dumas, "I've got their back"). Fear of rejection may not be a very noble cause of conformity, but fear is possibly one motive for our own morality. And the importance of loyalty is considered a noble virtue in many quarters—the US Marine Corps motto is "Semper Fidelis." Identifying these faulty beliefs may be necessary before a youngster can be persuaded by counterargument that it is actually better for one's ingroup and their corresponding respect for one to resist peer pressure and refuse to take part in antisocial, harmful, and dangerous actions.

Counterargument

The British programmer Paul Graham (2008) has proposed that the interactive Internet affords everyone much more opportunity to disagree with others' thoughts and has suggested a hierarchy of disagreement from name-calling at the bottom to refuting the central point at the top. Near the top is counterargument, which is backing up a contradiction with reasoning or supporting evidence. While we can certainly improve the quality of disagreement with clients, we do not really want therapeutic persuasion to sound like an argument. Many clients resist being controlled by someone else, as I detailed at some length in *How and Why People Change* (Evans, 2013). Clients are used to other people trying to persuade them that their ideas and beliefs are totally wrong. Just think of the arguments that an eating-disordered teen has had with her parents before ever getting into therapy. So a good recommendation is not to attempt to change a client's thoughts by direct confrontation and argumentative-sounding assertions. Doing so also makes it hard for therapists not to take a somewhat defensive position and insist on the correctness of their views. They may like closure too, and have a need for structure. The literature indicates that therapists' own ego involvement in verbal conflicts also represents motivated closed-mindedness, unless they are very willing to use the standard deflecting tactic: "You could be right." There is a wonderful country-western song popularized by Tanya Tucker, which starts with these words:

> There's a tree out in the backyard
> That never has been broken by the wind
> And the reason it's still standing
> It was strong enough to bend.

The third verse, showing a remarkable knowledge of 5th-century BC Buddhist philosophy (Dao De Jing; see Roberts, 2001), reveals the metaphor's meaning:

> When you say something that you can't take back
> Big wind blows and you hear a little crack
> When you say, "Hey, well, I might be wrong"
> You can sway with the wind till the storm is gone.

I can anticipate a little rolling of the eyes from those of you wanting and expecting science and being exposed to slightly clichéd song lyrics, but as we have seen throughout this book it is metaphorical language and poetry that taps into emotional systems—the way Teasdale (1999) has described so well. So even if you do not use this imagery to remind you not to directly contradict clients, the Dao De Jing advice that "the rigid and inflexible will surely fail while the soft and flowing will prevail" might still be useful for clients caught up in relationship conflicts. Other strategies of disputation are needed by therapists, as well as clients. One, for example, often attributed to Benjamin Franklin, is to pose the counterargument as though it were coming from somewhere else ("What would you say to someone who suggested . . .?"). In this way the therapist and the client are on one side of the debate and the counterargument ideas are on the other. The key thing to remember is that clients' cognitive resistance comes from needing to protect their egos (Baumeister, Smart, & Boden, 1996).

Many clients, however, are not closed-minded and are perfectly open to new perspectives and points of view. There has been much interest therapeutically in anxiety sensitivity, but perhaps we need also to consider a dimension such as threat sensitivity, particularly in people with posttraumatic stress disorder (Miller, 2003). For those who find lack of control and lack of certainty threatening and highly aversive, it might be useful to provide as much information as possible regarding what will happen in therapy and assured agreement as to what the outcome of therapy will look like. Also, therapists are not immune to closed-mindedness despite scientific training, because, I think it is fair to say, many of us find uncertainty creates anxiety. As Artemus Ward quipped: "It ain't what you don't know that gets you into trouble. It's what you know for sure that just ain't so" (Gilovich, 1991).

Metacognition: Reducing the Worry About Worry and the Depression About Depression

A common theme in acceptance and commitment therapy, but implicitly in other cognitive therapies as well, is that a problem for achieving therapeutic success is that clients are inflexible. That seems a bit like saying we have just concluded that life in the Arctic is hard because it is kind of cold up there. If people were flexible, if they did not resist change and showed cognitive resilience, they would not become clients. But let us for now accept that psychological inflexibility is a characteristic of some clients and that helping them reduce it would facilitate their gaining the lives (lifestyles) they value. Experiential avoidance is an example of inflexibility. Bond et al.'s (2011) scale to measure this construct contains items such as "I'm afraid of my feelings" and "Emotions cause problems in my life." I would propose that "experiential avoidance" is a general term meaning warding off new or aversive experiences and thoughts *because* the person has a low tolerance for the resulting negative feelings. This low tolerance is sometimes called *anxiety sensitivity* or *fear of fear* when the situation is threatening. In depression the phenomenon is called *aversion sensitivity*. Depressed mothers, for example, are thought to have low tolerance for conflict and make efforts not to think about aversive behavior in their children, resulting in their parenting often being unresponsive (Dix, Moed, & Anderson, 2014). There are no exact equivalents for other negative emotions such as anger or grief; however, people find chronic anger exhausting, and some grief is so painful the thought of experiencing it a second time can cause people to be less willing to commit to romantic relationships or feel too deeply for another person or child.

It is widely recognized that the cognitive anticipation of symptoms themselves can be aversive; relapses are dreaded, and clients seek safety in monotonous activities and routines. People who experience psychotic episodes remember them afterward with embarrassment and shame, unless surrounded with compassion. In other words, because negative thoughts, emotions, and remembered aversive experiences are difficult for some people to endure, clients go to considerable lengths to avoid them. This accounts for a great many maladaptive behaviors that make one feel better (or less bad) but only in the short run. Pertinent examples for clients who have endured sexual abuse as children are emotional detachment (numbing of feelings), drug use, checking, self-harm, blaming and attacking others, and promiscuous relationships (Pechtel, Evans, & Podd, 2011). Despite harmful physical consequences, purging immediately minimizes the fearful thought of weight gain in clients with bulimia. Trying hard not to think about a traumatic experience, ruminating about how the trauma could have been prevented or getting even with an assailant, staying up until very late to avoid nightmares or to stay vigilant to intruders, and giving up pleasurable activities because one might be punished again or will be reminded of the trauma and not be able to manage the emotions are all common but dysfunctional avoidance strategies for people with posttraumatic stress disorder (Ehlers & Clark, 2000). Thus encouraging clients to be less avoidant and more tolerant (accepting) of negative thoughts and affect is a fairly general psychotherapeutic technique, particularly in behavior therapy and now in CBT.

Using Words to Manage Moods and Feelings

In children, cognitively seeking further information in situations of doubt is sometimes recommended as a useful strategy to break negatively reinforcing traps (Chen, Zeltzer, Craske, & Katz, 1999), but it has its downside. Asking a parent or a nurse in a medical procedure "Is this going to hurt?" will usually result in reassurance that it will not, or only a little bit. If that turns out to be incorrect, the child's appraisal of the value of adult information will be compromised. So we need to be careful about the information provided to counteract irrational fears, and this can be done in tandem with a memory reappraisal strategy when the child has had prior experiences of potentially aversive medical procedures (Chen, Zeltzer, Craske, & Katz, 2000). The child's questions about the coming experience, for example, can be responded to in ways such as, "Remember the last time you were here in the hospital, what happened then? Yes it was unpleasant, but you were very brave, and afterwards you said it wasn't as bad as you thought it might be. Remember how the doctor said you had done great? And the nurse gave you a lollipop because you were so brave."

Just as name-calling is hurtful, so getting positive names shows the coping potential of words in the management of feelings: in the tolerance of, not necessarily removal of, all anxiety or other negative affect. A delightful example comes from the charitable project Being Brave. A representative story is recounted by a young woman who had to undergo numerous heart operations as a child, each one making her more scared. But then she realized that among her family she was the one who could chase away insects, go down the really tall slide in the playground, and eat gummy worms with impunity. So when she was four she told her mother:

> "It's okay. You don't have to call me Elizabeth anymore. You can call me Brave Girl." She did, and she helped me to be brave. I held onto that name I had given myself. . . . If I was going to make it through the medicine and the machines again, I had to be brave. There was no other choice. I'm 23 years old now, and my heart is doing well. But every time I go into the doctor's office for a yearly check-up, I remember how it felt to be small and scared. I remember how it felt to need to be brave. (http://being-brave.com/)

In the developmental psychology literature, this kind of approach is called "emotion talk" (Gottman, Katz, & Hooven, 1997). Parents who see emotional distress in their children as a teachable moment, an opportunity to develop self-regulation strategies using internalized thoughts and problem-solving cognitions, have children who are better able to regulate their feelings. My colleague Shane Harvey and I have shown how emotion talk is used by emotionally intelligent teachers or can be taught to those who are unfamiliar with the idea (Evans & Harvey, 2012). We gave teachers a five-step plan. The first step is to for teachers to recognize their own and their students' emotions and second to see emotion as an opportunity to teach social and emotional skills. Third, they should help students label their feelings—a key ingredient of affect regulation by thought, as it is hard to have thoughts without words and labels. Empathizing with the child is the fourth step, important for validating the child's feelings. (Think how often as parents or teachers we do the opposite: negate children's reality by saying to an upset child, "Oh, come on! It wasn't that bad. No need to cry; you're not really hurt!") Finally, teachers should offer simple solutions for future occurrences of the situation that led to the negative feelings, preferably based on their own experience.

Offering a New Narrative

There has always been an uncomplicated yet convincing rationale for cognitive perspectives on emotional problems, and Beck has illustrated this basic model with elegant simplicity. The established value of treatments based on the essential elements of Beck's theories of depression and anxiety provided the impetus for him to explore another vital dimension of human emotional dysfunction, one outside the usual province of mental health yet inside the province of forensic/correctional psychology: anger, hatred, and violence. Beck's analysis is identical to other perspectives I have introduced, even if the words might be slightly different. Cognitive errors and distortions arise from "primal thinking." This is the rapid, hot, System 1 level of information processing when confronted with a threat:

> personally relevant details are taken out of context, the meanings tending to be excessively egocentric and the conclusions too broad. Consequently, the thinking is unbalanced: it may be satisfactory for true life-or-death emergencies, but it is disruptive to the smooth functioning of everyday life and to the solution of normal interpersonal problems. (Beck, 1999, p. 73)

But there is no equally simple and straightforward translation of these basic ideas to treatment strategies. Ironically, there does seem to be a therapeutic effect of simply explaining these basic assumptions to clients, at least those who are reasonably inquisitive, self-analytic, and open-minded. Acceptance of a new model of how thoughts, while powerful, do not have to be in control of feelings and actions that are unwanted does not come easily to clients, for the numerous reasons we have examined. When thoughts have the property of beliefs, especially around faith and moral rules, the constructivist philosophy implicit in cognitive therapy is useful. When clients' thoughts are constrained by absolutist beliefs, exposing them educationally to societies, cultures, or times in history when very different beliefs were held is one nonargumentative way of revealing how thoughts that seem to be truisms are always socially constructed.

An alternative strategy is not to appraise or encourage self-assessment of negative things done or undesirable characteristics revealed. Instead it might be possible to encourage explicit and active attempts to show positive feelings toward one's own behavior independent of any judgment as to whether these are intrinsically good or bad. This is a strategy that Neff (2003) has advocated as "self-compassion." These are thoughts that explicitly promote forgiveness of one's own weaknesses or misdemeanors. It might seem somewhat self-indulgent unless the self-compassion is tied to (motivates) subsequent efforts to improve: to behave closer to one's own values and standards in the future. Self-compassion involves the linking of explicitly positive (positive affectively laden) thoughts to self, regardless of the nature of one's self characteristics.

Neff (2003) has described self-compassion as a healthy form of self-acceptance. She suggests three components of the construct. One is being kind and understanding to oneself when experiencing suffering or judging oneself negatively. Another is a broader recognition that across all humanity pain and failure are common and unavoidable experiences. Finally, self-compassion encompasses our old friend in cognitive therapy, the acceptance rather than avoidance of painful thoughts and feelings—but without exaggerated affect such as drama and self-pity. It is a catchy concept that can readily be explained to clients who are excessively self-critical and judgmental. Therefore, like all other therapy techniques, there are features of the idea (especially for clients whose moral and religious beliefs acknowledge forgiveness rather than retribution) that help create the kind of generalized self-worth viewpoint that is valued in American and probably other cultures.

Compassion is the key emotion emphasized in what is now a distinctive form of cognitive therapy: compassionate mind training. Like other specific therapies within the cognitive stable, Paul Gilbert (2005) developed this one in the context of a certain type of clinical problem—shame, guilt, and self-deprecation. A long time ago, before homosexuality and the gay lifestyle became highly acceptable in America and Western Europe and before the AIDS epidemic, I was consulted by a gay client, Claude, a man in his 50s, whose depression was expressed in the form of self-hatred. He judged himself to be too weak to resist urges, he felt disgusted at his behavior in public toilets and the bathhouses he frequented, he criticized openly gay people, and he despised the young men whom he occasionally paid for sex. My approach at the time was to focus on what I saw as his limited social skills in meeting men of his own age and social status, with similar refined cultural interests, who would be mutually seeking longer term, more meaningful relationships. This was moderately successful in decreasing the impersonal, promiscuous activities that he was most ashamed of. And hopefully he sensed no negative judgment on my part, even though I insisted in a very directive tone that inviting rent boys back to his apartment was reckless behavior. However, had Gilbert's (2005) compassion-based therapy been around to inspire me with ideas, I would most certainly have adopted his model as the guiding treatment rationale.

Compassionate therapy, like any other cognitive approach, is multifaceted, but there are some distinctive features that would have been relevant in Claude's case. First, a compassionate, accepting relationship with the client is important. I had that, and he expressed surprise sometimes that I was not shocked or repulsed by his revelations. But today, following Gilbert's (2005) work, I would spend more time differentiating between acceptance and nonjudgmental evaluation of which activities had potentially harmful consequences and needed to be changed—like anonymous oral sex encounters in public toilets that ran the risk of arrest. I would present Gilbert's model of Claude's self-criticism being a self-to-self relationship (despite my reservations about dualism) and seek explanations for the function of the critical self. I would trace the origins of his negative attitude toward homosexuality, in family history, in his religion (Catholic), in school experiences of bullying and teasing, in the hundreds of pejorative terms for gay people used in the media, and in the insults he experienced during a short, failed marriage. I would point out that the self-hatred and criticism was not functional—that it had no effect on his behavior nor permitted him to lead a life closer to his expressed values. I would teach a strategy for self-soothing, such as using imagery of a perfect nurturer, perhaps an angel or Christ forgiving sinners. I would suggest that his internal, critical self was perpetuating such bullying and prejudice and encourage some kind of writing activity, such as composing a compassionate letter to a friend who had come out of the closet to the great distress of his family. I would identify self-attacking thoughts, have Claude write them down, encourage him to use introspection to determine where they came from, and construct a compassionate reframe involving self-nurturing. I would have him read biographies of great humanists who have benefitted their society who were known to be homosexual in order to separate thoughts about homosexuality from thoughts about worthlessness. I would encourage empathy and compassion directly by having Claude generate instances of his ability to feel warmth toward others independent of any judgment as to their worthiness, morality, or social value. I would promote thoughts of belonging to a greater identity—humanity—rather than a subgroup of people: White, male, homosexual Catholics. While all of these are merely a smattering of the techniques encompassed in compassionate mind training, they give a sense of how Gilbert's ideas can be individualized for different client concerns.

Individualizing Cognitive Therapy and Making It Memorable

One of the big problems for a unified science of cognitive therapy and change is that the most popular and well-validated treatment manuals have strategies that are then confused with treatment principles. Meditation themes and mindfulness imagery are good examples of content trumping the therapeutic function of cognitive imagery, which should vary according to client needs. Such imagery might be to temporarily calm a stressed client; it might be to offer vivid imaginal scenes that serve to distract a client form negative thoughts; it might be part of a mindfulness training exercise to refocus attention away from threat cues. Or, because therapy needs to establish some new or changed schemata, often in competition with a long history of emotional experiences that have shaped a client's thinking, all treatment plans need to be memorable. This is where poetry, song lyrics, inspirational quotes, greeting cards, and posters all come in handy, as props, not as techniques.

In clinical contexts the thoughts that need to change or be changed are those that are serving directly to cause or prolong distressing negative feelings or those that interfere with the performance of adaptive and meaningful behaviors contributing to a person living a full and satisfying life. The kinds of changes that are needed, therefore, are in the frequency of those dysfunctional thoughts, in their content, or in the meaning and value that their content has for the person. Equally important is to discover and change the processes whereby experiences and situations that could easily be interpreted in a positive or at least neutral way are interpreted in a negative way. So taking the common self-deprecating thought "I am a failure" we want to (a) change its frequency; (b) change its content to "I did not succeed on that task"; (c) change its value ("I'm a failure, but I don't care"); (d) change the process for reaching the conclusion ("I did not succeed on that task; it was a hard one, and I did my best, and it is the trying that counts"); and (e) change the relationship with the incentive ("It made me feel disappointed in myself at first, but I can live with not succeeding on *that* task because now I know the next time I need to prepare better and get more help").

The fundamental limitation in designing cognitive therapy treatments is that while we know our own thoughts and can usually communicate them reasonably well, conscious experiences are

> but a sliver of the stuff the mind does. [Conscious thought] is the only aspect of the mind we subjectively experience, and hence the only aspect we believe exists. The truth is that thoughts, feelings, and behavior operate largely without deliberation or conscious recognition. It is the routinized, automatic, classically conditioned,

> precompiled aspects of our thoughts and feelings that make up a large part of who we are. We don't know what motivates us, even though we are certain we know just why we do the things we do, choose as we do, take action as we do. We have no idea that our perceptions and judgments are incorrect (as measured objectively), because we aren't confronted with such evidence, precisely because it remains outside conscious awareness. We don't recognize that our behavior is often at variance with our own intentions and aspirations. (Banaji, 2007a, pp. 263–264)

Clinicians need to be especially interested in why thoughts do *not* change, and one obvious reason is that what I have been describing as automatic inferences and appraisals of situations occur at a nonconscious level. Our ability to introspectively understand the way our judgments of others are dominated by System 1 processes is limited. How can we become more aware of these influences on our thoughts? One strategy was suggested by Banaji (2007a, 2007b) and others (see Chapter 8), and that is we can do two things when tempted by highly positive stimuli: one is to focus our thoughts on neutral, "cool," nonconsummatory aspects of the stimulus, and the other is to form implementation intentions regarding how one is going to act when presented with the tempting stimulus.

The Interrelationship of Cognitive Constructs

If we can agree that at least four elements of thought (content, process/function, structure, and personality/cognitive trait) are found in the standard portrayals of CBT rationales, the reality remains that we know little about how they interrelate in adverse life circumstances or respond interactively to therapeutic intervention. Take one of the central constructs in all cognitive therapies: acceptance. At the trait level, we have Ellis's notion of unconditional self-acceptance. Presumably this trait (cognitive style) is manifest in a context: when encountering adversity or making a mistake, a person lacking this characteristic would be self-critical and thus prone to negative moods. Beck too would doubtless argue that if one's global beliefs were to attribute adversity to external forces (external locus of control), no self-blame should occur. However, there are other cognitive styles that have been hypothesized. For example, when people able to show self-compassion do hurtful or harmful things, they should use their compassionate style to reduce any prolonged negative affect. Similarly, people who have been taught in therapy to eliminate their experiential avoidance (Hayes's key construct) might have negative thoughts and affect after adversity or error but then simply accept such thoughts and feelings, rather than avoid them, resulting in no continuation of distress. In truth the way similar theories using slightly different constructs make the development of a cohesive cognitive theory of the origins of dysfunctional thoughts seem remote at this point in time.

One reason for this is that the operational definitions of most cognitive constructs developed in CBT have not advanced as quickly as has the development of treatment protocols. Studies still have to rely on self-report questionnaires that are inadequate as measurement devices of subjective and often unknowable internal and implicit processes. Thus it is not surprising that psychometric measures of the supposedly quite different constructs of *conditional (low) self-acceptance, experiential avoidance, dysfunctional attitudes, global irrationality,* and *negative automatic thoughts* all correlate quite highly with each other (Cristea, Mongomery, Szamoskozi, & David, 2013). When a series of closely related variables interact with each other, or play mediating and moderating roles, it typically means, however, that therapy needs either to address all of the variables in the interacting system or carefully target those that are "keystones" that sustain the interaction pattern (Voeltz & Evans, 1982). Even if the exact order and sequence of the interactions can only be guessed at, it is a widely recognized rule of thumb when constructing case conceptualization models that interventions need to be directed to as many of the hypothesized relationships as possible (Evans, 1985; Persons, 1989). Next I offer two examples of what this might look like in practice.

Two Client Illustrations

Imagine you have a woman client who is clinically depressed. Depressed mood renders negative elements of any situation more salient and thus tends to make her more likely to formulate self-deprecating and hopeless remarks to herself and others. When these constitute a major part of her internal stream of everyday thoughts, they are likely to evoke an even more negative mood—a classic self-defeating spiral of thought–emotion interaction. This client may feel pessimistic about the benefits of cognitive psychotherapy, may not be in a good frame of mind to listen to the therapist's words, and may have core beliefs that are not easily altered by counterarguments. The client may also have limited insight into these causal processes because the negative affect is providing feedback that the world is bad and life truly hopeless; otherwise why would she be feeling this way? And indeed, because the client's mood is negative, she is engaging in few potentially reinforcing behaviors, and so there is no new contradictory evidence based on experience. Worse still, the limited behavioral repertoire means her stream of consciousness is not about planning, thinking of others, and constructively working out problems in her head, and her social communications and exchange of ideas with others is equally limited to melancholic themes.

Based on this picture, I list here some ideas you can consider and things you can do as her therapist, not necessarily in the sequence in which you would do them but starting off with the more distal, general kinds of influences.

You want the client to have greater insight—not in the traditional sense of where the depression originated but in the sense of having a better understanding of psychological processes. Thus you might offer a conceptualization of what you think is going on, but do not insist on the client accepting it right away. The model, however, will be the framework you keep returning to.

You want the client's mood to improve—that seems only too obvious, as that is the desired outcome of therapy, but in this case the goal is not a cure but some simple, short-term gains. This will not be achieved by telling the client about all the good things in her life (persuasion), but you might ask her to construct some herself, list them and read them out loud. Give her feedback when she uses words with negative connotations rather than more positive synonyms, some of which you can suggest to her.

Encourage her to savor any everyday experience, however trivial, like her first crunchy bite of her breakfast toast, and use mindfulness training to allow any thoughts about her situation to enter consciousness in a nonjudgmental way.

Facilitate her entertaining new beliefs by means of the strategy described in which examples of how major societal ideas have changed even within her lifetime.

Each time she says something blatantly irrational, stop her and ask her to generate an alternative, more rational version. Ask her to write it down and rehearse the statement at home.

Each time she blames herself for things that have gone wrong in her life, explain to her the importance of being self-compassionate.

Offer her a short lesson on the psychology of thoughts and elucidate the difference between automatic (hot) and controlled (cool) thinking.

Probe for past experiences in which she has built up an image of herself and look at the words, constructs, and metaphorical terms with which she represents her identity. Use this discussion to restructure some of her emotional memories or schemas.

Ask for memories of past experiences of episodes of depression and allow her to describe emotively how these episodes felt. Follow that by suggesting that efforts to avoid these negative experiences and her apparent failure to do so are making her both fearful of the next outcome (damaging family relationships, being hospitalized, having suicidal thoughts) and making her ruminate despondently about her present situation. Explain the phenomenon of depression about depression.

Does this list look like an eclectic hodge-podge of everything that has ever been proposed across a variety of different cognitive therapies? It is not, really. It is just a plan, based on concepts that are all drawn from our analysis of how thoughts are controlled and how they can change. They are not mutually exclusive nor equally important nor equally difficult or time-consuming, and the timing of them is something of an art and depends on the individual's circumstances, how many sessions are available, and how much the client seems drawn to you and is engaged in therapy. Also, this collection does not constitute a full psychological treatment, since it says little about behavioral activation, solving some of the real problems and stressors in the client's life, and especially modifying her social environment, and so on—all of the things well known to be part of the effective treatment of depression (actually treating any syndrome "transdiagnostically"), described in *How and Why People Change* (Evans, 2013).

Furthermore, these suggestions are hardly original and are certainly lacking in detail as to how they should actually be done, which may be where the devil lies. Still, the techniques you use would also depend on how much weight you give to the many devilish cognitive principles outlined in this book. You would also need to adjust your discourse (words used) to the verbal abilities, style of information processing, and core beliefs, attitudes, interests, and prejudices revealed by the client. You would need to practice mind-mindedness in order to be able to appreciate and accept the client's cognitive perspective on things. If you want to influence her thoughts, you would need to know what she daydreams about, what she reads, what she watches on TV, what her family say to her, and so on. It would be important to have a sense of what her life goals and values are and what a worthwhile therapeutic outcome really means to her. You could try strengthening self-improvement goal pursuits by having her fantasize good outcomes and contrasting fantasies and thoughts about difficulties and plausible barriers.

As a second and different case example, we return to the client who I used as an illustration in Chapter 1: the sex offender about to be paroled. I cannot imagine that a successful outcome could possibly be achieved unless the local probation or rehabilitation service has a wrap-around program of supports that will help this man find a suitable place to live where there are risk-reduction protections in place against reoffending (close monitoring) but no community disclosure that results in stigma and discrimination. He will also need a job and, depending on the length of his sentence and previous employment, some reskilling. If he has a drinking or drug problem, that will need to be considered as well. If he has no ongoing partner he may need help with social skills and opportunities to meet people that are normative (a church social or sporting club, rather than a bar or casino) and that offer suitable choices of women to date. If he has a spouse and children, he will need workable strategies for how to manage family interactions. If he is a member of a minority ethnic group, it will be helpful if his probation office is of the same ethnicity, has prestige in the local community, and is possibly a bit older. All of that is a standard, though not always achieved, clinical treatment plan upon release.

Without that plan you cannot expect as his therapist to accomplish much, but that plan alone will not succeed at all if there is no significant shift in his cognitions. Thus the cognitive therapy component can start to be addressed while he is still incarcerated. It has elements of a relapse prevention plan, but its primary focus is to prevent reoffending. Relapse prevention strategies involve identifying the external environmental triggers, as well as the internal thoughts and ruminations that make a deliberate plan of criminal action more probable. In this client's case (let's assume), it is related to his drinking problem, because when inebriated he is disinhibited and shows less self-control. We also know that his sexual fantasies and the pornography to which he masturbates regularly usually involve themes of force, coercion, and opportunistic sex. We would try to change that. Let us presume that he has erroneous beliefs about women having tempted him in the past, and he also has some narcissistic thoughts that he is desirable to women, as well as grandiose ideas that he deserves their attention. Let us also assume that he has a problem controlling anger and that you have managed to construct a fairly detailed offense chain depicting the events and thoughts that led up to his most recent offense—a sexual assault. What would you do?

In my case, being a white, middle-class, educated male, I want to learn more about his educational level, his understanding of abstract concepts, his implicit theories about the world, his religion, his gang affiliations, and, because he is from an indigenous culture, I would enlist some support from a cultural advisor. I would ask for ideas, myths, stories, songs, and engrained historical traditions from his culture that would give me a source of symbols and archetypes to incorporate into my own narrative with this client. To obtain his own concepts rather than any cultural stereotypes to which he may not resonate at all, I would let him talk, maybe for a session or two, about his background, his family, his childhood, his experiences at school, his friends, his partner, his moral code, and whether he has any passionate interests that I can use later for metaphorical or poetic analogies. I will surprise him by being nonjudgmental, and if he notices I will introduce ideas of self-acceptance and self-compassion. I will emphasize that compassion is not about offering excuses or avoidance but taking responsibility for approaching new resolutions never to reoffend. If he articulates vague goals of being a better person, I will steer his discourse toward making implementation intentions. I will listen closely for irrational beliefs, unwise clichés, prejudicial attitudes, and defensive posturing, like justifications for his antisocial behavior. I want to find out whether in the various programs he has undertaken he has recognized whether and how his thinking has changed—these self-recognized improvements in his thoughts will be what are consistently reinforced with encouragement and approval in order to restructure his recalled memories of moments of effective treatment.

It might be useful to start a simple program that will help him better interpret the thoughts (desires, intentions, and fears) of others. We want him to recognize that others will think differently than he does, even if they appear to be giving off signals he thinks he can read. This can be done with hypothetical "emotional intelligence" exercises (e.g., "Mary said she was feeling sad because her dog was killed by a hit-and-run driver and she asked you to give her a hug. You held her tight. What could you say that would make her feel better?") or in the context of therapy ("When you told me that you were mad at me for canceling our last session, how do you think that made *me* feel?"). The goal is to encourage perspective-taking with prosocial themes that encourage acceptance of other viewpoints. We should address his characteristic narcissism when thinking about others, whom he habitually puts down. Beck (1999) offers some examples of shifting themes from narcissistic-expansive to altruistic-humanistic, such as "Their lives are expendable" to "All lives are sacred." His grandiose beliefs about his own importance need not be challenged as being irrational, because they serve the reinforcing function of sustaining the perception of self-respect and the respect of others that he craves. He needs an alternative narrative regarding what makes him a worthwhile person—not a message that he has a life of no value and thus his self-esteem is unwarranted.

Sexual assault is likely to be motivated by more than one of the dominant belief systems tendered in Chapter 1. While he may have erroneous beliefs about women's desire for him, he may well also have hostility toward women, especially when he misinterprets their responses to him as putting him down, belittling him, or threatening his masculinity by talking about other men and triggering an emotion like jealousy. A combination of thoughts of hostility and jealousy provides a fertile backdrop for anger, with coercive sex used as a form of violence. Beck (1999, p. 250) provides a detailed offense chain of thoughts (misinterpretations) and feelings that I paraphrase for this offender: the woman is critical or refuses sex; the man interprets this as "she thinks I'm a nobody"; the man feels belittled and feels like a victim; anger is aroused and there is a desire to retaliate, to show her who is boss; the man feels entitled because the woman deserves to be put in her place; the man initiates coercive sexual approach. Each of these stages in the process are automatic thoughts, and Beck would argue that as the client's thought chain is probed, the origins in earlier schemata are explicated. Conditional beliefs ("If she doesn't want to have sex with me, it means she doesn't respect me as a man") need to be corrected; imperatives ("She should desire me; I'm great in bed") can be questioned by whether such beliefs are reasonable or have a logical foundation. I would never suggest that the perceived rejection was not in fact disrespectful or not intended to cause the client to stop making advances. Very often this *is* a correct interpretation of other people's desires and intentions. Therefore the thought is not irrational at all but has to be accepted. Acceptance is easier if the client uses rejection experiences as a motivator for self-improvement goals, such as refining his social skills, to be more appealing by being empathetic and enhancing communication, and to be more honest and less self-serving.

One difference between this type of client and the depressed client previously considered is that the sex-offending client has powerful behavioral habits that need to be controlled for the sake of the broader society, rather than feeling the misery of dysfunctional emotions. Thus the role of thought in regulating behavior rather than regulating feelings takes center stage. Return to Chapter 7 and see where self-regulation and better choice-making is discussed. Anger, Beck argues, is a negative affect that should have information value—it should be a signal or a warning *not* to take action. I would suggest possible distractions to this client, such as reinterpreting the assumed disrespect or using a self-control strategy such as a relaxation procedure to lower arousal. I might implement social norms theory, using respected members of this man's own community to emphasize what mainstream cultural beliefs and standards actually are.

Reflection

I hope it is convincing by now that it is possible to change people's thoughts and that, as a result, their characteristic feelings and behaviors will change as well. It is also true that interpersonal or social verbal processes (as input) will change thoughts (the output) and that that fact supports and essentially validates the usefulness and purpose of cognitive psychotherapy, since it is a phenomenon of verbal interaction between therapist and client. There are many ways in which this verbal influence on thoughts can be achieved, and there is no one true way or even any one unique way. None of the supposedly different cognitive "therapies" has a special method for changing thoughts that the others do not have. However, there are some methods for changing thoughts that none of them have, which is where the research literature is important and why we continue to claim to be scientist-practitioners. If you know the research literature, you can deduce your own techniques, and so you should.

That is a strong summary statement of facts and may well be disputed and resisted by those who are convinced that their therapeutic methods are special. However, for cognitive therapy as a whole it is very good news. It means that cognitive therapy is one thing, not many, and we can focus our interest on meaningful processes of change and not get too bound up with the special terminology of individual theorists. It is great news for trainees because it demystifies all of the different therapies that supposedly require long hours of training and initiation rites.

Clients' thoughts are both bounded, in Herbert Simon's (1983) sense of being specific to the present context (situation or task), and free-floating, in the daydreamy sense of consisting of streams of plans, worries, images, and memories not related to the current situation. Thus thoughts of the moment are changed by changed situations and thoughts of the future are changed by changed experiences. New experiences give us new memories and with them new ways of thinking about ourselves and our circumstances that are designed to be inconsistent with previously learned beliefs, ideas, and attitudes that are no longer helping us meet our personal needs. Cognitive psychotherapy is one of those experiences that is especially focused on old and new thoughts, probing for them, asking for their reexamination (metacognition), and reality testing (ways of disconfirming incorrect inferences or confirming positive expectations). In this social interaction the client's attention is focused strongly on what he or she typically thinks about emotionally laden and life-relevant events. The therapist's task is to ensure that this kind of metacognition is in the forefront of the therapeutic interaction. In that way it is noticeably different in both theory and purpose from more traditional behavior therapy, where there is a similar emphasis on what clients are doing—what their habits are, what skills they have, how they might change their typical practices, and how they can develop behaviors that better serve their goals. Goals in a clinical context, of course, can be either approach oriented (be happier, have more friends, get better grades at school, have a more exciting sex life) or avoidance oriented (be less depressed, no longer feel anxiety, stop hearing voices, reduce conflict within the family), but in the end are all related to having a less stressful, less distressing, more fulfilling life, more under one's own control and likely to lead to accomplishment of bigger issues, such as being a good parent, being a productive scientist, or leading a "life of value."

If the underlying emotive influence is changed, then one assumes that the negative thought that is influenced by this emotion will be reduced. This process is not always obvious in cognitive therapy, as it is the thought to be changed that is assumed to lead to the emotion that makes the client a client. But the sequence is probably more complicated than that. The client states he is depressed (mood or feeling) and expresses the thought that he is a failure at work. The therapist judges that such a thought ("I am a failure") is irrational, not based on factual evidence, and is thus contributing to his depressed mood. But further analysis might reveal that his thought that he is a failure comes from a tendency to notice his errors at work and to discount his successes. The therapist then assumes that such a bias in processing experiential information comes about because the client is overly focused on not making errors. This mental focus comes about because of another thought–emotion connection, which is the belief that one needs to be perfect (the client is a perfectionist and errors are upsetting). That too might be judged irrational but related possibly to a need to please strict parents in his early childhood, whose love was conditional on success. That could be a schema, a core belief, a personality trait, an implicit belief—it probably does not matter what we call it but we need to understand its function. So our persuasive reasoning with the client will address more than the irrational thought "I'm a failure" and also address the thought "I have to be perfect."

If this underlying belief and its origins ring true for the client, then the therapist's explanation leads to new insights. But does insight alone lead to a change in an emotion? I think not. The acceptance of "I am a perfectionist because my parents punished my failures" is not guaranteed to eliminate the emotion (guilt or fear depending on the type of parenting experience) when failure occurs. Cognitive therapy addresses the functional but unconscious influence of past learning in a number of ways, including diminishing the emotional power of the thought ("I have to be perfect") and restructuring the schema that determines its emotional (affective) valence.

Cognitive *skills*, meaning the better use of our rational thought (Kida, 2006), underlie a range of therapeutic methods. These include having more rational judgment and being able to focus one's thinking on important things in life rather than less important negative feelings that achieve little. They also include problem-solving skills and self-control techniques that allow people to manage urges and resist temptation, when surrendering to such enticements would not, in the long run, be in their best interests. Changing our thoughts also allows us to plan, to make better decisions about the future, and allows parents and teachers to appreciate children in all their variety rather than be continually exasperated by them. New thoughts resolve guilt, increase compassion, and enable one to enjoy the moment. Most important, changed thoughts about the nature of thought allow for a reappraisal of feelings we accepted as inevitable and valid.

There is growing recognition across a range of psychiatric and psychological opinion that there is more commonality among syndromes in the *Diagnostic and Statistical Manual of Mental Disorders* (fifth edition; American Psychiatric Association, 2013) than has been recognized in the past. Ideas are emerging about transdiagnostics and the role of personality types underlying a range of disorders (Barlow, Sauer-Zavala, Carl, Bullis, & Ellard, 2014; Caspi et al., 2014). Clinical psychological disorders truly are *emotional* disorders rather than cognitive disorders (Oatley & Johnson-Laird, 2014). People are unhappy or afraid or feel powerless or unaccepted or plotted against, and on the basis of these negative feelings, their behavior (their typical patterns of social and interpersonal responding) but especially their cognitions (beliefs, biases, attitudes, memories, inferences, judgments) cause further distress to themselves and much distress to others.

Behavior therapists have in the past relied on basic learning principles to account for the development and remediation of these intense feelings. But human consciousness makes us different from the zebras. We inherently make sense of all our experiences, we interpret them (often incorrectly), we remember them (not always precisely), we think about them (sometimes too much), we develop beliefs about them (usually with insufficient evidence), and we get trapped by all these cognitive processes influencing emotion, but at the same time we let emotion influence the processes and the thoughts, often responding too rapidly on the basis of biases, prejudices, and motivational needs. To help people out of those cognitive-emotional traps we as therapists need to be able to change (a) the content of their thoughts and how they derive them and/or (b) the emotional meaning attached to those thoughts that have not worked well for them in the past. This is the broadest possible interpretation of what cognitive therapy is all about.

REFERENCES

Abramson, L. Y., Seligman, M. E. P., & Teasdale, J. (1978). Learned helplessness in humans: Critique and reformulation. *Journal of Abnormal Psychology, 87*, 49–74.

Adams, G. R., Abraham, K. G., & Markstrom, C. A. (1987). The relations among identity development, self-consciousness, and self-focusing during middle and late adolescence. *Developmental Psychology, 23*, 292–297.

Adams, R. (1972). *Watership Down: A novel.* London, England: Rex Collings.

Addis, M. E., & Martell, C. R. (2004). *Overcoming depression one step at a time: The new behavioral activation approach to getting your life back.* New York, NY: New Harbinger.

Alloy, L. B., & Abramson, L. Y. (1979). Judgment of contingency in depressed and nondepressed students: Sadder but wiser? *Journal of Experimental Psychology, General, 108*, 441–485.

American Psychiatric Association. (2000). *Diagnostic and statistical manual of mental disorders* (4th ed., text rev.). Washington, DC: Author.

American Psychiatric Association. (2013). *Diagnostic and statistical manual of mental disorders* (5th ed.). Washington, DC: Author.

Anonymous. (2012). An overview of obsessive compulsive disorder: Written by a sufferer. Retrieved from https://sites.google.com/site/uncertaintyanxiety/home

Arch, J., Eifert, G. H., Davies, C., Plumb, J. C., Rose, R. D., & Craske, M. G. (2012). Randomized clinical trial of cognitive behavioral therapy (CBT) versus acceptance and commitment therapy (ACT) for mixed anxiety disorders *Journal of Consulting and Clinical Psychology, 80*, 750–765.

Arendt, H. (1966). *The origins of totalitarianism.* New York, NY: Harcourt Brace Jovanovich.

Aspinwall, L. G. (2005). The psychology of future-oriented thinking: From achievement to proactive coping, adaptation, and aging. *Motivation and Emotion, 29*, 203–235.

Bagby, R. M., Rector, N. A., Bacchiochi, J. R., & McBride, C. (2004). The stability of the Response Styles Questionnaire Rumination Scale in a sample of patients with major depression. *Cognitive Therapy and Research, 28*, 527–538.

Baltes, P. B., & Staudinger, U. M. (2000). Wisdom: A metaheuristic (pragmatic) to orchestrate mind and virtue toward excellence. *American Psychologist, 55*, 122–136.

Banaji, M. R. (2007a). The limits of introspection. In J. Brockman (Ed.), *What is your dangerous idea?* (pp. 263–265). New York, NY: Harper Perennial.

Banaji, M. R. (2007b). Unraveling beliefs. In J. Brockman (Ed.), *What are you optimistic about?* (pp. 266–268). New York, NY: Harper Collins.

Bandura, A. (1977). Self-efficacy: Toward a unifying theory of behavior change. *Psychological Review, 84*, 191–215.

Bandura, A. (2006). Toward a psychology of human agency. *Perspectives on Psychological Science, 1*, 164–180.

Banerjee, R., Watling, D., & Caputi, M. (2011). Peer relations and the understanding of faux pas: Longitudinal evidence for bidirectional associations. *Child Development, 82*, 1887–1905.

Bannister, D., & Fransella, F. (1971). *Inquiring man: Theory of personal constructs*. London, England: Croom Helm.

Barch, D. M., & Berenbaum, H. (1996). Language production and thought disorder in schizophrenia. *Journal of Abnormal Psychology, 105*, 81–88.

Barlow, D. H. (2002). *Anxiety and its disorders: The nature and treatment of anxiety and panic* (2nd ed.). New York, NY: Guilford Press.

Barlow, D. H., Allen, L. B., & Choate, M. L. (2004). Toward a unified treatment for emotional disorders. *Behavior Therapy, 35*, 205–230.

Barlow, D. H., Sauer-Zavala, S., Carl, J. R., Bullis, J. R., & Ellard, K. K. (2014). The nature, diagnosis, and treatment of neuroticism: Back to the future. *Clinical Psychological Science, 2*, 344–365.

Bartlett, F. C. (1932). *Remembering: A study in experimental and social psychology*. Cambridge, England: Cambridge University Press.

Baron-Cohen, S. (1995). *Mindblindness: An essay on autism and theory of mind*. Boston, MA: MIT Press.

Baron-Cohen, S., Leslie, A. M., & Frith, U. (1985) Does the autistic child have a "theory of mind"? *Cognition, 21*, 37–46.

Basson, R. (2007). Sexual desire/arousal disorders in women. In S. R. Leiblum (Ed.), *Principles and practice of sex therapy* (4th ed., pp. 25–53). New York, NY: Guilford Press.

Bateman, A., & Fonagy, P. (2006). *Mentalization based treatment: A practical guide*. Oxford, England: Oxford University Press.

Bateman, A., & Fonagy, F. (2013). Mentalization-based treatment. *Psychoanalytic Inquiry, 33*, 595–613.

Baumeister, R. F., Smart, L., & Boden, J. M. (1996). Relation of threatened egotism to violence and aggression: The dark side of high self-esteem. *Psychological Review, 103*, 5–33.

Baumeister, R. F., Vohs, K. D., DeWall, C. N., & Zhang, L. (2007). How emotion shapes behavior: Feedback, anticipation, and reflection, rather than direct causation. *Personality and Social Psychology Review, 11*, 167–203.

Beck, A. T. (1952). Successful outpatient psychotherapy of a chronic schizophrenic with a delusion based on borrowed guilt. *Psychiatry, 15*, 305–312.

Beck, A. T. (1964). Thinking and depression: II. Theory and therapy. *Archives of General Psychiatry, 10*, 561–571.

Beck, A. T. (1967). *Depression: Clinical, experimental, and theoretical aspects*. New York, NY: Harper & Row.

Beck, A. T. (1975). *Cognitive therapy and the emotional disorders*. Madison, CT: International Universities Press.

Beck, A. T. (1991). Cognitive therapy: A 30-year retrospective. *American Psychologist, 46*, 368–375.

Beck, A. T. (1996). Beyond belief: A theory of modes, personality, and psychopathology. In P. Salkovskis (Ed.), *Frontiers of cognitive therapy* (pp. 1–25). New York, NY: Guilford Press.

Beck, A. T. (1999). *Prisoners of hate: The cognitive basis of anger, hostility, and violence*. New York, NY: HarperCollins.

Beck, A. T., Brown, G., Steer, R. A., Eidelson, J. I., & Riskind, I. H. (1987). Differentiating anxiety and depression: A test of the cognitive content-specificity hypothesis. *Journal of Abnormal Psychology, 96*, 1–5.

Beck, A. T., & Freeman, A. (1990). *Cognitive therapy of personality disorders*. New York, NY: Guilford Press.

Beck, A. T., & Rector, N. A. (2005). Cognitive approaches to schizophrenia: Theory and therapy. *Annual Review of Clinical Psychology, 1*, 577–606.

Beck, J. S. (2011). *Cognitive behavior therapy: Basics and beyond* (2nd ed.). New York, NY: Guilford Press.

Beck, L., Kumschick, I. R., Eid, M., & Klann-Delius, G. (2012). Relationship between language competence and emotional competence in middle childhood. *Emotion, 12*, 503–514.

Beilock, S. (2010). *Choke: What the secrets of the brain reveal about getting it right when you have to*. New York, NY: Free Press.

Berkowitz, A. D. (2004). *The social norms approach: Theory, research, and annotated bibliography*. Retrieved from http://alanberkowitz.com/articles/social_norms.pdf

Berridge, K. C., & Kringelbach, M. L. (2011). Building a neuroscience of pleasure and well-being. *Psychology of Well-Being: Theory, Research and Practice, 1*, 1–26.

Berry, K., Ford, S., Jellicoe-Jones, L., & Haddock, G. (2013). PTSD symptoms associated with the experiences of psychosis and hospitalisation: A review of the literature. *Clinical Psychology Review, 33*, 526–538.

Birchwood, M., & Trower, P. (2006). The future of cognitive-behavioural therapy for psychosis: Not a quasi-neuroleptic. *British Journal of Psychiatry, 188*, 107–108.

Bishop, S. R., Lau, M., Shapiro, S., Carlson, L., Anderson, N. D., Carmody, J., . . . Devins, G. (2004). Mindfulness: A proposed operational definition. *Clinical Psychology: Science and Practice, 11*, 230–241.

Blackledge, J. T. (2007). Disrupting verbal processes: Cognitive defusion in acceptance and commitment therapy and other mindfulness-based psychotherapies. *The Psychological Record, 57*, 555–576.

Blair, I. V., Ma, J. E., & Lenton, A. P. (2001). Imagining stereotypes away: The moderation of implicit stereotypes through mental imagery. *Journal of Personality and Social Psychology, 81*, 828–841.

Bond, F. W., Hayes, S. C., Baer, R. A., Carpenter, K. M., Guenole, N., Orcutt, H. K., . . . Zettle, R. D. (2011). Preliminary psychometric properties of the Acceptance and Action Questionnaire–II: A revised measure of psychological inflexibility and experiential avoidance. *Behavior Therapy, 42*, 676–688.

Bohner, G., Siebler, F., & Schmelcher, J. (2006). Social norms and the likelihood of raping: Perceived rape myth acceptance of others affects men's rape proclivity. *Personality and Social Psychology Bulletin, 32*, 286–297.

Borkovec, T. D., & Inz, J. (1990). The nature of worry in generalized anxiety disorder: A predominance of thought activity. *Behaviour Research and Therapy, 28*, 153–158.

Borsari, B., & Carey, K. B. (2001). Peer influences on college drinking: A review of the research. *Journal of Substance Abuse, 13*, 391–424.

Borsari, B., & Carey, K. B. (2003). Descriptive and injunctive norms in college drinking: A meta-analytic integration. *Journal of Studies on Alcohol and Drugs, 64*, 331–341.

Boud, D., Keogh, R., & Walker, D. (1985). Promoting reflection in learning: A model. In D. Boud, R. Keogh, & D. Walker (Eds.), *Reflection: Turning experience into learning* (pp. 18–40). New York, NY: Nichols.

Bowen, S., Chawla, N., Collins, S. E., Witkiewitz, K., Hsu, S., Grow, J., . . . Marlatt, A. (2009). Mindfulness-based relapse prevention for substance use disorders: A pilot efficacy trial. *Substance Abuse, 30*, 295–305.

Bower, G. H. (1981). Mood and memory. *American Psychologist, 36*, 129–148.

Bowlby, J. (1969). *Attachment and loss*. New York, NY: Basic Books.

Boyer, P., & Bergstrom, B. (2011). Threat-detection in child development: An evolutionary perspective. *Neuroscience and Biobehavioral Reviews, 35*, 1034–1041.

Bretherton, I., Oppenheim, D., Emde, R. N., & the MacArthur Narrative Working Group (2003). The MacArthur Story Stem Battery. In R. N. Emde, D. P. Wolf, & D. Oppenheim (Eds.), *Revealing the inner worlds of young children: The MacArthur Story Stem Battery and parent–child narratives* (pp. 381–396). New York, NY: Oxford University Press.

Brown, J. R., & Dunn, J. (1996). Continuities in emotion understanding from 3–6 years. *Child Development, 67*, 789–802.

Bruner, J. (1960). *The process of education*. Cambridge, MA: Harvard University Press.

Buckingham, M. (2008). *The truth about you: Your secret to success*. Nashville, TN: Thomas Nelson.

Burkeman, O. (2007, August 11). Obituary: Albert Ellis, influential American psychologist who led the revolution in cognitive therapy. *The Guardian*, p. 43.

Butler, A. C., Chapman, J. E., Forman, E. M., & Beck, A. T. (2006). The empirical status of cognitive-behavioral therapy: A review of meta-analyses. *Clinical Psychology Review, 26*, 17–31.

Campbell, J. A. (2013). *Reasoning at the age of enlightenment: Nurturing wise minds.* (Unpublished master's thesis). School of Psychology, Massey University, Palmerston North, New Zealand.

Cannon, W. (1927). The James-Lange theory of emotions: A critical examination and an alternative theory. *The American Journal of Psychology, 39*, 106–124.

Cardoso, R., De Souza, E., Camano, L., & Leite, J. R. (2004). Meditation in health: An operational definition. *Brain Research Protocols, 14*, 58–60.

Caspi, A., Houts, R. M., Belsky, D. W., Goldman-Mellor, S. J., Harrington, H., Israel, S., . . . Moffitt, T. E. (2014). The *p* factor: One general psychopathology factor in the structure of psychiatric disorders? *Clinical Psychological Science, 2*, 119–137.

Chen, E., Zeltzer, L., Craske, M., & Katz, E. (1999). Alteration of memory in the reduction of children's distress during repeated aversive medical procedures. *Journal of Consulting and Clinical Psychology, 67*, 481–490.

Chen, E., Zeltzer, L., Craske, M., & Katz, E. (2000). Children's memories for painful cancer treatment procedures: Implications for distress. *Child Development, 71*, 933–947.

Chen, J., Liu, X., Rapee, R. M., & Pillay, P. (2013). Behavioural activation: A pilot trial of transdiagnostic treatment for excessive worry. *Behaviour Research and Therapy, 51*, 533–539.

Chiesa, A., & Serretti, A. (2009). Mindfulness-based stress reduction for stress management in healthy people: A review and meta-analysis. *The Journal of Alternative and Complementary Medicine, 15*, 593–600.

Chorpita, B. F., & Barlow, D. H. (1998). The development of anxiety: The role of control in the early environment. *Psychological Bulletin, 124*, 3–21.

Clark, A. (2008). *Supersizing the mind: Embodiment, action, and cognitive extension.* New York, NY: Oxford University Press.

Clark, D. M., & Wells, A. (1995). A cognitive model of social phobia. In R. G. Heimberg, M. R. Liebowitz, D. A. Hope, & F. R. Schneier (Eds.), *Social phobia: Diagnosis, assessment, and treatment* (pp. 69–93). New York, NY: Guilford Press.

Clarke, R. A. (2004). *Against all enemies: Inside America's war on terror.* New York, NY: Free Press.

Clerkin, E. M., & Teachman, B. A. (2008). Perceptual and cognitive biases in individuals with body dysmorphic disorder symptoms. *Cognition and Emotion, 22*, 1327–1339.

Clore, G. L., & Huntsinger, J. R. (2007). How emotions inform judgment and regulate thought. *Trends in Cognitive Science, 11*, 393–399.

Coelho, C. M., & Purkis, H. (2009). The origins of specific phobias: Influential theories and current perspectives. *Review of General Psychology, 13*, 335–348.

Coelho, H. F., Canter, P. H., & Ernst, E. (2007). Mindfulness-based cognitive therapy: Evaluating current evidence and informing future research. *Journal of Consulting and Clinical Psychology, 75*, 1000–1005.

Cohen, G. L., Sherman, D. K., Bastardi, A., Hsu, L., McGoey, M., & Ross, L. (2007). Bridging the partisan divide: Self-affirmation reduces ideological closed-mindedness and inflexibility in negotiation. *Journal of Personality and Social Psychology, 93*, 415–430.

Cohen, L. L. (2008). Behavioral approaches to anxiety and pain management for pediatric venous access. *Pediatrics, 122*, S134–S139.

Cordón, I. M., Pipe, M-E., Sayfan, L., Melinder, A., & Goodman, G. S. (2004). Memory for traumatic experiences in early childhood. *Developmental Review, 24*, 101–132.

Couch, C. M. (2010). *Balanced parenting with young children: Relationship focused parent training within a dialectical framework* (Doctoral thesis). School of Psychology, Massey University, Wellington, New Zealand.

Couch, C. M., & Evans, I. M. (2011). Relationship focused parent training within a dialectical framework: A case study. *Clinical Child Psychology and Psychiatry, 16*, 1–15.

Cristea, I. A., Montgomery, G. H., Szamoskozi, Ş., & David, D. (2013). Key constructs in "classical" and "new wave" cognitive behavioral psychotherapies: Relationships among each other and with emotional distress. *Journal of Clinical Psychology, 69*, 584–599.

Crombach, A., & Elbert, T. (2014). Controlling offensive behavior using narrative exposure therapy: A randomized controlled trial of former street children. *Clinical Psychological Science*. Advance online publication. doi:10.1177/2167702614534239

Csikszentmihalyi, M. (1997). *Finding flow: The psychology of engagement with everyday life*. New York, NY: Basic Books.

Csikszentmihalyi, M., & Figurski, T. J. (2006). Self-awareness and aversive experience in everyday life. *Journal of Personality, 50*, 15–28.

Dalenberg, C. J. (2009). The case for the study of "normal" dissociation. In P. F. Dell & J. A. O'Neil (Eds.), *Dissociation and the dissociative disorders*: DSM–V *and beyond* (pp. 145–154). New York, NY: Routledge.

Darrah, A. J. (2012). *The distressing case of modern mothering: Expectations, losses, and postnatal distress* (Unpublished doctoral thesis). School of Psychology, Massey University, Palmerston North, New Zealand.

Dash, S. R., Meeten, F., & Davey, G. C. L. (2013). Systematic information processing style and perseverative worry. *Clinical Psychology Review, 33*, 1041–1056.

Dawes, R. M., & Corrigan, B. (1974). Linear models in decision-making. *Psychological Bulletin, 81*, 95–106.

Delton, A. W., & Sell, A. (2014). The co-evolution of concepts and motivation. *Current Directions in Psychological Science, 23*, 115–120.

Denham, S. A., Caverly, S., Schmidt, M., Blair, K., DeMulder, E., Caal, S., . . . Mason, T. (2002). Preschool understanding of emotions: Contributions to classroom anger and aggression. *Journal of Child Psychology and Psychiatry, 43*, 901–916.

Dix, T., Moed, A., & Anderson, E. R. (2014). Mothers' depressive symptoms predict both increased and reduced negative reactivity: Aversion sensitivity and the regulation of emotion. *Psychological Science, 25*, 1353–1361. doi:10.1177/0956797614531025

Docherty, N. M., Evans, I. M., Sledge, W. H., Seibyl, J. P., & Krystal, J. H. (1994). Affective reactivity of language in schizophrenia. *The Journal of Nervous and Mental Disease, 182*, 98–102.

Dollard, J., & Miller, N. E. (1950). *Personality and psychotherapy*. New York, NY: McGraw-Hill.

Donker, T., Bennett, K., Bennett, A., Mackinnon, A., van Straten, A., Cuijpers, P., . . . Griffiths, K. M. (2013). Internet delivered interpersonal psychotherapy versus internet-delivered cognitive behavioral therapy for adults with depressive symptoms: Randomized controlled noninferiority trial. *Journal of Medical Internet Research, 15*(5), e82. doi:10.2196/jmir.2307

Dudley, R. E. J., John, C. H., Young, A. W., & Over, D. E. (1997). Normal and abnormal reasoning in people with delusions. *British Journal of Clinical Psychology, 36*, 243–258.

Dutra, L., Callahan, K., Forman, E., Mendelsohn, M., & Herman, J. (2008). Core schemas and sociality in a chronically traumatized population. *Journal of Nervous and Mental Disease, 196*, 71–74.

Dutton, D. G. (1986). Wife assaulters' explanations for assault: The neutralization of self-punishment. *Canadian Journal of Behavioral Science, 18*, 381–390.

Eels, T. D. (Ed.). (2007). *Handbook of psychotherapy case formulation* (2nd ed.). New York, NY: Guilford Press.

Ehlers, A., & Clark, D. M. (2000). A cognitive model of posttraumatic stress disorder. *Behaviour Research and Therapy, 38*, 319–345.

Ehlers, A., Clark, D. M., Hackmann, A., McManus, F., & Fennell, M. (2005). Cognitive therapy for post-traumatic stress disorder: Development and evaluation. *Behaviour Research and Therapy, 43*, 413–431.

Eifert, G. H. (1987). Language conditioning: Clinical issues and applications in behavior therapy. In H. J. Eysenck & I. Martin (Eds.), *Theoretical foundations of behavior therapy* (pp. 167–193). New York, NY: Plenum Press.

Eifert, G. H., McKay, M., & Forsyth, J. P. (2006). *ACT on life not on anger: The new acceptance and commitment therapy guide to problem anger*. Oakland, CA: New Harbinger.

Ellet, L., Freeman, D., & Garety, P. A. (2008). The psychological effect of an urban environment on individuals with persecutory ideation: The Camberwell walk study. *Schizophrenia Research*, *99*, 77–84.

Ellis, A. (1962). *Reason and emotion in psychotherapy*. New York, NY: Lyle Stuart.

Ellis, A. (1977). Psychotherapy and the value of a human being. In A. Ellis & R. Grieger (Eds.), *Handbook of rational-emotive therapy* (pp. 99–112). New York, NY: Springer.

Ellis, A. (1989). Comments on my critics. In M. E. Bernard & R. DiGuiseppe (Eds.), *Inside rational-emotive therapy* (pp. 199–233). San Diego, CA: Academic Press.

Ensor, R., Spencer, D., & Hughes, C. (2011). "You feel sad?" Emotion understanding mediates effects of verbal ability and mother-child mutuality on prosocial behaviors: Findings from 2 years to 4 years. *Social Development*, *20*, 93–110.

Evans, I. M. (1972). A conditioning model of a common neurotic pattern—fear of fear. *Psychotherapy: Theory, Research and Practice*, *9*, 238–241.

Evans, I. M. (1976). Classical conditioning. In M. P. Feldman & A. Broadhurst (Eds.), *Theoretical and experimental bases of the behaviour therapies* (pp. 71–83). London, England: Wiley.

Evans, I. M. (1985). Building systems models as a strategy for target behavior selection in clinical assessment. *Behavioral Assessment*, *7*, 21–32.

Evans, I. M. (2010). Positive affective priming: A behavioral technique to facilitate therapeutic engagement by families, caregivers, and teachers. *Child & Family Behavior Therapy*, *32*, 257–271.

Evans, I. M. (2013). *How and why people change: Foundations of psychological therapy*. New York, NY: Oxford University Press.

Evans, I. M., & Falchi, C. (2013). *Achieving positive stepfamily relationships: Negotiating fairness, forgiveness, and acceptance*. Final report to the Families Commission, Wellington, New Zealand.

Evans, I. M., & Fletcher, A. (2013). Focus on change: Implications for the understanding and evaluation of psychological interventions. *Psychologia*, *56*, 113–130.

Evans, I. M., & Galyer, K. (2009). Are you sure there isn't a monster in the closet? Regulation of children's worrying in uncertain contexts. *Child & Family Behavior Therapy*, *31*, 38–53.

Evans, I. M., & Harvey, S. T. (2012). *Warming the emotional climate of the primary school classroom*. Auckland, New Zealand: Dunmore.

Evans, I. M., & Pechtel, P. (2010). Phagophobia: Behavioral treatment of a complex case involving fear of fear. *Clinical Case Studies*, *10*, 37–52.

Evans, I. M., & Weiss, A. A. (1978). Process studies of language conditioning: II. The role of semantic relevance in conditioning negative emotional responses. *Journal of Behavior Therapy and Experimental Psychiatry*, *9*, 121–124.

Evans, J. St. B. T. (1982). *The psychology of deductive reasoning*. London, England: Routledge.

Eysenck, H. J. (1952). The effects of psychotherapy: An evaluation. *Journal of Consulting Psychology*, *16*, 319–324.

Eysenck, H. J. (1967). *The biological basis of personality*. Springfield, IL: Charles C. Thomas.

Eysenck, H. J. (1968). A theory of the incubation of anxiety/fear responses. *Behaviour Research and Therapy*, *6*, 309–321.

Eysenck, M. W., Derakshan, N., Santos, R., & Calvo, M. G. (2007). Anxiety and cognitive performance: Attentional control theory. *Emotion*, *7*, 336–353.

Fairburn, C. G. (2008). *Cognitive behavior therapy and eating disorders*. New York, NY: Guilford Press.

Fairburn, C. G., & Wilson, G. T. (1993). *Binge eating: Nature, assessment, and treatment*. New York, NY: Guilford Press.

Falchi, C. (2008). *Children's perceptions of fairness within families: The influence of the step-parenting experience* (Unpublished honor's thesis). Massey University, Wellington, New Zealand.

Feeney, J. (2005). Hurt feelings in couple relationships: Exploring the role of attachment and perceptions of personal injury. *Personal Relationships*, *12*, 253–272.

Fernandez, M. (2013, August 20). Fort Hood gunman told his superiors of concerns. *New York Times*. Retrieved from http://www.nytimes.com/2013/08/21/us/fort-hood-gunman-nidal-malik-hasan.html?ref=nidalmalikhasan&_r=0

Flanagan, J. (2001, November 11). South African men rape babies as a "cure" for AIDS. *The Telegraph*. Retrieved from http://www.telegraph.co.uk/news/worldnews/africaandindianocean/southafrica/1362134/South-African-men-rape-babies-as-cure-for-Aids.html

Foa, E. B., & Kozak, M. J. (1986). Emotional processing of fear: Exposure to corrective information. *Psychological Bulletin, 99*, 20–35.

Foa, E. B., & Rothbaum, B. O. (1998). *Treating the trauma of rape: Cognitive-behavioral therapy for PTSD*. New York, NY: Guilford Press.

Fodor, J. A. (1975). *The language of thought*. New York, NY: Crowell.

Fonagy, P., Gergely, G., Jurist, E. L., & Target, M. (2002). *Affect regulation, mentalization and the development of the self*. New York, NY: Other Press.

Fontaine, J. R. J., Scherer, K. R., & Soriano, C. (Eds.). (2013). *Components of emotional meaning: A sourcebook*. New York, NY: Oxford University Press.

Forman, E. M., Herbert, J. D., Moitra, E., Yeomans, P. D., & Geller, P. A. (2007). A randomized controlled effectiveness trial of acceptance and commitment therapy and cognitive therapy for anxiety and depression. *Behavior Modification, 31*, 772–799.

Fox, J. E., & Houston, B. K. (1981), Efficacy of self-instructional training in reducing children's anxiety in an evaluative situation. *Behaviour Research and Therapy, 19*, 509–515.

Frank, J. D. (1961). *Persuasion and healing: A comparative study of psychotherapy*. Baltimore, MD: Johns Hopkins University Press.

Frankl, V. (1959). *Man's search for meaning* (1984 ed.). New York, NY: Simon and Schuster.

Fredrickson, B. L. (2001). The role of positive emotion in positive psychology: The broaden-and-build theory of positive emotions. *American Psychologist, 56*, 218–226.

Galotti, K. M. (2007). Decision structuring in important real-life choices. *Psychological Science, 18*, 320–325.

Galotti, K. M., & Tinkelenberg, C. E. (2009). Real-life decision making: Parents choosing a first-grade placement. *American Journal of Psychology, 122*, 455–468.

Garland, E. L., Fredrickson, B., Kring, A. M., Johnson, D. P., Meyer, P. S., & Penn, D. L. (2010). Upward spirals of positive emotions counter downward spirals of negativity: Insights from the broaden-and-build theory and affective neuroscience on the treatment of emnotion dysfunctions and deficits in psychopathology. *Clinical Psychology Review, 30*, 849–864.

Garrett-Peters, P. T., & Fox, N. A. (2007). Cross-cultural differences in children's emotional reaction to a disappointing situation. *International Journal of Behavioral Development, 31*, 161–169.

Gaw, A. C., & Bernstein, R. L. (1992). Classification of amok in *DSM-IV. Hospital and Community Psychiatry, 43*, 789–793.

Gazendam, F. J., Kamphuis, J. H., Eigenhuis, A., Huizenga, H. M. H., Soeter, M., Bos, M. G. N., . . . Kindt, M. (2014). Personality predicts individual variation in fear learning: A multilevel growth modeling approach. *Clinical Psychological Science*. Advance online publication. doi:10.1177/2167702614535914

Gibbs, N. (2009, November 11).The Fort Hood killer: Terrified . . . or terrorist? *Time*.

Giambra, L. M. (1979). Sex differences in daydreaming and related mental activity from the late teens to the early nineties. *The International Journal of Aging and Human Development, 10*, 1–34.

Gibbs, J. C., Barriga, A. Q., & Potter, G. B. (2001). *How I Think (HIT) questionnaire*. Champaign, IL: Research Press.

Gilbert, P. (Ed.). (2005), *Compassion: Conceptualisations, research and use in psychotherapy*. East Sussex, England: Routledge.

Gilovich, T. (1991). *How we know what isn't so: The fallibility of human reason in everyday life*. New York, NY: Free Press.

Glasser, W. (1965). *Reality therapy: A new approach to psychiatry*. New York, NY: Harper & Row.

Glasser, W. (1969). *Schools without failure*. New York, NY: Harper & Row.

Glick, B., & Gibbs, J. C. (2010). *Aggression Replacement Training: A comprehensive intervention for aggressive youth* (3rd ed.). Champaign, IL: Research Press.

Goldfried, M. R., Castonguay, L. G., Hayes, A. M., Drozd, J. F., & Shapiro, D. A. (1997). A comparative analysis of the therapeutic focus in cognitive-behavioral and psychodynamic-interpersonal sessions. *Journal of Consulting and Clinical Psychology, 65*, 740–748.

Gollwitzer, P. M., & Bayer, U. (1999). Deliberative versus implemental mindsets in the control of action. In S. Chaiken & Y. Trope (Eds.), *Dual process theories in social psychology* (pp. 403–432). New York, NY: Guilford Press.

Gollwitzer, P. M., & Sheeran, P. (2006). Implementation intentions and goal achievement: A meta-analysis of effects and processes. *Advances in Experimental Social Psychology, 38*, 69–119.

Gonzales, A. L., Hancock, J. T., & Pennebaker, J. W. (2010). Language style matching as a predictor of social dynamics in small groups. *Communications Research, 31*, 3–19.

Gottman, J. M., Katz, L. F., & Hooven, C. (1997). *Meta-emotion: How families communicate emotionally*. Mahwah, NJ: Lawrence Erlbaum.

Grammont, F., Legrand, D., & Livet, P. (Eds.). (2010). *Naturalizing intention in action*. Cambridge, MA: MIT Press.

Graham, P. (2008). *How to disagree*. Retrieved from http://www.paulgraham.com/disagree.html

Greco, L. A., Lambert, W., & Baer, R. A. (2008). Psychological inflexibility in childhood and adolescence: Development and evaluation of the Avoidance and Fusion Questionnaire for Youth. *Psychological Assessment, 20*, 93–102.

Greenberger, D., & Padesky, C. A. (1995). *Mind over mood: A cognitive therapy treatment manual for clients*. New York, NY: Guilford Press.

Guerin, B. (2003). Language use as social strategy: A review and analytic framework for the social sciences. *Review of General Psychology, 7*, 251–298.

Haaga, D. A. F., & Davison, G. C. (1993). An appraisal of rational-emotive therapy. *Journal of Consulting and Clinical Psychology, 61*, 215–220.

Haeffel, G. J., & Hames, J. L. (2014). Cognitive vulnerability to depression can be contagious. *Clinical Psychological Science, 2*, 75–85.

Hall, P. L., & Tarrier, N. (2003). The cognitive-behavioural treatment of low self-esteem in psychotic patients: A pilot study. *Behaviour Research and Therapy, 41*, 317–332.

Hampton, J. A. (1981). An investigation of the nature of abstract concepts. *Memory & Cognition, 9*, 149–156.

Hampton, J. A. (2012). Thinking intuitively: The rich (and at times illogical) world of concepts. *Psychological Science, 21*, 398–402.

Hansell, S., Mechanic, D., & Brondolo, E. (1986). Introspectiveness and adolescent development. *Journal of Youth and Adolescence, 15*, 115–132.

Hariton, E. B., & Singer, J. L. (1974). Women's fantasies during sexual intercourse: Normative and theoretical implications. *Journal of Consulting and Clinical Psychology, 42*, 313–322.

Hayes, A. M., Laurenceau, J.-P., Feldman, G., Strauss, J. L., & Cardaciotto, L. (2007). Change is not always linear: The study of nonlinear and discontinuous patterns of change in psychotherapy. *Clinical Psychology Review, 27*, 715–723.

Hayes, S. C. (2004). Acceptance and commitment therapy, relational frame theory, and the third wave of behavioral and cognitive therapies. *Behavior Therapy, 35*, 639–665.

Hayes, S. C., & Lillis, J. (2012). *Acceptance and commitment therapy*. Washington, DC: American Psychological Association.

Hayes, S. C., Pistorello, J., & Levin, M. E. (2012). Acceptance and commitment therapy as a unified model of behavior change. *The Counseling Psychologist, 40*, 976–1002.

Hayes, S. C., Strosahl, K. D., & Wilson, K. G. (2012). *Acceptance and commitment therapy: The process and practice of mindful change* (2nd ed.). New York, NY: Guilford Press.

Heiby, E. M., & Staats, A. W. (1990). Depression: Classification, explanation, and treatment. In G. H. Eifert & I. M. Evans (Eds.), *Unifying behavior therapy: Contributions of paradigmatic behaviorism* (pp. 220–246). New York, NY: Springer.

Heyes, C. (2014). Submentalizing: I am not really reading your mind. *Perspectives on Psychological Science, 9*, 131–143.

Higgins, E. T., Bond, R. N., Klein, R., & Strauman, T. (1986). Self-discrepancies and emotional vulnerability: How magnitude, accessibility, and type of discrepancy influence affect. *Journal of Personality and Social Psychology, 51*, 5–15.

Hofmann, S. G. (2011). *An introduction to modern CBT: Psychological solutions to mental health problems*. Oxford, England: Wiley-Blackwell.

Hofmann, S. G., Asmundson, G. J. G., & Beck, A. T. (2013). The science of cognitive therapy. *Behavior Therapy, 44*, 199–212.

Hofmann, S. G., Asnaani, A., Vonk, I. J. J., Sawyer, A. T., & Fang, A. (2012). The efficacy of cognitive behavioral therapy: A review of meta-analyses. *Cognitive Therapy and Research, 36*, 427–440.

Hofmann, W., Deutsch, R., Lancaster, K., & Banaji, M. R. (2010). Cooling the heat of temptation: Mental self-control and the automatic evaluation of tempting stimuli. *European Journal of Social Psychology, 40*, 17–25.

Hookway, C. (2010). Pragmatism. In E. N. Zalat (Ed.), *The Stanford encyclopedia of philosophy*. Retrieved from http://plato.stanford.edu/archives/spr2010/entries/pragmatism/.

Hope, D. A., Heimberg, R. G., & Turk, C. L. (2010). *Managing social anxiety: A cognitive-behavioral therapy approach* (2nd ed.). New York, NY: Oxford University Press.

Hormuth, S. E. (2006). The sampling of experiences *in situ*. *Journal of Personality, 54*, 262–293.

Hoyer, J., & Klein, A. (2000). Self-reflection and well-being: Is there a healthy amount of introspection? *Psychological Reports, 86*, 135–141.

Huffington Post. (2013, December 12). Birther movement capitalizes on Loretta Fuddy's tragic death. Retrieved from http://www.huffingtonpost.com/2013/12/12/birther-movement-loretta-fuddy_n_4435768.html

Hugdahl, K., & Öhman, A. (1977). Effects of instruction on acquisition and extinction of electrodermal responses to fear-relevant stimuli. *Journal of Experimental Psychology: Human Learning and Memory, 3*, 609–618.

Hume, D. (1962). *A treatise of human nature*. Cleveland, OH: World. (Original work published in 1739)

Hurley, S. (1998). *Consciousness in action*. Boston, MA: Harvard University Press.

Ireland, M. E., Slatcher, R. B., Eastwick, P. W., Scissors, L. E., Finkel, E. J., & Pennebaker, J. W. (2011). Language style matching predicts relationship initiation and stability. *Psychological Science, 22*(1), 39–44. doi:10.1177/0956797610392928

Jacobson, N. S., Christensen, A., Prince, S. E., Cordova, J., & Eldridge, K. (2000). Integrative behavioral couple therapy: An acceptance-based, promising new treatment for couple discord. *Journal of Consulting and Clinical Psychology, 68*, 351–355.

James, W. (1975). *Pragmatism: A new name for some old ways of thinking*. Cambridge, MA: Harvard University Press. (Original work published in 1907)

Jarvis, A. N. (1996). *Taking a break: Preliminary investigations into the psychology of epiphanies as discontinuous change experiences* (Unpublished doctoral dissertation). University of Massachusetts, Amherst. Retrieved from http://scholarworks.umass.edu/dissertations/AAI9709611

Jesinoski, M. S. (2010). *Young's schema theory: Exploring the direct and indirect links between negative childhood experiences and temperament to negative affectivity in adulthood* (Doctoral dissertation). Utah State University, Logan. Retrieved from http://digitalcommons.usu.edu/etd/845

Johnson-Laird, P. N. (2012). Inference with mental models. In K. J. Holyoak & R. G. Morrison (Eds.), *The Oxford handbook of thinking and reasoning* (pp. 134–154). New York, NY: Oxford University Press.

Jones, E. E., & Pulos, S. M. (1993). Comparing the process in psychodynamic and cognitive-behavioral therapies. *Journal of Consulting and Clinical Psychology*, *61*, 306–316.

Jost, J. T. (2006). The end of the end of ideology. *American Psychologist*, *61*, 651–670.

Jost, J. T., & Amodio, D. M. (2012). Political ideology as motivated social cognition: Behavioral and neuroscientific evidence. *Motivation and Emotion*, *36*, 55–64.

Jost, J. T., Glaser, J., Kruglanski, A. W., & Sulloway, F. J. (2003). Political conservatism as motivated social cognition. *Psychological Bulletin*, *129*, 339–375.

Jost, J. T., Napier, J. L., Thorisdottire, H., Golsing, S. D., Palfai, D. T., & Ostafin, B. (2007). Are needs to manage uncertainty and threat associated with political conservatism or ideological extremity? *Personality and Social Psychology Bulletin*, *33*, 989–1007.

Jung, C. G. (1910). The association method. *American Journal of Psychology*, *31*, 219–269.

Jung, C. G. (1967). *The development of personality*. London, England: Routledge.

Jurado, M. B., & Rosselli, M. (2007). The elusive nature of executive functions: A review of our current understanding. *Neuropsychology Review*, *17*, 213–233.

Kabat-Zinn, J. (1982). An outpatient program in behavioral medicine for chronic pain patients based on the practice of mindfulness meditation: Theoretical considerations and preliminary results. *General Hospital Psychiatry*, *4*, 33–47.

Kabat-Zinn, J. (1990). *Full catastrophe living: Using the wisdom of your body and mind to face stress, pain, and illness*. New York, NY: Delacorte.

Kabat-Zinn, J. (1994). *Wherever you go, there you are: Mindfulness meditation in everyday life*. New York, NY: Hyperion.

Kahneman, D. (2011). *Thinking, fast and slow*. London, England: Penguin Books.

Kanai, Y., Sasagawa, S., Chen, J., Shimada, H., & Sakano, Y. (2010). Interpretation bias for ambiguous social behavior among individuals with high and low levels of social anxiety. *Cognitive Therapy and Research*, *34*, 229–240.

Kashdan, T., & Ciarrochi, J. (2013). *Mindfulness, acceptance, and positive psychology: The seven foundations of well-being*. Oakland, CA: Context Press.

Kazantzis, N., Fairburn, C. G., Padesky, C. A., Reinecke, M., & Teesson, M. (2014). Unresolved issues regarding the research and practice of cognitive behavior therapy: The case of guided discovery using Socratic questioning. *Behaviour Change*, *31*, 1–17.

Kazdin, A. E. (2001). Progression of therapy research and clinical application of treatment require better understanding of the change process. *Clinical Psychology: Science and Practice*, *8*, 143–151.

Kazdin, A. E., & Nock, M. K. (2003). Delineating mechanisms of change in child and adolescent therapy: Methodological issues and research recommendations. *Journal of Child Psychology and Psychiatry*, *44*, 1116–1129.

Keijsers, G. P. J., Schaap, C. P. D. R., & Hoogduin, C. A. L. (2000). The impact of interpersonal patient and therapist behavior on outcome in cognitive-behavior therapy: A review of empirical studies. *Behavior Modification*, *24*, 264–297.

Kelly, G. (1955). *The psychology of personal constructs*. New York, NY: Norton.

Kelly, V. L., Barker, H., Field, A. P., Wilson, C., & Reynolds, S. (2010). Can Rachman's indirect pathways be used to un-learn fear? A prospective paradigm to test whether children's fears can be reduced using positive information and modelling a non-anxious response. *Behaviour Research and Therapy*, *48*, 164–170.

Kendall, P. C., & Hedtke, K. A. (2006). *Cognitive-behavioral therapy for anxious children: Therapist manual* (3rd ed.). Ardmore, PA: Workbook Publishing.

Kida, T. (2006). *Don't believe everything you think: The 6 basic mistakes we make in thinking*. Amherst, NY: Prometheus Books.

Kingdon, D. G. (2009, May 2). Cognitive-behavioral therapy for severe mental illness [Podcast]. *Psychiatric Times*. Retrieved from http://www.psychiatrictimes.com%2Fcognitive-behavioral-therapy-severe-mental-illness

Kingdon, D. G., & Turkington, D. (2005). *Cognitive therapy of schizophrenia*. New York, NY: Guilford Press.

Kirsh, D., & Maglio P. (1994). On distinguishing epistemic from pragmatic action. *Cognitive Science, 18*, 513–549.

Kleim, B., Graham, B., Fihosy, S., Stott, R., & Ehlers, A. (2014). Reduced specificity in episodic future thinking in posttraumatic stress disorder. *Clinical Psychological Science, 2*, 165–173.

Klein, M. (1926). Infant analysis. *International Journal of Psychoanalysis, 7*, 31–63.

Klinger, E. (1971). *Structure and functions of fantasy*. New York, NY: Wiley.

Klinger, E. (1977). *Meaning and void: Inner experience and the incentives in people's lives*. Minneapolis: University of Minnesota Press.

Klinger, E. (2012). Daydreaming and fantasizing: Thought flow and motivation. In K. D. Markman, W. M. P. Klein, & J. A. Suhr (Eds.), *Handbook of imagination and mental simulation* (pp. 225–239). New York, NY: Psychology Press.

Klinger, E., Murphy, M. D., Ostrem, J. L., & Stark-Wroblewsky, K. (2004). Disclosing daydreams versus real experiences: Attitudes, emotional reactions, and personality correlates. *Imagination, Cognition and Personality, 24*, 101–138.

Knoll, J. L. (2010). The "pseudocommando" mass murderer: Part 1. The psychology of revenge and obliteration. *Journal of American Academy of Psychiatry and Law, 38*, 87–94.

Kohlenberg, R. J., & Tsai, M. (1991). *Functional analytic psychotherapy*. New York, NY: Plenum Press.

Kolb, D. A. 1984. *Experiential learning: Experience as the source of learning and development*. Upper Saddle River, NJ: Prentice-Hall.

Kross, E., Ayduk, O., & Mischel, W. (2005). When asking "why" does not hurt: Distinguishing rumination from reflective processing of negative emotions. *Psychological Science, 16*, 709–715.

Kruglanski, A. W. (2004). *The psychology of closed-mindedness*. New York, NY: Psychology Press.

Lalumière, M. L., Harris, G. T., Quinsey, V. L., & Rice, M. E. (2005). *The causes of rape: Understanding individual differences in male propensity for sexual aggression*. Washington, DC: American Psychological Association.

Lane, R. D., & Schwartz, G. E. (1992). Levels of emotional awareness: Implications for psychotherapeutic integration. *Journal of Psychotherapy Integration, 2*, 1–18.

Lang, P. J. (1985). The cognitive psychopathology of emotion: Fear and anxiety. In A. H. Tuma & J. D. Maser (Eds.), *Anxiety and the anxiety disorders* (pp. 131–170). Hillsdale, NJ: Lawrence Erlbaum.

Lazarus, R. S. (1966). *Psychological stress and the coping process*. New York, NY: McGraw-Hill.

Leary, M. R., & Springer, C. (2001). Hurt feelings: The neglected emotion. In R. M. Kowalski (Ed.), *Behaving badly: Aversive behaviors in interpersonal relationships* (pp. 151–175). Washington, DC: American Psychological Association.

LeDoux, J. E., & Gorman, J. M. (2001). A call to action: Overcoming anxiety through active coping. *American Journal of Psychiatry, 158*, 1953–1955.

Leitenberg, H., & Henning, K. (1995). Sexual fantasy. *Psychological Bulletin, 117*, 469–496.

Levelt, W. J. M. (1989). *Speaking: From intention to articulation*. Cambridge, MA: MIT Press.

Levy, B. J., & Anderson, M. C. (2008). Individual differences in the suppression of unwanted memories: The executive deficit hypothesis. *Acta Psychologica, 127*, 623–635.

Levy, B. S., & Farber, B. A. (1986). Clinical implications of adolescent introspection. *Psychotherapy, 23*, 570–577.

Lifton, R. J. (1961). *Thought reform and the psychology of totalism: A study of "brainwashing" in China*. New York, NY: W. W. Norton.

Linehan, M. M. (1993). *Cognitive-behavioral treatment of borderline personality disorder*. New York, NY: Guilford Press.

Linehan, M. M., Cochran, B. N., Mar, C. M., Levensky, E. R. & Comtois, K. A. (2000). Therapeutic burnout among borderline personality disordered clients and their therapists: Development and evaluation of two adaptations of the Maslach Burnout Inventory. *Cognitive and Behavioral Practice, 7*, 329–337.

Liu, Y., & Wang, Z. (2014). Positive affect and cognitive control: Approach-motivation intensity influences the balance between cognitive flexibility and stability. *Psychological Science, 25*(5), 1116–1123. doi:10.1177/0956797614525213

Lohr, J. M., & Hamberger, L. K. (1990). Verbal, emotional, and imagery repertoires in the regulation of dysfunctional behavior: An integrative conceptual framework for cognitive-behavioral disorders and interventions. In G. H. Eifert & I. M. Evans (Eds.), *Unifying behavior therapy: Contributions of paradigmatic behaviorism* (pp. 153–172). New York, NY: Springer.

Loo, R. (2000). A psychometric evaluation of the General Decision-Making Style Inventory. *Personality and Individual Differences, 29*, 895–905.

Lucas, M (2010, January 21). Rewire your brain for love [Web log post]. *Psychology Today.* Retrieved from http://www.psychologytoday.com/blog/rewire-your-brain-love/201001/meditation-and-the-false-lure-zoning-out.

Macdonald, D., Rodger, S., Abbott, R., Ziviani, J., & Jones, J. (2005). "I could do with a pair of wings": Perspectives on physical activity, bodies and health from young Australian children. *Sport, Education and Society, 10*, 195–209.

MacLeod, C., & Mathews, A. (2012). Cognitive bias modification approaches to anxiety. *Annual Review of Clinical Psychology, 8*, 189–217.

Mahoney, M. J. (1993). Theoretical developments in the cognitive psychotherapies. *Journal of Consulting and Clinical Psychology, 61*, 187–193.

Mahoney, M. J. (2002). Constructivism and positive psychology. In C. R. Snyder & S. J. Lopez (Eds.), *Handbook of positive psychology* (pp. 745–750). Oxford, England: Oxford University Press.

Mair, M. (2012). Enchanting psychology: The poetry of personal inquiry. *The Journal of Constructivist Psychology, 25*, 189–209.

Manicavasagar, V., Perich, T., & Parker, G. (2012). Cognitive predictors of change in cognitive behavior therapy and mindfulness-based cognitive therapy for depression. *Behavioural and Cognitive Psychotherapy, 40*, 227–232.

Markus, H., & Nurius, P. (1986). Possible selves. *American Psychologist, 41*, 954–969.

Masley, S. A., Gillanders, D. T., Simpson, S. G., & Taylor, M. A. (2012). A systematic review of the evidence base for schema therapy. *Cognitive Behaviour Therapy, 41*, 185–202.

Mathews, A., & Mackintosh, B. (1998). A cognitive model of selective processing in anxiety. *Cognitive Therapy and Research, 22*, 539–560.

Matthews, G. (2009). Personality and performance: Cognitive processes and models. In P. J. Corr & G. Matthews (Eds.), *The Cambridge handbook of personality psychology* (pp. 400–426). New York, NY: Cambridge University Press.

Matthews, G., & Wells, A. (2000). Attention, automaticity and affective disorder. *Behavior Modification, 24*, 69–93.

McAdams, D. P., & Constantian, C. A. (1983). Intimacy and affiliation motives in daily living: An experience sampling analysis. *Journal of Personality and Social Psychology, 45*, 851–861.

McClintock, J. M., & Evans, I. M. (2001). The underlying psychopathology of eating disorders and social phobia: A structural equation analysis. *Eating Behaviors, 2*, 247–261.

McDonald, M. G. (2008). The nature of epiphanic experience. *Journal of Humanistic Psychology, 48*, 89–115.

McElwee, R. O. B., & Haugh, J. A. (2010). Thinking clearly versus frequently about the future self: Exploring this distinction and its relation to possible selves. *Self and Identity, 9*, 298–321.

McIvor, J. A. (2014). *"Stupid little pointy needle!" Dismantling a cognitive-behavioural treatment for chronically ill children with needle-related distress* (Unpublished doctoral thesis). School of Psychology, Massey University, Wellington, New Zealand.

McGinn, L. K., & Young, J. E. (1996). Schema-focused therapy. In P. M. Salkovskis (Ed.), *Frontiers of cognitive therapy* (pp. 182–207). New York, NY: Guilford Press.

McNally, R. (2006). Cognitive abnormalities in post-traumatic stress disorder. *Trends in Cognitive Sciences, 10*, 271–277.

Meel, B. L. (2003). The myth of child rape as a cure for HIV/AIDS in the Transkei: A case report. *Medicine, Science and the Law. 43*, 85–88.

Meichenbaum, D. (1977). *Cognitive behavior modification: An integrative approach.* New York, NY: Plenum.

Meichenbaum, D., & Goodman, J. (1971). Training impulsive children to talk to themselves: A means of developing self-control. *Journal of Abnormal Psychology, 77*, 115–126.

Meins, E. (1997). *Security of attachment and the social development of cognition.* Hove, England: Psychology Press.

Merckelbach, H., & Jelicic, M. (2004). Dissociative symptoms are related to endorsement of vague trauma items. *Comprehensive Psychiatry, 45*, 70–75.

Merckelbach, H., Muris, P., & Rasin, X. (1999). Fantasy proneness and cognitive failures as correlates of dissociative experiences. *Personality & Individual Differences, 26*, 961–967.

Merckelbach, H., & van de Ven, V. (2001). Another White Christmas: Fantasy proneness and reports of "hallucinatory experiences" in undergraduate students. *Journal of Behavior Therapy and Experimental Psychiatry, 32*, 137–144.

Metcalfe, J., & Mischel, W. (1999). A hot/cool-system analysis of delay of gratification: Dynamics of will power. *Psychological Review, 106*, 3–19.

Mewton, L., Smith, J., Rossouw, P., & Andrews, G. (2014). Current perspectives on Internet-delivered cognitive behavioral therapy for adults with anxiety and related disorders. *Psychology Research and Behavior Management, 4*, 37–46.

Meyer, L. H., & Evans, I. M. (2012). *The school leader's guide to restorative school discipline.* Thousand Oaks, CA: Corwin Press.

Mikels, J. A., Cheung, E., Cone, J., & Gilovich, T. (2013). The dark side of intuition: Aging and increases in nonoptimal intuitive decisions. *Emotion, 13*, 189–195.

Miller, G. A., Galanter, E., & Pribram, K. H. (1960). *Plans and the organization of behavior.* New York, NY: Holt, Rinehart and Winston.

Miller, M. W. (2003). Personality and the etiology and expression of PTSD: A three-factor model perspective. *Clinical Psychology: Science and Practice, 10*, 373–393.

Mischel, W. (1974). Processes in delay of gratification. In R. Berkowitz (Ed.), *Advances in experimental social psychology* (Vol. 7, pp. 249–293). New York, NY: Academic Press.

Moore S. A., & Zoellner L. A. (2007). Overgeneral autobiographical memory and traumatic events: An evaluative review. *Psychological Bulletin, 133*, 419–437.

Mor, N., & Winquist, J. (2002). Self-focused attention and negative affect: A meta-analysis. *Psychological Bulletin, 128*, 638–662.

Morrison, A. K. (2009). Cognitive behavior therapy for people with schizophrenia. *Psychiatry, 6*, 32–39.

Morrison, A. P., French, P., Walford, L., Lewis, S. W., Kilcommons, A., Green, J., . . . Bentall, R. P. (2004). Cognitive therapy for the prevention of psychosis in people at ultra-high risk: Randomised control trial. *British Journal of Psychiatry, 185*, 291–297.

Muñoz Larroa, L. (2013). *What do I want to do and how do I get there? A possible selves approach to motivation in education* (Unpublished clinical doctoral thesis). School of Psychology, Massey University, Wellington, New Zealand. Retrieved from http://mro.massey.ac.nz/bitstream/handle/10179/4781/02_whole.pdf?sequence=1

Muris, P., & Field, A. P. (2010). The role of verbal threat information in the development of childhood fear. "Beware the Jabberwok!" *Clinical Child and Family Psychology Review, 13*, 129–150.

Nairne, J. S., & Pandeirada, J. N. S. (2010). Adaptive memory: Ancestral priorities and the mnemonic value of survival processing. *Cognitive Psychology, 61*, 1–22.

Nairne, J. S., Pandeirada, J. N. S., Gregory, K. J., & Van Arsdall, J. E. (2009). Adaptive memory: Fitness-relevance and the hunter-gatherer mind. *Psychological Science, 19*, 176–180.

Neuberg, S. L., Judice, T. N., & West, S. G. (1997). What the Need for Closure Scale measures and what it does not: Toward differentiating among related epistemic motives. *Journal of Personality and Social Psychology, 72*, 1396–1412.

Nezu, A. M. (2004). Problem solving and behavior therapy revisited. *Behavior Therapy, 35*, 1–33.

Nisbett, R. E., & Wilson, T. D. (1977). Telling more than we can know: Verbal reports on mental processes. *Psychological Review, 134*, 231–259.

Nolen-Hoeksema, S. (1991). Responses to depression and their effects on the duration of depressive episodes. *Journal of Abnormal Psychology, 100*, 569–582.

Nolen-Hoeksema, S. (2000). The role of rumination in depressive disorders and mixed anxiety/depressive symptoms. *Journal of Abnormal Psychology, 109*, 504–511.

Nolen-Hoeksema, S., Wisco, B. E., & Lyubomirsky, S. (2008). Rethinking rumination. *Perspectives on Psychological Science, 3*, 400–424.

Nock, M. K., Park, J. M., Finn, C. T., Deliberto, T. L., Dour, H. J., & Banaji, M. R. (2010). Measuring the suicidal mind: Implicit cognition predicts suicidal behavior. *Psychological Science, 21*, 511–517.

Oatley, K., & Johnson-Laird, P. N. (2014). Cognitive approaches to emotions. *Trends in Cognitive Sciences, 18*(3), 134–140.

O'Donohue, W., & Fisher, J. E. (2008). *Cognitive behavior therapy: Applying empirically supported techniques to your practice* (2nd ed.). Hoboken, NJ: Wiley.

Oei, T. P. S., & Baranoff, J. (2007). Young Schema Questionnaire: Review of psychometric and measurement issues. *Australian Journal of Psychology, 59*, 78–86.

Oettingen, G., & Mayer, D. (2002). The motivating function of thinking about the future: Expectations versus fantasies. *Journal of Personality and Social Psychology, 83*, 1198–1212.

Oettingen, G., Mayer, D., Thorpe, J. S., Janetzke, H., & Lorenz, S. (2005). Turning fantasies about positive and negative futures into self-improvement goals. *Motivation and Emotion, 29*, 237–267.

Oettingen, G., Stephens, E. J., Mayer, D., & Brinkmann, B. (2010). Mental contrasting and the self-regulation of helping relations. *Social Cognition, 28*, 490–508.

Öhman, A., & Mineka, S. (2001). Fears, phobias, and preparedness: Toward an evolved module of fear and fear learning. *Psychological Review, 108*, 483–522.

Öhman, A., & Soares, J. J. F. (1998). Emotional conditioning to masked stimuli: Expectancies for aversive outcomes following nonrecognized fear-relevant stimuli. *Journal of Experimental Psychology: General, 127*, 69–82.

Ollendick, T. H., & King, N. J. (1998). Empirically supported treatments for children with phobic and anxiety disorders: Current status. *Journal of Clinical Child Psychology, 27*, 156–167.

Olsson, A., Ebert, J. P., Banaji, M. R., & Phelps, E. A. (2005). The role of social groups in the persistence of learned fear. *Science, 309*, 785–787.

Olver, M. E., & Wong, S. C. P. (2013). A description and research review of the Clearwater Sex Offender Treatment Program. *Psychology, Crime & Law, 19*, 477–492.

Oppenheim, D. (2006). Child, parent, and parent–child emotion narratives: Implications for developmental psychopathology. *Development and Psychopathology, 18*, 771–790.

Ortony, A., Clore, G. L., & Collins, A. (1988). *The cognitive structure of emotions*. New York, NY: Cambridge University Press.

Osgood, C. E., Suci, G., & Tannenbaum, P. (1957). *The measurement of meaning*. Champaign: University of Illinois Press.

Ospina, M. B., Bond, K., Karkhaneh, M., Buscemi, N., Dryden, D. M., Barnes, V., . . . Shannahoff-Khalsa, D. (2008). Clinical trials of meditation practices in health care: Characteristics and quality. *The Journal of Alternative and Complementary Medicine, 14*, 1199–1213.

Oyserman, D., Bybee, D., Terry, K., & Hart-Johnson, T. (2004). Possible selves as road maps. *Journal of Research in Personality, 38*, 130–149.

Padesky, C. A. (1993, September). *Socratic questioning: Changing minds or guiding discovery?* Keynote address delivered at the European Congress of Behavioural and Cognitive Therapies, London, England.

Padesky, C. A., & Mooney, K. A. (1990). Clinical tip: Presenting the cognitive model to clients. *International Cognitive Therapy Newsletter, 6*, 13–14.

Paki, D. P. (2012). *"I've got your back!" The emotional influence of loyalty and fear of rejection on conformity and group compliance among adolescents* (Unpublished master's thesis). School of Psychology, Massey University, Palmerston North, New Zealand.

Pape, H. (2012). Young people's overestimation of peer substance use: An exaggerated phenomenon? *Addiction, 107*, 878–884.

Pavlov, I. P. (1961). The types of higher nervous activity in connection with neuroses and psychoses and the physiological mechanisms of neurotic and psychotic symptoms. *The essential works of Pavlov*. New York, NY: Bantam Books. (Original work published in 1935.)

Payne, J. W., Bettman, J. R., & Johnson, E. J. (1993). *The adaptive decision maker*. New York, NY: Cambridge University Press.

Pechtel, P., Evans, I. M., & Podd, J. V. (2011). Conceptualizations of the complex outcomes of sexual abuse: A signal detection analysis. *Journal of Child Sexual Abuse, 20*, 677–694.

Perkins, H. W., & Berkowitz, A. D. (1986). Perceiving the community norms of alcohol use among students: Some research implications for campus alcohol education programming. *International Journal of the Addiction, 21*, 961–976.

Persons, J. B. (1989). *Cognitive therapy in practice: A case formulation approach*. New York, NY: W. W. Norton.

Peterson, C. (2006). *A primer in positive psychology*. New York, NY: Oxford University Press.

Pierce, C. S. (1878). How to make our ideas clear. *Popular Science Monthly, 12*, 286–302.

Purdon, C., & Clark, D. A. (1993). Obsessive intrusive thoughts in nonclinical subjects: Part 1. Content and relation with depressive, anxious and obsessional symptoms. *Behaviour Research and Therapy, 31*, 713–720.

Prevedini, A. B., Presti, G., Rabitti, E., Miselli, G., & Moderato, P. (2011). Acceptance and commitment therapy (ACT): The foundation of the therapeutic model and an overview of its contribution to the treatment of patients with chronic physical diseases. *Giornale Italiano di Medicina del Lavoro ed Ergonomia, 33*, 53–63.

Prochaska, J. O., & DiClemente, C. C. (1983). Stages and processes of self-change of smoking: Toward an integrative model of change. *Journal of Consulting and Clinical Psychology, 51*, 390–395.

Puhl, R. M., Andreyeva, T., & Brownell, K. D. (2008). Perceptions of weight discrimination: Prevalence and comparison to race and gender discrimination in America. *International Journal of Obesity, 32*(6), 992–1000. doi:10.1038/ijo.2008.22

Rachman, S. (1997). The evolution of cognitive behaviour therapy. In D. M. Clark & C. G. Fairburn (Eds.), *Science and practice of cognitive behaviour therapy* (pp. 3–26). Oxford, England: Oxford University Press.

Rachman, S. (1998). A cognitive theory of obsessions: Elaborations. *Behaviour Research and Therapy, 36*, 385–401.

Rae, A. J. (2010). *Psychologists' intentional use of reflection as a tool for enquiry* (Unpublished doctoral thesis). Massey University, Palmerston North, New Zealand. Retrieved from http://hdl.handle.net/10179/2484

Ravenscroft, I. (2010). Folk psychology as a theory. In E. N. Zalta (Ed.), *The Stanford encyclopedia of philosophy*. Retrieved from http://plato.stanford.edu/archives/fall2010/entries/folkpsych-theory/

Read, J., Mosher, L., & Bentall, R. (Eds.). (2004). *Models of madness: Psychological, social and biological approaches to schizophrenia*. London, England: Taylor & Francis.

Reber, A. S., & Reber, E. S. (2001). *The Penguin dictionary of psychology* (3rd ed.). London, England: Penguin Books.

Reeves, M., & Taylor, J. (2007). Specific relationships between core beliefs and personality disorder symptoms in a non-clinical sample. *Clinical Psychology & Psychotherapy, 14*, 96–104.

Renaud, C. A., & Byers, E. S. (1999). Exploring the frequency, diversity, and content of university students' positive and negative sexual cognitions. *Canadian Journal of Human Sexuality, 8*, 17–30.

Renaud, C. A., & Byers, S. E. (2006). Positive and negative cognitions of sexual submission: Relationship to sexual violence. *Archives of Sexual Behavior, 35*, 483–490.

Reynolds, A. C. (2013). *Introspectiveness during adolescence: An investigation of a personality trait and its relationship with psychological well-being* (Unpublished doctoral dissertation). School of Psychology, Massey University at Wellington, New Zealand.

Roberts, M. (Trans.). (2001). *Laozi's Dao de Jing: The book of the way.* Berkeley: University of California Press.

Robinson, J. L. (2007). Story stem narratives with young children: Moving to clinical research and practice. *Attachment & Human Development, 9*, 179–185.

Roskes, M., Elliot, A. J., & De Dreu, C. K. W. (2014). Why is avoidance motivation problematic, and what can be done about it? *Current Directions in Psychological Science, 23*, 133–138.

Roth, M. S. (2014). *Beyond the university: Why liberal education matters.* New Haven, CT: Yale University Press.

Russell, B. (1938). *Power: A new social analysis.* London, England: Allen & Unwin.

Russell, J. A. (2003). Core affect and the psychological construction of emotion. *Psychological Review, 110*, 145–172.

Rusting, C. L., & Nolen-Hoeksema, S. (1998). Regulating responses to anger: Effects of rumination and distraction on angry mood. *Journal of Personality and Social Psychology, 74*, 790–803.

Safran, J. D., Vallis, T. M., Segal, Z. V., & Shaw, B. F. (1986). Assessment of core cognitive processes in cognitive therapy. *Cognitive Therapy and Research, 10*, 509–526.

Salkovskis, P. M. (1989). Cognitive-behavioural factors and the persistence of obsessional problems. *Behaviour Research and Therapy, 27*, 677–682.

Salkovskis, P. M. (1996). Cognitive therapy and Aaron T. Beck. In P. M. Salkovskis (Ed.), *Frontiers of cognitive therapy* (pp. 531–540). New York, NY: Guilford Press.

Salmon, K., Evans, I. M., Moskowitz, S., Grouden, M., Parkes, F., & Miller, E. (2013). The components of young children's emotion knowledge: Which are enhanced by adult emotion talk? *Social Development, 22*, 94–110.

Sapolsky, R. M. (1998). *Why zebras don't get ulcers: An updated guide to stress, stress related diseases, and coping* (2nd ed.). New York, NY: Freeman.

Savulich, G., Shergill, S., & Yiend, J. (2012). Biased cognition in psychosis. *Journal of Experimental Psychopathology, 3*, 514–536.

Seligman, M. E. P., Rashid, T., & Parks, A. C. (2006). Positive psychotherapy. *American Psychologist, 61*, 774–788.

Selye, H. (1956). *The stress of life.* New York, NY: McGraw-Hill.

Schachter, S., & Singer, J. L. (1962). Cognitive, social, and physiological determinants of emotional state. *Psychological Review, 69*, 379–399.

Schauer, M., Neuner, F., & Elbert, T. (2011). *Narrative exposure therapy: A short-term treatment for traumatic stress disorders.* Toronto, ON: Hogrefe & Huber.

Scherer, K. R., Schorr, A., & Johnstone, T. (2001). *Appraisal processes in emotion: Theory, methods, research.* New York, NY: Oxford University Press.

Schneider, W., & Chein, J. M. (2003). Controlled & automatic processing: Behavior, theory, and biological mechanisms. *Cognitive Science, 27*, 525–559.

Schneider, W., & Shiffrin, R. M. (1977). Controlled and automatic human information processing: I. Detection, search, and attention. *Psychological Review, 84*, 1–66.

Schwarz, N. (2004). Meta-cognitive experiences in consumer judgment and decision making. *Journal of Consumer Psychology, 14*, 332–348.

Scoones, C., Willis, G. M., & Grace, R. C. (2012). Beyond static and dynamic risk factors: The incremental predictive validity of release planning in sex offender risk assessment. *Journal of Interpersonal Violence, 27*, 222–238.

Scott, S. G., & Bruce, R. A. (1995). Decision-making style: The development and assessment of a new measure. *Educational and Psychological Measurement, 55*, 818–831.

Segal, Z. V., Williams, J. M. G., & Teasdale, J. (2002). *Mindfulness-based cognitive therapy for depression: A new approach to preventing relapse.* New York, NY: Guilford Press.

Shafran, R., & Rachman, S, (2004). Thought-action fusion: A review. *Journal of Behavior Therapy and Experimental Psychiatry*, *35*, 87–107.

Shane, S. (2013, April 21). Suspects with a foot in 2 worlds, perhaps echoing plots of past. *New York Times*, p. 1.

Sherwell, P., & Spillius, A. (2009, November 7). Fort Hood shooting: Texas army killer linked to September 11 terrorists. *Daily Telegraph*.

Shields, D., & Salerno, S. (2013). *Salinger*. New York, NY: Simon and Schuster.

Shikina, R. (2013, March 30). Labor official who sided with players began career in isles. *Star Advertiser*, B1, p. 3.

Shiv, B., & Fedorikhin, A. (1999). Heart and mind in conflict: The interplay of affect and cognition in consumer decision making. *Journal of Consumer Research*, *26*, 278–291.

Shulman, R. G. (2013, May 19). Dangerous assumptions in neuroscience [Web log post]. *OUP Blog*. Retrieved from http://blog.oup.com/2013/05/dangerous-assumptions-in-neuroscience/

Shure, M. B., & Spivack, G. (1982). Interpersonal problem-solving in young children: A cognitive approach to prevention. *American Journal of Community Psychology*, *10*, 341–356.

Simon, H. A. (1983). *Reason in human affairs*. Stanford, CA: Stanford University Press.

Singer, J. L. (1966). *Daydreaming: An introduction to the experimental study of inner experience*. New York, NY: Random House.

Singer, J. L. (1975). Navigating the stream of consciousness: Research in daydreaming and related inner experience. *American Psychologist*, *30*, 727–738.

Singer, J. L., & Antrobus, J. S. (1972). Daydreaming, imaginal processes, and personality: A normative study. In P. Sheehan (Ed.), *The function and nature of imagery* (pp. 172–202). New York, NY: Academic Press.

Skinner, B. F. (1957. *Verbal behavior*. Upper Saddle River, NJ: Prentice Hall.

Smallwood, J., & Schooler, J. W. (2006). The restless mind. *Psychological Bulletin*, *132*, 946–958.

Smythe, T., & Dewar, T. (2009). *Raising the village: How individuals and communities can work together to give our children a stronger start in life*. Toronto, ON: BPS Books.

Solomon, R. C. (2006). *True to our feelings: What our emotions are really telling us*. New York, NY: Oxford University Press.

Spiegel, D., Loewenstein, R. J., Lewis-Fernández, R., Sar, V., Simeon, D., Vermetten, E., . . . Dell, P. F. (2011). Dissociative disorders in *DSM-5*. *Depression and Anxiety*, *28*, 17–45.

Staats, A. W. (1968). *Learning, language and cognition*. New York, NY: Holt, Rinehart and Winston.

Staats, A. W. (1972). Language behavior therapy: A derivative of social behaviorism. *Behavior Therapy*, *3*, 165–192.

Staats, A. W. (1983). *Psychology's crisis of disunity*. New York, NY: Praeger.

Staats, A. W. (2012). *The marvelous learning animal: What makes human nature unique*. Amherst, NY: Prometheus Books.

Staats, A. W., & Eifert, G. H. (1990). A psychological behaviorism theory of emotions: A basis for unification. *Clinical Psychology Review*, *10*, 1–40.

Staats, A. W., & Lohr, J. M. (1979). Images, language, emotion, and personality: Social behaviorism's theory. *Journal of Mental Imagery*, *3*, 85–106.

Stanovich, K. E. (1999). *Who is rational? Studies of individual differences in reasoning*. Mahwah, NJ: Lawrence Erlbaum.

Stanovich, K. E., & Toplak, M. E. (2012). Defining features versus incidental correlates of Type 1 and Type 2 processing. *Mind & Society*, *11*, 3–13.

Stanovich, K. E., & West, R. F. (2000). Individual differences in reasoning: Implications for the rationality debate? *Behavioral & Brain Sciences*, *23*, 645–726.

Stawarczyk, D., Majerus, S., Maj, M., Van der Linden, M., & D'Argembeau, A. (2011). Mind-wandering: Phenomenology and function as assessed with a novel experience. *Acta Psychologica*, *136*, 370–381.

Stewart, B. D., & Payne, B. K. (2008). Bringing automatic stereotyping under control: Implementation intentions as an efficient means of thought control. *Personality and Social Psychology Bulletin*, *34*, 1332–1345.

Strassberg, D. S., & Lockerd, L. K. (1998). Force in women's sexual fantasies. *Archives of Sexual Behavior, 27*, 403–414.

Suarez, E., & Gadalla, T. M. (2010). Stop blaming the victim: A meta-analysis on rape myths. *Journal of Interpersonal Violence, 25*, 2010–2035.

Suddendorf, T., & Corballis, M. C. (2007). The evolution of foresight: What is mental time travel, and is it unique to humans? *Behavioral and Brain Sciences, 30*, 299–351.

Tai, S., & Turkington, D. (2009). The evolution of cognitive behavior therapy for schizophrenia: Current practice and recent developments. *Schizophrenia Bulletin, 35*, 865–873.

Tak, J., & van Bon, W. (2005). Pain- and distress-reducing interventions for venipuncture in children. *Child Care, Health and Development, 32*, 257–268.

Tang, T. Z., & DeRubeis, R. J. (1999). Sudden gains and critical sessions in cognitive-behavioral therapy for depression. *Journal of Consulting and Clinical Psychology, 67*, 894–904.

Tang, T. Z., DeRubeis, R. J., Beberamn, R., & Pham, T. (2005). Cognitive changes, critical sessions, and sudden gains in cognitive-behavioral therapy for depression. *Journal of Consulting and Clinical Psychology, 73*, 168–172.

Tannen, D. (1990). *You just don't understand: Men and women in conversation*. New York, NY: William Morrow.

Tarrier, N., Lewis, S. W., Haddock, G., Bentall, R., Drake, R., Kinderman, P., . . . Dunn, G. (2004). Cognitive-behavioural therapy in first-episode and early schizophrenia: 18 month follow-up of a randomised controlled trail. *British Journal of Psychiatry, 184*, 231–239.

Tavris, C. (2012). How to spot pseudoneuroscience and biobunk. *APS Observer, 25*(6). Retrieved from http://www.psychologicalscience.org/index.php/video/how-to-spot-pseudoneuroscience-and-biobunk.html

Taylor, L (2012). *The brain supremacy*. London, England: Oxford University Press.

Taylor, S. E., & Brown, J. D. (1988). Illusion and well-being: A social psychological perspective on mental health. *Psychological Bulletin, 103*, 193–210.

Teasdale, J. D. (1993). Emotion and two kinds of meaning: Cognitive therapy and applied cognitive science. *Behaviour Research and Therapy, 31*, 339–354.

Teasdale, J. D. (1999). Multi-level theories of cognition-emotion relations. In T. Dalgleish & M. Power (Eds.), *Handbook of cognition and emotion* (pp. 665–681). Chichester, England: Wiley.

Teasdale, J. D., & Barnard, P. J. (1993). *Affect, cognition, and change*. Hillsdale, NJ: Lawrence Erlbaum.

Teasdale, J. D., & Fennell, M. J. V. (1982). Immediate effects on depression of cognitive therapy interventions. *Cognitive Therapy and Research, 6*, 343–351.

Teasdale, J. D., Proctor, L., Llloyd, C. A., & Baddeley, A. D. (1993). Working memory and stimulus-independent thought: Effects of memory load and presentation rate. *European Journal of Cognitive Psychology, 5*, 417–433.

Teasdale, J. D., Williams, M. G., & Segal, Z. V. (2014). *The mindful way workbook: An 8-week program to free yourself from depression and emotional distress*. New York, NY: Guilford Press.

Thakker, J., Ward, T., & Chu, C. M. (2013). The Good Lives Model of offender rehabilitation. In W. T. O'Donohue (Ed.), *Case studies in sexual deviance: Toward evidence based practice* (pp. 79–101). Florence, KY: Routledge.

Thaler, R. H. (2000) From Homo Economicus to Homo Sapiens. *Journal of Economic Perspectives, 14*, 114–142.

Tharp, R. G. (2012). *Delta theory and psychosocial systems: The practice of influence and change*. New York, NY: Cambridge University Press.

Thompson, M. M., & Zanna, M. P. (1995). The conflicted individual: Personality-based and domain-specific antecedents of ambivalent social attitudes. *Journal of Personality, 63*, 259–288.

Thouless, R. H. (1932). *Straight and crooked thinking*. New York, NY: Simon and Schuster.

Tolin, D. F. (2010). Is cognitive-behavioral therapy more effective than other therapies? A meta-analytic review. *Clinical Psychology Review, 30*, 710–720.

Trower, P., Birchwood, M., & Meaden, A. (2004). Cognitive therapy for command hallucinations: Randomised control trial. *British Journal of Psychiatry, 184*, 312–320.

Turkington, D., & Kingdon, D. (2000). Cognitive-behavioural techniques for general psychiatrists in the management of patients with psychoses. *British Journal of Psychiatry, 177*, 101–106.

Turner, S. M., Beidel, D. C., & Stanley, M. A. (1992). Are obsessional thoughts and worry different cognitive phenomena? *Clinical Psychology Review, 12*, 257–270.

Tversky, A., & Kahneman, D. (1974). Judgment under uncertainty: Heuristics and biases. *Science, 185*, 1124–1131.

Tversky, A., & Kahneman, D. (1983). Extensional versus intuitive reasoning: The conjunction fallacy in probability judgment. *Psychological Review, 90*, 293–315.

Unger, W., Evans, I. M., Rourke, P., & Levis, D. J. (2003). The S-S construct of expectancy versus the S-R construct of fear: Which motivates the acquisition of avoidance behavior? *The Journal of General Psychology, 130*, 131–147.

Velten, E. Jr. (1968). A laboratory task for the induction of mood states. *Behaviour Research and Therapy, 6*, 473–482.

Vera, A. H., & Simon, H. A. (1993). Situated action: A symbolic interpretation. *Cognitive Science, 17*, 7–48.

Voeltz, L. M., & Evans, I. M. (1982). The assessment of behavioral interrelationships in child behavior therapy. *Behavioral Assessment, 4*, 131–165.

Wachtel, P. L. (1977). *Psychoanalysis and behavior therapy: Toward an integration*. New York, NY: Basic Books.

Ward, T. (2000). Sexual offenders' cognitive distortions as implicit theories. *Aggression and Violent Behavior, 5*, 491–507.

Ward, T., & Casey, A. (2010). Extending the mind into the world: A new theory of cognitive distortions in sex offenders. *Aggression and Violent Behavior, 15*, 49–58.

Ward, T., Louden, K., Hudson, S. M., & Marshall, W. L. (1995). A descriptive model of the offense chain for child molesters. *Journal of Interpersonal Violence, 10*, 452–472.

Ward, T., Mann, R. E., & Gannon, T. A. (2007). The Good Lives Model of offender rehabilitation: Clinical implications. *Aggression and Violent Behavior, 12*, 87–107.

Watkins, E. R., Baeyens, C. B., & Read, R. (2009). Concreteness training reduces dysphoria: Proof-of-principle for repeated cognitive bias modification in depression. *Journal of Abnormal Psychology, 118*, 55–64.

Weaver, K., Garcia, S. M., Schwartz, N., & Miller, D. T. (2007). Inferring the popularity of an opinion from its familiarity: A repetitive voice can sound like a chorus. *Journal of Personality and Social Psychology, 92*, 821–833.

Wegner, D. M., & Bargh, J. A. (1998). Control and automaticity in social life. In D. Gilbert, S. T. Fiske, & G. Lindzey (Eds.), *Handbook of social psychology* (pp. 446–496). New York, NY: McGraw Hill.

Wegner, D. M., Schneider, D. J., Carter, S. R., & White, T. L. (1987). Paradoxical effects of thought suppression. *Journal of Personality and Social Psychology, 53*, 5–13.

Weiner, B. (1972). Attribution theory, achievement motivation, and the educational process. *Review of Educational Research, 42*, 203–215.

Weishaar, M. E. (1993). *Aaron T. Beck*. London, England: Sage.

Wells, A. (2000). *Emotional disorders and metacognition: Innovative cognitive therapy*. Chichester, England: Wiley.

Wells, A. (2002). GAD, metacognition, and mindfulness: An information processing analysis. *Clinical Psychology: Science and Practice, 9*, 95–100.

Wells, A. (2009). *Metacognitive therapy for anxiety and depression*. New York, NY: Guilford Press.

Wells, A., & King, P. (2006). Metacognitive therapy for generalized anxiety disorder: An open trial. *Journal of Behavior Therapy and Experimental Psychiatry, 37*, 206–212.

Wenzel, A. & Rubin, D. C. (Eds.). (2005). *Cognitive methods in clinical research*. Washington, DC: American Psychological Association.

Whisman, M. A. (1993). Mediators and moderators of change in cognitive therapy of depression. *Psychological Bulletin, 114*, 248–265.

Wiers, R. W., Gladwin, T. E., Hofmann, W., Salemink, E., & Ridderinkhof, K. R. (2013). Cognitive bias modification and cognitive control training in addiction and related psychopathology: Mechanisms, clinical perspectives, and ways forward. *Clinical Psychological Science, 1*, 192–212.

Williams, J. M. G. (1996). Memory processes in psychotherapy. In P. M. Salkovskis (Ed.), *Frontiers of cognitive therapy* (pp. 97–113). New York, NY: Guilford Press.

Williams, M., Teasdale, J., Segal, Z., & Kabat-Zinn, J. (2007). *The mindful way through depression: Freeing yourself from chronic unhappiness*. New York, NY: Guilford Press.

Wilson, D. B., Bouffard, L. A., & Mackenzie, D. L. (2005). A quantitative review of structured, group-oriented, cognitive-behavioral programs for offenders. *Criminal Justice and Behavior, 32*, 172–204.

Wilson, N. J., Kilgour, G., & Polaschek, D. L. L. (2013). Treating high-risk rapists in a New Zealand intensive prison programme. *Psychology, Crime & Law, 19*, 527–547.

Wilson, G. T., Wilfley, D. E., & Agras, W. S. (2010). Psychological treatments of binge eating disorder. *Archives of General Psychiatry, 67*, 94–101.

Wilson, K. G., Hayes, S. C., & Gifford, E. V. (1997). Cognition in behavior therapy: Agreements and differences. *Journal of Behavior Therapy and Experimental Psychiatry, 28*, 53–63.

Witkiewitz, K., & Bowen, S. (2010). Depression, craving, and substance use following a randomized trial of mindfulness-based relapse prevention. *Journal of Consulting and Clinical Psychology, 78*, 362–374.

Witkiewitz, K. A., & Marlatt, G. A. (Eds.). (2007). *Therapist's guide to evidence-based relapse prevention*. Burlington, MA: Academic Press/Elsevier.

Wong, Q. J. J., & Moulds, M. L. (2009). Impact of rumination versus distraction on anxiety and maladaptive self-beliefs in socially anxious individuals. *Behaviour Research and Therapy, 47*, 861–867.

Wong, Q. J. J., & Moulds, M. L. (2011). A new measure of the maladaptive self-beliefs in social anxiety: Psychometric properties in a non-clinical sample. *Journal of Psychopathology and Behavioral Assessment, 33*, 285–297.

Woodworth, R. S., & Schlosberg, H. (1954). *Experimental psychology* (rev. ed.). New York, NY: Holt.

Yeung, N. (2013). Conflict monitoring and cognitive control. In K. Ochsner & S. Kosslyn (Eds.), *Oxford handbook of cognitive neuroscience* (Vol. 2, pp. 275–299). New York, NY: Oxford University Press.

Yoon, G., & Vargas, P. T. (2014). Know thy avatar: The unintended effect of virtual-self representation on behavior. *Psychological Science, 25*(4), 1043–1045. doi:10.1177/0956797613519271

Young, J. E. (1994). *Cognitive therapy for personality disorders: A schema-focused approach* (rev. ed.). Sarasota, FL: Professional Resource Press.

Young, J. E., & Brown, G. (1994). Young Schema Questionnaire (2nd ed.). In J. E. Young (Ed.), *Cognitive therapy for personality disorders: A schema-focused approach* (rev. ed., pp. 63–76). Sarasota, FL: Professional Resource Press.

Young, J. E., Klosko, J. S., & Weishaar, M. E. (2003). *Schema therapy: A practitioner's guide*. New York, NY: Guilford Press.

Zhang, Y., & Epley, N. (2012). Exaggerated, mispredicted, and misplaced: When "it's the thought that counts" in gift exchanges. *Journal of Experimental Psychology: General, 141*, 667–681.

Zimbardo, P. G., & Boyd, J. N. (1999). Putting time in perspective: A valid, reliable, individual-differences metric. *Journal of Personality and Social Psychology, 77*, 1271–1288.

ABOUT THE AUTHOR

Ian Evans, who was born in England and grew up in South Africa, has always considered himself fortunate to have been a doctoral student of the legendary Hans J. Eysenck between 1966 and 1970 at the Institute of Psychiatry, London University. Eysenck was deeply interested in the broad conceptual and experimental basis of the rapidly emerging field of behavior therapy. After completing his PhD, Evans joined the clinical faculty at the University of Hawai'i, attracted by the magisterial work of Arthur Staats and Roland Tharp, both of whom have been devoted to the unification of behavioral, cognitive, and culturally responsive clinical practice. Evans's own research focused on principles of assessment and systemic methods for positive approaches to behavior problems at home and at school in children with autism and serious developmental disabilities. An especially important feature of his life in Honolulu was conducting a small part-time private practice and practicum teaching in the state's community mental health and developmental disability systems. He then moved to upstate New York as Director of Clinical Training at Binghamton University (State University of New York) where he continued to collaborate with his wife, Professor Luanna Meyer, and other special education colleagues on inclusive, positive community-wide programs to promote restorative school discipline for challenging behavior and to link home and school for the prevention of dropout. After one deep snowfall too many, and seeking further adventures and better wine, he accepted a position as professor and director of clinical training at the University of Waikato in New Zealand, later becoming head of the School of Psychology at Massey University, from which he has recently retired as emeritus professor. His research interests in New Zealand extended to many aspects of children's emotional development, particularly their sense of fairness in family relationships. In 2013 he returned to his old stomping grounds on O'ahu to seriously retire, write books such as this one, and entertain the grandchildren. Happily he had not been forgotten by former students and colleagues and has been teaching occasional courses as an Affiliate of the University of Hawai'i's clinical studies program, where the excellent graduate students keep him on his mental toes and he gets to wear sharp aloha shirts. Evans is a fellow of the American Psychological Association (Division 12), Association for Psychological Science, and the Royal Society of New Zealand.

INDEX